Practical
Business
Math
Procedures

Practical Business Math Procedures

Brief Tenth Edition

JEFFREY SLATER

North Shore Community College
Danvers, Massachusetts

SHARON MEYER

Pikes Peak Community College
Contributor

McGraw-Hill
Irwin

McGraw-Hill
Irwin

PRACTICAL BUSINESS MATH PROCEDURES, BRIEF TENTH EDITION
Published by McGraw-Hill/Irwin, a business unit of The McGraw-Hill Companies, Inc., 1221 Avenue of the Americas, New York, NY, 10020. Copyright © 2011, 2008, 2006, 2003, 2000, 1997, 1994, 1993, 1991, 1987 by The McGraw-Hill Companies, Inc. All rights reserved. No part of this publication may be reproduced or distributed in any form or by any means, or stored in a database or retrieval system, without the prior written consent of The McGraw-Hill Companies, Inc., including, but not limited to, in any network or other electronic storage or transmission, or broadcast for distance learning.

Some ancillaries, including electronic and print components, may not be available to customers outside the United States.

This book is printed on acid-free paper.

6 7 8 9 0 DOW/DOW 1 0 9 8 7 6 5 4 3 2

ISBN   978-0-07-732793-4 (student edition)
MHID   0-07-732793-4 (student edition)
ISBN   978-0-07-732785-9 (teacher's edition)
MHID   0-07-732785-3 (teacher's edition)

Vice president and editor-in-chief: *Brent Gordon*
Editorial director: *Stewart Mattson*
Executive editor: *Richard T. Hercher, Jr.*
Director of development: *Ann Torbert*
Managing development editor: *Gail Korosa*
Vice president and director of marketing: *Robin J. Zwettler*
Marketing director: *Sankha Basu*
Vice president of editing, design and production: *Sesha Bolisetty*
Lead project manager: *Pat Frederickson*
Lead production supervisor: *Michael R. McCormick*
Interior designer: *JoAnne Schopler*
Senior photo research coordinator: *Jeremy Cheshareck*
Photo research: *Teri Stratford*
Media project manager: *Jennifer Lohn*
Cover design: *Joanne Schopler*
Interior design: *Joanne Schopler*
Typeface: *10/12 Times Roman*
Compositor: *Aptara®, Inc.*
Printer: *R. R. Donnelley*

Library of Congress Cataloging-in-Publication Data

Slater, Jeffrey, 1947-
      Practical business math procedures / Jeffrey Slater. — Brief 10th ed.
         p. cm.
      Includes index.
      ISBN-13: 978-0-07-732793-4 (student edition : alk. paper)
      ISBN-10: 0-07-732793-4 (student edition : alk. paper)
      ISBN-13: 978-0-07-732785-9 (teacher's edition : alk. paper)
      ISBN-10: 0-07-732785-3 (teacher's edition : alk. paper)
      1. Business mathematics—Problems, exercises, etc. I. Title.
   HF5694.S57 2011b
   650.01'513—dc22
                                        2009050027

Dedication

To Shelley,
my best friend
—Love, PaPa Jeff

ROADMAP TO SUCCESS

How to use this book and the Total Slater Learning System.

Step 1: **Each chapter broken down into Learning Units. You should read one learning unit at a time.**

How do I know if I understand it?

- Try the practice quiz. All the worked out solutions are provided. If you still have questions, watch the author on your DVD (comes with your text) and work each problem out.
- Need more practice? Try the extra practice quiz provided. Worked-out solutions are in Appendix B.
- Go on to next Learning Unit in chapter.

Step 2: **Review the "Chapter Organizer" at the end of the chapter.**

How do I know if I understand it?

- Cover over the second or third column and see if you can explain the key points or the examples.

Step 3: **Do assigned problems at the end of the chapter (or Appendix A). These may include discussion questions, drill, word problems, challenge problems, video cases, as well as projects from the Business Math Scrapbook and Kiplinger's magazine.**

Can I check my homework?

- Appendix C has check figures for all the odd-numbered problems.

Step 4: **Take the Summary Practice Test.**

Can I check my progress?

- Appendix C has check figures for all problems.

What do I do if I do not match check figures?

- Review the video tutorial on the student DVD—the author works out each problem.

To aid you in studying the book, I have developed the following color code:

Blue: Movement, cancellations, steps to solve, arrows, blueprints

Gold: Formulas and steps

Green: Tables and forms

Red: Key items we are solving for

If you have difficulty with any text examples, pay special attention to the red and the blue. These will help remind you what you are looking for as well as what the procedures are.

FEATURES   Features students have told me have helped them the most.

Blueprint Aid Boxes   For the first eight chapters (not in Chapter 4), blueprint aid boxes are available to help you map out a plan to solve a word problem. I know that often the hardest thing to do in solving word problems is where to start. Use the blueprint as a model to get started.

Business Math Handbook   This reference guide contains all the tables found in the text. It makes homework, exams, etc. easier to deal with than flipping back and forth through the text.

Chapter Organizer   At the end of each chapter is a quick reference guide called the Chapter Organizer. Key points, formulas, and examples are provided. A list of vocabulary terms is also included, as well as Check Figures for Extra Practice Quizzes. All have page references. (A complete glossary is found at the end of the text.) Think of the chapter organizer as your set of notes and use it as a reference when doing homework problems, and to review before exams.

DVD-ROM   The DVD packaged with the text includes practice quizzes, links to Web sites listed in the Business Math Internet Resource Guide, the Excel® templates, PowerPoint, videocases, and tutorial videos—which cover all the Learning Unit Practice Quizzes and Summary Practice Tests.

The Business Math Web site   Visit the site at www.mhhe.com/slater10e and find the Internet Resource Guide with hot links, tutorials, practice quizzes, Excel® workbook and templates, and other study materials useful for the course.

Video Cases   There are four video cases applying business math concepts to real companies such as American President Lines, FedEx, Noodles & Company and Washburn Guitars. These are included on the student DVD. Some background case information and assignment problems incorporating information on the companies are included at the end of Chapters 6, 7, 8, and 9.

Business Math Scrapbook   At the end of each chapter you will find clippings from *The Wall Street Journal* and various other publications. These articles will give you a chance to use the theory provided in the chapter to apply to the real world. It allows you to put your math skills to work.

Group Activity: Personal Finance, a Kiplinger Approach   In each chapter you can debate a business math issue based on a *Kiplinger's Personal Finance* magazine article that is presented. This is great for critical thinking, as well as improving your writing skills.

Spreadsheet Templates   Excel® templates are available for selected end-of-chapter problems. You can run these templates as is or enter your own data. The templates also include an interest table feature that enables you to input any percentage rate and any terms. The program will then generate table values for you.

Cumulative Reviews   At the end of Chapters 3 and 8 are word problems that test your retention of business math concepts and procedures. Check figures for *all* cumulative review problems are in Appendix C.

Vocabulary   On each chapter opener is a Vocabulary Preview covering the key terms in the chapter you need to know. The Chapter Organizer includes page references to the terms. There's also a glossary at the end of the text.

Academic Experts, Contributors

Eric Ball	Patrick Cunningham	Jeff Hong	Gabrielle Serrano
Ellen Benowitz	Stanley Dabrowski	Deanna Knight	Jeneen Smith Sims
Tom Bilyeu	Dorothy Dean	Amy McAnally	Margene Sunderland
Sylvia Brown	Michael Discello	Jeffrey Rabish	Leslie Thompson
Richard Bruce	Jacqueline Donovan	Stan Rickert	Judith Toland
Lisa Bryde	Mary Frey	Lawrence Roman	Patricia Tyunaitis
Charles Bunn, Jr.	Joe Hanson	Tim Samolis	Peter VanderWeyst
Linda Cress	Jennifer Herrera	Ellen Sawyer	

Special thanks to Sharon Meyer for all the help she provided in the revision of the text.

Company/Applications

Chapter 1

Dunkin' Donuts—*Problem solving*

Coca-Cola Co—*Reading, writing and rounding numbers*

Salary.com—*Rounding numbers*

Tootsie Roll Industries—*Dissecting word problems and rounding*

Flexcar/Zipcar—*Adding and subtracting whole numbers*

Starbucks—*Rounding all the way*

Hershey—*Subtraction of whole numbers*

United Airlines—*Multiplying and dividing whole numbers*

Disney, InGrid, Alarm.com, AT&T—*Applying your skills*

Chapter 2

Apple—*Fractions*

M&M's Mars—*Fractions and multiplication*

Google—*Adding and subtracting fractions*

Albertsons—*Dissecting word problems with fractions*

M&M's Mars—*Multiplying and dividing fractions*

IRS, Canyons Grand Summit, Four Seasons, Ritz Carlton, Stowe Mountain Lodge, Whiteface Lodge, Gap—*Applying your skills*

Chapter 3

Starbucks—*International currency*

American Airlines, Lufthansa—*Subtracting decimals*

Toyota—*Shortcuts for multiples of 10*

Gap, H&R Block, McDonalds, Roto-Rooter—*Applying your skills*

Chapter 4

Bank of America—*Overdraft fees*

Comerica Inc—*New social security debit cards*

Wells Fargo, Citigroup, Regions, Financial, Sun Trust, Key Corp, Fifth Third

PNC Financial, U.S. Bancorp, BB&T, Capital One—*Stress test by government*

HSBC Holdings, First National of Nebraska, ING Group—*Online banking*

Bank of America, Apple, Wells Fargo, JPMorgan Chase, Banc Plus—*Applying your skills*

Chapter 5

Google—*Formulas*

McDonald's—*International sales*

Marvel Entertainment, Scholastic Inc—*Solving for the unknown*

Webmath.com—*Applying your skills*

Chapter 6

Chrysler Corp., Toyota—*Concept of percents*

Motorola, Coca-Cola, PepsiCo, Red Bull—*Concept of percents*

IRS—*Reading percents*

Apple—*Converting percents to decimal*

M&M's Mars—*Base, rate, and portion*

National Energy Assistance Directors Association—*Percent increase and decrease*

National Association of Realtors—*Applying your skills*

Chapter 7

BillQ Plus, Rudder.com—*Insight into discounts*

Shopstyle.com, Glimpse.com, Anheuser-Busch—*Trade discounts*

McGraw-Hill Publishers—*Trade discount*

DHL, UPS, FedEx—*Freight terms*

Desa LLC,—*Freight costs*

Walmart, Folcroft, Enterprise, Target, Sears Holdings—*Applying your skills*

Chapter 8

Zara, Gap—*International retailing*

Gap—*Markup on cost and selling price*

Macy's, JCPenney, Lord & Taylor—*Applying your skills*

Chapter 9

Walt Disney Co.—*Layoffs*

Walmart—*Payroll settlement*

Yum Brands, McDonald's—*Labor laws*

Goodyear Tire & Rubber Co.—*Pay scales*

IRS—*Circular E tables*

FedEx, Janus Capital Group Inc.—*Applying your skills*

Chapter 10

Quiznos, Cold Stone Creamery, Curves, Domino's Pizza—*Intro to bad loans*

Citigroup, Wachovia, Bank of America, JPMorgan Chase—*Simple interest*

Cash and More, SIM Corp., Citigroup—*Applying your skills*

Chapter 11

JPMorgan Chase—*Short sales for financial troubled borrowers*

Goodyear—*Credit lines*

U.S. Treasury—*Buying treasuries*

Talbots, Bank of America, HSBC Holdings—*Credit lines*

Hewlett-Packard, Baker and Hughes, Verizon—*Applying your skills*

Chapter 12

Quicken—*Overview of compounding of money*

Kiplinger Magazine—*Magic of compounding*

Dow Jones—*Applying your skills*

Contents

Because Money Matters...

Get *Kiplinger's Personal Finance* at a Special Low Student Rate, Just $1 a Month!

Practical Business Math Procedures

WHOLE NUMBERS: HOW TO DISSECT AND SOLVE WORD PROBLEMS

Hillary Price, Rymes with Orange, © 2008

Wall Street Journal © 2009

LU 1–1: Reading, Writing, and Rounding Whole Numbers

1. Use place values to read and write numeric and verbal whole numbers (p. 4).
2. Round whole numbers to the indicated position (p. 6).
3. Use blueprint aid for dissecting and solving a word problem (p. 8).

LU 1–2: Adding and Subtracting Whole Numbers

1. Add whole numbers; check and estimate addition computations (p. 10).
2. Subtract whole numbers; check and estimate subtraction computations (p. 11).

LU 1–3: Multiplying and Dividing Whole Numbers

1. Multiply whole numbers; check and estimate multiplication computations (p. 14).
2. Divide whole numbers; check and estimate division computations (p. 16).

VOCABULARY PREVIEW

Here are the key terms in this chapter. When you finish the chapter, if you feel you know the term, place a checkmark within the parentheses following the term. If you are not certain of the definition, look it up and write the page number where it can be found in the text. The chapter organizer includes page references to the terms. There is also a complete glossary at the end of the text.

addends . ( ) decimal point . ( ) decimal system . ( ) difference . ( ) dividend . ( ) divisor . ( ) minuend . ( )
multiplicand . ( ) multiplier . ( ) partial products . ( ) partial quotient . ( ) product . ( ) quotient . ( )
remainder . ( ) rounding all the way . ( ) subtrahend . ( ) sum . ( ) whole number . ( )

People of all ages make personal business decisions based on the answers to number questions. Numbers also determine most of the business decisions of companies. For example, click on your computer, go to the Web site of a company such as Dunkin' Donuts and note the importance of numbers in the company's business decision-making process.

GLOBAL

The following *Wall Street Journal* clipping "Dunkin' Donuts Targets Shanghai" announces plans to expand into China:

Dunkin' Donuts Targets Shanghai

Dunkin' Donuts plans to open in Shanghai this spring as part of a push into China.

The coffee-and-bakery chain, **Dunkin' Brands** Inc. unit, says it plans to open fewer than 10 locations in the Shanghai area this year, with an additional 10 in the area, and possibly other Chinese cities, in 2009. Dunkin' Donuts first opened a handful of stores in China during the 1990s, but closed them.

In the U.S., Dunkin' has expanded in recent years on the success of its coffee drinks while emphasizing its convenience as a no-frills coffee destination. In China, its locations will have more seating, and they are expected to sell more food than beverages, said Will Kussell, president and chief brand officer for Dunkin' Donuts Worldwide.

China has become an increasingly important market for U.S.-based coffee chains because of its rapidly growing middle class and affinity for Western brands. **Starbucks** Corp. has said it wants to make China its largest market outside the U.S. Dunkin' started its push into the region last year by opening a store in Taiwan, where it now has 10 locations.

In Shanghai, Dunkin' plans to build its drinks around coffee while offering a variety of teas.

Oilai Shen/Bloomberg News/Landov

Wall Street Journal © 2008

Companies often follow a general problem-solving procedure to arrive at a change in company policy. Using Dunkin' Donuts as an example, the following steps illustrate this procedure:

Step 1. State the problem(s).   Increase market share and profitability.

Step 2. Decide on the best methods to solve the problem(s).   Expand operations in China.

Step 3. Does the solution make sense?   Adapt to Chinese eating habits—more food than beverages.

Step 4. Evaluate the results.   Dunkin' Donuts will evaluate new plan.

Your study of numbers begins with a review of basic computation skills that focuses on speed and accuracy. You may think, "But I can use my calculator." Even if your instructor allows you to use a calculator, you still must know the basic computation skills. You need these skills to know what to calculate, how to interpret your calculations, how to make estimates to recognize errors you made in using your calculator, and how to make calculations when you do not have a calculator.

The United States' numbering system is the **decimal system** or *base 10 system*. Your calculator gives the 10 single-digit numbers of the decimal system—0, 1, 2, 3, 4, 5, 6, 7, 8, and 9. The center of the decimal system is the **decimal point.** When you have a number with a decimal point, the numbers to the left of the decimal point are **whole numbers** and the numbers to the right of the decimal point are decimal numbers (discussed in Chapter 3). When you have a number *without* a decimal, the number is a whole number and the decimal is assumed to be after the number.

This chapter discusses reading, writing, and rounding whole numbers; adding and subtracting whole numbers; and multiplying and dividing whole numbers.

Learning Unit 1–1: Reading, Writing, and Rounding Whole Numbers

Coca-Cola over the years has acquired many companies. In 2008 Coke acquired a Chinese maker of juices for 2 billion, 300 million dollars. Numerically we can write this as 2,300,000,000. In 2009 Chinese regulaters blocked the acquisition.

Now let's begin our study of whole numbers.

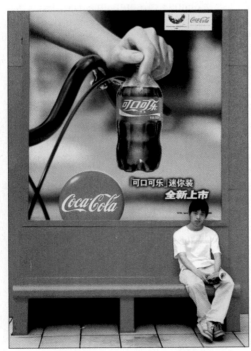

GLOBAL

ImagineChina/AP Images

Reading and Writing Numeric and Verbal Whole Numbers

The decimal system is a *place-value system* based on the powers of 10. Any whole number can be written with the 10 digits of the decimal system because the position, or placement, of the digits in a number gives the value of the digits.

To determine the value of each digit in a number, we use a place-value chart (Figure 1.1) that divides numbers into named groups of three digits, with each group separated by a comma. To separate a number into groups, you begin with the last digit in the number and insert commas every three digits, moving from right to left. This divides the number into the named groups (units, thousands, millions, billions, trillions) shown in the place-value chart. Within each group, you have a ones, tens, and hundreds place. Keep in mind that the leftmost group may have fewer than three digits.

In Figure 1.1, the numeric number 1,605,743,891,412 illustrates place values. When you study the place-value chart, you can see that the value of each place in the chart is 10 times the value of the place to the right. We can illustrate this by analyzing the last four digits in the number 1,605,743,891,412 :

$$1,412 = (1 \times 1,000) + (4 \times 100) + (1 \times 10) + (2 \times 1)$$

So we can also say, for example, that in the number 745, the "7" means seven hundred (700); in the number 75, the "7" means 7 tens (70).

To read and write a numeric number in verbal form, you begin at the left and read each group of three digits as if it were alone, adding the group name at the end (except the last units group and groups of all zeros). Using the place-value chart in Figure 1.1, the number 1,605,743,891,412 is read as one trillion, six hundred five billion, seven hundred forty-three million, eight hundred ninety-one thousand, four hundred twelve. You do not read zeros. They fill vacant spaces as placeholders so that you can correctly state the number values. Also,

FIGURE 1.1

Whole number place-value chart

Whole Number Groups

Trillions				Billions				Millions				Thousands				Units			
Hundred trillions	Ten trillions	Trillions	Comma	Hundred billions	Ten billions	Billions	Comma	Hundred millions	Ten millions	Millions	Comma	Hundred thousands	Ten thousands	Thousands	Comma	Hundreds	Tens	Ones (units)	Decimal Point
		1	,	6	0	5	,	7	4	3	,	8	9	1	,	4	1	2	.

the numbers twenty-one to ninety-nine must have a hyphen. And most important, when you read or write whole numbers in verbal form, do not use the word *and*. In the decimal system, *and* indicates the decimal, which we discuss in Chapter 3.

By reversing this process of changing a numeric number to a verbal number, you can use the place-value chart to change a verbal number to a numeric number. Remember that you must keep track of the place value of each digit. The place values of the digits in a number determine its total value.

Before we look at how to round whole numbers, we should look at how to convert a number indicating parts of a whole number to a whole number. We will use the following *Wall Street Journal* clip "Coke Sets China Deal" as an example.

GLOBAL

Coke Sets China Deal

BY BETSY McKAY

Coca-Cola Co. said it plans to acquire a Chinese maker of juices and nectars for $2.3 billion, the second-largest acquisition in the Atlanta company's history.

The planned acquisition of **China Huiyuan Juice Group** Ltd. also represents a major investment by a foreign company in China.

Coke has been steadily acquiring companies around the world in recent years that make juice, water and other noncarbonated drinks, to broaden its portfolio and beat back competitors.

Coke's largest acquisition is its $4.1 billion purchase in 2007 of Energy Brands Inc., the Whitestone, N.Y., maker of Vitaminwater.

Huiyuan is "highly complementary to the Coca-Cola China business," Coke's chief executive officer, Muhtar Kent, said in a statement.

Huiyuan said the deal would help it develop its brand. "The business combination of Coca-Cola and Huiyuan creates a win-win partnership that combines Coca-Cola's expertise as a global beverage company with Huiyuan's knowledge and understanding of the China beverage market," company Chairman Zhu Xinli said in a statement.

Coke said the purchase of Huiyuan requires approval from Chinese regulators, who have blocked some recent foreign acquisitions.

Wall Street Journal © 2008

The $2,300,000,000 Coca-Cola plans to pay for a Chinese maker of juices could be written as $2.3 billion. This amount is two billion plus three hundred million of an additional billion. The following steps explain how to convert these decimal numbers into a regular whole number:

CONVERTING PARTS OF A MILLION, BILLION, TRILLION, ETC., TO A REGULAR WHOLE NUMBER
Step 1. Drop the decimal point and insert a comma.
Step 2. Add zeros so the leftmost digit ends in the word name of the amount you want to convert. Be sure to add commas as needed.

EXAMPLE   Convert 2.3 billion to a regular whole number.

Step 1. 2.3 billion

2,3   Change the decimal point to a comma.

Step 2. 2,300,000,000   Add zeros and commas so the whole number indicates billion.

Rounding Whole Numbers

Many of the whole numbers you read and hear are rounded numbers. Government statistics are usually rounded numbers. The financial reports of companies also use rounded numbers. All rounded numbers are *approximate* numbers. The more rounding you do, the more you approximate the number.

Rounded whole numbers are used for many reasons. With rounded whole numbers you can quickly estimate arithmetic results, check actual computations, report numbers that change quickly such as population numbers, and make numbers easier to read and remember.

Numbers can be rounded to any identified digit place value, including the first digit of a number (rounding all the way). To round whole numbers, use the following three steps:

ROUNDING WHOLE NUMBERS

Step 1. Identify the place value of the digit you want to round.

Step 2. If the digit to the right of the identified digit in Step 1 is 5 or more, increase the identified digit by 1 (round up). If the digit to the right is less than 5, do not change the identified digit.

Step 3. Change all digits to the right of the rounded identified digit to zeros.

EXAMPLE 1   Round 9,362 to the nearest hundred.

Step 1. 9,362   The digit 3 is in the hundreds place value.

Step 2.   The digit to the right of 3 is 5 or more (6). Thus, 3, the identified digit in Step 1, is now rounded to 4. You change the identified digit only if the digit to the right is 5 or more.

9,462

Step 3. 9,400   Change digits 6 and 2 to zeros, since these digits are to the right of 4, the rounded number.

By rounding 9,362 to the nearest hundred, you can see that 9,362 is closer to 9,400 than to 9,300.

Next, we show you how to round to the nearest thousand.

EXAMPLE 2   Round 67,951 to the nearest thousand.

Step 1. 67,951   The digit 7 is in the thousands place value.

Step 2.   Digit to the right of 7 is 5 or more (9). Thus, 7, the identified digit in Step 1, is now rounded to 8.

68,951

Step 3. 68,000   Change digits 9, 5, and 1 to zeros, since these digits are to the right of 8, the rounded number.

By rounding 67,951 to the nearest thousand, you can see that 67,951 is closer to 68,000 than to 67,000.

Now let's look at **rounding all the way.** To round a number all the way, you round to the first digit of the number (the leftmost digit) and have only one nonzero digit remaining in the number.

EXAMPLE 3   Round 7,843 all the way.

Step 1. 7,843   Identified leftmost digit is 7.

Step 2.   Digit to the right of 7 is greater than 5, so 7 becomes 8.

8,843

Step 3. 8,000   Change all other digits to zeros.

Rounding 7,843 all the way gives 8,000.

Remember that rounding a digit to a specific place value depends on the degree of accuracy you want in your estimate. For example, In the *Wall Street Journal* clip "A Mother's Pay? $117,000" rounds all the way to $100,000 because the digit to the right of 1 (leftmost digit) is less than 5. The $100,000 is $17,000 less than the original $117,000. You would be more accurate if you rounded $117,000 to the ten thousand place value of 1 identified digit, which is $120,000.

Before concluding this unit, let's look at how to dissect and solve a word problem.

Ariel Skelley/Getty Images

A Mother's Pay? $117,000

If a stay-at-home mom could be financially compensated, she would bring home nearly $117,000 a year.

That is according to an annual study for U.S. Mother's Day Sunday issued by Salary.com, which studies workplace compensation. For the past eight years, Salary.com has calculated mothers' market value by studying pay for tasks such as child care and housekeeping. This year's stay-at-home mom figure is $116,805 per year, while the working-mom figure is $68,405. Both are down from last year because of a change in study methodology. The numbers are based on a survey of moms who averaged a 94-hour workweek. If moms were in the workplace, they would be spending more than half their working hours on overtime.

Wall Street Journal © 2008

How to Dissect and Solve a Word Problem

As a student, your author found solving word problems difficult. Not knowing where to begin after reading the word problem caused the difficulty. Today, students still struggle with word problems as they try to decide where to begin.

Solving word problems involves *organization* and *persistence*. Recall how persistent you were when you learned to ride a two-wheel bike. Do you remember the feeling of success you experienced when you rode the bike without help? Apply this persistence to word problems. Do not be discouraged. Each person learns at a different speed. Your goal must be to FINISH THE RACE and experience the success of solving word problems with ease.

To be organized in solving word problems, you need a plan of action that tells you where to begin—a blueprint aid. Like a builder, you will refer to this blueprint aid constantly until you know the procedure. The blueprint aid for dissecting and solving a word problem follows on page 8. Note that the blueprint aid serves an important function—**it decreases your math anxiety.**

Blueprint Aid for Dissecting and Solving a Word Problem

The facts	Solving for?	Steps to take	Key points

LO 3

David Young Wolff/Photoedit

Now let's study this blueprint aid. The first two columns require that you *read* the word problem slowly. Think of the third column as the basic information you must know or calculate before solving the word problem. Often this column contains formulas that provide the foundation for the step-by-step problem solution. The last column reinforces the key points you should remember.

It's time now to try your skill at using the blueprint aid for dissecting and solving a word problem.

The Word Problem   On the 100th anniversary of Tootsie Roll Industries, the company reported sharply increased sales and profits. Sales reached one hundred ninety-four million dollars and a record profit of twenty-two million, five hundred fifty-six thousand dollars. The company president requested that you round the sales and profit figures all the way.

Study the following blueprint aid and note how we filled in the columns with the information in the word problem. You will find the organization of the blueprint aid most helpful. Be persistent! You *can* dissect and solve word problems! When you are finished with the word problem, make sure the answer seems reasonable.

The facts	Solving for?	Steps to take	Key points
Sales: One hundred ninety-four million dollars. *Profit:* Twenty-two million, five hundred fifty-six thousand dollars.	Sales and profit rounded all the way.	Express each verbal form in numeric form. Identify leftmost digit in each number.	Rounding all the way means only the leftmost digit will remain. All other digits become zeros.

Steps to solving problem

1. Convert verbal to numeric.
   One hundred ninety-four million dollars ──────────────────➤ $194,000,000
   Twenty-two million, five hundred fifty-six thousand dollars ──────────➤ $ 22,556,000

2. Identify leftmost digit of each number.
   $1|94,000,000 $2|2,556,000

3. Round.
   $200,000,000 $20,000,000

Note that in the final answer, $200,000,000 and $20,000,000 have only one nonzero digit.

Remember that you cannot round numbers expressed in verbal form. You must convert these numbers to numeric form.

Now you should see the importance of the information in the third column of the blueprint aid. When you complete your blueprint aids for word problems, do not be concerned if the order of the information in your boxes does not follow the order given in the text boxes. Often you can dissect a word problem in more than one way.

Your first Practice Quiz follows. Be sure to study the paragraph that introduces the Practice Quiz.

LU 1–2 PRACTICE QUIZ

Complete this **Practice Quiz** to see how you are doing.

1. Add by totaling each separate column:
   8,974
   6,439
   + 6,941

2. Estimate by rounding all the way (do not round the total of estimate) and then do the actual computation:
   4,241
   8,794
   + 3,872

3. Subtract and check your answer:
   9,876
   − 4,967

4. Jackson Manufacturing Company projected its year 2011 furniture sales at $900,000. During 2011, Jackson earned $510,000 in sales from major clients and $369,100 in sales from the remainder of its clients. What is the amount by which Jackson over- or under-estimated its sales? Use the blueprint aid, since the answer will show the completed blueprint aid.

Solutions with Step-by-Step Help on DVD

✓ Solutions

1.   14
      14
      2 2
      20
      22,354

2. | Estimate | Actual |
   |---|---|
   | 4,000 | 4,241 |
   | 9,000 | 8,794 |
   | + 4,000 | + 3,872 |
   | **17,000** | **16,907** |

3.   8 18 6 16
      9,876
      − 4,967
      4,909

   Check
      4,909
      + 4,967
      9,876

4. Jackson Manufacturing Company over- or underestimated sales:

The facts	Solving for?	Steps to take	Key points
Projected 2011 sales: $900,000. Major clients: $510,000. Other clients: $369,100.	How much were sales over- or underestimated?	Total projected sales − Total actual sales = Over- or underestimated sales.	Projected sales (minuend) − Actual sales (subtrahend) = Difference.

Steps to solving problem

1. Calculate total actual sales.
   $510,000
   + 369,100
   $879,100

2. Calculate overestimated or underestimated sales.
   $900,000
   − 879,100
   $ 20,900 (overestimated)

LU 1–2a EXTRA PRACTICE QUIZ WITH WORKED-OUT SOLUTIONS

Need more practice? Try this **Extra Practice Quiz** (check figures in Chapter Organizer, p. 20). Worked-out Solutions can be found in Appendix B at end of text.

1. Add by totaling each separate column:
   9,853
   7,394
   +8,843

2. Estimate by rounding all the way (do not round the total of estimate) and then do the actual computation:
   3,482
   6,981
   +5,490

3. Subtract and check your answer:

$$9,787$$
$$-5,968$$

4. Jackson Manufacturing Company projected its year 2011 furniture sales at $878,000. During 2011, Jackson earned $492,900 in sales from major clients and $342,000 in sales from the remainder of its clients. What is the amount by which Jackson over- or under-estimated its sales?

Learning Unit 1–3: Multiplying and Dividing Whole Numbers

LO 1

The *Wall Street Journal* clip "United to Charge Some Fliers $25 per Extra Checked Bag" shows a new charge facing passengers. If you fly on United and have 6 extra bags to check it would cost you an additional $150:

$$\$25 \times 6 \text{ bags} = \$150$$

If you divide $150 by $25 per bag you get 6 bags.

This unit will sharpen your skills in two important arithmetic operations—multiplication and division. These two operations frequently result in knowledgeable business decisions.

United to Charge Some Fliers $25 per Extra Checked Bag; Others Consider Similar Move

By Susan Carey

BUCKING CONVENTION, United Airlines plans to charge passengers buying its cheapest, nonrefundable tickets for domestic and Canadian flights $25 to check a second piece of luggage—unless the travelers have elite status in its Mileage Plus frequent-flier program.

Until this change, all United passengers could check two 50-pound suitcases free of charge, the in-

Wall Street Journal © 2008

Multiplication of Whole Numbers—Shortcut to Addition

From calculating your cost of checking extra baggage you know that multiplication is a *shortcut to addition:*

$$\$25 \times 6 = \$150 \quad \text{or} \quad \$25 + \$25 + \$25 + \$25 + \$25 + \$25 = \$150$$

Before learning the steps used to multiply whole numbers with two or more digits, you must learn some multiplication terminology.

Note in the following example that the top number (number we want to multiply) is the **multiplicand.** The bottom number (number doing the multiplying) is the **multiplier.** The final number (answer) is the **product.** The numbers between the multiplier and the product are **partial products.** Also note how we positioned the partial product 2090. This number is the result of multiplying 418 by 50 (the 5 is in the tens position). On each line in the partial products, we placed the first digit directly below the digit we used in the multiplication process.

EXAMPLE

	418 ←	Top number (multiplicand)
Partial products	× 52 ←	Bottom number (multiplier)
	836	
	20 90	
	21,736 ←	Product answer

$$2 \times 418 = \quad 836$$
$$50 \times 418 = \underline{+\ 20,900}$$
$$21,736$$

We can now give the following steps for multiplying whole numbers with two or more digits:

MULTIPLYING WHOLE NUMBERS WITH TWO OR MORE DIGITS
Step 1. Align the multiplicand (top number) and multiplier (bottom number) at the right. Usually, you should make the smaller number the multiplier.
Step 2. Begin by multiplying the right digit of the multiplier with the right digit of the multiplicand. Keep multiplying as you move left through the multiplicand. Your first partial product aligns at the right with the multiplicand and multiplier.
Step 3. Move left through the multiplier and continue multiplying the multiplicand. Your partial product right digit or first digit is placed directly below the digit in the multiplier that you used to multiply.
Step 4. Continue Steps 2 and 3 until you have completed your multiplication process. Then add the partial products to get the final product.

Checking and Estimating Multiplication

We can check the multiplication process by reversing the multiplicand and multiplier and then multiplying. Let's first estimate 52 × 418 by rounding all the way.

EXAMPLE

$$
\begin{array}{r}
50 \leftarrow \quad 52 \\
\times \ 400 \leftarrow \times 418 \\
\hline
20{,}000 \quad \ 416 \\
52 \\
20\ 8 \\
\hline
\boxed{21{,}736}
\end{array}
$$

By estimating before actually working the problem, we know our answer should be about 20,000. When we multiply 52 by 418, we get the same answer as when we multiply 418 × 52—and the answer is about 20,000. Remember, if we had not rounded all the way, our estimate would have been closer. If we had used a calculator, the rounded estimate would have helped us check the calculator's answer. Our commonsense estimate tells us our answer is near 20,000—not 200,000.

Before you study the division of whole numbers, you should know (1) the multiplication shortcut with numbers ending in zeros and (2) how to multiply a whole number by a power of 10.

MULTIPLICATION SHORTCUT WITH NUMBERS ENDING IN ZEROS
Step 1. When zeros are at the end of the multiplicand or the multiplier, or both, disregard the zeros and multiply.
Step 2. Count the number of zeros in the multiplicand and multiplier.
Step 3. Attach the number of zeros counted in Step 2 to your answer.

EXAMPLE

$$
\begin{array}{r}
65{,}000 \\
\times \ \ 420 \\
\hline
\end{array}
\qquad
\begin{array}{r}
65 \\
\times \ \ 42 \\
\hline
1\ 30 \\
26\ 0 \\
\hline
27{,}300{,}000
\end{array}
\qquad
\begin{array}{r}
3 \text{ zeros} \\
+\ 1 \text{ zero} \\
\hline
4 \text{ zeros}
\end{array}
$$

No need to multiply rows of zeros

$$
\begin{array}{r}
65{,}000 \\
\times \ \ \ \ 420 \\
\hline
00\ 000 \\
1\ 300\ 00 \\
26\ 000\ 0 \\
\hline
\boxed{27{,}300{,}000}
\end{array}
$$

MULTIPLYING A WHOLE NUMBER BY A POWER OF 10
Step 1. Count the number of zeros in the power of 10 (a whole number that begins with 1 and ends in one or more zeros such as 10, 100, 1,000, and so on).
Step 2. Attach that number of zeros to the right side of the other whole number to obtain the answer. Insert comma(s) as needed every three digits, moving from right to left.

EXAMPLE

99 × 10   = 99<u>0</u>   = $\boxed{990}$ ← Add 1 zero

99 × 100   = 9,9<u>00</u>   = $\boxed{9{,}900}$ ← Add 2 zeros

99 × 1,000 = 99,<u>000</u> = $\boxed{99{,}000}$ ← Add 3 zeros

When a zero is in the center of the multiplier, you can do the following:

EXAMPLE

$$
\begin{array}{r}
658 \\
\times \ \ 403 \\
\hline
1\ 974 \\
263\ 2\square \\
\hline
\boxed{265{,}174}
\end{array}
\qquad
\begin{array}{r}
3 \times 658 = \quad 1{,}974 \\
400 \times 658 = +\ 263{,}200 \\
\hline
\boxed{265{,}174}
\end{array}
$$

Division of Whole Numbers

LO 2

Division is the reverse of multiplication and a time-saving shortcut related to subtraction. For example, in the introduction of this learning unit you determined you would pay $150 extra to check 6 additional bags. You can also multiply $25 × 6 to get $150. Since division is the reverse of multiplication you can say that $150 ÷ 6 = $25.

Universal Press Syndicate © 2008

Division can be indicated by the common symbols ÷ and $\overline{)}$, or by the bar — in a fraction and the forward slant / between two numbers, which means the first number is divided by the second number. Division asks how many times one number **(divisor)** is contained in another number **(dividend).** The answer, or result, is the **quotient.** When the divisor (number used to divide) doesn't divide evenly into the dividend (number we are dividing), the result is a **partial quotient,** with the leftover amount the **remainder** (expressed as fractions in later chapters). The following example illustrates *even division* (this is also an example of *long division* because the divisor has more than one digit).

EXAMPLE

$$
\begin{array}{r}
18 \leftarrow \text{Quotient} \\
\text{Divisor} \longrightarrow 15\overline{)270} \leftarrow \text{Dividend} \\
\underline{15} \\
120 \\
\underline{120}
\end{array}
$$

This example divides 15 into 27 once with 12 remaining. The 0 in the dividend is brought down to 12. Dividing 120 by 15 equals 8 with no remainder; that is, even division. The following example illustrates *uneven division with a remainder* (this is also an example of *short division* because the divisor has only one digit).

EXAMPLE

$$
\begin{array}{r}
24\,\text{R}1 \leftarrow \text{Remainder} \\
7\overline{)169} \\
\underline{14} \\
29 \\
\underline{28} \\
1
\end{array}
$$

Check

$(7 \quad \times \quad 24) \quad + \quad 1 \quad = \quad 169$

Divisor × Quotient + Remainder = Dividend

Note how doing the check gives you assurance that your calculation is correct. When the divisor has one digit (short division) as in this example, you can often calculate the division mentally as illustrated in the following examples:

EXAMPLES

$$
\begin{array}{r}
108 \\
8\overline{)864}
\end{array}
\qquad
\begin{array}{r}
16\,\text{R}6 \\
7\overline{)118}
\end{array}
$$

Next, let's look at the value of estimating division.

Estimating Division

Before actually working a division problem, estimate the quotient by rounding. This estimate helps check the answer. The example that follows is rounded all the way. After you make an estimate, work the problem and check your answer by multiplication.

EXAMPLE
<table>
<tr><td>36 R111</td><td>**Estimate**</td><td>**Check**</td></tr>
</table>

```
         36 R111          Estimate          Check
    138)5,079                  50              138
      4 14               100)5,000          ×  36
      ─────                                  ────
        939                                   828
        828                                  4 14
        ───                                  ─────
        111                                  4,968
                                           +  111  ←── Add remainder
                                            ─────
                                            5,079
```

Now let's turn our attention to division shortcuts with zeros.

Division Shortcuts with Zeros

The steps that follow show a shortcut that you can use when you divide numbers with zeros.

DIVISION SHORTCUT WITH NUMBERS ENDING IN ZEROS
Step 1. When the dividend and divisor have ending zeros, count the number of ending zeros in the divisor.
Step 2. Drop the same number of zeros in the dividend as in the divisor, counting from right to left.

Note the following examples of division shortcut with numbers ending in zeros. Since two of the symbols used for division are ÷ and $\overline{)}$, our first examples show the zero shortcut method with the ÷ symbol.

EXAMPLES

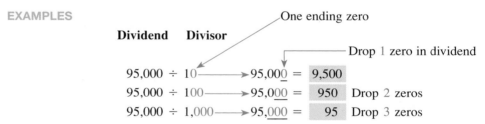

```
Dividend   Divisor                    One ending zero
                                    ┌───── Drop 1 zero in dividend
95,000 ÷ 10 ──────→ 95,000 =  9,500
95,000 ÷ 100 ─────→ 95,000 =   950    Drop 2 zeros
95,000 ÷ 1,000 ───→ 95,000 =    95    Drop 3 zeros
```

In a long division problem with the $\overline{)}$ symbol, you again count the number of ending zeros in the divisor. Then drop the same number of ending zeros in the dividend and divide as usual.

EXAMPLE
```
6,500)88,000 ←── Drop 2 zeros              13 R35
                                        65)880
                                           65
                                          ───
                                          230
         65)880 ←┘                        195
                                          ───
                                           35
```

You are now ready to practice what you learned by dissecting and solving a word problem.

How to Dissect and Solve a Word Problem

The blueprint aid on page 18 will be your guide to dissecting and solving the following word problem.

The Word Problem Dunkin' Donuts sells to four different companies a total of $3,500 worth of doughnuts per week. What is the total annual sales to these companies? What is the yearly sales per company? (Assume each company buys the same amount.) Check your answer to show how multiplication and division are related.

The facts	Solving for?	Steps to take	Key points
Sales per week: $3,500. Companies: 4.	Total annual sales to all four companies. Yearly sales per company.	Sales per week × Weeks in year (52) = Total annual sales. Total annual sales ÷ Total companies = Yearly sales per company.	Division is the reverse of multiplication.

Steps to solving problem

1. Calculate total annual sales. $3,500 × 52 weeks = $182,000

2. Calculate yearly sales per company, $182,000 ÷ 4 = $45,500

   Check

   $45,500 × 4 = $182,000

It's time again to check your progress with a Practice Quiz.

LU 1–3   PRACTICE QUIZ

Complete this **Practice Quiz** to see how you are doing.

1. Estimate the actual problem by rounding all the way, work the actual problem, and check:

   Actual   **Estimate**   **Check**
   3,894
   × 18

2. Multiply by shortcut method: 3. Multiply by shortcut method:
   77,000   95 × 10,000
   × 1,800

4. Divide by rounding all the way, complete the actual calculation, and check, showing remainder as a whole number.
   $26\overline{)5,325}$

5. Divide by shortcut method:
   $4,000\overline{)96,000}$

6. Assume General Motors produces 960 Chevrolets each workday (Monday through Friday). If the cost to produce each car is $6,500, what is General Motors' total cost for the year? Check your answer.

Solutions with Step-by-Step Help on DVD

✓ Solutions

1. **Estimate**   **Actual**   **Check**
   4,000   3,894   8 × 3,894 =   31,152
   ×   20   ×   18   10 × 3,894 =   + 38,940
   80,000   31 152   70,092
                            38 94
                            70,092

2. 77 × 18 = 1,386 + 5 zeros = 138,600,000   3. 95 + 4 zeros = 950,000

4. **Rounding**   **Actual**   **Check**
        166 R20   204 R21   26 × 204 = 5,304
   $30\overline{)5,000}$ $26\overline{)5,325}$ +   21
        3 0   5 2   5,325
        2 00   125
        1 80   104
         200   21
         180
          20

5. Drop 3 zeros = $\dfrac{\boxed{24}}{4\overline{)96}}$

6. General Motors' total cost per year:

The facts	Solving for?	Steps to take	Key points
Cars produced each workday: 960. *Workweek:* 5 days. *Cost per car:* $6,500.	Total cost per year.	Cars produced per week × 52 = Total cars produced per year. Total cars produced per year × Total cost per car = Total cost per year.	Whenever possible, use multiplication and division shortcuts with zeros. Multiplication can be checked by division.

Steps to solving problem

1. Calculate total cars produced per week.   5 × 960 = 4,800 cars produced per week

2. Calculate total cars produced per year.   4,800 cars × 52 weeks = 249,600 total cars produced per year

3. Calculate total cost per year.   249,600 cars × $6,500 = **$1,622,400,000**
(multiply 2,496 × 65 and add zeros)

Check

$1,622,400,000 ÷ 249,600 = $6,500 (drop 2 zeros before dividing)

LU 1–3a   **EXTRA PRACTICE QUIZ WITH WORKED-OUT SOLUTIONS**

Need more practice? Try this **Extra Practice Quiz** (check figures in Chapter Organizer, p. 20). Worked-out Solutions can be found in Appendix B at end of text.

1. Estimate the actual problem by rounding all the way, work the actual problem, and check:

Actual	**Estimate**	**Check**
4,938		
× 19		

2. Multiply by shortcut method:
86,000
× 1,900

3. Multiply by shortcut method:
86 × 10,000

4. Divide by rounding all the way, complete the actual calculation, and check, showing remainder as a whole number.
26$\overline{)6,394}$

5. Divide by the shortcut method:
3,000$\overline{)99,000}$

6. Assume General Motors produces 850 Chevrolets each workday (Monday through Friday). If the cost to produce each car is $7,000, what is General Motors's total cost for the year? Check your answer.

CHAPTER ORGANIZER AND REFERENCE GUIDE

Topic	Key point, procedure, formula	Example(s) to illustrate situation
Reading and writing numeric and verbal whole numbers, p. 4	Placement of digits in a number gives the value of the digits (Figure 1.1). Commas separate every three digits, moving from right to left. Begin at left to read and write number in verbal form. Do not read zeros or use *and*. Hyphenate numbers twenty-one to ninety-nine. Reverse procedure to change verbal number to numeric.	462 → Four hundred sixty-two 6,741 → Six thousand, seven hundred forty-one
Rounding whole numbers, p. 6	1. Identify place value of the digit to be rounded. 2. If digit to the right is 5 or more, round up; if less than 5, do not change. 3. Change all digits to the right of rounded identified digit to zeros.	643 to nearest ten 4 in tens place value. 3 is not 5 or more Thus, 643 rounds to 640.
Rounding all the way, p. 7	Round to first digit of number. One nonzero digit remains. In estimating, you round each number of the problem to one nonzero digit. The final answer is not rounded.	468,451 ⟶ 500,000 The 5 is the only nonzero digit remaining.
Adding whole numbers, p. 10	1. Align numbers at the right. 2. Add units column. If sum more than 9, carry tens digit. 3. Moving left, repeat Step 2 until all place values are added. Add from top to bottom. Check by adding bottom to top or adding each column separately and combining.	$$\begin{array}{r} 65 \\ + 47 \\ \hline 112 \end{array} \quad \begin{array}{r} 12 \\ +10 \\ \hline 112 \end{array}$$ Checking sum of each digit
Subtracting whole numbers, p. 11	1. Align minuend and subtrahend at the right. 2. Subtract units digits. If necessary, borrow 1 from tens digit in minuend. 3. Moving left, repeat Step 2 until all place values are subtracted. Minuend less subtrahend equals difference.	**Check** $$\begin{array}{r} {}^{5\,18} \\ \cancel{685} \\ -492 \\ \hline 193 \end{array} \quad \begin{array}{r} 193 \\ +492 \\ \hline 685 \end{array}$$
Multiplying whole numbers, p. 14	1. Align multiplicand and multiplier at the right. 2. Begin at the right and keep multiplying as you move to the left. First partial product aligns at the right with multiplicand and multiplier. 3. Move left through multiplier and continue multiplying multiplicand. Partial product right digit or first digit is placed directly below digit in multiplier. 4. Continue Steps 2 and 3 until multiplication is complete. Add partial products to get final product. **Shortcuts:** (a) When multiplicand or multiplier, or both, end in zeros, disregard zeros and multiply; attach same number of zeros to answer. If zero in center of multiplier, no need to show row of zeros. (b) If multiplying by power of 10, attach same number of zeros to whole number multiplied.	$$\begin{array}{r} 223 \\ \times\ 32 \\ \hline 446 \\ 6\ 69 \\ \hline 7,136 \end{array}$$ a. $\begin{array}{r} 48,000 \\ \times\ 40 \end{array}$ $\begin{array}{r} 48 \\ 4 \end{array}$ $\begin{array}{r} 3 \text{ zeros} \\ +1 \text{ zero} \\ \hline 4 \text{ zeros} \end{array}$ 1,920,000 $\begin{array}{r} 524 \\ \times\ 206 \\ \hline 3\ 144 \\ 104\ 8 \\ \hline 107,944 \end{array}$ b. 14 × 10 = 140 (attach 1 zero) 14 × 1,000 = 14,000 (attach 3 zeros)

(continues)

CHAPTER ORGANIZER AND REFERENCE GUIDE

Topic	Key point, procedure, formula	Example(s) to illustrate situation
Dividing whole numbers, p. 16	**1.** When divisor is divided into the dividend, the remainder is less than divisor. **2.** Drop zeros from dividend right to left by number of zeros found in the divisor. Even division has no remainder; uneven division has a remainder; divisor with one digit is short division; and divisor with more than one digit is long division.	**1.** $\begin{array}{r} 5\ R6 \\ 14\overline{)76} \\ 70 \\ \hline 6 \end{array}$ **2.** $5{,}000 \div 100 = 50 \div 1 = \boxed{50}$ $5{,}000 \div 1{,}000 = 5 \div 1 = \boxed{5}$

KEY TERMS	addends, *p. 10* decimal point, *p. 4* decimal system, *p. 4* difference, *p. 11* dividend, *p. 16* divisor, *p. 16*	minuend, *p. 11* multiplicand, *p. 14* multiplier, *p. 14* partial products, *p. 14* partial quotient, *p. 16* product, *p. 14*	quotient, *p. 16* remainder, *p. 16* rounding all the way, *p. 7* subtrahend, *p. 11* sum, *p. 10* whole number, *p. 4*

CHECK FIGURE FOR EXTRA PRACTICE QUIZZES WITH PAGE REFERENCES. (WORKED-OUT SOLUTIONS IN APPENDIX B.)	LU 1–1a (p. 9) **1.** A. Eight thousand, six hundred eighty-two; B. Fifty-six thousand, two hundred ninety-five; C. Seven hundred thirty-two billion, three hundred ten million, four hundred forty-four thousand, eight hundred eighty-eight **2.** A. 40; B. 700; C. 7,000; D. 6,000 **3.** 3,000,000; 400,000	LU 1–2a (p. 13) **1.** 26,090 **2.** 15,000; 15,953 **3.** 3,819 **4.** 43,100 (over)	LU 1–3a (p. 19) **1.** 100,000; 93,822 **2.** 163,400,000 **3.** 860,000 **4.** 245 R24 **5.** 33 **6.** $1,547,000,000

Critical Thinking Discussion Questions

1. List the four steps of the decision-making process. Do you think all companies should be required to follow these steps? Give an example.

2. Explain the three steps used to round whole numbers. Pick a whole number and explain why it should not be rounded.

3. How do you check subtraction? If you were to attend a movie, explain how you might use the subtraction check method.

4. Explain how you can check multiplication. If you visit a local supermarket, how could you show multiplication as a short-cut to addition?

5. Explain how division is the reverse of multiplication. Using the supermarket example, explain how division is a timesaving shortcut related to subtraction.

Classroom Notes

Check figures for odd-numbered problems in Appendix C

Name _____   Date _____

DRILL PROBLEMS

Add the following:

1–1.   99
           + 15

1–2.   790
          + 755

1–3.   88
          + 88

1–4.   88
          + 75

1–5.   6,251
          + 7,329

1–6.   59,481
            51,411
          + 70,821

1–7.   78,159
            15,850
          + 19,681

Subtract the following:

1–8.   68
           −19

1–9.   80
           −42

1–10.   287
            −199

1–11.   9,000
            −5,400

1–12.   9,800
            −8,900

1–13.   1,622
            − 548

Multiply the following:

1–14.   75
            × 8

1–15.   510
            × 61

1–16.   800
            × 200

1–17.   677
            × 503

1–18.   309
            × 850

1–19.   450
            × 280

Divide the following by short division:

1–20. 6)1,200

1–21. 9)810

1–22. 4)164

Divide the following by long division. Show work and remainder.

1–23. 6)520

1–24. 62)8,915

Add the following without rearranging:

1–25. 87 + 325

1–26. 1,055 + 88

1–27. 666 + 950

1–28. 1,011 + 17

1–29. Add the following and check by totaling each column individually without carrying numbers:

Check

```
  8,539
  6,842
+ 9,495
```

Estimate the following by rounding all the way and then do actual addition:

	Actual	Estimate			Actual	Estimate
1–30.	7,700			**1–31.**	6,980	
	9,286				3,190	
	+ 3,900				+ 7,819	

Subtract the following without rearranging:

1–32. $190 - 66$

1–33. $950 - 870$

1–34. Subtract the following and check answer:

```
  591,001
− 375,956
```

Multiply the following horizontally:

1–35. 17×8 **1–36.** 84×8 **1–37.** 27×8 **1–38.** 17×6

Divide the following and check by multiplication:

1–39. $45\overline{)876}$ **Check** **1–40.** $46\overline{)1,950}$ **Check**

Complete the following:

1–41.	9,200	**1–42.**	3,000,000
	− 1,510		− 769,459
	− 700		− 68,541

1–43. Estimate the following problem by rounding all the way and then do the actual multiplication:

Actual	Estimate
870	
× 81	

Divide the following by the shortcut method:

1–44. $1,000\overline{)950,000}$ **1–45.** $100\overline{)70,000}$

24

1–46. Estimate actual problem by rounding all the way and do actual division:

Actual   **Estimate**

$$695\overline{)8{,}950}$$

WORD PROBLEMS

1–47. Home Heating Service, Inc., out of Colorado Springs is offering a special on winter maintenance advertised in the Gazette Telegraph for household furnaces for the fall of 2009. The offer is buy one service for $95 or two services (this year and next year) for $150. What is the per service cost if the two-year service is purchased?

1–48. An education can be the key to higher earnings. In a U.S. Census Bureau study, high school graduates earned $30,400 per year. Associate's degree graduates averaged $38,200 per year. Bachelor's degree graduates averaged $52,200 per year. Assuming a 50-year work-life, calculate the lifetime earnings for a high school graduate, associate's degree graduate, and bachelor's degree graduate. What's the lifetime income difference between a high school and associate's agree? What about the lifetime difference between a high school and bachelor's degree?

1–49. Assume season-ticket prices in the lower bowl for the Buffalo Bills will rise from $480 for a 10-game package to $600. Fans sitting in the best seats in the upper deck will pay an increase from $440 to $540. Don Manning plans to purchase 2 season tickets for either lower bowl or upper deck. **(a)** How much more will 2 tickets cost for lower bowl? **(b)** How much more will 2 tickets cost for upper deck? **(c)** What will be his total cost for a 10-game package for lower bowl? **(d)** What will be his total cost for a 10-game package for upper deck?

1–50. Some ticket prices for *Grease* on Broadway were $50, $75, $100, and $150. For a family of four, estimate the cost of the $75 tickets by rounding all the way and then do the actual multiplication:

1–51. Walt Disney World Resort and United Vacations got together to create a special deal. The air-inclusive package features accommodations for three nights at Disney's All-Star Resort, hotel taxes, and a four-day unlimited Magic Pass. Prices are $609 per person traveling from Washington, DC, and $764 per person traveling from Los Angeles. **(a)** What would be the cost for a family of four leaving from Washington, DC? **(b)** What would be the cost for a family of four leaving from Los Angeles? **(c)** How much more will it cost the family from Los Angeles?

1–52. NTB Tires bought 910 tires from its manufacturer for $36 per tire. What is the total cost of NTB's purchase? If the store can sell all the tires at $65 each, what will be the store's gross profit, or the difference between its sales and costs (Sales − Costs = Gross profit)?

1–53. What was the total average number of visits for these Internet Web sites?

Web site	Average daily unique visitors
1. Orbitz.com	1,527,000
2. Mypoints.com	1,356,000
3. Americangreetings.com	745,000
4. Bizrate.com	503,000
5. Half.com	397,000

1–54. Lee Wong bought 5,000 shares of GE stock. She held the stock for 6 months. Then Lee sold 190 shares on Monday, 450 shares on Tuesday and again on Thursday, and 900 shares on Friday. How many shares does Lee still own? The average share of the stock Lee owns is worth $48 per share. What is the total value of Lee's stock?

1–55. A report from the Center for Science in the Public Interest—a consumer group based in Washington, DC—released a study listing calories of various ice cream treats sold by six of the largest ice cream companies. The worst treat tested by the group was 1,270 total calories. People need roughly 2,200 to 2,500 calories per day. Using a daily average, how many additional calories should a person consume after eating the ice cream?

1–56. At Rose State College, Alison Wells received the following grades in her online accounting class: 90, 65, 85, 80, 75, and 90. Alison's instructor, Professor Clark, said he would drop the lowest grade. What is Alison's average?

1–57. Lee Wills, professor of business, has 18 students in Accounting I, 26 in Accounting II, 22 in Introduction to Computers, 23 in Business Law, and 29 in Introduction to Business. What is the total number of students in Professor Wills's classes? If 12 students withdraw, how many total students will Professor Wills have?

1–58. Ron Alf, owner of Alf's Moving Company, bought a new truck. On Ron's first trip, he drove 1,200 miles and used 80 gallons of gas. How many miles per gallon did Ron get from his new truck? On Ron's second trip, he drove 840 miles and used 60 gallons. What is the difference in miles per gallon between Ron's first trip and his second trip?

1–59. If Office Depot reduced its $450 Kodak digital camera by $59, what is the new selling price of the digital camera? If Office Depot sold 1,400 cameras at the new price, what were the store's digital camera dollar sales?

1–60. Assume Barnes and Noble.com has 289 business math texts in inventory. During one month, the online bookstore ordered and received 1,855 texts; it also sold 1,222 on the Web. What is the bookstore's inventory at the end of the month? If each text costs $59, what is the end-of-month inventory cost?

1–61. Assume Cabot Company produced 2,115,000 cans of paint in August. Cabot sold 2,011,000 of these cans. If each can cost $18, what were Cabot's ending inventory of paint cans and its total ending inventory cost?

1–62. A local community college has 20 faculty members in the business department, 40 in psychology, 26 in English, and 140 in all other departments. What is the total number of faculty at this college? If each faculty member advises 25 students, how many students attend the local college?

1–63. Hometown Buffet had 90 customers on Sunday, 70 on Monday, 65 on Tuesday, and a total of 310 on Wednesday to Saturday. How many customers did Hometown Buffet serve during the week? If each customer spends $9, what were the total sales for the week?

If Hometown Buffet had the same sales each week, what were the sales for the year?

1–64. A local travel agency projected its year 2009 sales at $880,000. During 2009, the agency earned $482,900 sales from its major clients and $116,500 sales from the remainder of its clients. How much did the agency overestimate its sales?

1–65. Ryan Seary works at US Airways and earned $71,000 last year before tax deductions. From Ryan's total earnings, his company subtracted $1,388 for federal income taxes, $4,402 for Social Security, and $1,030 for Medicare taxes. What was Ryan's actual, or net, pay for the year?

1–66. Assume Macy's received the following invoice amounts from some of its local suppliers. How much does the company owe?

Per item	
22 paintings	$210
39 rockers	75
40 desk lamps	65
120 coffee tables	155

1–67. Roger Company produces beach balls and operates three shifts. Roger produces 5,000 balls per shift on shifts 1 and 2. On shift 3, the company can produce 6 times as many balls as on shift 1. Assume a 5-day workweek. How many beach balls does Roger produce per week and per year?

1–68. Assume 6,000 children go to Disneyland today. How much additional revenue will Disneyland receive if it raises the cost of admission from $31 to $41 and lowers the age limit for adults from 12 years old to 10 years old?

1–69. Moe Brink has a $900 balance in his checkbook. During the week, Moe wrote the following checks: rent, $350; telephone, $44; food, $160; and entertaining, $60. Moe also made a $1,200 deposit. What is Moe's new checkbook balance?

1–70. A local Sports Authority store, an athletic sports shop, bought and sold the following merchandise:

	Cost	Selling price
Tennis rackets	$ 2,900	$ 3,999
Tennis balls	70	210
Bowling balls	1,050	2,950
Sneakers	+ 8,105	+ 14,888

What was the total cost of the merchandise bought by Sports Authority? If the shop sold all its merchandise, what were the sales and the resulting gross profit (Sales − Costs = Gross profit)?

1–71. Rich Engel, the bookkeeper for Engel's Real Estate, and his manager are concerned about the company's telephone bills. Last year the company's average monthly phone bill was $32. Rich's manager asked him for an average of this year's phone bills. Rich's records show the following:

January	$ 34	July	$ 28
February	60	August	23
March	20	September	29
April	25	October	25
May	30	November	22
June	59	December	41

What is the average of this year's phone bills? Did Rich and his manager have a justifiable concern?

1–72. On Monday, a local True Value Hardware sold 15 paint brushes at $3 each, 6 wrenches at $5 each, 7 bags of grass seed at $3 each, 4 lawn mowers at $119 each, and 28 cans of paint at $8 each. What were True Value's total dollar sales on Monday?

1–73. While redecorating, Lee Owens went to Carpet World and bought 150 square yards of commercial carpet. The total cost of the carpet was $6,000. How much did Lee pay per square yard?

1–74. Washington Construction built 12 ranch houses for $115,000 each. From the sale of these houses, Washington received $1,980,000. How much gross profit (Sales − Costs = Gross profit) did Washington make on the houses?

The four partners of Washington Construction split all profits equally. How much will each partner receive?

CHALLENGE PROBLEMS

1–75. Douglas and Mallori Rouse have the following monthly budget items: mortgage, $1,252; car payment, $458; food, $325; insurance, $112; cable, $75; cell phones, $80; utilities, $295; credit card payment, $50; cash donations, $100; gym fee, $25; car and home maintenance, $250; gasoline, $200; and savings, $500. Douglas earns $2,800 and Mallori earns $1,000 per month. Mallori wants to quit her job and go back to school. Can they afford for her to do this? Explain using math calculations.

1–76. Paula Sanchez is trying to determine her 2011 finances. Paula's actual 2010 finances were as follows:

Income:		Assets:		
Gross income	$69,000	Checking account	$ 1,950	
Interest income	450	Savings account	8,950	
Total	$69,450	Automobile	1,800	
Expenses:		Personal property	14,000	
Living	$24,500	Total	$26,700	
Insurance premium	350	Liabilities:		
Taxes	14,800	Note to bank	4,500	
Medical	585	Net worth	$22,200	($26,700 − $4,500)
Investment	4,000			
Total	$44,235			

Net worth = Assets − Liabilities
(own)   (owe)

Paula believes her gross income will double in 2011 but her interest income will decrease $150. She plans to reduce her 2011 living expenses by one-half. Paula's insurance company wrote a letter announcing that her insurance premiums would triple in 2011. Her accountant estimates her taxes will decrease $250 and her medical costs will increase $410. Paula also hopes to cut her investments expenses by one-fourth. Paula's accountant projects that her savings and checking accounts will each double in value. On January 2, 2011, Paula sold her automobile and began to use public transportation. Paula forecasts that her personal property will decrease by one-seventh. She has sent her bank a $375 check to reduce her bank note. Could you give Paula an updated list of her 2011 finances? If you round all the way each 2010 and 2011 asset and liability, what will be the difference in Paula's net worth?

 SUMMARY PRACTICE TEST

1. Translate the following verbal forms to numbers and add. *(p. 4)*

   a. Four thousand, eight hundred thirty-nine

   b. Seven million, twelve

   c. Twelve thousand, three hundred ninety-two

2. Express the following number in verbal form. *(p. 4)*

   9,622,364

3. Round the following numbers. *(p. 6)*

Nearest ten	Nearest hundred	Nearest thousand	Round all the way
a. 68	**b.** 888	**c.** 8,325	**d.** 14,821

4. Estimate the following actual problem by rounding all the way, work the actual problem, and check by adding each column of digits separately. *(pp. 7, 10)*

Actual   **Estimate**   **Check**

   1,886
   9,411
+ 6,395

5. Estimate the following actual problem by rounding all the way and then do the actual multiplication. *(pp. 7, 14)*

Actual   **Estimate**

   8,843
×   906

6. Multiply the following by the shortcut method. *(p. 15)*

$829,412 \times 1,000$

7. Divide the following and check the answer by multiplication. *(p. 14)*

                        Check

$39\overline{)14,800}$

8. Divide the following by the shortcut method. *(p. 17)*

$6,000 \div 60$

9. Ling Wong bought a $299 iPod that was reduced to $205. Ling gave the clerk 3 $100 bills. What change will Ling receive? *(p. 11)*

10. Sam Song plans to buy a $16,000 Ford Focus with an interest charge of $4,000. Sam figures he can afford a monthly payment of $400. If Sam must pay 40 equal monthly payments, can he afford the Ford Focus? *(pp. 10, 14)*

11. Lester Hal has the oil tank at his business filled 20 times per year. The tank has a capacity of 200 gallons. Assume **(a)** the price of oil fuel is $3 per gallon and **(b)** the tank is completely empty each time Lester has it filled. What is Lester's average monthly oil bill? Complete the following blueprint aid for dissecting and solving the word problem. *(pp. 10, 14, 16)*

The facts	Solving for?	Steps to take	Key points

Steps to solving problem

An Early Look at Retirement

At 43, Steve Gurney spent a week in a retirement community and was surprised by what he found. **AS TOLD TO MARY BETH FRANKLIN**

WHY DID YOU MAKE THE MOVE? During my 20 years publishing the *Guide to Retirement Living SourceBook* (www .retirement-living.com), I've visited more than 500 communities. But I felt I didn't understand what it was like to be a resident. I wanted to experience moving into a retirement home so I could help my readers prepare themselves and make more-informed choices.

WERE THERE ANY SURPRISES? Lots of them. As I walked through my house deciding what I would take into a one-bedroom apartment and what I would leave behind, I realized how my memories were tied to my belongings. I felt a bit of the loss that elders must feel when they have to cull a lifetime of possessions.

WHAT ABOUT COSTS? It really hit home that my monthly rent, including dining and housekeeping services, would be more than the mortgage payment on my four-bedroom house. At the retirement community I moved into, rates range from $2,700 to $4,000 a month for independent living and up to $6,300 a month for assisted living.

WHAT WAS THE HARDEST PART? Adjusting to a new environment. Just like being the new kid at school, it was a bit unnerving at first to decide where to sit at dinner. Some of the residents who volunteer to help newcomers transition invited me to join them in the dining room.

WHAT WAS THE BEST PART? The people. Many of them have lived fascinating lives, and I'd often get an interesting nugget of information or a history lesson from someone who actually experienced an event.

HOW HAS THE EXPERIENCE CHANGED YOU? I learned to slow down. One day I went with a group to visit a museum and I did something I had never done before: I read every single word at the exhibit. Although it seems as though the sky is falling these days, an exhibit on the Civil War reminded me that our country has overcome much worse challenges. It helped put today's bad news in perspective.

WHAT'S NEXT? I hope to repeat the project in other types of communities, including a nursing home and an Alzheimer's facility. ▪

From Kiplinger's Personal Finance, p. 80.

▪ WHEN GURNEY FELT LIKE THE NEW KID ON THE BLOCK, RESIDENTS OF PAUL SPRING RETIREMENT COMMUNITY, IN ALEXANDRIA, VA., MADE HIM WELCOME.

BUSINESS MATH ISSUE

Rates at resident communities for assisted living make retirement impossible.

1. List the key points of the article and information to support your position.
2. Write a group defense of your position using math calculations to support your view.

PROJECT A

Write each attendance number numerically and calculate total attendance.

Misadventure?

Attendance at Disney theme parks in 2006:

Park	Attendance (in millions)
Magic Kingdom (Florida)	16.64
Disneyland (California)	14.73
Tokyo Disneyland	12.90
Tokyo Disney Sea	12.10
Disneyland Paris	10.60
Epcot (Florida)	10.46
Disney-MGM Studios (Florida)	9.10
Animal Kingdom (Florida)	8.91
California Adventure	**5.95**
Hong Kong Disneyland	5.20
Walt Disney Studios Paris	2.20

Source: TEA/ERA Theme Park Attendance Report

The 'Tower of Terror' ride at Disney's California Adventure.

Wall Street Journal © 2008

PROJECT B

Assuming you set up a home safety system for 12 months, what would be the difference in cost between InGrid and iControl?

Home, Safe Home

A comparison of basic features offered by wireless home-security systems, in which homeowners can arm/disarm the sensors via the Internet and receive alerts through email and text messaging.

	Installation	Features	Cost
InGrid	Do-it-yourself installation.	Integrated smoke/fire sensors; weather forecasts and severe-weather alerts.	$299 hardware cost plus $30 in monthly fees*
iControl	Professional installation in most cases, though some security dealers sell do-it-yourself versions.	Video monitoring; smoke-detection sensors; Can also activate lights, change or schedule thermostat settings to save energy.	$100 hardware cost plus $15 monthly fees
Alarm. com	Professional installation in most cases.	Video monitoring; temperature, water, motion sensors; uses cellular technology, so no broadband connection is needed.	$200 hardware cost plus $20 to $30 in monthly fees
AT&T	Do-it-yourself installation.	Temperature and water sensors; sends live video to Internet-connected PC or AT&T mobile device.	$200 hardware cost plus $10 in monthly fees*

* With a one-year commitment

Wall Street Journal © 2008

Internet Projects: See text Web site (www.mhhe.com/slater10e) and The Business Math Internet Resource Guide.

Tuesday, June 9, 2009 **B1**

Apple's Philip Schiller took the stage Monday to unveil the iPhone 3G S.

To Sustain iPhone, Apple Halves Price

BY YUKARI IWATANI KANE

Apple Inc. halved the price of its entry-level iPhone to $99 and rolled out a next-generation model, looking to sustain the momentum for its popular smart phone amid the recession and fresh competition.

Apple also announced several new lower-priced notebook computers at its annual conference for software developers, which kicked off Monday. Chief Executive Steve Jobs, who went on medical leave in January, didn't make an appearance.

LEARNING UNIT OBJECTIVES

LU 2–1: Types of Fractions and Conversion Procedures

1. Recognize the three types of fractions *(pp. 36–37)*.
2. Convert improper fractions to whole or mixed numbers and mixed numbers to improper fractions *(pp. 37–38)*.
3. Convert fractions to lowest and highest terms *(pp. 38–39)*.

LU 2–2: Adding and Subtracting Fractions

1. Add like and unlike fractions *(pp. 41–42)*.
2. Find the least common denominator by inspection and prime numbers *(pp. 42–43)*.
3. Subtract like and unlike fractions *(p. 44)*.
4. Add and subtract mixed numbers with the same or different denominators *(pp. 44–46)*.

LU 2–3: Multiplying and Dividing Fractions

1. Multiply and divide proper fractions and mixed numbers *(pp. 47–48)*.
2. Use the cancellation method in the multiplication and division of fractions *(pp. 48–49)*.

VOCABULARY PREVIEW

Here are the key terms in this chapter. When you finish the chapter, if you feel you know the term, place a checkmark within the parentheses following the term. If you are not certain of the definition, look it up and write the page number where it can be found in the text. The chapter organizer includes page references to the terms. There is also a complete glossary at the end of the text.

Cancellation . ( ) Common denominator . ( ) Denominator . ( ) Equivalent . ( ) Fraction . ( ) Greatest common divisor . ( ) Higher terms . ( ) Improper fraction . ( ) Least common denominator (LCD) . ( ) Like fractions . ( ) Lowest terms . ( ) Mixed numbers . ( ) Numerator . ( ) Prime numbers . ( ) Proper fractions . ( ) Reciprocal . ( ) Unlike fractions . ( )

Paid Leave: Workers Like It, But Some Businesses May Not

BY SARA SCHAEFER MUÑOZ

New Jersey's Senate recently passed legislation that would give employees the right to take paid leave to care for a newborn or a sick relative. Those taking the leave would be eligible for two-thirds of their salary—up to $524 a week—for six weeks. It would be financed by payroll deductions, costing every worker around $33 a year.

"I would be happy to pay for [this], even though I will probably not be using the benefits it provides. I think overall it is a benefit to society."

Wall Street Journal © 2008

[1]Off 1 due to rounding.

The following *Wall Street Journal* clipping "Paid Leave: Workers Like It, But Some Businesses May Not" illustrates the use of a fraction. From the clipping you learn that two-thirds ($\frac{2}{3}$) of an employee's salary would be paid when taking leave to care for a newborn or sick relative.

Now let's look at Milk Chocolate M&M's® candies as another example of using fractions.

As you know, M&M's® candies come in different colors. Do you know how many of each color are in a bag of M&M's®? If you go to the M&M's website, you learn that a typical bag of M&M's® contains approximately 17 brown, 11 yellow, 11 red, and 5 each of orange, blue, and green M&M's®.[1]

The 1.69-ounce bag of M&M's® shown here contains 55 M&M's®. In this bag, you will find the following colors:

18 yellow	9 blue	6 brown
10 red	7 orange	5 green

55 pieces in the bag

The number of yellow candies in a bag might suggest that yellow is the favorite color of many people. Since this is a business math text, however, let's look at the 55 M&M's® in terms of fractional arithmetic.

Of the 55 M&M's® in the 1.69-ounce bag, 5 of these M&M's® are green, so we can say that 5 parts of 55 represent green candies. We could also say that 1 out of 11 M&M's® is green. Are you confused?

For many people, fractions are difficult. If you are one of these people, this chapter is for you. First you will review the types of fractions and the fraction conversion procedures. Then you will gain a clear understanding of the addition, subtraction, multiplication, and division of fractions.

Learning Unit 2–1: Types of Fractions and Conversion Procedures

LO 1

GLOBAL

This chapter explains the parts of whole numbers called **fractions.** With fractions you can divide any object or unit—a whole—into a definite number of equal parts. For example, the bag of 55 M&M's® shown at the beginning of this chapter contains 6 brown candies. If you eat only the brown M&M's®, you have eaten 6 parts of 55, or 6 parts of the whole bag of M&M's®. We can express this in the following fraction:

$$\frac{6}{55}$$

6 is the **numerator,** or top of the fraction. The numerator describes the number of equal parts of the whole bag that you ate.

55 is the **denominator,** or bottom of the fraction. The denominator gives the total number of equal parts in the bag of M&M's®.

Before reviewing the arithmetic operations of fractions, you must recognize the three types of fractions described in this unit. You must also know how to convert fractions to a workable form.

Types of Fractions

When you read the *Wall Street Journal* clipping "Hewlett-Packard to Lay Off 24,600" you see that Hewlett-Packard is planning to make one-half ($\frac{1}{2}$) of the job cuts in the United States. The fraction $\frac{1}{2}$ is a proper fraction.

Hewlett-Packard to Lay Off 24,600

*Nearly Half in U.S.;
Firm Restructures
After Buying EDS*

BY JUSTIN SCHECK
AND BEN CHARNY

HEWLETT-PACKARD Co. said it will cut 24,600 jobs as part of its plan to integrate tech-services giant Electronic Data Systems Corp., providing the first details of how extensive its restructuring of the combined company will be.

The cuts are intended to combined work force. Before the $13.25 billion acquisition of EDS, which was finalized last month, H-P had 178,000 employees and EDS had 142,000.

The staff cuts will be spread across both companies, H-P said, with nearly half coming in the U.S. The company added that it "expects to replace roughly half of these positions over the next three years to create a global work force."

PROPER FRACTIONS

A **proper fraction** has a value less than 1; its numerator is smaller than its denominator.

EXAMPLES $\quad \dfrac{1}{4}, \dfrac{1}{2}, \dfrac{1}{10}, \dfrac{1}{12}, \dfrac{1}{3}, \dfrac{4}{7}, \dfrac{9}{10}, \dfrac{12}{13}, \dfrac{18}{55}$

Boston Globe © 2009

IMPROPER FRACTIONS

An **improper fraction** has a value equal to or greater than 1; its numerator is equal to or greater than its denominator.

EXAMPLES $\quad \dfrac{14}{14}, \dfrac{7}{6}, \dfrac{15}{14}, \dfrac{22}{19}$

MIXED NUMBERS

A **mixed number** is the sum of a whole number greater than zero and a proper fraction.

EXAMPLES $\quad 5\dfrac{1}{6}, 5\dfrac{9}{10}, 8\dfrac{7}{8}, 33\dfrac{5}{6}, 139\dfrac{9}{11}$

Conversion Procedures

In Chapter 1 we worked with two of the division symbols ($\div$ and $\overline{)}\,$). The horizontal line (or the diagonal) that separates the numerator and the denominator of a fraction also indicates division. The numerator, like the dividend, is the number we are dividing into. The denominator, like the divisor, is the number we use to divide. Then, referring to the 6 brown M&M's® in the bag of 55 M&M's® ($\frac{6}{55}$) shown at the beginning of this unit, we can say that we are dividing 55 into 6, or 6 is divided by 55. Also, in the fraction $\frac{3}{4}$, we can say that we are dividing 4 into 3, or 3 is divided by 4.

Working with the smaller numbers of simple fractions such as $\frac{3}{4}$ is easier, so we often convert fractions to their simplest terms. In this unit we show how to convert improper fractions to whole or mixed numbers, mixed numbers to improper fractions, and fractions to lowest and highest terms.

Converting Improper Fractions to Whole or Mixed Numbers

Business situations often make it necessary to change an improper fraction to a whole number or mixed number. You can use the following steps to make this conversion:

CONVERTING IMPROPER FRACTIONS TO WHOLE OR MIXED NUMBERS

LO 2

Step 1. Divide the numerator of the improper fraction by the denominator.

Step 2. a. If you have no remainder, the quotient is a whole number.

   b. If you have a remainder, the whole number part of the mixed number is the quotient. The remainder is placed over the old denominator as the proper fraction of the mixed number.

EXAMPLES

$$\frac{15}{15} = 1 \qquad \frac{16}{5} = 3\frac{1}{5} \qquad \begin{array}{r} 3\ R1 \\ 5\overline{)16} \\ \underline{15} \\ 1 \end{array}$$

Converting Mixed Numbers to Improper Fractions

By reversing the procedure of converting improper fractions to mixed numbers, we can change mixed numbers to improper fractions.

CONVERTING MIXED NUMBERS TO IMPROPER FRACTIONS
Step 1. Multiply the denominator of the fraction by the whole number.
Step 2. Add the product from Step 1 to the numerator of the old fraction.
Step 3. Place the total from Step 2 over the denominator of the old fraction to get the improper fraction.

EXAMPLE $\quad 6\frac{1}{8} = \frac{(8 \times 6) + 1}{8} = \frac{49}{8}$ ——Note that the denominator stays the same.

Converting (Reducing) Fractions to Lowest Terms

When solving fraction problems, you always reduce the fractions to their lowest terms. This reduction does not change the value of the fraction. For example, in the bag of M&M's®, 5 out of 55 were green. The fraction for this is $\frac{5}{55}$. If you divide the top and bottom of the fraction by 5, you have reduced the fraction to $\frac{1}{11}$ without changing its value. Remember, we said in the chapter introduction that 1 out of 11 M&M's® in the bag of 55 M&M's® represents green candies. Now you know why this is true.

To reduce a fraction to its lowest terms, begin by inspecting the fraction, looking for the largest whole number that will divide into both the numerator and the denominator without leaving a remainder. This whole number is the **greatest common divisor,** which cannot be zero. When you find this largest whole number, you have reached the point where the fraction is reduced to its **lowest terms.** At this point, no number (except 1) can divide evenly into both parts of the fraction.

LO 3

REDUCING FRACTIONS TO LOWEST TERMS BY INSPECTION
Step 1. By inspection, find the largest whole number (greatest common divisor) that will divide evenly into the numerator and denominator (does not change the fraction value).
Step 2. Now you have reduced the fraction to its lowest terms, since no number (except 1) can divide evenly into the numerator and denominator.

EXAMPLE $\quad \dfrac{24}{30} = \dfrac{24 \div 6}{30 \div 6} = \dfrac{4}{5}$

Using inspection, you can see that the number 6 in the above example is the greatest common divisor. When you have large numbers, the greatest common divisor is not so obvious. For large numbers, you can use the following step approach to find the greatest common divisor:

STEP APPROACH FOR FINDING GREATEST COMMON DIVISOR
Step 1. Divide the smaller number (numerator) of the fraction into the larger number (denominator).
Step 2. Divide the remainder of Step 1 into the divisor of Step 1.
Step 3. Divide the remainder of Step 2 into the divisor of Step 2. Continue this division process until the remainder is a 0, which means the last divisor is the greatest common divisor.

EXAMPLE

$$
\frac{24}{30}
$$

Step 1

$$
24\overline{)30} \\
\underline{24} \\
6
$$

$$
\begin{array}{r}
1 \\
24\overline{)30}
\end{array}
$$

Step 2

$$
\begin{array}{r}
4 \\
6\overline{)24} \\
\underline{24} \\
0
\end{array}
$$

$$
\frac{24 \div \boxed{6}}{30 \div \boxed{6}} = \frac{4}{5}
$$

Reducing a fraction by inspection is to some extent a trial-and-error method. Sometimes you are not sure what number you should divide into the top (numerator) and bottom (denominator) of the fraction. The following reference table on divisibility tests will be helpful. Note that to reduce a fraction to lowest terms might result in more than one division.

Will divide evenly into number if →

Examples →

2	3	4	5	6	10
Last digit is 0, 2, 4, 6, 8.	Sum of the digits is divisible by 3.	Last two digits can be divided by 4.	Last digit is 0 or 5.	The number is even and 3 will divide into the sum of the digits.	The last digit is 0.
$\dfrac{12}{14} = \dfrac{6}{7}$	$\dfrac{36}{69} = \dfrac{12}{23}$ $3 + 6 = 9 \div 3 = 3$ $6 + 9 = 15 \div 3 = 5$	$\dfrac{140}{160} = \dfrac{1(40)}{1(60)}$ $= \dfrac{35}{40} = \dfrac{7}{8}$	$\dfrac{15}{20} = \dfrac{3}{4}$	$\dfrac{12}{18} = \dfrac{2}{3}$	$\dfrac{90}{100} = \dfrac{9}{10}$

Converting (Raising) Fractions to Higher Terms

Later, when you add and subtract fractions, you will see that sometimes fractions must be raised to **higher terms.** Recall that when you reduced fractions to their lowest terms, you looked for the largest whole number (greatest common divisor) that would divide evenly into both the numerator and the denominator. When you raise fractions to higher terms, you do the opposite and multiply the numerator and the denominator by the same whole number. For example, if you want to raise the fraction $\frac{1}{4}$, you can multiply the numerator and denominator by 2.

EXAMPLE $\dfrac{1}{4} \times \dfrac{2}{2} = \boxed{\dfrac{2}{8}}$

The fractions $\frac{1}{4}$ and $\frac{2}{8}$ are **equivalent** in value. By converting $\frac{1}{4}$ to $\frac{2}{8}$, you only divided it into more parts.

Let's suppose that you have eaten $\frac{4}{7}$ of a pizza. You decide that instead of expressing the amount you have eaten in 7ths, you want to express it in 28ths. How would you do this?

To find the new numerator when you know the new denominator (28), use the steps that follow.

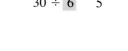

$ MONEY TIPS

Do you want to save $\frac{1}{5}$ or so of your income? Cancel your cable; get rid of a second vehicle; eat, drink coffee, and entertain at home; wear out your clothing; rent out a room; and cancel your cell phone (use a prepaid phone plan instead).

RAISING FRACTIONS TO HIGHER TERMS WHEN DENOMINATOR IS KNOWN

Step 1. Divide the *new* denominator by the *old* denominator to get the common number that raises the fraction to higher terms.

Step 2. Multiply the common number from Step 1 by the old numerator and place it as the new numerator over the new denominator.

EXAMPLE $\dfrac{4}{7} = \dfrac{?}{28}$

Step 1. Divide 28 by 7 = 4.

Step 2. Multiply 4 by the numerator 4 = 16.

       Result:

$$
\frac{4}{7} = \boxed{\frac{16}{28}} \qquad \left(\textit{Note:} \text{ This is the same as multiplying } \frac{4}{7} \times \frac{4}{4}. \right)
$$

Note that the $\frac{4}{7}$ and $\frac{16}{28}$ are equivalent in value, yet they are different fractions.

Now try the following Practice Quiz to check your understanding of this unit.

LU 2–1   PRACTICE QUIZ

Complete this **Practice Quiz** to see how you are doing.

1. Identify the type of fraction—proper, improper, or mixed:

    a. $\dfrac{4}{5}$ b. $\dfrac{6}{5}$ c. $19\dfrac{1}{5}$ d. $\dfrac{20}{20}$

2. Convert to a mixed number:

    $\dfrac{160}{9}$

3. Convert the mixed number to an improper fraction:

    $9\dfrac{5}{8}$

4. Find the greatest common divisor by the step approach and reduce to lowest terms:

    a. $\dfrac{24}{40}$ b. $\dfrac{91}{156}$

5. Convert to higher terms:

    a. $\dfrac{14}{20} = \dfrac{}{200}$ b. $\dfrac{8}{10} = \dfrac{}{60}$

Solutions with Step-by-Step Help on DVD

✓ **Solutions**

1. a. Proper
    b. Improper
    c. Mixed
    d. Improper

2. $\begin{array}{r} 17\frac{7}{9} \\ 9\overline{)160} \\ 9 \\ \hline 70 \\ 63 \\ \hline 7 \end{array}$

3. $\dfrac{(9 \times 8) + 5}{8} = \dfrac{77}{8}$

4. a. $\begin{array}{r} 1 \\ 24\overline{)40} \\ 24 \\ \hline 16 \end{array} \quad \begin{array}{r} 1 \\ 16\overline{)24} \\ 16 \\ \hline 8 \end{array} \quad \begin{array}{r} 2 \\ 8\overline{)16} \\ 16 \\ \hline 0 \end{array}$ **8** is greatest common divisor.

    $\dfrac{24 \div 8}{40 \div 8} = \dfrac{3}{5}$

    b. $\begin{array}{r} 1 \\ 91\overline{)156} \\ 91 \\ \hline 65 \end{array} \quad \begin{array}{r} 1 \\ 65\overline{)91} \\ 65 \\ \hline 26 \end{array} \quad \begin{array}{r} 2 \\ 26\overline{)65} \\ 52 \\ \hline 13 \end{array} \quad \begin{array}{r} 2 \\ 13\overline{)26} \\ 26 \\ \hline 0 \end{array}$ **13** is greatest common divisor.

    $\dfrac{91 \div 13}{156 \div 13} = \dfrac{7}{12}$

5. a. $\begin{array}{r} 10 \\ 20\overline{)200} \end{array}$ $10 \times 14 = 140$ $\dfrac{14}{20} = \dfrac{140}{200}$

    b. $\begin{array}{r} 6 \\ 10\overline{)60} \end{array}$ $6 \times 8 = 48$ $\dfrac{8}{10} = \dfrac{48}{60}$

LU 2–1a   EXTRA PRACTICE QUIZ WITH WORKED-OUT SOLUTIONS

Need more practice? Try this **Extra Practice Quiz** (check figures in Chapter Organizer, p. 53). Worked-out Solutions can be found in Appendix B at end of text.

1. Identify the type of fraction—proper, improper, or mixed:

    a. $\dfrac{2}{5}$ b. $\dfrac{7}{6}$ c. $18\dfrac{1}{3}$ d. $\dfrac{40}{40}$

2. Convert to a mixed number (do not reduce):

    $\dfrac{155}{7}$

3. Convert the mixed number to an improper fraction:

    $8\dfrac{7}{9}$

4. Find the greatest common divisor by the step approach and reduce to lowest terms:

    a. $\dfrac{42}{70}$ **b.** $\dfrac{96}{182}$

5. Convert to higher terms:

    a. $\dfrac{16}{30} = \dfrac{}{300}$ **b.** $\dfrac{9}{20} = \dfrac{}{60}$

Learning Unit 2–2: Adding and Subtracting Fractions

Wall Street Journal © 2005

The *Wall Street Journal* clipping shows how more teachers are using online video-sharing sites that are modeled after Google Inc.'s YouTube. Note in clip how a fraction lesson is shown on TeacherTube. Note these fractions can be added because the fractions have the same denominator. These are called *like fractions*.

In this unit you learn how to add and subtract fractions with the same denominators (**like fractions**) and fractions with different denominators (**unlike fractions**). We have also included how to add and subtract mixed numbers.

Addition of Fractions

LO 1

When you add two or more quantities, they must have the same name or be of the same denomination. You cannot add 6 quarts and 3 pints unless you change the denomination of one or both quantities. You must either make the quarts into pints or the pints into quarts. The same principle also applies to fractions. That is, to add two or more fractions, they must have a **common denominator.**

Adding Like Fractions

In our video-sharing clipping at the beginning of this unit we stated that because the fractions had the same denominator, or a common denominator, they were *like fractions*. Adding like fractions is similar to adding whole numbers.

ADDING LIKE FRACTIONS
Step 1. Add the numerators and place the total over the original denominator.
Step 2. If the total of your numerators is the same as your original denominator, convert your answer to a whole number; if the total is larger than your original denominator, convert your answer to a mixed number.

EXAMPLE $\dfrac{1}{7} + \dfrac{4}{7} = \boxed{\dfrac{5}{7}}$

The denominator, 7, shows the number of pieces into which some whole was divided. The two numerators, 1 and 4, tell how many of the pieces you have. So if you add 1 and 4, you get 5, or $\frac{5}{7}$.

Adding Unlike Fractions

Since you cannot add *unlike fractions* because their denominators are not the same, you must change the unlike fractions to *like fractions*—fractions with the same denominators. To do this, find a denominator that is common to all the fractions you want to add. Then look for the **least common denominator (LCD).**[2] The LCD is the smallest nonzero whole

---

[2]Often referred to as the *lowest common denominator.*

number into which all denominators will divide evenly. You can find the LCD by inspection or with prime numbers.

Finding the Least Common Denominator (LCD) by Inspection The example that follows shows you how to use inspection to find an LCD (this will make all the denominators the same).

EXAMPLE $\dfrac{3}{7} + \dfrac{5}{21}$

Inspection of these two fractions shows that the smallest number into which denominators 7 and 21 divide evenly is 21. Thus, 21 is the LCD.

You may know that 21 is the LCD of $\frac{3}{7} + \frac{5}{21}$, but you cannot add these two fractions until you change the denominator of $\frac{3}{7}$ to 21. You do this by building (raising) the equivalent of $\frac{3}{7}$, as explained in Learning Unit 2–1. You can use the following steps to find the LCD by inspection:

Step 1. Divide the new denominator (21) by the old denominator (7): $21 \div 7 = 3$.

Step 2. Multiply the 3 in Step 1 by the old numerator (3): $3 \times 3 = 9$. The new numerator is 9.

Result:

$$\frac{3}{7} = \frac{9}{21}$$

Now that the denominators are the same, you add the numerators.

$$\frac{9}{21} + \frac{5}{21} = \frac{14}{21} = \frac{2}{3}$$

Note that $\frac{14}{21}$ is reduced to its lowest terms $\frac{2}{3}$. Always reduce your answer to its lowest terms.

You are now ready for the following general steps for adding proper fractions with different denominators. These steps also apply to the following discussion on finding LCD by prime numbers.

LO 2

ADDING UNLIKE FRACTIONS
Step 1. Find the LCD.
Step 2. Change each fraction to a like fraction with the LCD.
Step 3. Add the numerators and place the total over the LCD.
Step 4. If necessary, reduce the answer to lowest terms.

As of 9/4/06
9,808,358 is the number of digits in the largest known prime number.

Finding the Least Common Denominator (LCD) by Prime Numbers When you cannot determine the LCD by inspection, you can use the prime number method. First you must understand prime numbers.

PRIME NUMBERS
A **prime number** is a whole number greater than 1 that is only divisible by itself and 1. The number 1 is not a prime number.

EXAMPLES   2, 3, 5, 7, 11, 13, 17, 19, 23, 29, 31, 37, 41, 43

Note that the number 4 is not a prime number. Not only can you divide 4 by 1 and by 4, but you can also divide 4 by 2. A whole number that is greater than 1 and is only divisible by itself and 1 has become a source of interest to some people.

EXAMPLE $\dfrac{1}{3} + \dfrac{1}{8} + \dfrac{1}{9} + \dfrac{1}{12}$

Step 1. Copy the denominators and arrange them in a separate row.

3   8   9   12

Step 2. Divide the denominators in Step 1 by prime numbers. Start with the smallest number that will divide into at least two of the denominators. Bring down any number that is not divisible. Keep in mind that the lowest prime number is 2.

$$2 \, \overline{)\, 3 \quad 8 \quad 9 \quad 12}$$
$$\phantom{2 \, \overline{)}} \, 3 \quad 4 \quad 9 \quad 6$$

Note: The 3 and 9 were brought down, since they were not divisible by 2.

Step 3. Continue Step 2 until no prime number will divide evenly into at least two numbers.

Note: The 3 is used, since 2 can no longer divide evenly into at least two numbers.

$$2 \, \overline{)\, 3 \quad 8 \quad 9 \quad 12}$$
$$2 \, \overline{)\, 3 \quad 4 \quad 9 \quad 6}$$
$$3 \, \overline{)\, 3 \quad 2 \quad 9 \quad 3}$$
$$\phantom{3 \, \overline{)}} \, 1 \quad 2 \quad 3 \quad 1$$

Step 4. To find the LCD, multiply all the numbers in the divisors (2, 2, 3) and in the last row (1, 2, 3, 1).

$$\boxed{2 \times 2 \times 3} \times \boxed{1 \times 2 \times 3 \times 1} = \boxed{72} \text{ (LCD)}$$

Divisors   ×   Last row

Step 5. Raise each fraction so that each denominator will be 72 and then add fractions.

$$\frac{1}{3} = \frac{?}{72} \qquad 72 \div 3 = 24$$
$$\qquad\qquad\qquad 24 \times 1 = 24$$

$$\frac{24}{72} + \frac{9}{72} + \frac{8}{72} + \frac{6}{72} = \frac{47}{72}$$

$$\frac{1}{8} = \frac{?}{72} \qquad 72 \div 8 = 9$$
$$\qquad\qquad\qquad 9 \times 1 = 9$$

The above five steps used for finding LCD with prime numbers are summarized as follows:

FINDING LCD FOR TWO OR MORE FRACTIONS
Step 1. Copy the denominators and arrange them in a separate row.
Step 2. Divide the denominators by the smallest prime number that will divide evenly into at least two numbers.
Step 3. Continue until no prime number divides evenly into at least two numbers.
Step 4. Multiply all the numbers in divisors and last row to find the LCD.
Step 5. Raise all fractions so each has a common denominator and then complete the computation.

Adding Mixed Numbers

The following steps will show you how to add mixed numbers:

ADDING MIXED NUMBERS
Step 1. Add the fractions (remember that fractions need common denominators, as in the previous section).
Step 2. Add the whole numbers.
Step 3. Combine the totals of Steps 1 and 2. Be sure you do not have an improper fraction in your final answer. Convert the improper fraction to a whole or mixed number. Add the whole numbers resulting from the improper fraction conversion to the total whole numbers of Step 2. If necessary, reduce the answer to lowest terms.

Using prime numbers to find LCD of example

```
2 / 20   5   4
2 / 10   5   2
5 /  5   5   1
     1   1   1
2 × 2 × 5 = 20 LCD
```

EXAMPLE

$$4\frac{7}{20} \qquad 4\frac{7}{20}$$

$$6\frac{3}{5} \qquad 6\frac{12}{20}$$

$$+7\frac{1}{4} \qquad +7\frac{5}{20}$$

$$\frac{3}{5} = \frac{?}{20}$$

$$20 \div 5 = \quad 4$$
$$\times \ 3$$
$$\overline{\quad 12}$$

Step 1 → $\quad \frac{24}{20} = 1\frac{4}{20}$

Step 2 → $\quad + \ 17$

Step 3 → $\quad = 18\frac{4}{20} = \boxed{18\frac{1}{5}}$

Subtraction of Fractions

The subtraction of fractions is similar to the addition of fractions. This section explains how to subtract like and unlike fractions and how to subtract mixed numbers.

Subtracting Like Fractions

To subtract like fractions, use the steps that follow.

LO 3

SUBTRACTING LIKE FRACTIONS
Step 1. Subtract the numerators and place the answer over the common denominator.
Step 2. If necessary, reduce the answer to lowest terms.

EXAMPLE $\quad \dfrac{9}{10} - \dfrac{1}{10} = \dfrac{8 \div 2}{10 \div 2} = \boxed{\dfrac{4}{5}}$

$\qquad\qquad\qquad\qquad\qquad\quad \uparrow \qquad \uparrow$

Step 1 **Step 2**

Subtracting Unlike Fractions

Now let's learn the steps for subtracting unlike fractions.

SUBTRACTING UNLIKE FRACTIONS
Step 1. Find the LCD.
Step 2. Raise the fraction to its equivalent value.
Step 3. Subtract the numerators and place the answer over the LCD.
Step 4. If necessary, reduce the answer to lowest terms.

EXAMPLE

$$\frac{5}{8} \qquad \frac{40}{64}$$

$$-\frac{2}{64} \qquad -\frac{2}{64}$$

$$\qquad\qquad \frac{38}{64} = \boxed{\frac{19}{32}}$$

By inspection, we see that LCD is 64.
Thus $64 \div 8 = 8 \times 5 = 40$.

Subtracting Mixed Numbers

When you subtract whole numbers, sometimes borrowing is not necessary. At other times, you must borrow. The same is true of subtracting mixed numbers.

LO 4

SUBTRACTING MIXED NUMBERS	
When Borrowing Is Not Necessary	*When Borrowing Is Necessary*
Step 1. Subtract fractions, making sure to find the LCD.	**Step 1.** Make sure the fractions have the LCD.
	Step 2. Borrow from the whole number of the minuend (top number).
Step 2. Subtract whole numbers.	
Step 3. Reduce the fraction(s) to lowest terms.	**Step 3.** Subtract the whole numbers and fractions.
	Step 4. Reduce the fraction(s) to lowest terms.

EXAMPLE   Where borrowing is not necessary: Find LCD of 2 and 8. LCD is 8.

$$6\frac{1}{2}\qquad\qquad\qquad 6\frac{4}{8}$$
$$-\ \frac{3}{8}\qquad\qquad\qquad -\ \frac{3}{8}$$
$$\overline{\qquad\qquad}\qquad\qquad \overline{6\frac{1}{8}}$$

EXAMPLE   Where borrowing is necessary:

$$3\frac{1}{2}=\qquad 3\frac{2}{4}=\qquad 2\frac{6}{4}\ \left(\frac{4}{4}+\frac{2}{4}\right)$$
$$-\ 1\frac{3}{4}=\qquad -\ 1\frac{3}{4}=\qquad -\ 1\frac{3}{4}$$
$$\overline{\text{LCD is }4.}\qquad \overline{\qquad}\qquad \overline{1\frac{3}{4}}$$

Since $\frac{3}{4}$ is larger than $\frac{2}{4}$, we must borrow 1 from the 3. This is the same as borrowing $\frac{4}{4}$. A fraction with the same numerator and denominator represents a whole. When we add $\frac{4}{4}+\frac{2}{4}$, we get $\frac{6}{4}$. Note how we subtracted the whole number and fractions, being sure to reduce the final answer if necessary.

How to Dissect and Solve a Word Problem

Let's now look at how to dissect and solve a word problem involving fractions.

The Word Problem   The Albertsons grocery store has $550\frac{1}{4}$ total square feet of floor space. Albertsons' meat department occupies $115\frac{1}{2}$ square feet, and its deli department occupies $145\frac{7}{8}$ square feet. If the remainder of the floor space is for groceries, what square footage remains for groceries?

Rick Bowmer/AP Images

The facts	Solving for?	Steps to take	Key points
Total square footage: $550\frac{1}{4}$ sq. ft. Meat department: $115\frac{1}{2}$ sq. ft. Deli department: $145\frac{7}{8}$ sq. ft.	Total square footage for groceries.	Total floor space − Total meat and deli floor space = Total grocery floor space.	Denominators must be the same before adding or subtracting fractions. $\frac{8}{8}=1$ Never leave improper fraction as final answer.

Steps to solving problem

1. Calculate total square footage of the meat and deli departments.

$$\begin{array}{lll}\text{Meat:} & 115\frac{1}{2}= & 115\frac{4}{8}\\[4pt]\text{Deli:} & +\ 145\frac{7}{8}= & +\ 145\frac{7}{8}\\ \hline & & 260\frac{11}{8}=261\frac{3}{8}\text{ sq. ft.}\end{array}$$

2. Calculate total grocery square footage.

Check

$$\begin{array}{lll}550\frac{1}{4}= & 550\frac{2}{8}= & 549\frac{10}{8}\\[4pt]-\ 261\frac{3}{8}= & -\ 261\frac{3}{8}= & -\ 261\frac{3}{8}\quad\left(\frac{2}{8}+\frac{8}{8}\right)\\ \hline & & 288\frac{7}{8}\text{ sq. ft.}\end{array}$$

$$\begin{array}{l}261\frac{3}{8}\\ +\ 288\frac{7}{8}\\ \hline 549\frac{10}{8}=550\frac{2}{8}=550\frac{1}{4}\text{ sq. ft.}\end{array}$$

Note how the above blueprint aid helped to gather the facts and identify what we were looking for. To find the total square footage for groceries, we first had to sum the areas for meat and deli. Then we could subtract these areas from the total square footage. Also note that in Step 1 above, we didn't leave the answer as an improper fraction. In Step 2, we borrowed from the 550 so that we could complete the subtraction.

It's your turn to check your progress with a Practice Quiz.

LU 2–2 PRACTICE QUIZ

Complete this **Practice Quiz** to see how you are doing.

1. Find LCD by the division of prime numbers:
   12, 9, 6, 4

2. Add and reduce to lowest terms if needed:

   a. $\dfrac{3}{40} + \dfrac{2}{5}$ b. $2\dfrac{3}{4} + 6\dfrac{1}{20}$

3. Subtract and reduce to lowest terms if needed:

   a. $\dfrac{6}{7} - \dfrac{1}{4}$ b. $8\dfrac{1}{4} - 3\dfrac{9}{28}$ c. $4 - 1\dfrac{3}{4}$

4. Computerland has $660\frac{1}{4}$ total square feet of floor space. Three departments occupy this floor space: hardware, $201\frac{1}{8}$ square feet; software, $242\frac{1}{4}$ square feet; and customer service, _____ square feet. What is the total square footage of the customer service area? You might want to try a blueprint aid, since the solution will show a completed blueprint aid.

Solutions with Step-by-Step Help on DVD

✓ Solutions

1.
```
2 / 12   9   6   4
2 /  6   9   3   2
3 /  3   9   3   1
     1   3   1   1
```
   $LCD = 2 \times 2 \times 3 \times 1 \times 3 \times 1 \times 1 = \boxed{36}$

2. a. $\dfrac{3}{40} + \dfrac{2}{5} = \dfrac{3}{40} + \dfrac{16}{40} = \boxed{\dfrac{19}{40}}$

   $\left(\begin{array}{l} \dfrac{2}{5} = \dfrac{?}{40} \\ 40 \div 5 = 8 \times 2 = 16 \end{array} \right)$

   b.
   $\begin{array}{r} 2\dfrac{3}{4} \\ + 6\dfrac{1}{20} \\ \hline \end{array}$ $\begin{array}{r} 2\dfrac{15}{20} \\ + 6\dfrac{1}{20} \\ \hline 8\dfrac{16}{20} = \boxed{8\dfrac{4}{5}} \end{array}$

   $\dfrac{3}{4} = \dfrac{?}{20}$

   $20 \div 4 = 5 \times 3 = 15$

3. a.
   $\begin{array}{r} \dfrac{6}{7} = \dfrac{24}{28} \\ -\dfrac{1}{4} = -\dfrac{7}{28} \\ \hline \boxed{\dfrac{17}{28}} \end{array}$

   b.
   $\begin{array}{r} 8\dfrac{1}{4} = 8\dfrac{7}{28} = 7\dfrac{35}{28} \\ -3\dfrac{9}{28} = -3\dfrac{9}{28} = -3\dfrac{9}{28} \\ \hline 4\dfrac{26}{28} = \boxed{4\dfrac{13}{14}} \end{array}$ $\left(\dfrac{28}{28} + \dfrac{7}{28} \right)$

   c.
   $\begin{array}{r} 3\dfrac{4}{4} \\ -1\dfrac{3}{4} \\ \hline \boxed{2\dfrac{1}{4}} \end{array}$ Note how we showed the 4 as $3\dfrac{4}{4}$.

4. Computerland's total square footage for customer service:

The facts	Solving for?	Steps to take	Key points
Total square footage: $660\frac{1}{4}$ sq. ft. *Hardware:* $201\frac{1}{8}$ sq. ft. *Software:* $242\frac{1}{4}$ sq. ft.	Total square footage for customer service.	Total floor space − Total hardware and software floor space = Total customer service floor space.	Denominators must be the same before adding or subtracting fractions.

Steps to solving problem

1. Calculate the total square footage of hardware and software.

$$20\tfrac{1}{8} = 20\tfrac{1}{8} \text{ (hardware)}$$
$$+\ 242\tfrac{1}{4} = +\ 242\tfrac{2}{8} \text{ (software)}$$
$$\overline{443\tfrac{3}{8}}$$

2. Calculate the total square footage for customer service.

$$660\tfrac{1}{4} = 660\tfrac{2}{8} = 659\tfrac{10}{8} \text{ (total square footage)}$$
$$-443\tfrac{3}{8} = -443\tfrac{3}{8} = -443\tfrac{3}{8} \text{ (hardware plus software)}$$
$$216\tfrac{7}{8} \text{ sq. ft. (customer service)}$$

LU 2–2a   EXTRA PRACTICE QUIZ WITH WORKED-OUT SOLUTIONS

Need more practice? Try this **Extra Practice Quiz** (check figures in Chapter Organizer, p. 53). Worked-out Solutions can be found in Appendix B at end of text.

1. Find the LCD by the division of prime numbers:
   10, 15, 9, 4

2. Add and reduce to lowest terms if needed:

   a. $\dfrac{2}{25} + \dfrac{3}{5}$ b. $3\dfrac{3}{8} + 6\dfrac{1}{32}$

3. Subtract and reduce to lowest terms if needed:

   a. $\dfrac{5}{6} - \dfrac{1}{3}$ b. $9\dfrac{1}{8} - 3\dfrac{7}{32}$ c. $6 - 1\dfrac{2}{5}$

4. Computerland has $985\tfrac{1}{4}$ total square feet of floor space. Three departments occupy this floor space: hardware, $209\tfrac{1}{8}$ square feet; software, $382\tfrac{1}{4}$ square feet; and customer service, _____ square feet. What is the total square footage of the customer service area?

Learning Unit 2–3: Multiplying and Dividing Fractions

LO 1

The following recipe for Coconutty "M&M's"® Brownies makes 16 brownies. What would you need if you wanted to triple the recipe and make 48 brownies?

Coconutty "M&M's"® Brownies

6 squares (1 ounce each) semi-sweet chocolate
½ cup (1 stick) butter
¾ cup granulated sugar
2 large eggs
1 tablespoon vegetable oil
1 teaspoon vanilla extract
1¼ cups all-purpose flour
3 tablespoons unsweetened cocoa powder
1 teaspoon baking powder
½ teaspoon salt
1½ cups "M&M's"® Chocolate Mini Baking Bits, divided
Coconut Topping (recipe follows)

© 2000 Mars, Incorporated

Preheat oven to 350°F. Grease 8 × 8 × 2-inch pan; set aside. In small saucepan combine chocolate, butter, and sugar over low heat; stir constantly until smooth. Remove from heat; let cool. In bowl beat eggs, oil, and vanilla; stir in chocolate mixture until blended. Stir in flour, cocoa powder, baking powder, and salt. Stir in 1 cup "M&M's"® Chocolate Mini Baking Bits. Spread batter in prepared pan. Bake 35 to 40 minutes or until toothpick inserted in center comes out clean. Cool. Prepare a coconut topping. Spread over brownies; sprinkle with $\frac{1}{2}$ cup "M&M's"® Chocolate Mini Baking Bits.

In this unit you learn how to multiply and divide fractions.

Multiplication of Fractions

Multiplying fractions is easier than adding and subtracting fractions because you do not have to find a common denominator. This section explains the multiplication of proper fractions and the multiplication of mixed numbers.

MULTIPLYING PROPER FRACTIONS[3]
Step 1. Multiply the numerators and the denominators.
Step 2. Reduce the answer to lowest terms or use the cancellation method.

First let's look at an example that results in an answer that we do not have to reduce.

EXAMPLE $\quad \dfrac{1}{7} \times \dfrac{5}{8} = \dfrac{5}{56}$

In the next example, note how we reduce the answer to lowest terms.

EXAMPLE $\quad \dfrac{5}{1} \times \dfrac{1}{6} \times \dfrac{4}{7} = \dfrac{20}{42} = \dfrac{10}{21}$ $\qquad$ Keep in mind $\dfrac{5}{1}$ is equal to 5.

We can reduce $\frac{20}{42}$ by the step approach as follows:

$$\begin{array}{r} 2 \\ 20\overline{)42} \\ 40 \\ \hline 2 \end{array} \qquad \begin{array}{r} 10 \\ 2\overline{)20} \\ 20 \\ \hline 0 \end{array}$$

We could also have found the greatest common divisor by inspection.

$$\dfrac{20 \div 2}{42 \div 2} = \dfrac{10}{21}$$

As an alternative to reducing fractions to lowest terms, we can use the **cancellation** technique. Let's work the previous example using this technique.

LO 2

EXAMPLE $\quad \dfrac{5}{1} \times \dfrac{1}{\overset{}{\underset{3}{6}}} \times \dfrac{\overset{2}{4}}{7} = \dfrac{10}{21}$ $\qquad$ 2 divides evenly into 4 twice and into 6 three times.

Note that when we cancel numbers, we are reducing the answer before multiplying. We know that multiplying or dividing both numerator and denominator by the same number gives an equivalent fraction. So we can divide both numerator and denominator by any number that divides them both evenly. It doesn't matter which we divide first. Note that this division reduces $\frac{10}{21}$ to its lowest terms.

Multiplying Mixed Numbers

The following steps explain how to multiply mixed numbers:

MULTIPLYING MIXED NUMBERS
Step 1. Convert the mixed numbers to improper fractions.
Step 2. Multiply the numerators and denominators.
Step 3. Reduce the answer to lowest terms or use the cancellation method.

EXAMPLE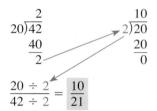

$$2\frac{1}{3} \times 1\frac{1}{2} = \frac{7}{\underset{1}{3}} \times \frac{\overset{1}{3}}{2} = \frac{7}{2} = 3\frac{1}{2}$$

$\qquad$ Step 1 $\qquad$ Step 2 $\qquad$ Step 3

[3]You would follow the same procedure to multiply improper fractions.

Division of Fractions

When you studied whole numbers in Chapter 1, you saw how multiplication can be checked by division. The multiplication of fractions can also be checked by division, as you will see in this section on dividing proper fractions and mixed numbers.

Dividing Proper Fractions

The division of proper fractions introduces a new term—the **reciprocal.** To use reciprocals, we must first recognize which fraction in the problem is the divisor—the fraction that we divide by. Let's assume the problem we are to solve is $\frac{1}{8} \div \frac{2}{3}$. We read this problem as "$\frac{1}{8}$ divided by $\frac{2}{3}$." The divisor is the fraction after the division sign (or the second fraction). The steps that follow show how the divisor becomes a reciprocal.

DIVIDING PROPER FRACTIONS
Step 1. Invert (turn upside down) the divisor (the second fraction). The inverted number is the *reciprocal.*
Step 2. Multiply the fractions.
Step 3. Reduce the answer to lowest terms or use the cancellation method.

Do you know why the inverted fraction number is a reciprocal? Reciprocals are two numbers that when multiplied give a product of 1. For example, 2 (which is the same as $\frac{2}{1}$) and $\frac{1}{2}$ are reciprocals because multiplying them gives 1.

EXAMPLE $\frac{1}{8} \div \frac{2}{3}$ $\frac{1}{8} \times \frac{3}{2} = \boxed{\frac{3}{16}}$

Dividing Mixed Numbers

Now you are ready to divide mixed numbers by using improper fractions.

DIVIDING MIXED NUMBERS
Step 1. Convert all mixed numbers to improper fractions.
Step 2. Invert the divisor (take its reciprocal) and multiply. If your final answer is an improper fraction, reduce it to lowest terms. You can do this by finding the greatest common divisor or by using the cancellation technique.

EXAMPLE $8\frac{3}{4} \div 2\frac{5}{6}$

Step 1. $\dfrac{35}{4} \div \dfrac{17}{6}$

Step 2. $\dfrac{35}{\overset{}{\underset{2}{4}}} \times \dfrac{\overset{3}{6}}{17} = \dfrac{105}{34} = \boxed{3\frac{3}{34}}$ Here we used the cancellation technique.

How to Dissect and Solve a Word Problem

The Word Problem Jamie Slater ordered $5\frac{1}{2}$ cords of oak. The cost of each cord is $150. He also ordered $2\frac{1}{4}$ cords of maple at $120 per cord. Jamie's neighbor, Al, said that he would share the wood and pay him $\frac{1}{5}$ of the total cost. How much did Jamie receive from Al?

Note how we filled in the blueprint aid columns. We first had to find the total cost of all the wood before we could find Al's share—$\frac{1}{5}$ of the total cost.

The facts	Solving for?	Steps to take	Key points
Cords ordered: $5\frac{1}{2}$ at \$150 per cord; $2\frac{1}{4}$ at \$120 per cord. Al's cost share: $\frac{1}{5}$ the total cost.	What will Al pay Jamie?	Total cost of wood $\times$ $\frac{1}{5}$ = Al's cost.	Convert mixed numbers to improper fractions when multiplying. Cancellation is an alternative to reducing fractions.

Steps to solving problem

1. Calculate the cost of oak.

$$5\frac{1}{2} \times \$150 = \frac{11}{2} \times \overset{\$75}{\cancel{\$150}} = \$825$$

2. Calculate the cost of maple.

$$2\frac{1}{4} \times \$120 = \frac{9}{4} \times \overset{\$30}{\cancel{\$120}} = +270$$

$$\overline{\$1,095} \text{ (total cost of wood)}$$

3. What Al pays.

$$\frac{1}{5} \times \overset{\$219}{\cancel{\$1,095}} = \boxed{\$219}$$

You should now be ready to test your knowledge of the final unit in the chapter.

LU 2–3 PRACTICE QUIZ

Complete this **Practice Quiz** to see how you are doing.

1. Multiply (use cancellation technique):

  a. $\dfrac{4}{8} \times \dfrac{4}{6}$ b. $35 \times \dfrac{4}{7}$

2. Multiply (do not use canceling; reduce by finding the greatest common divisor):

  $\dfrac{14}{15} \times \dfrac{7}{10}$

3. Complete the following. Reduce to lowest terms as needed.

  a. $\dfrac{1}{9} \div \dfrac{5}{6}$ b. $\dfrac{51}{5} \div \dfrac{5}{9}$

4. Jill Estes bought a mobile home that was $8\frac{1}{8}$ times as expensive as the home her brother bought. Jill's brother paid \$16,000 for his mobile home. What is the cost of Jill's new home?

Solutions with Step-by-Step Help on DVD

✓ **Solutions**

1. a. $\dfrac{\overset{1}{\overset{1}{\cancel{4}}}}{\underset{2}{\underset{1}{\cancel{8}}}} \times \dfrac{\overset{1}{\cancel{4}}}{\underset{3}{\cancel{6}}} = \dfrac{1}{3}$ b. $\overset{5}{\cancel{35}} \times \dfrac{4}{\underset{1}{\cancel{7}}} = \boxed{20}$

2. $\dfrac{14}{15} \times \dfrac{7}{10} = \dfrac{98 \div 2}{150 \div 2} = \boxed{\dfrac{49}{75}}$

$$
\begin{array}{ccccccc}
\overset{1}{98\overline{)150}} & & \overset{1}{52\overline{)98}} & & \overset{1}{46\overline{)52}} & & \overset{7}{6\overline{)46}} & & \overset{1}{4\overline{)6}} & & \overset{2}{2\overline{)4}} \\
\underline{98} & & \underline{52} & & \underline{46} & & \underline{42} & & \underline{4} & & \underline{4} \\
52 & & 46 & & 6 & & 4 & & 2 & & 0
\end{array}
$$

3. a. $\dfrac{1}{9} \times \dfrac{6}{5} = \dfrac{6 \div 3}{45 \div 3} = \boxed{\dfrac{2}{15}}$ b. $\dfrac{51}{5} \times \dfrac{9}{5} = \dfrac{459}{25} = \boxed{18\dfrac{9}{25}}$

4. Total cost of Jill's new home:

The facts	Solving for?	Steps to take	Key points
Jill's mobile home: $8\frac{1}{8}$ as expensive as her brother's. Brother paid: \$16,000.	Total cost of Jill's new home.	$8\frac{1}{8} \times$ Total cost of Jill's brother's mobile home = Total cost of Jill's new home.	Canceling is an alternative to reducing.

Steps to solving problem

1. Convert $8\frac{1}{8}$ to a mixed number. $\frac{65}{8}$

2. Calculate the total cost of Jill's home. $\frac{65}{8} \times$ ~~$16,000~~ $^{\$2,000}$ = $\boxed{\$130,000}$

LU 2–3a	EXTRA PRACTICE QUIZ WITH WORKED-OUT SOLUTIONS

Need more practice? Try this **Extra Practice Quiz** (check figures in Chapter Organizer, p. 53). Worked-out Solutions can be found in Appendix B at end of text.

1. Multiply (use cancellation technique):

   a. $\frac{6}{8} \times \frac{3}{6}$ b. $42 \times \frac{1}{7}$

2. Multiply (do not use canceling; reduce by finding the greatest common divisor):

   $\frac{13}{117} \times \frac{9}{5}$

3. Complete the following. Reduce to lowest terms as needed.

   a. $\frac{1}{8} \div \frac{4}{5}$ b. $\frac{61}{6} \div \frac{6}{7}$

4. Jill Estes bought a mobile home that was $10\frac{1}{8}$ times as expensive as the home her brother bought. Jill's brother paid $10,000 for his mobile home. What is the cost of Jill's new home?

CHAPTER ORGANIZER AND REFERENCE GUIDE

Topic	Key point, procedure, formula	Example(s) to illustrate situation
Types of fractions, p. 36	*Proper:* Value less than 1; numerator smaller than denominator. *Improper:* Value equal to or greater than 1; numerator equal to or greater than denominator. *Mixed:* Sum of whole number greater than zero and a proper fraction.	$\frac{3}{5}, \frac{7}{9}, \frac{8}{15}$ $\frac{14}{14}, \frac{19}{18}$ $6\frac{3}{8}, 9\frac{8}{9}$
Fraction conversions, p. 37	*Improper to whole or mixed:* Divide numerator by denominator; place remainder over *old* denominator. *Mixed to improper:* $\frac{\text{Whole number} \times \text{Denominator} + \text{Numerator}}{\text{Old denominator}}$	$\frac{17}{4} = 4\frac{1}{4}$ $4\frac{1}{8} = \frac{32 + 1}{8} = \frac{33}{8}$
Reducing fractions to lowest terms, p. 38	1. Divide numerator and denominator by largest possible divisor (does not change fraction value). 2. When reduced to lowest terms, no number (except 1) will divide evenly into both numerator and denominator.	$\frac{18 \div 2}{46 \div 2} = \frac{9}{23}$
Step approach for finding greatest common denominator, p. 39	1. Divide smaller number of fraction into larger number. 2. Divide remainder into divisor of Step 1. Continue this process until no remainder results. 3. The last divisor used is the greatest common divisor.	$\begin{array}{r} \\ 15 \longrightarrow \\ 65 \end{array} \begin{array}{r} 4 \\ 15\overline{)65} \\ 60 \\ \hline 5 \end{array} \quad \begin{array}{r} 3 \\ 5\overline{)15} \\ 15 \\ \hline 0 \end{array}$ 5 is greatest common divisor.
Raising fractions to higher terms, p. 39	Multiply numerator and denominator by same number. Does not change fraction value.	$\frac{15}{41} = \frac{?}{410}$ $410 \div 41 = 10 \times 15 = \boxed{150}$

(continues)

CHAPTER ORGANIZER AND REFERENCE GUIDE

Topic	Key point, procedure, formula	Example(s) to illustrate situation
Adding and subtracting like and unlike fractions, p. 41	When denominators are the same (like fractions), add (or subtract) numerators, place total over original denominator, and reduce to lowest terms. When denominators are different (unlike fractions), change them to like fractions by finding LCD using inspection or prime numbers. Then add (or subtract) the numerators, place total over LCD, and reduce to lowest terms.	$\dfrac{4}{9} + \dfrac{1}{9} = \boxed{\dfrac{5}{9}}$ $\dfrac{4}{9} - \dfrac{1}{9} = \dfrac{3}{9} = \boxed{\dfrac{1}{3}}$ $\dfrac{4}{5} + \dfrac{2}{7} = \dfrac{28}{35} + \dfrac{10}{35} = \dfrac{38}{35} = \boxed{1\dfrac{3}{35}}$
Prime numbers, p. 42	Whole numbers larger than 1 that are only divisible by itself and 1.	2, 3, 5, 7, 11
LCD by prime numbers, p. 42	1. Copy denominators and arrange them in a separate row. 2. Divide denominators by smallest prime number that will divide evenly into at least two numbers. 3. Continue until no prime number divides evenly into at least two numbers. 4. Multiply all the numbers in the divisors and last row to find LCD. 5. Raise fractions so each has a common denominator and complete computation.	$\dfrac{1}{3} + \dfrac{1}{6} + \dfrac{1}{8} + \dfrac{1}{12} + \dfrac{1}{9}$ $\begin{array}{l} 2\ \underline{/\ 3\quad 6\quad 8\quad 12\quad 9} \\ 2\ \underline{/\ 3\quad 3\quad 4\quad 6\quad 9} \\ 3\ \underline{/\ 3\quad 3\quad 2\quad 3\quad 9} \\ 1\quad 1\quad 2\quad 1\quad 3 \end{array}$ $2 \times 2 \times 3 \times 1 \times 1 \times 2 \times 1 \times 3 = \boxed{72}$
Adding mixed numbers, p. 43	1. Add fractions. 2. Add whole numbers. 3. Combine totals of Steps 1 and 2. If denominators are different, a common denominator must be found. Answer cannot be left as improper fraction.	$1\dfrac{4}{7} + 1\dfrac{3}{7}$ Step 1: $\dfrac{4}{7} + \dfrac{3}{7} = \dfrac{7}{7}$ Step 2: $1 + 1 = 2$ Step 3: $2\dfrac{7}{7} = \boxed{3}$
Subtracting mixed numbers, p. 44	1. Subtract fractions. 2. If necessary, borrow from whole numbers. 3. Subtract whole numbers and fractions if borrowing was necessary. 4. Reduce fractions to lowest terms. If denominators are different, a common denominator must be found.	$12\dfrac{2}{5} - 7\dfrac{3}{5}$ $11\dfrac{7}{5} - 7\dfrac{3}{5}$ $= \boxed{4\dfrac{4}{5}}$ Due to borrowing $\dfrac{5}{5}$ from number 12 $\dfrac{5}{5} + \dfrac{2}{5} = \dfrac{7}{5}$ The whole number is now 11.
Multiplying proper fractions, p. 48	1. Multiply numerators and denominators. 2. Reduce answer to lowest terms or use cancellation method.	$\dfrac{4}{\overset{7}{\cancel{7}}_{1}} \times \dfrac{\overset{1}{\cancel{7}}}{9} = \boxed{\dfrac{4}{9}}$
Multiplying mixed numbers, p. 48	1. Convert mixed numbers to improper fractions. 2. Multiply numerators and denominators. 3. Reduce answer to lowest terms or use cancellation method.	$1\dfrac{1}{8} \times 2\dfrac{5}{8}$ $\dfrac{9}{8} \times \dfrac{21}{8} = \dfrac{189}{64} = \boxed{2\dfrac{61}{64}}$
Dividing proper fractions, p. 49	1. Invert divisor. 2. Multiply. 3. Reduce answer to lowest terms or use cancellation method.	$\dfrac{1}{4} \div \dfrac{1}{8} = \dfrac{1}{\underset{1}{\cancel{4}}} \times \dfrac{\overset{2}{\cancel{8}}}{1} = \boxed{2}$

(continues)

CHAPTER ORGANIZER AND REFERENCE GUIDE

Topic	Key point, procedure, formula	Example(s) to illustrate situation
Dividing mixed numbers p. 49	1. Convert mixed numbers to improper fractions. 2. Invert divisor and multiply. If final answer is an improper fraction, reduce to lowest terms by finding greatest common divisor or using the cancellation method.	$1\frac{1}{2} \div 1\frac{5}{8} = \frac{3}{2} \div \frac{13}{8}$ $= \frac{3}{2} \times \frac{\overset{4}{\cancel{8}}}{13}$ $= \frac{12}{13}$

KEY TERMS	Cancellation, *p. 48* Common denominator, *p. 41* Denominator, *p. 36* Equivalent, *p. 39* Fraction, *p. 36* Greatest common divisor, *p. 38*	Higher terms, *p. 39* Improper fraction, *p. 37* Least common denominator (LCD), *p. 41* Like fractions, *p. 41* Lowest terms, *p. 38* Mixed numbers, *p. 37*	Numerator, *p. 36* Prime numbers, *p. 42* Proper fractions, *p. 37* Reciprocal, *p. 49* Unlike fractions, *p. 41*

CHECK FIGURE FOR EXTRA PRACTICE QUIZZES WITH PAGE REFERENCES. (WORKED-OUT SOLUTIONS IN APPENDIX B.)	LU 2–1a (p. 40) 1. a. P b. I c. M d. I 2. $22\frac{1}{7}$ 3. $\frac{79}{9}$ 4. a. 14; $\frac{3}{5}$ b. 2; $\frac{48}{91}$ 5. a. 160; b. 27	LU 2–2a (p. 47) 1. 180 2. a. $\frac{17}{25}$ b. $9\frac{13}{32}$ 3. a. $\frac{1}{2}$ b. $5\frac{29}{32}$ c. $4\frac{3}{5}$ 4. $393\frac{7}{8}$ ft.	LU 2–3a (p. 51) 1. a. $\frac{3}{8}$ b. 6 2. $117;\frac{1}{5}$ 3. a. $\frac{5}{32}$ b. $11\frac{31}{36}$ 4. $101,250

Critical Thinking Discussion Questions

1. What are the steps to convert improper fractions to whole or mixed numbers? Give an example of how you could use this conversion procedure when you eat at Pizza Hut.

2. What are the steps to convert mixed numbers to improper fractions? Show how you could use this conversion procedure when you order doughnuts at Dunkin' Donuts.

3. What is the greatest common divisor? How could you use the greatest common divisor to write an advertisement showing that 35 out of 60 people prefer MCI to AT&T?

4. Explain the step approach for finding the greatest common divisor. How could you use the MCI–AT&T example in question 3 to illustrate the step approach?

5. Explain the steps of adding or subtracting unlike fractions. Using a ruler, measure the heights of two different-size cans of food and show how to calculate the difference in height.

6. What is a prime number? Using the two cans in question 5, show how you could use prime numbers to calculate the LCD.

7. Explain the steps for multiplying proper fractions and mixed numbers. Assume you went to Staples (a stationery superstore). Give an example showing the multiplying of proper fractions and mixed numbers.

Classroom Notes

Check figures for odd-numbered problems in Appendix C   Name _____ Date _____

DRILL PROBLEMS

Identify the following types of fractions:

2–1. $11\frac{1}{7}$

2–2. $\frac{12}{11}$

2–3. $\frac{3}{7}$

Convert the following to mixed numbers:

2–4. $\frac{89}{9} =$

2–5. $\frac{921}{15} =$

Convert the following to improper fractions:

2–6. $8\frac{7}{8}$

2–7. $19\frac{2}{3}$

Reduce the following to the lowest terms. Show how to calculate the greatest common divisor by the step approach.

2–8. $\frac{16}{38}$

2–9. $\frac{44}{52}$

Convert the following to higher terms:

2–10. $\frac{9}{10} = \frac{}{70}$

Determine the LCD of the following (a) by inspection and (b) by division of prime numbers:

2–11. $\frac{3}{4}, \frac{7}{12}, \frac{5}{6}, \frac{1}{5}$ **Check**

       Inspection

2–12. $\frac{5}{6}, \frac{7}{18}, \frac{5}{9}, \frac{2}{72}$ **Check**

       Inspection

2–13. $\frac{1}{4}, \frac{3}{32}, \frac{5}{48}, \frac{1}{8}$ **Check**

       Inspection

Add the following and reduce to lowest terms:

2–14. $\frac{3}{9} + \frac{3}{9}$

2–15. $\frac{3}{7} + \frac{4}{21}$

2–16. $6\frac{1}{8} + 4\frac{3}{8}$

2–17. $6\frac{3}{8} + 9\frac{1}{24}$

2–18. $9\frac{9}{10} + 6\frac{7}{10}$

Subtract the following and reduce to lowest terms:

2–19. $\dfrac{11}{12} - \dfrac{1}{12}$

2–20. $14\dfrac{3}{8} - 10\dfrac{5}{8}$

2–21. $12\dfrac{1}{9} - 4\dfrac{2}{3}$

Multiply the following and reduce to lowest terms. Do not use the cancellation technique for these problems.

2–22. $17 \times \dfrac{4}{2}$

2–23. $\dfrac{5}{6} \times \dfrac{3}{8}$

2–24. $8\dfrac{7}{8} \times 64$

Multiply the following. Use the cancellation technique.

2–25. $\dfrac{4}{10} \times \dfrac{30}{60} \times \dfrac{6}{10}$

2–26. $3\dfrac{3}{4} \times \dfrac{8}{9} \times 4\dfrac{9}{12}$

Divide the following and reduce to lowest terms. Use the cancellation technique as needed.

2–27. $\dfrac{12}{9} \div 4$

2–28. $18 \div \dfrac{1}{5}$

2–29. $4\dfrac{2}{3} \div 12$

2–30. $3\dfrac{5}{6} \div 3\dfrac{1}{2}$

WORD PROBLEMS

2–31. Michael Wittry has been investing in his Roth IRA retirement account for 20 years. Two years ago, his account was worth $215,658. After losing $\frac{1}{3}$ of its original value, it then gained $\frac{1}{2}$ of its new value back, what is the current value of his Roth IRA?

2–32. Delta pays Pete Rose $180 per day to work in the maintenance department at the airport. Pete became ill on Monday and went home after $\frac{1}{6}$ of a day. What did he earn on Monday? Assume no work, no pay.

2–33. Britney Summers visited Curves and lost $2\frac{1}{4}$ pounds in week 1, $1\frac{3}{4}$ pounds in week 2, and $\frac{5}{8}$ pound in week 3. What is the total weight loss for Britney?

2–34. Joy Wigens, who works at Putnam Investments, received a check for $1,600. She deposited $\frac{1}{4}$ of the check in her Citibank account. How much money does Joy have left after the deposit?

$$\frac{3}{4} \times \frac{1,600}{1} = \frac{48,000}{4}$$

2–54. Shelly Van Doren hired a contractor to refinish her kitchen. The contractor said the job would take $49\frac{1}{2}$ hours. To date, the contractor has worked the following hours:

Monday	$4\frac{1}{4}$
Tuesday	$9\frac{1}{8}$
Wednesday	$4\frac{1}{4}$
Thursday	$3\frac{1}{2}$
Friday	$10\frac{5}{8}$

How much longer should the job take to be completed?

ADDITIONAL SET OF WORD PROBLEMS

2–55. An issue of *Taunton's Fine Woodworking* included plans for a hall stand. The total height of the stand is $81\frac{1}{2}$ inches. If the base is $36\frac{5}{16}$ inches, how tall is the upper portion of the stand?

2–56. Albertsons grocery planned a big sale on apples and received 750 crates from the wholesale market. Albertsons will bag these apples in plastic. Each plastic bag holds $\frac{1}{9}$ of a crate. If Albertsons has no loss to perishables, how many bags of apples can be prepared?

2–57. Frank Puleo bought 6,625 acres of land in ski country. He plans to subdivide the land into parcels of $13\frac{1}{4}$ acres each. Each parcel will sell for \$125,000. How many parcels of land will Frank develop? If Frank sells all the parcels, what will be his total sales?

If Frank sells $\frac{3}{5}$ of the parcels in the first year, what will be his total sales for the year?

2–58. A local Papa Gino's conducted a food survey. The survey showed that $\frac{1}{9}$ of the people surveyed preferred eating pasta to hamburger. If 5,400 responded to the survey, how many actually favored hamburger?

2–59. Tamara, Jose, and Milton entered into a partnership that sells men's clothing on the Web. Tamara owns $\frac{3}{8}$ of the company, and Jose owns $\frac{1}{4}$. What part does Milton own?

2–60. *Quilters Newsletter Magazine* gave instructions on making a quilt. The quilt required $4\frac{1}{2}$ yards of white-on-white print, 2 yards blue check, $\frac{1}{2}$ yard blue-and-white stripe, $2\frac{3}{4}$ yards blue scraps, $\frac{3}{4}$ yard yellow scraps, and $4\frac{7}{8}$ yards lining. How many total yards are needed?

2–61. A trailer carrying supplies for a Krispy Kreme from Virginia to New York will take $3\frac{1}{4}$ hours. If the truck traveled $\frac{1}{5}$ of the way, how much longer will the trip take?

2–62. Land Rover has increased the price of a FreeLander by $\frac{1}{5}$ from the original price. The original price of the FreeLander was $30,000. What is the new price?

CHALLENGE PROBLEMS

2–63 A recipe calls for $2\frac{1}{2}$ cups flour, 1 cup sugar, $1\frac{1}{2}$ cups butter, 4 eggs, 1 teaspoon baking soda, $\frac{1}{2}$ teaspoon salt, and $1\frac{1}{2}$ teaspoon vanilla. If you need to cut the recipe in half, how much of each will you need?

2–64. Jack MacLean has entered into a real estate development partnership with Bill Lyons and June Reese. Bill owns $\frac{1}{4}$ of the partnership, while June has a $\frac{1}{5}$ interest. The partners will divide all profits on the basis of their fractional ownership.

   The partnership bought 900 acres of land and plans to subdivide each lot into $2\frac{1}{4}$ acres. Homes in the area have been selling for $240,000. By time of completion, Jack estimates the price of each home will increase by $\frac{1}{3}$ of the current value. The partners sent a survey to 12,000 potential customers to see whether they should heat the homes with oil or gas. One-fourth of the customers responded by indicating a 5-to-1 preference for oil. From the results of the survey, Jack now plans to install a 270-gallon oil tank at each home. He estimates that each home will need 5 fills per year. Current price of home heating fuel is $1 per gallon. The partnership estimates its profit per home will be $\frac{1}{8}$ the selling price of each home.

   From the above, please calculate the following:

a. Number of homes to be built.

b. Selling price of each home.

c. Number of people responding to survey.

d. Number of people desiring oil.

e. Average monthly cost to run oil heat per house.

f. Amount of profit Jack will receive from the sale of homes.

SUMMARY PRACTICE TEST

Identify the following types of fractions. *(p. 36)*

1. $5\frac{1}{8}$

2. $\frac{2}{7}$

3. $\frac{20}{19}$

4. Convert the following to a mixed number. *(p. 37)*

$\frac{163}{9}$

5. Convert the following to an improper fraction. *(p. 37)*

$8\frac{1}{8}$

6. Calculate the greatest common divisor of the following by the step approach and reduce to lowest terms. *(p. 39)*

$$\frac{63}{90}$$

7. Convert the following to higher terms. *(p. 39)*

$$\frac{16}{94} = \frac{?}{376}$$

8. Find the LCD of the following by using prime numbers. Show your work. *(p. 41)*

$$\frac{1}{8} + \frac{1}{3} + \frac{1}{2} + \frac{1}{12}$$

9. Subtract the following. *(p. 44)*

$$15\frac{4}{5}$$
$$-8\frac{19}{20}$$

Complete the following using the cancellation technique. *(p. 48)*

10. $\dfrac{3}{4} \times \dfrac{2}{4} \times \dfrac{6}{9}$ **11.** $7\dfrac{1}{9} \times \dfrac{6}{7}$ **12.** $\dfrac{3}{7} \div 6$

13. A trip to Washington from Boston will take you $5\frac{3}{4}$ hours. If you have traveled $\frac{1}{3}$ of the way, how much longer will the trip take? *(p. 48)*

14. Quiznos produces 640 rolls per hour. If the oven runs $12\frac{1}{4}$ hours, how many rolls will the machine produce? *(p. 49)*

15. A taste-testing survey of Zing Farms showed that $\frac{2}{3}$ of the people surveyed preferred the taste of veggie burgers to regular burgers. If 90,000 people were in the survey, how many favored veggie burgers? How many chose regular burgers? *(p. 48)*

16. Jim Janes, an employee of Enterprise Co., worked $9\frac{1}{4}$ hours on Monday, $4\frac{1}{2}$ hours on Tuesday, $9\frac{1}{4}$ hours on Wednesday, $7\frac{1}{2}$ hours on Thursday, and 9 hours on Friday. How many total hours did Jim work during the week? *(p. 41)*

17. JCPenney offered a $\frac{1}{3}$ rebate on its \$39 hair dryer. Joan bought a JCPenney hair dryer. What did Joan pay after the rebate? *(p. 48)*

MAJOR MARKDOWNS
THESE HOMES ARE PRICED TO SELL.

NAPA VALLEY, CAL.
3 BR, 2.5 BA, in gated community
LAST SOLD FOR: $1,071,200
CURRENT PRICE: $654,900

LAKEVILLE, MINN.
4 BR, 3.5 BA, on nearly an acre
LAST SOLD FOR: $473,989
CURRENT PRICE: $335,500

HALLANDALE, FLA.
3 BR, 3 BA, oceanfront condo
LAST SOLD FOR: $1,002,800
CURRENT PRICE: $785,000

HUNTINGTON, N.Y.
5 BR, 3 BA, heated pool
LAST SOLD FOR: $1,450,000
CURRENT PRICE: $1,039,000

THIS ARTICLE WAS WRITTEN BY **JESSICA ANDERSON, THOMAS M. ANDERSON, JANE BENNETT CLARK, LAURA COHN, PATRICIA MERTZ ESSWEIN, MARY BETH FRANKLIN, CANDICE LEE JONES, JEFFREY R. KOSNETT, DAVID LANDIS, ELIZABETH ODY, STACY RAPACON** AND **ANDREW TANZER.**

From Kiplinger's Personal Finance, August 2009, p. 62.

DEL POSTO

DEALS ON FANCY MEALS
RITZY RESTAURANTS ARE DRUMMING UP BUSINESS WITH SPECIAL PROMOTIONS AND *PRIX FIXE* MENUS.

And you thought *you* were having a bad year. High wholesale prices and newly cost-conscious consumers have created "the most challenging environment for the restaurant industry in several decades," says Hudson Riehle, of the National Restaurant Association. Even high-end restaurants, including those operated by big-name chefs such as Mario Batali, have responded to weak sales by offering diners reduced prices, *prix fixe* meals, nightly specials, free appetizers or desserts, and small plates at (relatively) low cost. Restaurateurs who try to hold out for *le prix scandaleux* do so at their peril, says Riehle. "With the competition so intense, consumers are quick to vote with their feet."

What constitutes a bargain at a ritzy restaurant? At Batali's Del Posto, in New York City, that would be the tasting menu, recently reduced from $175 to $125 for a seven-item assortment that includes gourmet ingredients such as foie gras and truffles. The *prix fixe* lunch goes for a mere $32.

But it's not just pricey Manhattan eateries that are dishing out savings. Splash!, a seafood restaurant in Tampa, draws bottom feeders with such weeknight "stimulus" specials as the shrimp jambalaya for $5 (plus the price of a beverage)—about one-fifth the price of the seafood risotto from the regular menu. Ruth's Chris Steakhouse, where the average dinner tab runs $74, recently introduced a *prix fixe* meal that includes an appetizer, a side, a 16-ounce strip steak and dessert for $40.

WINE AT A PALATABLE PRICE FORGET FRANCE AND CALIFORNIA. THINK RED, WHITE AND BUBBLY FROM SPAIN AND ARGENTINA.

Argentina is the fastest-growing exporter of wine to the U.S. market. It's not hard to see why: The country is producing impressive wines at reasonable prices. Wines made with Malbec grapes—lesser blending grapes from Bordeaux that have flourished in Argentina's soil since they were transplanted there in the 19th century—are particularly hot. One elegant example is **Bodega Luigi Bosca Malbec Reserva Lujan de Cuyo 2006** ($15 to $18), an inky red wine with raspberry and tobacco notes.

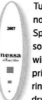

Tucked away in the northwest corner of Spain, Galicia is bottling some stunning white wines at affordable prices. The region's Albarino grape produces crisp, dry, aromatic wines that pair perfectly with shellfish and other seafood and make a refreshing summer aperitif. You can find many fine examples of Albarino wines in the $10-to-$20 price range. One is **Nessa Albarino Rias Baixas 2007** ($13 to $15), a fragrant wine with citrus and mineral overtones and enough acidity to cut through that fish oil.

Champagne, the effervescent wine of northern France, has been priced out of sight due to sturdy global demand and tight supply. The French government simply will not expand the region's tightly delineated boundaries. But you can do very well at a fraction of the price with a sparkling wine from Spain, such as **Mont Marcal Brut Reserva Cava 2005 (or 2006)**, which costs about $15. Mont Marcal is made mostly from indigenous Spanish grapes you've never heard of, but it is a delicate, refined potion.

BUSINESS MATH ISSUE

Lowering food prices by 4/5 means a business will always turn a profit.

1. List the key points of the article and information to support your position.
2. Write a group defense of your position using math calculations to support your view.

Slater's Business Math Scrapbook

Applying Your Skills

PROJECT A
At Whiteface Lodge what is the selling cost of a whole unit?

PROJECT B
Convert these tax facts to fractions.

TAX FACTS

Odds that your individual tax return was audited by the IRS in 2008, by income level.

Under $200,000	1 in 100
Between $200,000 and $1 million	1 in 37
Over $1 million	1 in 18

Source: WSJ calculations based on IRS data

A Piece of the Mountain

More mountain resorts are offering fractional ownerships alongside standard hotel fare. Prices are for a standard double-occupancy room in the summer, except where indicated.

NAME / LOCATION / PRICE	COMMENTS
The Canyons Grand Summit Park City, Utah / $194	365-room hotel has both fractional and whole-ownership units, offered as hotel rooms when not being used by owners. Open in summer, but some restaurants close in off-season. Quarter shares in studios from $60K.
Four Seasons Jackson Hole Teton Village, Wyo. / $525	This 124-unit hotel operates fully in summer. The 12 Residence Club units start from $185K.
Ritz-Carlton Bachelor Gulch Avon, Colo. / $375	Resort, with 180 rooms and 54 fractional. units, offers patrons the chance to borrow Bachelor, the hotel's yellow Labrador. Fractionals start at $220K. One restaurant is closed until November.
Stowe Mountain Lodge Stowe, Vt. / $435 (at fall opening)	New 139-room hotel won't be ready until late November at the earliest; the 34 additional fractional suites, with 1/8 shares starting at $349K, won't be available for rental.
Whiteface Lodge Lake Placid, N.Y. / $490	All 94 units are sold as fractionals, starting at $120K for a 1/12 share. Owners can make units available for rental through the hotel.

—Ben Casselman

Wall Street Journal © 2007

PROJECT C
Assume Gap had 120,000 customers ordering online today. How many customers can it expect to sell across its brand lines?

Gap Links 4 Web Sites to Spur Sales

BY JENNIFER SARANOW

In an effort to get shoppers to use all four of its Web sites, **Gap** Inc. is allowing them to move more easily between the sites, fill one virtual shopping bag and pay one shipping fee.

Until now, shoppers had to visit the company's Gap, Banana Republic, Old Navy and Piperlime sites separately to make purchases.

By integrating the sites, the San Francisco-based company hopes to encourage shoppers to purchase products from more than one of its brands. Gap says about a third of its online orders are placed by customers who shopped at more than one of its Web sites in the past year.

"We are creating an extremely compelling advantage for our customers to stay within our family and shop multiple sites," said Toby Lenk, president of Gap Inc. Direct. "In one sense, it's one big Web site now, whereas before it was four completely separate Web

At checkout, each brand is displayed; the items will be shipped together.

sites." Gap announced the feature in emails sent to customers early Tuesday morning.

Wall Street Journal © 2008

Internet Projects: See text Web site (www.mhhe.com/slater10e) and The Business Math Internet Resource Guide.

ARBITRAGE

The Price of a 'Grande' Coffee Frappuccino at Starbucks

CITY	CURRENCY	US$
Tokyo	¥440	$3.72
Hong Kong	HK$31	3.96
New York	$4.25	4.25
London	£2.60	5.23
Frankfurt	€4.40	5.99
Vienna	€4.40	5.99
Paris	€4.50	6.12

Note: Prices, including taxes, as provided by retailers in each city, averaged and converted to the nearest U.S. dollar

Wall Street Journal © 2007

Pepper . . . and Salt
THE WALL STREET JOURNAL

"$4.75. Why? It takes many years to develop a new coffee."

Wall Street Journal © 2009

Frappuccino®
Ice Blended Beverage

แมงโกซีทรัสและครีมแฟรปปูชิโ

Whipped Cream
วิปครีม

Cream Frappu
ครีมแฟ

Mango Citrus
แมงโกซีทรัส

Icy and Smoo
น้ำแข็งบ

frappuccino
ICE BLENDED BEVERAGES

LU 3–1: Rounding Decimals; Fraction and Decimal Conversions

1. Explain the place values of whole numbers and decimals; round decimals (pp. 66, 67).

2. Convert decimal fractions to decimals, proper fractions to decimals, mixed numbers to decimals, and pure and mixed decimals to decimal fractions (pp. 68–70).

LU 3–2: Adding, Subtracting, Multiplying, and Dividing Decimals

1. Add, subtract, multiply, and divide decimals (pp. 71–73).

2. Complete decimal applications in foreign currency (pp. 73–74).

3. Multiply and divide decimals by shortcut methods (pp. 74–75).

VOCABULARY PREVIEW

Here are the key terms in this chapter. When you finish the chapter, if you feel you know the term, place a checkmark within the parentheses following the term. If you are not certain of the definition, look it up and write the page number where it can be found in the text. The chapter organizer includes page references to the terms. There is also a complete glossary at the end of the text.

Decimal . ( ) Decimal fraction . ( ) Decimal point . ( ) Mixed decimal . ( ) Pure decimal . ( ) Repeating decimal . ( ) Rounding decimals . ( )

Oh, the Fees You'll Pay . . .

Here are two sample air tickets with taxes, fees and surcharges broken out.

	Boston-San Diego on American	Chicago-Frankfurt on Lufthansa
Base fare	$593.49	$1,191.00
U.S. federal tax	58.51	30.80
Security fees	10.00	12.67
Airport charges	18.00	36.68
Fuel surcharge	NA	200.00
Customs, immigration and agriculture inspection fees	NA	17.50
Total taxes and fees	86.51	297.65
Total ticket cost	680.00	1,488.65

Source: the airlines.   NA=not applicable

Wall Street Journal © 2008

Are you looking to vacation in San Diego or Frankfurt? As you can see from the *Wall Street Journal* clip "Oh, the Fees You'll Pay" airplane ticket prices do vary. The difference in cost between the American and Lufthansa routes is $808.65.

Lufthansa: $1,488.65
American: − 680.00
$ 808.65

TABLE	3.1

Analyzing a bag of M&M's®

LO 1

Color*	Fraction	Decimal
Yellow	$\frac{18}{55}$	.33
Red	$\frac{10}{55}$	.18
Blue	$\frac{9}{55}$	.16
Orange	$\frac{7}{55}$	.13
Brown	$\frac{6}{55}$	.11
Green	$\frac{5}{55}$	.09
Total	$\frac{55}{55} = 1$	1.00

*The color ratios currently given are a sample used for educational purposes. They do not represent the manufacturer's color ratios.

Sharon Hoogstraten

Chapter 2 introduced the 1.69-ounce bag of M&M's® shown in Table 3.1. In Table 3.1, the six colors in the 1.69-ounce bag of M&M's® are given in fractions and their values expressed in decimal equivalents that are rounded to the nearest hundredths.

This chapter is divided into two learning units. The first unit discusses rounding decimals, converting fractions to decimals, and converting decimals to fractions. The second unit shows you how to add, subtract, multiply, and divide decimals, along with some shortcuts for multiplying and dividing decimals. Added to this unit is a global application of decimals dealing with foreign exchange rates. One of the most common uses of decimals occurs when we spend dollars and cents, which is a *decimal number*.

A **decimal** is a decimal number with digits to the right of a *decimal point,* indicating that decimals, like fractions, are parts of a whole that are less than one. Thus, we can interchange the terms *decimals* and *decimal numbers.* Remembering this will avoid confusion between the terms *decimal, decimal number,* and *decimal point.*

Learning Unit 3–1: Rounding Decimals; Fraction and Decimal Conversions

Remember to read the decimal point as *and.*

In Chapter 1 we stated that the **decimal point** is the center of the decimal numbering system. So far we have studied the whole numbers to the left of the decimal point and the parts of whole numbers called fractions. We also learned that the position of the digits in a whole number gives the place values of the digits (Figure 1.1, p. 5). Now we will study the position (place values) of the digits to the right of the decimal point (Figure 3.1, p. 67). Note that the words to the right of the decimal point end in *ths.*

You should understand why the decimal point is the center of the decimal system. If you move a digit to the left of the decimal point by place (ones, tens, and so on), *you increase its value 10 times for each place (power of 10).* If you move a digit to the right of the decimal point by place (tenths, hundredths, and so on), *you decrease its value 10 times for each place.*

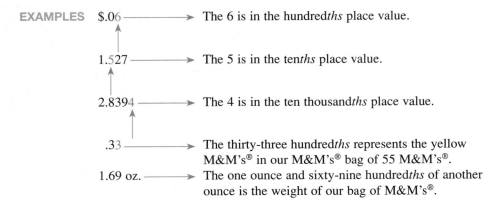

EXAMPLES $.06 \longrightarrow$ The 6 is in the hundred*ths* place value.

1.527 $\longrightarrow$ The 5 is in the ten*ths* place value.

2.8394 $\longrightarrow$ The 4 is in the ten thousand*ths* place value.

.33 $\longrightarrow$ The thirty-three hundred*ths* represents the yellow M&M's® in our M&M's® bag of 55 M&M's®.

1.69 oz. $\longrightarrow$ The one ounce and sixty-nine hundred*ths* of another ounce is the weight of our bag of M&M's®.

FIGURE **3.1**

Decimal place-value chart

Whole Number Groups					Decimal Place Values				
Thousands	Hundreds	Tens	Ones (units)	Decimal point (and)	Tenths	Hundredths	Thousandths	Ten thousandths	Hundred thousandths
1,000	100	10	1	and	$\frac{1}{10}$	$\frac{1}{100}$	$\frac{1}{1,000}$	$\frac{1}{10,000}$	$\frac{1}{100,000}$

Do you recall from Chapter 1 how you used a place-value chart to read or write whole numbers in verbal form? To read or write decimal numbers, you read or write the decimal number as if it were a whole number. Then you use the name of the decimal place of the last digit as given in Figure 3.1. For example, you would read or write the decimal .0796 as seven hundred ninety-six ten thousandths (the last digit, 6, is in the ten thousandths place).

To read a decimal with four or fewer whole numbers, you can also refer to Figure 3.1. For larger whole numbers, refer to the whole-number place-value chart in Chapter 1 (Figure 1.1, p. 5). For example, from Figure 3.1 you would read the number 126.2864 as one hundred twenty-six and two thousand eight hundred sixty-four ten thousandths. Remember that the *and* is the decimal point.

Now let's round decimals. Rounding decimals is similar to the rounding of whole numbers that you learned in Chapter 1.

Rounding Decimals

From Table 3.1, you know that the 1.69-ounce bag of M&M's® introduced in Chapter 2 contained $\frac{18}{55}$, or .33, yellow M&M's®. The .33 was rounded to the nearest hundredth. **Rounding decimals** involves the following steps:

ROUNDING DECIMALS TO A SPECIFIED PLACE VALUE
Step 1. Identify the place value of the digit you want to round.
Step 2. If the digit to the right of the identified digit in Step 1 is 5 or more, increase the identified digit by 1. If the digit to the right is less than 5, do not change the identified digit.
Step 3. Drop all digits to the right of the identified digit.

Let's practice rounding by using the $\frac{18}{55}$ yellow M&M's® that we rounded to .33 in Table 3.1. Before we rounded $\frac{18}{55}$ to .33, the number we rounded was .32727. This is an example of a **repeating decimal** since the 27 repeats itself.

EXAMPLE   Round .3272727 to nearest hundredth.

Step 1.   .3272727   The identified digit is 2, which is in the hundredths place (two places to the right of the decimal point).

Step 2.   The digit to the right of 2 is more than 5 (7). Thus, 2, the identified digit in Step 1, is changed to 3.

.3372727

Step 3.   .33   Drop all other digits to right of the identified digit 3.

We could also round the .3272727 M&M's® to the nearest tenth or thousandth as follows:

	Tenth	**or**	**Thousandth**
.3272727 ⟶	.3	.3272727 ⟶	.327

OTHER EXAMPLES

Round to nearest dollar:	$166.39	→	$166
Round to nearest cent:	$1,196.885	→	$1,196.89
Round to nearest hundredth:	$38.563	→	$38.56
Round to nearest thousandth:	$1,432.9981	→	$1,432.998

The rules for rounding can differ with the situation in which rounding is used. For example, have you ever bought one item from a supermarket produce department that was marked "3 for $1" and noticed what the cashier charged you? One item marked "3 for $1" would not cost you $33\frac{1}{3}$ cents rounded to 33 cents. You will pay 34 cents. Many retail stores round to the next cent even if the digit following the identified digit is less than $\frac{1}{2}$ of a penny. In this text we round on the concept of 5 or more.

LO 2

Fraction and Decimal Conversions

In business operations we must frequently convert fractions to decimal numbers and decimal numbers to fractions. This section begins by discussing three types of fraction-to-decimal conversions. Then we discuss converting pure and mixed decimals to decimal fractions.

Converting Decimal Fractions to Decimals

From Figure 3.1 you can see that a **decimal fraction** (expressed in the digits to the right of the decimal point) is a fraction with a denominator that has a power of 10, such as $\frac{1}{10}$, $\frac{17}{100}$, and $\frac{23}{1,000}$. To convert a decimal fraction to a decimal, follow these steps:

CONVERTING DECIMAL FRACTIONS TO DECIMALS

Step 1. Count the number of zeros in the denominator.

Step 2. Place the numerator of the decimal fraction to the right of the decimal point the same number of places as you have zeros in the denominator. (The number of zeros in the denominator gives the number of digits your decimal has to the right of the decimal point.) Do not go over the total number of denominator zeros.

Now let's change $\frac{3}{10}$ and its higher multiples of 10 to decimals.

EXAMPLES

Verbal form	Decimal fraction	Decimal[1]	Number of decimal places to right of decimal point
a. Three tenths	$\frac{3}{10}$	.3	1
b. Three hundredths	$\frac{3}{100}$	.03	2
c. Three thousandths	$\frac{3}{1,000}$	.003	3
d. Three ten thousandths	$\frac{3}{10,000}$	.0003	4

Note how we show the different values of the decimal fractions above in decimals. The zeros after the decimal point and before the number 3 indicate these values. If you add zeros after the number 3, you do not change the value. Thus, the numbers .3 , .30 , and .300 have the same value. So 3 tenths of a pizza, 30 hundredths of a pizza, and 300 thousandths of a pizza are the same total amount of pizza. The first pizza is sliced into 10 pieces. The second pizza is sliced into 100 pieces. The third pizza is sliced into 1,000 pieces. Also, we don't need to place a zero to the left of the decimal point.

---

[1]From .3 to .0003, the values get smaller and smaller, but if you go from .3 to .3000, the values remain the same.

Converting Proper Fractions to Decimals

Recall from Chapter 2 that proper fractions are fractions with a value less than 1. That is, the numerator of the fraction is smaller than its denominator. How can we convert these proper fractions to decimals? Since proper fractions are a form of division, it is possible to convert proper fractions to decimals by carrying out the division.

CONVERTING PROPER FRACTIONS TO DECIMALS
Step 1. Divide the numerator of the fraction by its denominator. (If necessary, add a decimal point and zeros to the number in the numerator.)
Step 2. Round as necessary.

EXAMPLES

$$\frac{3}{4} = 4\overline{)3.00} \quad \frac{.75}{}$$

$$\begin{array}{r} .75 \\ 4\overline{)3.00} \\ \underline{2\,8} \\ 20 \\ \underline{20} \end{array}$$

$$\frac{3}{8} = \begin{array}{r} .375 \\ 8\overline{)3.000} \\ \underline{2\,4} \\ 60 \\ \underline{56} \\ 40 \\ \underline{40} \end{array}$$

$$\frac{1}{3} = \begin{array}{r} .33\overline{3} \\ 3\overline{)1.000} \\ \underline{9} \\ 10 \\ \underline{9} \\ 10 \\ \underline{9} \\ 1 \end{array}$$

Note that in the last example $\frac{1}{3}$, the 3 in the quotient keeps repeating itself (never ends). The short bar over the last 3 means that the number endlessly repeats.

Converting Mixed Numbers to Decimals

A mixed number, you will recall from Chapter 2, is the sum of a whole number greater than zero and a proper fraction. To convert mixed numbers to decimals, use the following steps:

CONVERTING MIXED NUMBERS TO DECIMALS
Step 1. Convert the fractional part of the mixed number to a decimal (as illustrated in the previous section).
Step 2. Add the converted fractional part to the whole number.

EXAMPLE

$$8\frac{2}{5} = \textbf{(Step 1)} \quad \begin{array}{r} .4 \\ 5\overline{)2.0} \\ \underline{2\,0} \end{array} \qquad \textbf{(Step 2)} = \begin{array}{r} 8.00 \\ +\ .40 \\ \hline 8.40 \end{array}$$

Now that we have converted fractions to decimals, let's convert decimals to fractions.

Converting Pure and Mixed Decimals to Decimal Fractions

A **pure decimal** has no whole number(s) to the left of the decimal point (.43, .458, and so on). A **mixed decimal** is a combination of a whole number and a decimal. An example of a mixed decimal follows.

EXAMPLE   737.592 = Seven hundred thirty-seven and five hundred ninety-two thousandths

Note the following conversion steps for converting pure and mixed decimals to decimal fractions:

CONVERTING PURE AND MIXED DECIMALS TO DECIMAL FRACTIONS
Step 1. Place the digits to the right of the decimal point in the numerator of the fraction. Omit the decimal point. (For a decimal fraction with a fractional part, see examples **c** and **d** below.)
Step 2. Put a 1 in the denominator of the fraction.
Step 3. Count the number of digits to the right of the decimal point. Add the same number of zeros to the denominator of the fraction. For mixed decimals, add the fraction to the whole number.

If desired, you can reduce the fractions in Step 3.

EXAMPLES		Step 1	Step 2	Places	Step 3
a.	.3	$\dfrac{3}{}$	$\dfrac{3}{1}$	1	$\dfrac{3}{10}$
b.	.24	$\dfrac{24}{}$	$\dfrac{24}{1}$	2	$\dfrac{24}{100}$
c.	$.24\frac{1}{2}$	$\dfrac{245}{}$	$\dfrac{245}{1}$	3	$\dfrac{245}{1,000}$

$ MONEY TIPS

It is always useful to know that $\frac{1}{8} = .125$, $\frac{3}{8} = .375$, $\frac{5}{8} = .625$, and $\frac{7}{8} = .875$ by memory. These commonly used fractions are as useful to know as are $\frac{1}{4}, \frac{1}{2}$, and $\frac{3}{4}$, which most of us know. These are especially handy when dealing with your personal finance.

Before completing Step 1 in example **c,** we must remove the fractional part, convert it to a decimal ($\frac{1}{2} = .5$), and multiply it by .01 (.5 × .01 = .005). We use .01 because the 4 of .24 is in the hundredths place. Then we add .005 + .24 = .245 (three places to right of the decimal) and complete Steps 1, 2, and 3.

d.	$.07\frac{1}{4}$	$\dfrac{725}{}$	$\dfrac{725}{1}$	4	$\dfrac{725}{10,000}$

In example **d,** be sure to convert $\frac{1}{4}$ to .25 and multiply by .01. This gives .0025. Then add .0025 to .07, which is .0725 (four places), and complete Steps 1, 2, and 3.

e.	17.45	$\dfrac{45}{}$	$\dfrac{45}{1}$	2	$\dfrac{45}{100} = 17\dfrac{45}{100}$

Example **e** is a mixed decimal. Since we substitute *and* for the decimal point, we read this mixed decimal as seventeen and forty-five hundredths. Note that after we converted the .45 of the mixed decimals to a fraction, we added it to the whole number 17.

The Practice Quiz that follows will help you check your understanding of this unit.

LU 3–1 | PRACTICE QUIZ

Complete this **Practice Quiz** to see how you are doing.

Write the following as a decimal number.

1. Four hundred eight thousandths

Name the place position of the identified digit:

2. 6.8241   **3.** 9.3942

Round each decimal to place indicated:

		Tenth	Thousandth
4.	.62768	**a.**	**b.**
5.	.68341	**a.**	**b.**

Convert the following to decimals:

6. $\dfrac{9}{10,000}$ **7.** $\dfrac{14}{100,000}$

Convert the following to decimal fractions (do not reduce):

8. .819   **9.** 16.93   **10.** $.05\frac{1}{4}$

Convert the following fractions to decimals and round answer to nearest hundredth:

11. $\dfrac{1}{6}$ **12.** $\dfrac{3}{8}$ **13.** $12\dfrac{1}{8}$

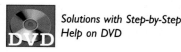

Solutions with Step-by-Step Help on DVD

✓ Solutions

1. .408 (3 places to right of decimal)
2. Hundredths   3. Thousandths
4. **a.** .6 (identified digit 6—digit to   **b.** .628 (identified digit 7—digit to
        right less than 5)   right greater than 5)
5. **a.** .7 (identified digit 6—digit to   **b.** .683 (identified digit 3—digit to
        right greater than 5)   right less than 5)
6. .0009 (4 places)   7. .00014 (5 places)
8. $\dfrac{819}{1,000}$ $\left(\dfrac{819}{1 + 3 \text{ zeros}}\right)$ 9. $16\dfrac{93}{100}$

10. $\dfrac{525}{10,000}$ $\left(\dfrac{525}{1 + 4 \text{ zeros}} \quad \dfrac{1}{4} \times .01 = .0025 + .05 = .0525\right)$

11. .16666 = .17   12. .375 = .38   13. 12.125 = 12.13

| LU 3–1a | EXTRA PRACTICE QUIZ WITH WORKED-OUT SOLUTIONS |

*Need more practice? Try this **Extra Practice Quiz** (check figures in Chapter Organizer, p. 78). Worked-out Solutions can be found in Appendix B at end of text.*

Write the following as a decimal number:
  1. Three hundred nine thousandths
Name the place position of the identified digit:
  2. 7.9324   3. 8.3682
      ↑   ↑

Round each decimal to place indicated:

	Tenth	Thousandth
4. .84361	**a.**	**b.**
5. .87938	**a.**	**b.**

Convert the following to decimals:

6. $\dfrac{8}{10,000}$ 7. $\dfrac{16}{100,000}$

Convert the following to decimal fractions (do not reduce):
  8. .938   9. 17.95   10. .03$\frac{1}{4}$

Convert the following fractions to decimals and round answer to nearest hundredth:

11. $\dfrac{1}{8}$ 12. $\dfrac{4}{7}$ 13. $13\dfrac{1}{9}$

Learning Unit 3–2: Adding, Subtracting, Multiplying, and Dividing Decimals

Would you like to save almost $2,000 per year? The *Wall Street Journal* clip "Some Workers Downsize Lunch" (p. 72) shows by brown-bagging you can save $5.45 each day. The following calculation shows that over one year savings could be $1,989.25.

Lunch from deli:	$10.69
Homemade lunch:	5.24
	$5.45 × 365 = $1,989.25

This learning unit shows you how to add, subtract, multiply, and divide decimals. You also make calculations involving decimals, including decimals used in foreign currency.

Addition and Subtraction of Decimals

Since you know how to add and subtract whole numbers, to add and subtract decimal numbers you have only to learn about the placement of the decimals. The following steps on page 72 will help you:

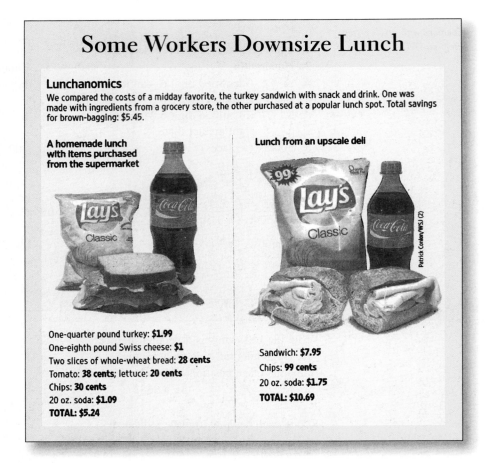

Some Workers Downsize Lunch

Lunchanomics

We compared the costs of a midday favorite, the turkey sandwich with snack and drink. One was made with ingredients from a grocery store, the other purchased at a popular lunch spot. Total savings for brown-bagging: $5.45.

A homemade lunch with items purchased from the supermarket

One-quarter pound turkey: **$1.99**
One-eighth pound Swiss cheese: **$1**
Two slices of whole-wheat bread: **28 cents**
Tomato: **38 cents**; lettuce: **20 cents**
Chips: **30 cents**
20 oz. soda: **$1.09**
TOTAL: $5.24

Lunch from an upscale deli

Sandwich: **$7.95**
Chips: **99 cents**
20 oz. soda: **$1.75**
TOTAL: $10.69

Wall Street Journal © 2008

ADDING AND SUBTRACTING DECIMALS

Step 1. Vertically write the numbers so that the decimal points align. You can place additional zeros to the right of the decimal point if needed without changing the value of the number.

Step 2. Add or subtract the digits starting with the right column and moving to the left.

Step 3. Align the decimal point in the answer with the above decimal points.

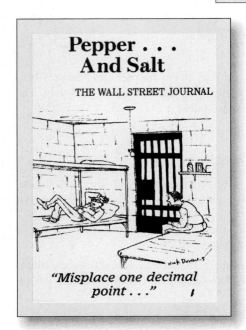

Pepper . . . And Salt

THE WALL STREET JOURNAL

"Misplace one decimal point . . ."

Wall Street Journal © 2008

EXAMPLES   Add $4 + 7.3 + 36.139 + .0007 + 8.22$.

Whole number to the right of the last digit is assumed to have a decimal.

$$
\begin{array}{r}
4.0000 \\
7.3000 \\
36.1390 \\
.0007 \\
8.2200 \\
\hline
55.6597
\end{array}
$$

Extra zeros have been added to make calculation easier.

Subtract $45.3 - 15.273$.

$$
\begin{array}{r}
{\scriptstyle 2\,9\,10} \\
45.\cancel{3}\cancel{0}\cancel{0} \\
- 15.273 \\
\hline
30.027
\end{array}
$$

Subtract $7 - 6.9$.

$$
\begin{array}{r}
{\scriptstyle 6\ 10} \\
\cancel{7}.\cancel{0} \\
- 6.9 \\
\hline
.1
\end{array}
$$

Multiplication of Decimals

The multiplication of decimal numbers is similar to the multiplication of whole numbers except for the additional step of placing the decimal in the answer (product). The steps that follow on page 73 simplify this procedure.

MULTIPLYING DECIMALS

Step 1. Multiply the numbers as whole numbers ignoring the decimal points.

Step 2. Count and total the number of decimal places in the multiplier and multiplicand.

Step 3. Starting at the right in the product, count to the left the number of decimal places totaled in Step 2. Place the decimal point so that the product has the same number of decimal places as totaled in Step 2. If the total number of places is greater than the places in the product, insert zeros in front of the product.

EXAMPLES

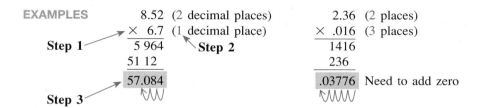

$$
\begin{array}{r}
8.52 \ \ \text{(2 decimal places)} \\
\times \ 6.7 \ \ \text{(1 decimal place)} \\
\hline
5\,964 \\
51\,12 \\
\hline
57.084
\end{array}
$$

Step 1 → Step 2

Step 3 →

$$
\begin{array}{r}
2.36 \ \ \text{(2 places)} \\
\times \ .016 \ \ \text{(3 places)} \\
\hline
1416 \\
236 \\
\hline
.03776
\end{array}
$$
Need to add zero

Division of Decimals

If the divisor in your decimal division problem is a whole number, first place the decimal point in the quotient directly above the decimal point in the dividend. Then divide as usual. If the divisor has a decimal point, complete the steps that follow.

DIVIDING DECIMALS

Step 1. Make the divisor a whole number by moving the decimal point to the right.

Step 2. Move the decimal point in the dividend to the right the same number of places that you moved the decimal point in the divisor (Step 1). If there are not enough places, add zeros to the right of the dividend.

Step 3. Place the decimal point in the quotient above the new decimal point in the dividend. Divide as usual.

EXAMPLE

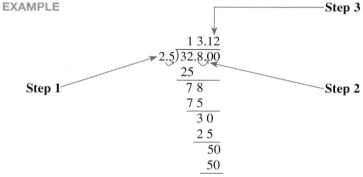

Step 3

$$
\begin{array}{r}
1\,3.12 \\
2.5\overline{)32.8.00} \\
25 \\
\hline
7\,8 \\
7\,5 \\
\hline
3\,0 \\
2\,5 \\
\hline
50 \\
50 \\
\hline
\end{array}
$$

Step 1   Step 2

Stop a moment and study the above example. Note that the quotient does not change when we multiply the divisor and the dividend by the same number. This is why we can move the decimal point in division problems and always divide by a whole number.

LO 2   **GLOBAL**   **Decimal Applications in Foreign Currency**

EXAMPLE

The *Wall Street Journal* clip shows in China the price of Microsoft Office was reduced to 199 yuan from an original price of 699 yuan. Using the currencies table (p. 74) lets us see what the original as well as sales price is in U.S. dollars. In the table 1 yuan equals $.1463. To find the original selling price you multiply the number of yuan (699) times $.1463.

$$699 \text{ yuan} \times \$.1463 = \$102.26$$

Software edition	Price change			Effective date
Windows Vista (Home basic)	1,521 yuan	→	499	Aug. 2007
Microsoft Office (Home and student)	699	→	199	Oct. 2008

Currencies

U.S.-dollar foreign-exchange rates in late New York trading

Country/currency	Wed in US$	per US$	US$ vs, YTD chg (%)	Country/currency	Wed in US$	per US$	US$ vs, YTD chg (%)
Americas				**Europe**			
Argentina peso*	.3100	3.2258	**2.4**	**Czech Rep.** koruna**	.04905	20.387	**12.2**
Brazil real	.4196	2.3832	**33.9**	**Denmark** krone	.1721	5.8106	**13.8**
Canada dollar	.7969	1.2549	**26.3**	**Euro area** euro	1.2830	.7794	**13.8**
1-mos forward	.7972	1.2544	**26.3**	**Hungary** forint	.004555	219.54	**26.7**
3-mos forward	.7988	1.2519	**26.1**	**Norway** krone	.1378	7.2569	**33.6**
6-mos forward	.7997	1.2505	**25.9**	**Poland** zloty	.3377	2.9612	**20.0**
Chile peso	.001556	642.67	**29.0**	**Russia** ruble‡	.03709	26.961	**9.7**
Colombia peso	.0004230	2364.07	**17.1**	**Slovak Rep** koruna	.04210	23.753	**3.2**
Ecuador US dollar	1	1	**unch**	**Sweden** krona	.1275	7.8431	**21.3**
Mexico peso*	.0721	13.8773	**27.2**	**Switzerland** franc	.8592	1.1639	**2.7**
Peru new sol	.3229	3.097	**3.3**	1-mos forward	.8601	1.1627	**2.8**
Uruguay peso†	.04380	22.83	**5.9**	3-mos forward	.8614	1.1609	**3.0**
Venezuela b. fuerte	.465701	2.1473	**0.1**	6-mos forward	.8621	1.1600	**3.3**
				Turkey lira**	.5902	1.6942	**45.1**
Asia-Pacific				**UK pound**	1.6241	.6157	**22.3**
Australian dollar	.6685	1.4959	**31.1**	1-mos forward	1.6215	.6167	**22.4**
China yuan	.1463	6.8348	**-6.4**	3-mos forward	1.6181	.6180	**22.5**
Hong Kong dollar	.1290	7.7527	**-0.6**	6-mos forward	1.6115	.6205	**22.6**
India rupiah	.02028	49.310	**25.1**				
Indonesia rupiah	.0001010	9901	**5.4**	**Middle East/Africa**			
Japan yen	.010235	97.70	**-12.3**	**Bahrain** dinar	2.6522	.3770	**0.3**
1-mos forward	.010259	97.48	**-12.2**	**Egypt** pound*	.1791	5.5832	**0.9**
3-mos forward	.010314	96.96	**-12.1**	**Israel** shekel	.2581	3.8745	**0.5**
6-mos forward	.010362	96.51	**-11.8**	**Jordan** dinar	1.4129	.7078	**-0.1**
Malaysia ringgit§	.2820	3.5461	**7.2**	**Kuwait** dinar	3.7122	.2694	**-1.5**
New Zealand dollar	.5838	1.7129	**31.3**	**Lebanon** pound	.0006662	1501.05	**-0.7**
Pakistan rupee	.01235	80.972	**31.3**	**Saudi Arabia** riyal	.2665	3.7523	**unch**
Philippines peso	.0206	48.662	**18.0**	**South Africa** rand	.0851	11.7509	**71.7**
Singapore dollar	.6667	1.4999	**4.1**	**UAE** dirham	.2723	3.6724	**unch**
South Korea won	.0007339	1362.58	**45.6**				
Taiwan dollar	.03034	32.960	**1.6**				
Thailand baht	.02897	34.519	**14.9**				
Vietnam dong	.00005940	16834	**5.0**	**SDR**††	1.4932	.6697	**5.7**

Wall Street Journal © 2008

The original selling price in U.S. dollars is $102.26. To find the new selling price in U.S. dollars, you multiply the number of yuan 199 times $.1463. The new selling price in U.S. dollars is $29.11.

$$199 \times \$.1463 = \$29.11$$

To check you could multiply the new price $29.11 in U.S. dollars times the table factor 6.8348.

$$\$29.11 \times 6.8348 = 198.96 \text{ yuan}$$
each $1 equals 6.8348 yuan

Multiplication and Division Shortcuts for Decimals

The shortcut steps that follow show how to solve multiplication and division problems quickly involving multiples of 10 (10, 100, 1,000, 10,000, etc.).

SHORTCUTS FOR MULTIPLES OF 10

Multiplication

Step 1. Count the zeros in the multiplier.

Step 2. Move the decimal point in the multiplicand the same number of places to the right as you have zeros in the multiplier.

Division

Step 1. Count the zeros in the divisor.

Step 2. Move the decimal point in the dividend the same number of places to the left as you have zeros in the divisor.

LO 3

In multiplication, the answers are *larger* than the original number.

EXAMPLE   If Toyota spends $60,000 for magazine advertising, what is the total value if it spends this same amount for 10 years? What would be the total cost?

$$\$60,000 \times 10 = \boxed{\$600,000} \qquad \text{(1 place to the right)}$$

OTHER EXAMPLES   6.89 × 10 = 68.9   (1 place to the right)

6.89 × 100 = 689.   (2 places to the right)

6.89 × 1,000 = 6,890.   (3 places to the right)

In division, the answers are *smaller* than the original number.

EXAMPLES   6.89 ÷ 10 = .689   (1 place to the left)

6.89 ÷ 100 = .0689   (2 places to the left)

6.89 ÷ 1,000 = .00689   (3 places to the left)

6.89 ÷ 10,000 = .000689   (4 places to the left)

Next, let's dissect and solve a word problem.

How to Dissect and Solve a Word Problem

The Word Problem May O'Mally went to Sears to buy wall-to-wall carpet. She needs 101.3 square yards for downstairs, 16.3 square yards for the upstairs bedrooms, and 6.2 square yards for the halls. The carpet cost $14.55 per square yard. The padding cost $3.25 per square yard. Sears quoted an installation charge of $6.25 per square yard. What was May O'Mally's total cost?

By completing the following blueprint aid, we will slowly dissect this word problem. Note that before solving the problem, we gather the facts, identify what we are solving for, and list the steps that must be completed before finding the final answer, along with any key points we should remember. Let's go to it!

The facts	Solving for?	Steps to take	Key points
Carpet needed: 101.3 sq. yd.; 16.3 sq. yd.; 6.2 sq. yd. Costs: Carpet, $14.55 per sq. yd.; padding, $3.25 per sq. yd.; installation, $6.25 per sq. yd.	Total cost of carpet	Total square yards × Cost per square yard = Total cost.	Align decimals. Round answer to nearest cent.

Steps to solving problem

1. Calculate the total number of square yards.

101.3
16.3
 6.2
———
123.8 square yards

2. Calculate the total cost per square yard.

$14.55
  3.25
  6.25
———
$24.05

3. Calculate the total cost of carpet.

123.8 × $24.05 = **$2,977.39**

It's time to check your progress.

LU 3–2   PRACTICE QUIZ

1. Rearrange vertically and add: 2. Rearrange and subtract:
   14, .642, 9.34, 15.87321   28.1549 − .885
3. Multiply and round the answer to the nearest tenth:
   28.53 × 17.4
4. Divide and round to the nearest hundredth:
   2,182 ÷ 2.83

Complete by the shortcut method:

5. 14.28 × 100   6. 9,680 ÷ 1,000   7. 9,812 ÷ 10,000

(cont. p. 76)

8. Could you help Mel decide which product is the "better buy"?
   Dog food A: $9.01 for 64 ounces   **Dog food B:** $7.95 for 50 ounces
   Round to the nearest cent as needed.
9. At Avis Rent-A-Car, the cost per day to rent a medium-size car is $39.99 plus 29 cents per mile. What will it cost to rent this car for 2 days if you drive 602.3 miles? Since the solution shows a completed blueprint, you might use a blueprint also.
10. A trip to Mexico cost 6,000 pesos. What would this be in U.S. dollars? Check your answer.

Solutions with Step-by-Step Help on DVD

✓ Solutions

1.
```
   14.00000
     .64200
    9.34000
   15.87321
   ─────────
   39.85521
```

2.
```
      7 101414
   28.1549
    −.8850
   ─────────
   27.2699
```

3.
```
      28.53
    × 17.4
    ───────
    11 412
   199 71
   285 3
   ───────
   496.422     = 496.4
```

4.
```
            771.024 = 771.02
   2.83)218200.000
        1981
        ────
         2010
         1981
         ────
          290
          283
          ───
          7 00
          5 66
          ─────
          1 340
          1 132
```

5. 14.28 = 1,428   6. 9.680 = 9.680   7. .9812 = .9812
8. **A:** $9.01 ÷ 64 = $.14   **B:** $7.95 ÷ 50 = $.16   **Buy A.**
9. Avis Rent-A-Car total rental charge:

The facts	Solving for?	Steps to take	Key points
Cost per day, $39.99. 29 cents per mile. Drove 602.3 miles. 2-day rental.	Total rental charge.	Total cost for 2 days' rental + Total cost of driving = Total rental charge.	In multiplication, count the number of decimal places. Starting from right to left in the product, insert decimal in appropriate place. Round to nearest cent.

Steps to solving problem

1. Calculate total costs for 2 days' rental. $39.99 × 2 = $79.98
2. Calculate the total cost of driving. $.29 × 602.3 = $174.667 = $174.67
3. Calculate the total rental charge.
```
      $ 79.98
    + 174.67
    ─────────
     $254.65
```

10. 6,000 × $.0721 = $432.60
    Check $432.60 × 13.8773 = 6003.3 pesos due to rounding

LU 3–2a   EXTRA PRACTICE QUIZ WITH WORKED-OUT SOLUTIONS

Need more practice? Try this **Extra Practice Quiz** (check figures in Chapter Organizer, p. 78). Worked-out Solutions can be found in Appendix B at end of text.

1. Rearrange vertically and add:
   16, .831, 9.85, 17.8321

2. Rearrange and subtract:
   29.5832 − .998

3. Multiply and round the answer to the nearest tenth:
   29.64 × 18.2

4. Divide and round to the nearest hundredth:
   $3,824 \div 4.94$
Complete by the shortcut method:
5. 17.48×100 6. $8,432 \div 1,000$ 7. $9,643 \div 10,000$
8. Could you help Mel decide which product is the "better buy"?
   Dog food A: $8.88 for 64 ounces   **Dog food B:** $7.25 for 50 ounces
Round to the nearest cent as needed:
9. At Avis Rent-A-Car, the cost per day to rent a medium-size car is $29.99 plus 22 cents per mile. What will it cost to rent this car for 2 days if you drive 709.8 miles?
10. A trip to Mexico costs 7,000 pesos. What would this be in U.S. dollars? Check your answer.

CHAPTER ORGANIZER AND REFERENCE GUIDE

Topic	Key point, procedure, formula	Example(s) to illustrate situation
Identifying place value, p. 67	$10, 1, \frac{1}{10}, \frac{1}{100}, \frac{1}{1,000}$, etc.	.439 in thousandths place value
Rounding decimals, p. 67	1. Identify place value of digit you want to round. 2. If digit to right of identified digit in Step 1 is 5 or more, increase identified digit by 1; if less than 5, do not change identified digit. 3. Drop all digits to right of identified digit.	.875 rounded to nearest tenth = .9 Identified digit
Converting decimal fractions to decimals, p. 68	1. Decimal fraction has a denominator with multiples of 10. Count number of zeros in denominator. 2. Zeros show how many places are in the decimal.	$\frac{8}{1,000} = .008$ $\frac{6}{10,000} = .0006$
Converting proper fractions to decimals, p. 69	1. Divide numerator of fraction by its denominator. 2. Round as necessary.	$\frac{1}{3}$ (to nearest tenth) = .3
Converting mixed numbers to decimals, p. 69	1. Convert fractional part of the mixed number to a decimal. 2. Add converted fractional part to whole number.	$6\frac{1}{4}$ $\frac{1}{4} = .25 + 6 = 6.25$
Converting pure and mixed decimals to decimal fractions, p. 69	1. Place digits to right of decimal point in numerator of fraction. 2. Put 1 in denominator. 3. Add zeros to denominator, depending on decimal places of original number. For mixed decimals, add fraction to whole number.	.984 (3 places) 1. $\frac{984}{}$ 2. $\frac{984}{1}$ 3. $\frac{984}{1,000}$
Adding and subtracting decimals, p. 71	1. Vertically write and align numbers on decimal points. 2. Add or subtract digits, starting with right column and moving to the left. 3. Align decimal point in answer with above decimal points.	Add $1.3 + 2 + .4$ 1.3 2.0 .4 3.7 Subtract $5 - 3.9$ 5.0 −3.9 1.1

(continues)

CHAPTER ORGANIZER AND REFERENCE GUIDE

Topic	Key point, procedure, formula	Example(s) to illustrate situation
Multiplying decimals, p. 72	1. Multiply numbers, ignoring decimal points. 2. Count and total number of decimal places in multiplier and multiplicand. 3. Starting at right in the product, count to the left the number of decimal places totaled in Step 2. Insert decimal point. If number of places greater than space in answer, add zeros.	2.48 (2 places) × .018 (3 places) 1 984 2 48 .04464
Dividing a decimal by a whole number, p. 73	1. Place decimal point in quotient directly above the decimal point in dividend. 2. Divide as usual.	1.1 42)46.2 42 42 42
Dividing if the divisor is a decimal, p. 73	1. Make divisor a whole number by moving decimal point to the right. 2. Move decimal point in dividend to the right the same number of places as in Step 1. 3. Place decimal point in quotient above decimal point in dividend. Divide as usual.	14.2 2.9)41.39 29 123 116 79 58 21
Shortcuts on multiplication and division of decimals, p. 74	When multiplying by 10, 100, 1,000, and so on, move decimal point in multiplicand the same number of places to the right as you have zeros in multiplier. For division, move decimal point to the left.	4.85 × 100 = 485 4.85 ÷ 100 = .0485
KEY TERMS	Decimal, p. 66 Decimal fraction, p. 68 Decimal point, p. 66	Mixed decimal, p. 69 Rounding decimals, p. 67 Pure decimal, p. 69 Repeating decimal, p. 67

CHECK FIGURES FOR EXTRA PRACTICE QUIZZES WITH PAGE REFERENCES. (WORKED-OUT SOLUTIONS IN APPENDIX B.)	LU 3–1a (p. 71)
	1. .309
	2. Hundredths
	3. Ten-thousandths
	4. A. .8
	   B. .844
	5. A. .9
	   B. .879
	6. .0008
	7. .00016
	8. $\frac{938}{1,000}$
	9. $17\frac{95}{100}$
	10. $\frac{325}{10,000}$
	11. .13
	12. .57
	13. 13.11
		LU 3–2a (p. 76)
		1. 44.5131 6. 8.432
		2. 28.5852 7. .9643
		3. 539.4 8. Buy A $.14
		4. 774.09 9. $216.14
		5. 1,748 10. $504.70

Note: For how to dissect and solve a word problem, see page 75.

Critical Thinking Discussion Questions

1. What are the steps for rounding decimals? Federal income tax forms allow the taxpayer to round each amount to the nearest dollar. Do you agree with this?

2. Explain how to convert fractions to decimals. If 1 out of 20 people buys a Land Rover, how could you write an advertisement in decimals?

3. Explain why .07, .70, and .700 are not equal. Assume you take a family trip to Disney World that covers 500 miles. Show that $\frac{8}{10}$ of the trip, or .8 of the trip, represents 400 miles.

4. Explain the steps in the addition or subtraction of decimals. Visit a car dealership and find the difference between two sticker prices. Be sure to check each sticker price for accuracy. Should you always pay the sticker price?

END-OF-CHAPTER PROBLEMS  www.mhhe.com/slater10e

Check figures for odd-numbered problems in Appendix C Name _____ Date _____

DRILL PROBLEMS

Identify the place value for the following:

3–1. 9.4391

3–2. 293.9438

Round the following as indicated:

	Tenth	**Hundredth**	**Thousandth**
3–3. .8466			
3–4. 6.8629			
3–5. 5.8312			
3–6. 6.8415			
3–7. 6.5555			
3–8. 75.9913			

Round the following to the nearest cent:

3–9. $4,822.775

3–10. $4,892.046

Convert the following types of decimal fractions to decimals (round to nearest hundredth as needed):

3–11. $\dfrac{6}{100}$

3–12. $\dfrac{4}{10}$

3–13. $\dfrac{61}{1,000}$

3–14. $\dfrac{610}{1,000}$

3–15. $\dfrac{82}{100}$

3–16. $\dfrac{979}{1,000}$

3–17. $16\dfrac{61}{100}$

Convert the following decimals to fractions. Do not reduce to lowest terms.

3–18. .7

3–19. .71

3–20. .009

3–21. .0125

3–22. .609

3–23. .825

3–24. .9999

3–25. .7065

Convert the following to mixed numbers. Do not reduce to the lowest terms.

3–26. 9.2

3–27. 28.48

3–28. 6.025

Write the decimal equivalent of the following:

3–29. Four thousandths

3–30. Three hundred three and two hundredths

3–31. Eighty-five ten thousandths

3–32. Seven hundred seventy-five thousandths

Rearrange the following and add:

3–33. .115, 10.8318, 4.7, 802.4811

3–34. .005, 2,002.181, 795.41, 14.0, .184

Rearrange the following and subtract:

3–35. 9.2 − 5.8

3–36. 7 − 2.0815

3–37. 3.4 − 1.08

Estimate by rounding all the way and multiply the following (do not round final answer):

3–38. 6.24 × 3.9

3–39. .413 × 3.07

Estimate

Estimate

3–40. 675 × 1.92

3–41. 4.9 × .825

Estimate

Estimate

Divide the following and round to the nearest hundredth:

3–42. .8931 ÷ 3

3–43. 29.432 ÷ .0012

3–44. .0065 ÷ .07

3–45. 7,742.1 ÷ 48

3–46. 8.95 ÷ 1.18

3–47. 2,600 ÷ .381

Convert the following to decimals and round to the nearest hundredth:

3–48. $\frac{1}{8}$

3–49. $\frac{1}{25}$

3–50. $\frac{5}{6}$

3–51. $\frac{5}{8}$

Complete these multiplications and divisions by the shortcut method (do not do any written calculations):

3–52. 96.7 ÷ 10

3–53. 258.5 ÷ 100

3–54. 8.51 × 1,000

3–55. .86 ÷ 100

3–56. 9.015 × 100

3–57. 48.6 × 10

3–58. 750 × 10

3–59. 3,950 ÷ 1,000

3–60. 8.45 ÷ 10

3–61. 7.9132 × 1,000

WORD PROBLEMS

As needed, round answers to the nearest cent.

3–62. A Ford Flex costs $24,000. What would it cost in London? Check your answer.

3–63. Ken Griffey Jr. got 7 hits out of 12 at bats. What was his batting average to the nearest thousandths place?

3–64. The August 17, 2009, *San Francisco Chronicle* reported on the rapid growth of Facebook.com. Facebook is becoming a social superpower with 120 million registered members who log in at least once daily. They share 1 billion photos and 10 million videos each month. What is the average number of photos and videos that each active member posts? Round to the nearest ten thousandth.

3–65. At the Party Store, Joan Lee purchased 21.50 yards of ribbon. Each yard costs 91 cents. What was the total cost of the ribbon? Round to the nearest cent.

3–66. Douglas Noel went to Home Depot and bought 4 doors at $42.99 each and 6 bags of fertilizer at $8.99 per bag. What was the total cost to Douglas? If Douglas had $300 in his pocket, what does he have left to spend?

3–67. The stock of Intel has a high of $30.25 today. It closed at $28.85. How much did the stock drop from its high?

3–68. Pete is traveling by car to a computer convention in San Diego. His company will reimburse him $.48 per mile. If Pete travels 210.5 miles, how much will Pete receive from his company?

3–69. Mark Ogara rented a truck from Avis Rent-A-Car for the weekend (2 days). The base rental price was $29.95 per day plus $14\frac{1}{2}$ cents per mile. Mark drove 410.85 miles. How much does Mark owe?

3–70. Nursing home costs are on the rise as consumeraffairs.com reports in their quarterly newsletter. The average cost is around $192 a day with an average length of stay of 2.5 years. Calculate the cost of the average nursing home stay.

3–71. Bob Ross bought a Blackberry on the Web for $89.99. He saw the same Blackberry in the mall for $118.99. How much did Bob save by buying on the Web?

3–72. Russell is preparing the daily bank deposit for his coffee shop. Before the deposit, the coffee shop had a checking account balance of $3,185.66. The deposit contains the following checks:

No. 1	$ 99.50	No. 3	$8.75
No. 2	110.35	No. 4	6.83

Russell included $820.55 in currency with the deposit. What is the coffee shop's new balance, assuming Russell writes no new checks?

3–73. Assume US Airways Express is offering a $190 round-trip fare for Chattanooga, Tennessee–New York for those who buy tickets in the next couple of weeks. Ticket prices had been running between $230 and $330 round-trip. Mark VanLoh, Airport Authority president, said the new fare is lower than the $219 ticket price offered by Southwest Airlines. How much would a family of four save using US Airways versus Southwest Airlines?

3–74. Randi went to Lowe's to buy wall-to-wall carpeting. She needs 110.8 square yards for downstairs, 31.8 square yards for the halls, and 161.9 square yards for the bedrooms upstairs. Randi chose a shag carpet that costs $14.99 per square yard. She ordered foam padding at $3.10 per square yard. The carpet installers quoted Randi a labor charge of $3.75 per square yard. What will the total job cost Randi?

3–75. Paul Rey bought 4 new Dunlop tires at Goodyear for $95.99 per tire. Goodyear charged $3.05 per tire for mounting, $2.95 per tire for valve stems, and $3.80 per tire for balancing. If Paul paid no sales tax, what was his total cost for the 4 tires?

3–76. Shelly is shopping for laundry detergent, mustard, and canned tuna. She is trying to decide which of two products is the better buy. Using the following information, can you help Shelly?

Laundry detergent A	**Mustard A**	**Canned tuna A**
$2.00 for 37 ounces	$.88 for 6 ounces	$1.09 for 6 ounces

Laundry detergent B	**Mustard B**	**Canned tuna B**
$2.37 for 38 ounces	$1.61 for $12\frac{1}{2}$ ounces	$1.29 for $8\frac{3}{4}$ ounces

3–77. Roger bought season tickets for weekend games to professional basketball games. The cost was $945.60. The season package included 36 home games. What is the average price of the tickets per game? Round to the nearest cent. Marcelo, Roger's friend, offered to buy 4 of the tickets from Roger. What is the total amount Roger should receive?

3–78. A nurse was to give each of her patients a 1.32-unit dosage of a prescribed drug. The total remaining units of the drug at the hospital pharmacy were 53.12. The nurse has 38 patients. Will there be enough dosages for all her patients?

3–79. Audrey Long went to Japan and bought an animation cel of Mickey Mouse. The price was 25,000 yen. What is the price in U.S. dollars? Check your answer.

ADDITIONAL SET OF WORD PROBLEMS

3–80. On Monday, the stock of Google closed at $488.40. At the end of trading on Tuesday, Google closed at $492.80. How much did the price of stock increase from Monday to Tuesday?

3–81. Tie Yang bought season tickets to the Boston Pops for $698.55. The season package included 38 performances. What is the average price of the tickets per performance? Round to nearest cent. Sam, Tie's friend, offered to buy 4 of the tickets from Tie. What is the total amount Tie should receive?

3–82. Morris Katz bought 4 new tires at Goodyear for $95.49 per tire. Goodyear also charged Morris $2.50 per tire for mounting, $2.40 per tire for valve stems, and $3.95 per tire for balancing. Assume no tax. What was Morris's total cost for the 4 tires?

3–83. The *Denver Post* reported that Xcel Energy is revising customer charges for monthly residential electric bills and gas bills. Electric bills will increase $3.32. Gas bills will decrease $1.74 a month. **(a)** What is the resulting new monthly increase for the entire bill? **(b)** If Xcel serves 2,350 homes, how much additional revenue would Xcel receive each month?

3–84. Steven is traveling to a auto show by car. His company will reimburse him $.29 per mile. If Steven travels 890.5 miles, how much will he receive from his company?

3–85. Gracie went to Home Depot to buy wall-to-wall carpeting for her house. She needs 104.8 square yards for downstairs, 17.4 square yards for halls, and 165.8 square yards for the upstairs bedrooms. Gracie chose a shag carpet that costs $13.95 per square yard. She ordered foam padding at $2.75 per square yard. The installers quoted Gracie a labor cost of $5.75 per square yard in installation. What will the total job cost Gracie?

CHALLENGE PROBLEMS

3–86. The DeQuarto family is planning a 14-day trip to Colorado. Debbie, Mike, and their three kids, Courtney, Alexis, and Andres, will be going. They want to compare costs between driving and flying. They found a flight for $210 round-trip per person. The airport is 15 miles from their home and charges $10 per night in parking. If they drove, they would be traveling 900 miles one way. Gas is $2.92 and their vehicle gets 24 miles a gallon. They would need to stay in a hotel two nights each way. The estimated hotel cost is $110 a night. Because they have to eat whether they drive or fly, they are not concerned with those costs. Do you recommend they fly or drive?

3–87. Jill and Frank decided to take a long weekend in New York. City Hotel has a special getaway weekend for $79.95. The price is per person per night, based on double occupancy. The hotel has a minimum two-night stay. For this price, Jill and Frank will receive $50 credit toward their dinners at City's Skylight Restaurant. Also included in the package is a $3.99 credit per person toward breakfast for two each morning.

Since Jill and Frank do not own a car, they plan to rent a car. The car rental agency charges $19.95 a day with an additional charge of $.22 a mile and $1.19 per gallon of gas used. The gas tank holds 24 gallons.

From the following facts, calculate the total expenses of Jill and Frank (round all answers to nearest hundredth or cent as appropriate). Assume no taxes.

Car rental (2 days):		Dinner cost at Skylight	$182.12
Beginning odometer reading	4,820	Breakfast for two:	
Ending odometer reading	4,940	Morning No. 1	24.17
Beginning gas tank: $\frac{3}{4}$ full.		Morning No. 2	26.88
Gas tank on return: $\frac{1}{2}$ full.			
Tank holds 24 gallons.			

 SUMMARY PRACTICE TEST

1. Add the following by translating the verbal form to the decimal equivalent. *(pp. 67, 71)*

Three hundred thirty-eight and seven hundred five thousandths
Nineteen and fifty-nine hundredths
Five and four thousandths
Seventy-five hundredths
Four hundred three and eight tenths

Convert the following decimal fractions to decimals. *(p. 68)*

2. $\dfrac{7}{10}$ **3.** $\dfrac{7}{100}$ **4.** $\dfrac{7}{1,000}$

Convert the following to proper fractions or mixed numbers. Do not reduce to the lowest terms. *(p. 69)*

5. .9   **6.** 6.97   **7.** .685

Convert the following fractions to decimals (or mixed decimals) and round to the nearest hundredth as needed. *(p. 69)*

8. $\dfrac{2}{7}$ **9.** $\dfrac{1}{8}$ **10.** $4\dfrac{4}{7}$ **11.** $\dfrac{1}{13}$

12. Rearrange the following decimals and add. *(p. 71)*

     5.93, 11.862, 284.0382, 88.44

13. Subtract the following and round to the nearest tenth. *(p. 72)*

     $13.111 - 3.872$

14. Multiply the following and round to the nearest hundredth. *(p. 73)*

     7.4821×15.861

15. Divide the following and round to the nearest hundredth. *(p. 73)*

     $203{,}942 \div 5.88$

Complete the following by the shortcut method. *(p. 74)*

16. $62.94 \times 1{,}000$

17. $8{,}322{,}249.821 \times 100$

18. The average pay of employees is $795.88 per week. Lee earns $820.44 per week. How much is Lee's pay over the average? *(p. 72)*

19. Lowes reimburses Ron $.49 per mile. Ron submitted a travel log for a total of 1,910.81 miles. How much will Lowes reimburse Ron? Round to the nearest cent. *(p. 73)*

20. Lee Chin bought 2 new car tires from Michelin for $182.11 per tire. Michelin also charged Lee $3.99 per tire for mounting, $2.50 per tire for valve stems, and $4.10 per tire for balancing. What is Lee's final bill? *(pp. 71, 73)*

21. Could you help Judy decide which of the following products is cheaper per ounce? *(p. 73)*

     Canned fruit A   **Canned fruit B**

     $.37 for 3 ounces $.58 for $3\frac{3}{4}$ ounces

22. Paula Smith bought an iPod for 350 euros. What is this price in U.S. dollars? *(p. 73)*

23. Google stock traded at a high of $438.22 and closed at $410.12. How much did the stock fall from its high? *(p. 72)*

Personal Finance

NATURAL GAS GLUT
PROFIT FROM THE SURPLUS WITH AN ETF.

Natural gas doesn't get much respect. In early June, domestic gas traded at $3.74 per million cubic feet, near its six-year low. Meanwhile, traders had pushed the price of oil to $69 a barrel, up from its recent low of $33 in December. In terms of the two carbon-based commodities' energy-equivalent prices, oil is now some three times costlier than gas. In an age of environmental awareness, that doesn't make sense: Gas is cleaner; it has a future as a fuel for buses, cars and trucks; and it's popular in heavy industry and for power generation. Right now, there's a glut of gas in storage, but energy surpluses have a habit of vanishing quickly. The easiest way to bet on the price of gas is exchange-traded **UNITED STATES NATURAL GAS** fund **(UNG)**, which tracks changes in the price of gas by buying futures contracts. Note, however, that the fund is set up as a limited partnership, so you may face tax hassles.

PENNY-PINCHING BROKERS
WE PICK FIRMS FOR TWO KINDS OF INVESTORS.

BEST FOR TRADERS:
JUST2TRADE
If low-cost trades are what you're after, look no further than Just-2Trade (www.just2trade.com). It charges just $2.50 for stock, exchange-traded-fund and mutual fund transactions on trades of any size. But don't expect many frills or access to outside research—this broker is bare-bones.

You can open an account with $2,500, and you won't pay account-maintenance or inactivity fees. The site courts market-savvy types, so it requires that new customers have at least two years' experience using another online broker.

BEST FOR AVERAGE INVESTORS: FIDELITY
Fidelity (www.fidelity.com) boasts reasonable commissions and no maintenance fees, plus a world of user-friendly extras. Stock commissions range from $8 per trade to $19.95 per transaction for up to 1,000 shares, depending on your account's size and how often you trade. You can invest in 1,400 funds without paying sales or transaction fees, although you'll get hit with a stiff $75 commission for straying from this list. But you also get access to stock research from 18 different firms and useful asset-allocation and retirement-planning tools.

COUPON QUEEN SAVING MONEY
WITH SCISSORS IS A PASSION, NOT A PAIN.

You may begin your weekend by perusing the newspaper and savoring a cup of coffee. Sara Moothart starts her Saturday by scouring the advertising circulars for the week's best deals and clipping coupons.

Moothart, 31, of Baltimore, began "couponing" as a way to stretch her graduate-student budget. She buys groceries for herself and a roommate, and the value of the coupons alone saves her almost $40 a month. She reckons that she has saved triple that amount by leveraging the coupons against store markdowns.

Each week, Moothart reviews the offerings of three local grocery stores as well as Target. She creates a list for each store, taking note of relevant coupons, and sorts her collection in an accordion organizer labeled by section of the store. She also visits CouponMom.com to find more discounts and links to other Web sites. Moothart uses coupons to buy only what she will use—for example, she and her roommate eat fresh foods, so she skips the ubiquitous coupons for processed products. She buys items in large quantities only if she can freeze them or if they're nonperishable and she'll use them quickly.

The savings, which Moothart records in a notebook, have fired her passion for more couponing. And she's been thinking about putting aside the money she saves for something special—say, airfare to visit her family on the West Coast or a weekend getaway.

TOP TIPS

Plan your shopping list **around sale items.**

Look for stores **that double or triple a coupon's value.**

If "buy one, get one free" means you **pay half price for each item, use two coupons.**

From Kiplinger's Personal Finance, August 2009, p. 65.

BUSINESS MATH ISSUE

Natural gas will never replace gasoline in automobiles.

1. List the key points of the article and information to support your position.
2. Write a group defense of your position using math calculations to support your view.

PROJECT A

Assuming you drove the Toyota Prius 15,000 miles this year, what would be your total gas cost assuming 48 miles per gallon?

Slater's Business Math Scrapbook

Applying Your Skills

Comparing Costs of Hybrid Cars

A look at 2008 hybrid models, which generally cost more than their gas-powered counterparts. Estimates are based on a car driven 15,000 miles annually, with gas that costs to break even—where fuel savings offset the premium paid for a hybrid model. An analysis shows the amount of time it would take a buyer $4.01 a gallon.

Mercury Mariner: 5.5 years

Toyota Prius: 3.5 years

Saturn Aura: 31 years

Wieck (3)

2008 model	Final net price**	Hybrid premium***	MPG (city/hwy)	Annual gas savings	Years to break even
Toyota Prius	$22,939	$3,708	48/45	$1,073	3.5
Nissan Altima°	22,666	1,879	35/33	499	3.8
GMC Yukon°	47,653	5,680	21/22	1,170	4.9
Toyota Camry	25,732	3,046	33/34	562	5.4
Mercury Mariner°	24,946	4,324	34/30	784	5.5
Ford Escape°	24,051	4,622	34/30	784	5.9
Honda Civic°	21,082	3,601	40/45	587	6.1

2008 model	Final net price	Hybrid premium	MPG (city/hwy)	Annual gas savings	Years to break even
Saturn Vue*	$24,445	$4,570	27/32	$661	6.9
Lexus RX400H	39,923	5,069	26/24	731	6.9
Chevy Malibu°	22,931	1,867	24/32	171	10.9
Chevy Tahoe°	46,862	11,058	21/22	800	13.8
Toyota Highlander	40,921	10,805	27/25	603	17.9
Saturn Aura°	22,990	5,295	24/32	171	31
Lexus LS600H	102,423	18,858	20/22	192	98.5

Source: Edmunds.com

*Vehicles with available tax credit; **Final net price is average national figure; ***Amount the car exceeds the cost of a comparable gas-powered model.

Wall Street Journal © 2008

Consumer Purchases

	2005	2006	2007
Single-Family Home Median resale price	$219,600[1]	$221,900[1]	$217,600[2]
Toyota Camry Manufacturer's suggested retail price for the LE manual transmission	$19,545	$19,725	$20,025
Unleaded Gasoline Average national price per gallon for all grades of unleaded gasoline combined, including taxes	$2.32	$2.60	$2.82
Pair of Jeans Gap's Easy Fit, stonewashed, starting price	$39.50	$39.50	$44.50
Internet Service Average monthly subscription cost for broadband cable service from Comcast, standard tier	$42.95	$42.95	$42.95
Tax Preparation Average cost of federal, state and local tax return preparation by H&R Block	$146.75[1]	$155.20[1]	$165.06
Hospital Stay Average cost of one day in a semiprivate room, including ancillary services except private physician's fee (Cleveland)	$4,848	$5,261	$5,504
McDonald's Big Mac Average price for company-owned restaurants. Prices vary at independently owned franchised locations.	$2.43[1]	$2.57[1]	$2.76[2]

PROJECT B

If you bought 25 movie tickets in 2007. How much more expensive were they than they were in 2005?

	2005	2006	2007
Clearing Clogged Sink Roto-Rooter sewer and drain service, residential nat'l avera	$212.00	$230.55[1]	$243.46[3]
Movie Ticket Average price for all tickets sold at all prices at all times	$6.41	$6.55	$6.82[4]
Airline Ticket Domestic round-trip, based on a 2,000-mile trip, excluding aviation taxes	$246	$260[1]	$258[3]
Birth Average hospital cost for mother and child, excluding private physician's fee (Cleveland)	$7,907	$8,162	$9,873
A Year in College In-state, including room and board and fees, undergraduate student at Penn State	$17,799	$19,014	$20,024
Funeral National average, excluding cemetery costs	$6,734[1]	$6,951[1]	$7,170

[1]Revised [2]Preliminary [3]Through October [4]Through September

Sources: National Association of Realtors; Lundberg Survey; National Association of Theatre Owners; Air Transport Association of America; Federated Funeral Directors of America; Medical Mutual of Ohio

Wall Street Journal © 2008

Internet Projects: See text Web site (www.mhhe.com/slater10e) and The Business Math Internet Resource Guide.

A Word Problem Approach—Chapters 1, 2, 3

1. The top rate at the Waldorf Towers Hotel in New York is $390. The top rate at the Ritz Carlton in Boston is $345. If John spends 9 days at the hotel, how much can he save if he stays at the Ritz? *(p. 10)*

2. Robert Half Placement Agency was rated best by 4 to 1 in an independent national survey. If 250,000 responded to the survey, how many rated Robert Half the best? *(p. 47)*

3. Of the 63.2 million people who watch professional football, only $\frac{1}{5}$ watch the commercials. How many viewers do not watch the commercials? *(p. 47)*

4. AT&T advertised a 10-minute call for $2.27. MCI WorldCom's rate was $2.02. Assuming Bill Splat makes forty 10-minute calls, how much could he save by using MCI WorldCom? *(p. 14)*

5. A square foot of rental space in New York City, Boston, and Rhode Island costs as follows: New York City, $6.25; Boston, $5.75; and Rhode Island, $3.75. If Compaq Computer wants to rent 112,500 square feet of space, what will Compaq save by renting in Rhode Island rather than Boston? *(p. 14)*

6. American Airlines has a frequent-flier program. Coupon brokers who buy and sell these awards pay between 1 and $1\frac{1}{2}$ cents for each mile earned. Fred Dietrich earned a 50,000-mile award (worth two free tickets to any city). If Fred decided to sell his award to a coupon broker, approximately how much would he receive? *(p. 71)*

7. Lillie Wong bought 4 new Firestone tires at $82.99 each. Firestone also charged $2.80 per tire for mounting, $1.95 per tire for valves, and $3.15 per tire for balancing. Lillie turned her 4 old tires in to Firestone, which charged $1.50 per tire to dispose of them. What was Lillie's final bill? *(p. 72)*

8. Tootsie Roll Industries bought Charms Company for $65 million. Some analysts believe that in 4 years the purchase price could rise to 3 times as much. If the analysts are right, how much did Tootsie Roll save by purchasing Charms immediately? *(p. 10)*

9. Today the average business traveler will spend $47.73 a day on food. The breakdown is dinner, $22.26; lunch, $10.73; breakfast, $6.53; tips, $6.23; and tax, $1.98. If Clarence Donato, an executive for Honeywell, spends only .33 of the average, what is Clarence's total cost for food for the day? If Clarence wanted to spend $\frac{1}{3}$ more than the average on the next day, what would be his total cost on the second day? Round to the nearest cent. *(p. 71)*

Be sure you use the fractional equivalent in calculating $.3\overline{3}$.

BANKING

Bank Suspends Overdraft Fee Increase

BY JANE J. KIM

Bank of America Corp. is suspending a previously announced rise in its overdraft fees. Earlier this month, the bank sent notices to customers, announcing pricing changes scheduled to go into effect June 5 that would have raised the overdraft fee to $39 from $35 per item. On Monday, citing the "increase in unemployment," the bank said it was suspending that increase and keeping the fee at $35, according to spokesman Jim Pierpoint.

The bank is also introducing a program for customers who have lost their jobs, where it will waive monthly account-maintenance fees for three months, and will refund or waive insufficient funds and overdraft fees for some customers on a case-by-case basis.

Among the other changes to take effect in June: Customers will be hit with another $35 fee if their account is overdrawn for more than five days. Meanwhile, the bank is raising monthly maintenance fees on certain checking accounts, as well as the balance requirements needed to avoid fees.

The changes represent the second time this year that Bank of America has tinkered with its overdraft program.

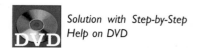 Solution with Step-by-Step Help on DVD

✓ **Solution**

No. *113*	$ *83.76*
June 5	20 *11*
To *Angel Corp.*	
For *Rent*	

	DOLLARS	CENTS
BALANCE	9,500	60
AMT. DEPOSITED	690	60
TOTAL	10,191	20
AMT. THIS CHECK	83	76
BALANCE FORWARD	10,107	44

Long Company
22 Aster Rd.
Salem, MA 01970

No. 113

PAY TO THE ORDER OF *Angel Corporation*   *June 5* 20 *11*   5-13/110 $ *83 76/100*

Eighty-three and 76/100 _____ DOLLARS

IPSWICHBANK
ipswichbank.com

Roland Small

MEMO *Rent*

⑆011000138⑆   14 0380 113

LU 4–1a   **EXTRA PRACTICE QUIZ WITH WORKED-OUT SOLUTIONS**

Need more practice? Try this **Extra Practice Quiz** (check figures in Chapter Organizer, p. 101). Worked-out Solutions can be found in Appendix B at end of text.

Complete the following check and stub for Long Company. Note the $10,800.80 balance brought forward on check stub No. 113. You must make an $812.88 deposit on May 3. Sign the check for Roland Small.

Date	Check No.	Amount	Payable to	For
July 8, 2011	113	$79.88	Lowe Corp	Advertising

No. *113*	$ ____
	20 ____
To ____	
For ____	

	DOLLARS	CENTS
BALANCE	10,800	80
AMT. DEPOSITED		
TOTAL		
AMT. THIS CHECK		
BALANCE FORWARD		

Long Company
22 Aster Rd.
Salem, MA 01970

No. 113

PAY TO THE ORDER OF *lowe Corp*   Jul 8, 20 11 $ 79.88   5-13/110

Seventy nine dollars 98/100 cents _____ DOLLARS

IPSWICHBANK
ipswichbank.com

Roland Small

MEMO *Advertising*

⑆011000138⑆   14 0380 113

Learning Unit 4–2: Bank Statement and Reconciliation Process; Trends in Online Banking

Trends in Banking Industry[1]

Since 2008 trends in banking have been changing rapidly. The government has been involved in many bailout packages due to the financial crises. Some banks have had to close or merge. The following *Wall Street Journal* clip on stress test for banks shows the results of stress tests that evaluate how big banks are doing and if they need more capital. Take a moment to look at the stress test scorecard on top of page 94.

The rest of this learning unit is divided into two sections: (1) bank statement and reconciliation process, and (2) trends in online banking. The bank statement discussion will teach you why it was important for Gracie's Natural Superstore to reconcile its checkbook balance with the balance reported on its bank balance. Note that you can also use this reconciliation process in reconciling your personal checking account and avoiding the expensive error of an overdrawn account.

---

[1]Check my Web site for the latest updates on banking bailouts and government intervention. www.mhhe.com/slater10e.

Stress Test Scorecard How key banks fared		Capital needed in billions	Worst-case loss estimates in billions
Bank of America		$33.9	$136.6
Wells Fargo	WELLS FARGO	13.7	86.1
Citigroup	citi	5.5	104.7
Regions Financial	R	2.5	9.2
SunTrust	SunTrust	2.2	11.8
KeyCorp		1.8	6.7
Fifth Third	5/3	1.1	9.1
PNC Financial		0.6	18.8
U.S. Bancorp	US	NONE	15.7
J.P. Morgan Chase	JPM	NONE	97.4
BB&T	BB&T	NONE	8.7
Capital One	tal One	NONE	13.4

Wall Street Journal © 2009

LO 2

Bank Statement and Reconciliation Process

Each month, Ipswich Bank sends Gracie's Natural Superstore a **bank statement** (Figure 4.4, p. 95). We are interested in the following:

1. Beginning bank balance.
2. Total of all the account increases. Each time the bank increases the account amount, it *credits* the account.
3. Total of all account decreases. Each time the bank decreases the account amount, it *debits* the account.
4. Final ending balance.

Due to differences in timing, the bank balance on the bank statement frequently does not match the customer's checkbook balance. Also, the bank statement can show transactions that have not been entered in the customer's checkbook. Figure 4.5, p. 95, tells you what to look for when comparing a checkbook balance with a bank balance.

Gracie's Natural Superstore is planning to offer to its employees the option of depositing their checks directly into each employee's checking account. This is accomplished through the **electronic funds transfer (EFT)**—a computerized operation that electronically transfers funds among parties without the use of paper checks. Gracie's, who sublets space in the store, receives rental payments by EFT. Gracie's also has the bank pay the store's health insurance premiums by EFT.

FIGURE 4.4

Bank statement

Ipswich Bank				Account Statement

Ipswich Bank
1 Pleasant St.
Bartlett, NH 01835

Gracie's Natural Superstore
80 Garfield St.
Bartlett, NH 01835

Checking Account: 881900662

Checking Account Summary as of 3/31/11

Beginning Balance	Total Deposits	Total Withdrawals	Service Charge	Ending Balance
$13,112.24	$8,705.28	$9,926.00	$28.50	$11,863.02

Checking Accounts Transactions

Deposits	Date	Amount
Deposit	3/05	2,000.00
Deposit	3/05	224.00
Deposit	3/09	389.20
EFT leasing: Bakery dept.	3/18	1,808.06
EFT leasing: Meat dept.	3/27	4,228.00
Interest	3/31	56.02

Charges	Date	Amount
Service charge: Check printing	3/31	28.50
EFT: Health insurance	3/21	722.00
NSF	3/21	104.00

Checks			Daily Balance			
Number	Date	Amount	Date	Balance	Date	Balance
301	3/07	200.00	2/28	13,112.24	3/18	10,529.50
633	3/13	6,000.00	3/05	15,232.24	3/21	9,807.50
634	3/13	300.00	3/07	14,832.24	3/28	14,035.50
635	3/11	200.00	3/09	15,221.44	3/31	11,863.02
636	3/18	200.00	3/11	15,021.44		
637	3/31	2,200.00	3/13	8,721.44		

FIGURE 4.5

Reconciling checkbook with bank statement

Checkbook balance		Bank balance
+ EFT (electronic funds transfer)	− NSF check	+ Deposits in transit
+ Interest earned	− Online fees	− Outstanding checks
+ Notes collected	− Automatic payments*	± Bank errors
+ Direct deposits	− Overdrafts†	
− ATM withdrawals	− Service charges	
− Automatic withdrawals	− Stop payments‡	
	± Book errors§	

*Preauthorized payments for utility bills, mortgage payments, insurance, etc.

†**Overdrafts** occur when the customer has no overdraft protection and a check bounces back to the company or person who received the check because the customer has written a check without enough money in the bank to pay for it.

‡A stop payment is issued when the writer of the check does not want the receiver to cash the check.

§If a $60 check is recorded at $50, the checkbook balance must be decreased by $10.

To reconcile the difference between the amount on the bank statement and in the checkbook, the customer should complete a **bank reconciliation.** Today, many companies and home computer owners are using software such as Quicken and QuickBooks to complete their bank reconciliation. However, you should understand the following steps for manually reconciling a bank statement.

RECONCILING A BANK STATEMENT

Step 1. Identify the outstanding checks (checks written but not yet processed by the bank). You can use the ✓ column in the check register (Figure 4.6) to check the canceled checks listed in the bank statement against the checks you wrote in the check register. The unchecked checks are the outstanding checks.

Step 2. Identify the deposits in transit (deposits made but not yet processed by the bank), using the same method in Step 1.

Step 3. Analyze the bank statement for transactions not recorded in the check stubs or check registers (like EFT).

Step 4. Check for recording errors in checks written, in deposits made, or in subtraction and addition.

Step 5. Compare the adjusted balances of the checkbook and the bank statement. If the balances are not the same, repeat Steps 1–4.

Molly uses a check register (Figure 4.6) to keep a record of Gracie's checks and deposits. By looking at Gracie's check register, you can see how to complete Steps 1 and 2 above. The explanation that follows for the first four bank statement reconciliation steps will help you understand the procedure.

FIGURE 4.6

Gracie's Natural Superstore check register

		RECORD ALL CHARGES OR CREDITS THAT AFFECT YOUR ACCOUNT							
NUMBER	DATE 2011	DESCRIPTION OF TRANSACTION	PAYMENT/DEBIT (−)		√	FEE (IF ANY) (−)	DEPOSIT/CREDIT (+)		BALANCE $
									12,912	24
	3/04	Deposit	$			$	$ 2,000	00	+ 2,000	00
									14,912	24
	3/04	Deposit					224	00	+ 224	00
									15,136	24
633	3/08	Staples Company	6,000	00	✓				− 6,000	00
									9,136	24
634	3/09	Health Foods Inc.	1,020	00	✓				− 1,020	00
									8,116	24
	3/09	Deposit					389	20	+ 389	20
									8,505	44
635	3/10	Liberty Insurance	200	00	✓				− 200	00
									8,305	44
636	3/18	Ryan Press	200	00	✓				− 200	00
									8,105	44
637	3/29	Logan Advertising	2,200	00	✓				− 2,200	00
									5,905	44
	3/30	Deposit					3,383	26	+ 3,383	26
									9,288	70
638	3/31	Sears Roebuck	572	00					− 572	00
									8,716	70
639	3/31	Flynn Company	638	94					− 638	94
									8,077	76
640	3/31	Lynn's Farm	166	00					− 166	00
									7,911	76
641	3/31	Ron's Wholesale	406	28					− 406	28
									7,505	48
642	3/31	Grocery Natural, Inc.	917	06					− 917	06
									$6,588	42

REMEMBER TO RECORD AUTOMATIC PAYMENTS/DEPOSITS ON DATE AUTHORIZED.

Step 1. Identify Outstanding Checks

Outstanding checks are checks that Gracie's Natural Superstore has written but Ipswich Bank has not yet recorded for payment when it sends out the bank statement. Gracie's treasurer identifies the following checks written on 3/31 as outstanding:

No. 638	$572.00
No. 639	638.94
No. 640	166.00
No. 641	406.28
No. 642	917.06

Step 2. Identify Deposits in Transit

Deposits in transit are deposits that did not reach Ipswich Bank by the time the bank prepared the bank statement. The March 30 deposit of $3,383.26 did not reach Ipswich Bank by the bank statement date. You can see this by comparing the company's bank statement with its check register.

Step 3. Analyze Bank Statement for Transactions Not Recorded in Check Stubs or Check Register

The bank statement of Gracie's Natural Superstore (Figure 4.4, p. 95) begins with the deposits, or increases, made to Gracie's bank account. Increases to accounts are known as credits. These are the result of a **credit memo (CM).** Gracie's received the following increases or credits in March:

1. *EFT leasing:* $1,808.06 and $4,228.00.

   Each month the bakery and meat departments pay for space they lease in the store.

2. *Interest credited:* $56.02.

   Gracie's has a checking account that pays interest; the account has earned $56.02.

When Gracie's has charges against her bank account, the bank decreases, or debits, Gracie's account for these charges. Banks usually inform customers of a debit transaction by a **debit memo (DM).** The following items will result in debits to Gracie's account:

1. *Service charge:* $28.50

   The bank charged $28.50 for printing Gracie's checks.

2. *EFT payment:* $722.

   The bank made a health insurance payment for Gracie's.

3. *NSF check:* $104.

   One of Gracie's customers wrote Gracie's a check for $104. Gracie's deposited the check, but the check bounced for **nonsufficient funds (NSF).** Thus, Gracie's has $104 less than it figured.

Step 4. Check for Recording Errors

The treasurer of Gracie's Natural Superstore, Molly Kate, recorded check No. 634 for the wrong amount—$1,020 (see the check register). The bank statement showed that check No. 634 cleared for $300. To reconcile Gracie's checkbook balance with the bank balance, Gracie's must add $720 to its checkbook balance. Neglecting to record a deposit also results in an error in the company's checkbook balance. As you can see, reconciling the bank's balance with a checkbook balance is a necessary part of business and personal finance.

Step 5. Completing the Bank Reconciliation

Now we can complete the bank reconciliation on the back side of the bank statement as shown in Figure 4.7 (p. 98). This form is usually on the back of a bank statement. If necessary, however, the person reconciling the bank statement can construct a bank reconciliation form similar to Figure 4.8 (p. 98).

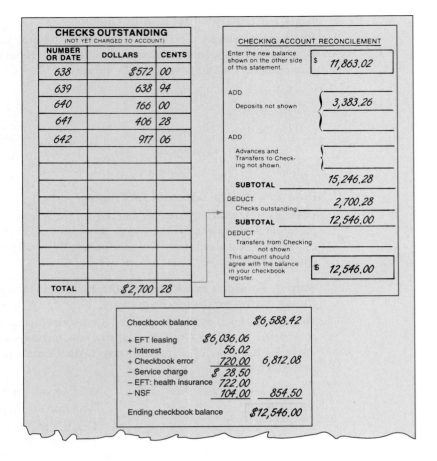

CHECKS OUTSTANDING
(NOT YET CHARGED TO ACCOUNT)

NUMBER OR DATE	DOLLARS	CENTS
638	8572	00
639	638	94
640	166	00
641	406	28
642	917	06
TOTAL	$2,700	28

CHECKING ACCOUNT RECONCILEMENT

Enter the new balance shown on the other side of this statement.	$ 11,863.02
ADD Deposits not shown	3,383.26
ADD Advances and Transfers to Checking not shown.	
SUBTOTAL	15,246.28
DEDUCT Checks outstanding	2,700.28
SUBTOTAL	12,546.00
DEDUCT Transfers from Checking not shown	
This amount should agree with the balance in your checkbook register.	$ 12,546.00

Checkbook balance		$6,588.42
+ EFT leasing	$6,036.06	
+ Interest	56.02	
+ Checkbook error	720.00	6,812.08
− Service charge	$ 28.50	
− EFT: health insurance	722.00	
− NSF	104.00	854.50
Ending checkbook balance		$12,546.00

GRACIE'S NATURAL SUPERSTORE
Bank Reconciliation as of March 31, 2011

Checkbook balance			Bank balance		
Gracie's checkbook balance		$6,588.42	Bank balance		$11,863.02
Add:			Add:		
EFT leasing: Bakery dept.	$1,808.06		Deposit in transit, 3/30		3,383.26
EFT leasing: Meat dept.	4,228.00				$15,246.28
Interest	56.02				
Error: Overstated check No. 634	720.00	$ 6,812.08			
		$13,400.50			
Deduct:			Deduct:		
Service charge	$ 28.50		Outstanding checks:		
NSF check	104.00		No. 638	$572.00	
EFT health insurance payment	722.00	854.50	No. 639	638.94	
			No. 640	166.00	
			No. 641	406.28	
			No. 642	917.06	2,700.28
Reconciled balance		$12,546.00	Reconciled balance		$12,546.00

LO 3

Trends in Online Banking: Pro and Con[2]

Did you know that banking online is quite safe? The *Wall Street Journal* clip "The Hold-up at Online Banks" states that out of $41.7 trillion, about $969 million was lost in fraud. Note in this clip the pros and cons of online banking are discussed. With more and more people banking online, read this article carefully.

FAMILY MONEY

The Holdup at Online Banks

At a time of uncertainty in nearly every market, I'm a big fan of online savings accounts, many of which are paying 3% to 4% interest right now. But they have a frustrating quirk: Transferring money between a savings account at one bank and a checking account at another easily takes two days—and sometimes as many as four.

This delay has become more apparent and more irritating during the continuing financial crisis, as consumers seek two basics: safety and yield. (Yields on these savings accounts have tended to be higher than those on money-market accounts.)

By Karen Blumenthal

Online accounts, like all bank accounts, are protected by the Federal Deposit Insurance Corp. up to $250,000 per account holder. Offerings from **HSBC Holdings** PLC's HSBC Direct, **Emigrant Bank**'s EmigrantDirect and **First National of Nebraska** Inc.'s FNBO Direct typically have low minimum-balance requirements. They can be good places for holding your cash reserves or earning interest on money set aside for tax payments or tuition, especially since interest-bearing checking accounts and traditional bank savings accounts typically pay well be-

low 1% interest.

But in a remarkably interconnected, instantaneous world, where a debit-card purchase shows up in our bank accounts right away, it's equally remarkable that online transfers can be so slow.

Here's the hitch: Funds transferred between two different banks or a bank and a brokerage firm aren't really sent "online" in the way we have come to expect. Instead, these large transfers move in steps. Banks have slowed down the process further to reduce the chance of fraud, even though such fraud is fairly rare. (Years ago, Congress forced banks to speed up the clearing of checks and the availability of deposits, but it hasn't addressed electronic payments.)

You may have seen this when you tried to move money to or from a brokerage account. I ran into it most recently when I went to my ING Direct savings account first thing on a Monday morning to transfer money for a new car to my Bank of America checking account. While it showed up as "pending" on Wednesday, it wasn't mine to spend until Thursday.

What happens during that time? ING sends transactions in batches during the day to an automated clearinghouse, which sorts them and moves them to the receiving bank in a matter of two to four hours, ac-

cording to Arkadi Kuhlmann, chief executive officer of ING Direct USA, a unit of **ING Groep** NV, and Elliott C. McEntee, chief executive of Nacha, the Electronic Payments Association, a not-for-profit group that oversees the automated clearinghouses.

In many cases, the receiving bank gets the transfer the same day. Under rules established by Nacha, money that moves on Monday should be available by the end of Tuesday. If the transfer slips to early Tuesday morning, the money should be available first thing Wednesday morning.

But the money isn't always available that quickly. **Bank of America** Corp. says such transfers typically take two to three days. EmigrantDirect says on its Web site that transfers take two to four days, while HSBC Direct says customers should expect transfers to take up to three days. The industry calls this a "three-day good funds model," says David Goeden, an HSBC executive vice president in personal financial services. That is, the bank wants to make sure our funds are good before it lets us have them.

[2]Be sure to read about mobile banking in Business Math Scrapbook.

LU 4–2   PRACTICE QUIZ

Complete the **Practice Quiz** to see how you are doing.

Rosa Garcia received her February 3, 2011, bank statement showing a balance of $212.80. Rosa's checkbook has a balance of $929.15. The bank statement showed that Rosa had an ATM fee of $12.00 and a deposited check returned fee of $20.00. Rosa earned interest of $1.05. She had three outstanding checks: No. 300, $18.20; No. 302, $38.40; and No. 303, $68.12. A deposit for $810.12 was not on her bank statement. Prepare Rosa Garcia's bank reconciliation.

Solution with Step-by-Step Help on DVD

✓ Solution

ROSA GARCIA					
Bank Reconciliation as of February 3, 2011					
Checkbook balance			**Bank balance**		
Rosa's checkbook balance		$929.15	Bank balance		$ 212.80
Add:			Add:		
Interest		1.05	Deposit in transit		810.12
		$930.20			$1,022.92
Deduct:			Deduct:		
Deposited check returned fee	$20.00		Outstanding checks:		
ATM	12.00	32.00	No. 300	$18.20	
			No. 302	38.40	
			No. 303	68.12	124.72
Reconciled balance		$898.20	Reconciled balance		$ 898.20

LU 4–2a   EXTRA PRACTICE QUIZ WITH WORKED-OUT SOLUTIONS

Need more practice? Try this **Extra Practice Quiz** (check figures in Chapter Organizer, p. 101). Worked-out Solutions can be found in Appendix B at end of text.

Earl Miller received his March 8, 2011, bank statement, which had a $300.10 balance. Earl's checkbook has a $1,200.10 balance. The bank statement showed a $15.00 ATM fee and a $30.00 deposited check returned fee. Earl earned $24.06 interest. He had three outstanding checks: No. 300, $22.88; No. 302, $15.90; and No. 303, $282.66. A deposit for $1,200.50 was not on his bank statement. Prepare Earl's bank reconciliation.

CHAPTER ORGANIZER AND REFERENCE GUIDE

Topic	Key point, procedure, formula	Example(s) to illustrate situation
Types of endorsements, p. 91	*Blank:* Not safe; can be further endorsed.	Jones Co. 21-333-9
	Full: Only person or company named in endorsement can transfer check to someone else.	Pay to the order of Regan Bank Jones Co. 21-333-9
	Restrictive: Check must be deposited. Limits any further negotiation of the check.	Pay to the order of Regan Bank. For deposit only. Jones Co. 21-333-9
Bank reconciliation, p. 95	**Checkbook balance** + EFT (electronic funds transfer) + Interest earned + Notes collected + Direct deposits − ATM withdrawals − NSF check − Online fees − Automatic withdrawals − Overdrafts − Service charges − Stop payments ± Book errors* CM—adds to balance DM—deducts from balance **Bank balance** + Deposits in transit − Outstanding checks ± Bank errors *If a $60 check is recorded as $50, we must decrease checkbook balance by $10.	**Checkbook balance** Balance $800 − NSF 40 $760 − Service charge 4 $756 **Bank balance** Balance $ 632 + Deposits in transit 416 $1,048 − Outstanding checks 292 $ 756
KEY TERMS	Automatic teller machine (ATM), *p. 89* Bank reconciliation, *p. 95* Bank statement, *p. 94* Blank endorsement, *p. 91* Check, *p. 90* Check register, *p. 91* Credit stub, *p. 91* Credit memo (CM), *p. 97* Debit card, *p. 89*	Debit memo (DM), *p. 97* Deposit slip, *p. 90* Deposits in transit, *p. 97* Draft, *p. 90* Drawee, *p. 91* Drawer, *p. 91* Electronic funds transfer (EFT), *p. 94* Endorse, *p. 91* Full endorsement, *p. 91* Nonsufficient funds (NSF), *p. 97* Outstanding checks, *p. 97* Overdrafts, *p. 95* Payee, *p. 91* Restrictive endorsement, *p. 91* Signature card, *p. 90*
CHECK FIGURES FOR EXTRA PRACTICE QUIZZES WITH PAGE REFERENCES. (WORKED-OUT SOLUTIONS IN APPENDIX B.)	LU 4–1a (p. 93) Ending Balance Forward $11,533.80	LU 4–2a (p. 102) Reconciled Balance $1,179.16

Critical Thinking Discussion Questions

1. Explain the structure of a check. The trend in bank statements is not to return the canceled checks. Do you think this is fair?

2. List the three types of endorsements. Endorsements are limited to the top $1\frac{1}{2}$ inches of the trailing edge on the back left side of your check. Why do you think the Federal Reserve made this regulation?

3. List the steps in reconciling a bank statement. Today, many banks charge a monthly fee for certain types of checking accounts. Do you think all checking accounts should be free? Please explain.

4. What are some of the trends in online banking? Will we become a cashless society in which all transactions are made with some type of credit card?

5. What do you think of the government's intervention in trying to bail out banks? Should banks be allowed to fail?

Check figures for odd-numbered problems in Appendix C Name _____ Date _____

DRILL PROBLEMS

4–1. Fill out the check register that follows with this information:

2010

July 7	Check No. 482	AOL	$143.50
15	Check No. 483	Staples	66.10
19	Deposit		800.00
20	Check No. 484	Sprint	451.88
24	Check No. 485	Krispy Kreme	319.24
29	Deposit		400.30

		RECORD ALL CHARGES OR CREDITS THAT AFFECT YOUR ACCOUNT						
NUMBER	DATE 2009	DESCRIPTION OF TRANSACTION	PAYMENT/DEBIT (−)	√	FEE (IF ANY) (−)	DEPOSIT/CREDIT (+)	BALANCE $	4,500 75
			$		$	$		

4–2. November 1, 2010, Payroll.com, an Internet company, has a $10,481.88 checkbook balance. Record the following transactions for Payroll.com by completing the two checks and check stubs provided. Sign the checks Garth Scholten, controller.

 a. November 8, 2010, deposited $688.10

 b. November 8, check No. 190 payable to Staples for office supplies—$766.88

 c. November 15, check No. 191 payable to Best Buy for computer equipment—$3,815.99.

No. _____ $ _____	PAYROLL.COM	No. 190
_____ 20 _____	1 LEDGER RD. ST. PAUL, MN 55113	
To _____ For _____		

PAY TO THE ORDER OF _Staples_   Nov 1, 20 10   5-13/110 $ 766.88

Seven hundred sixty six 88/100 _Cents_ DOLLARS

BALANCE / AMT. DEPOSITED / TOTAL / AMT. THIS CHECK / BALANCE FORWARD

IPSWICHBANK ipswichbank.com   MEMO _Office Supplies_   _Garth Scholten_

⑈011000138⑈ 25 11103 190

No. _____ $ _____	PAYROLL.COM	No. 191
_____ 20 _____	1 LEDGER RD. ST. PAUL, MN 55113	
To _____ For _____		

PAY TO THE ORDER OF _Best Buy_   Nov 15 20 10   5-13/110 $ 3,815.99

three thousand eight hundred fifteen 99/100 DOLLARS

BALANCE / AMT. DEPOSITED / TOTAL / AMT. THIS CHECK / BALANCE FORWARD

IPSWICHBANK ipswichbank.com   MEMO _Comp equip_   _Garth Scholten_

⑈011000138⑈ 25 11103 191

4–3. Using the check register in Problem 4–1 and the following bank statement, prepare a bank reconciliation for Lee.com.

BANK STATEMENT			
Date	Checks	Deposits	Balance
7/1 balance			$4,500.75
7/18	$143.50		4,357.25
7/19		$ 800.00	5,157.25
7/26	319.24		4,838.81
7/30	15.00 SC		4,823.01

WORD PROBLEMS

4–4. According to Bankrate's 2008 Checking Study (a survey of leading banks), ATM surcharges, bounced check fees, monthly service charges, and minimal balances are all increasing. To help reverse this trend, Hometown Bank offers a free checking account for up to 5 checks written a month. After five checks, they charge a fee of $.25 per check. Best Bank offers a checking account with a charge of $.10 per check. Sammy Smith typically writes 15 checks per month. Which bank should he go to for the lowest cost?

Best Bank for $.10 a check.

4–5. The U.S. Chamber of Commerce provides a free monthly bank reconciliation template at business.uschamber.com/tools/ bankre_m.asp. Annie Moats just received her bank statement notice online. She wants to reconcile her checking account with her bank statement and has chosen to reconcile her accounts manually. Her checkbook shows a balance of $698. Her bank statement reflects a balance of $1,348. Checks outstanding are No. 2146, $25; No. 2148, $58; No. 2152, $198; and No. 2153, $464. Deposits in transit are $100 and $50. There is a $15 service charge and $5 ATM charge in addition to notes collected of $50 and $25. Reconcile Annie's balances.

3. Felix Babic banks at Role Federal Bank. Today he received his March 31, 2010, bank statement showing a $762.80 balance. Felix's checkbook shows a balance of $799.80. The following checks have not cleared the bank: No. 140, $130.55; No. 149, $66.80; and No. 161, $102.90. Felix made a $820.15 deposit that is not shown on the bank statement. He has his $617.30 monthly mortgage payment paid through the bank. His $1,100.20 IRS refund check was mailed to his bank. Prepare Felix Babic's bank reconciliation. *(p. 95)*

4. On June 30, 2010, Wally Company's bank statement showed a $7,500.10 bank balance. Wally has a beginning checkbook balance of $9,800.00. The bank statement also showed that it collected a $1,200.50 note for the company. A $4,500.10 June 30 deposit was in transit. Check No. 119 for $650.20 and check No. 130 for $381.50 are outstanding. Wally's bank charges $.40 cents per check. This month, 80 checks were processed. Prepare a reconciled statement. *(p. 95)*

Personal Finance

WHEN TIMOTHY STITT OF LEEPER, PA., FIRST HEARD ABOUT A NEW CHECKING ACCOUNT at a small western Pennsylvania bank, he was intrigued. The "preferred account" from S&T Bank would give him free ATM transactions and a debit card with cash-back rewards. That appealed to Stitt because he frequently uses his debit card to purchase equipment for his landscaping business. So he signed up for an account.

"It was something I couldn't pass up," says Stitt. "It was a no-brainer."

The icing on the cake was the personal service: The bank's account executives took the time to answer all of his questions. And they helped him refinance his mortgage, to a 15-year fixed-rate loan at 5.5%.

Community banks, credit unions and online banks are luring refugees from the big money-center banks by offering lower fees, better rates on savings and a level of personal service that may remind you of George Bailey's building and loan. And just in case that's not enough, they're offering freebies to sweeten the deal—the 21st-century version of the free toaster.

For example, when you set up an account today, you may get a cash-back debit card or a free iPod. Key-Bank hands over a Garmin GPS device. BBVA Compass, of Birmingham, Ala., gives you the chance to win a Mini Cooper. If you refer a friend to Chevy Chase Bank, which serves the Washington, D.C., area, you'll be rewarded with a three-day getaway (not including airfare) to St. Thomas, Las Vegas, Orlando or another vacation spot. "This is a great time for consumers," says Jon Paul, president of Value Added Finance Resources, a consulting firm. "Banks are very hungry for your deposits."

Big banks want your money, too, but they're turning customers off with higher fees and tighter lending—not to mention stress tests and troubled assets. They continue to raise fees, even as the grab for business intensifies and consumers are more cost-conscious.

Bank of America recently raised the monthly maintenance fees on some of its checking accounts; for example,

fees for MyAccess Checking went from $5.95 a month to $8.95 a month. Wachovia, now a Wells Fargo company, boosted its transfer fee to cover checking-account overdrafts from $5 to $10 on some accounts. Charges for using credit cards overseas are also on the rise.

Bank customers are ready for a change. A survey by Aite Group found that just 2% of consumers have a high degree of trust in banks. And satisfaction with the major banks—such as Bank of America, Citigroup and JPMorgan Chase—has either leveled off or dropped, as measured by the American Customer Satisfaction Index and TowerGroup. "Banks are just not where they need to be," says Kathleen Khirallah, of TowerGroup.

●● FIND A BETTER DEAL

Community banks appeal to customers like Stitt because they have close ties to local residents and tend to offer more personal assistance than the big money-center banks. "Community banks are in the relationship-building business," says Karen Tyson, senior vice-president of the Independent Community Bankers of America. They tend to have fewer—and lower—fees than the major banks. And they generally offer lower rates on loans and higher yields on savings.

Likewise, credit unions are focused on their members. According to a study by the Credit Union National Association, credit unions charge an average of $25 for overdrafts; banks charge an average of $30. Similarly, banks sock you with a $35 fee if you're late paying your credit-card bill, but credit unions charge $20. Interest payments on a

$25,000, 60-month car loan from a credit union would be $184 a year less than they would be if you got the loan from a bank, according to an analysis by Datatrac. Over five years, that would save you nearly $1,000. And average closing costs on a mortgage are lower at a credit union: $2,280, versus $2,309 at banks.

Online banks are another good option, particularly if you want to avoid ATM fees. If you need to use a brick-and-mortar bank's ATM, many online banks will reimburse you for any fees it charges. For example, UFBDirect .com reimburses its free-checking-account customers up to $4.50 a month for ATM charges from other banks. If you open a checking account at Charles Schwab (www.schwab.com), you'll get a refund of all ATM fees.

From Kiplinger's Personal Finance, August 2009, p. 44.

BUSINESS MATH ISSUE

The government should allow large banks to fail.

1. List the key points of the article and information to support your position.
2. Write a group defense of your position using math calculations to support your view.

Slater's Business Math Scrapbook

Applying Your Skills

PROJECT A

Would you do mobile banking. What are the pros and cons?

Branching Out: Mobile Banking Finds New Users

Improved Technology Helps Attract Younger Customers, Even as Balances Dwindle

By Ben Worthen

You may not want to learn how much smaller your bank account has gotten. But banks are making it easier than ever for consumers to access account information on their mobile devices.

Big banks are offering new services or improving existing ones that allow people to access their accounts while on the go. In January, **Bank of America** Corp. launched an updated software application that allows consumers to check their balances and pay bills through **Apple** Inc.'s iPhone. **Wells Fargo** & Co. has begun promoting a service that lets business clients approve wire transfers through their cellphones. And mobile banking is at the center of a major new ad campaign from Chase, a division of **J.P. Morgan Chase** & Co, which is offering a service that lets customers check their balances and get other information via text messages.

Smaller banks are beginning to invest in mobile services as well. Bank-Plus, a subsidiary of **Banc-Plus** Corp. with 65 offices throughout Mississippi, unveiled a service last year that lets customers transfer funds and view their transaction history from their mobile phones. "We wanted to offer a service that the big boys offered," says Ike Aslam, vice president of information services at BankPlus, who adds that around 4,000 customers have signed up for the service.

Overall, the number of people in the U.S. that use mobile-banking services grew to 3.1 million in 2008 from 400,000 in 2007, and that number is expected to hit seven million this year, according to ABI Research, a technology-research firm based in New York. At the same time, the number of U.S. banks that offer mobile banking is expected to jump to 614 this year—about 4% of all banks in the country—from 245 in 2008, according to Aite Group, a Boston-based financial-services research firm.

The services are making banking more convenient for customers and small businesses. Customers can use their phones to check how much money they have in their accounts before making a purchase, or pay a bill while waiting to board a plane. Small-business owners can approve payments without having to turn on their computers. In most cases, banks are offering these services free.

Bank of America customers can check balances and pay bills on an Apple iPhone.

Internet Projects: See text Web site (www.mhhe.com/slater10e) and The Business Math Internet Resource Guide.

SOLVING FOR THE UNKNOWN: A HOW-TO APPROACH FOR SOLVING EQUATIONS

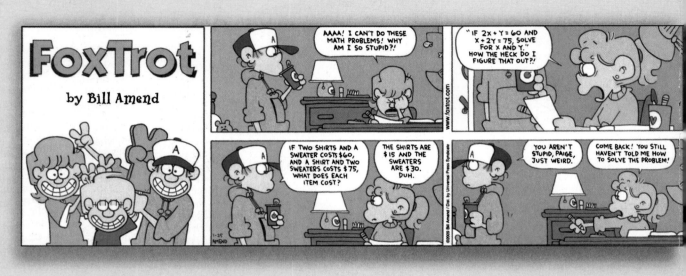

Marcio Jose Sanchez/AP Images

Google Searches for Staffing Answers

By Scott Morrison

Concerned a brain drain could hurt its long-term ability to compete, **Google** Inc. is tackling the problem with its typical tool: an algorithm.

The Internet search giant recently began crunching data from employee reviews and promotion and pay histories in a mathematical formula Google says can identify which of its 20,000 employees are most likely to quit.

Google officials are reluctant to share details of the formula, which is still being tested. The inputs include information from surveys and peer reviews, and Google says the algorithm already has identified employees who felt underused, a key complaint among those who contemplate leaving.

LU 5–1: Solving Equations for the Unknown

1. Explain the basic procedures used to solve equations for the unknown *(pp. 114–116)*.

2. List the five rules and the mechanical steps used to solve for the unknown in seven situations; know how to check the answers *(pp. 116–118)*.

LU 5–2: Solving Word Problems for the Unknown

1. List the steps for solving word problems *(p. 120)*.

2. Complete blueprint aids to solve word problems; check the solutions *(pp. 121–122)*.

VOCABULARY PREVIEW

Here are the key terms in this chapter. When you finish the chapter, if you feel you know the term, place a checkmark within the parentheses following the term. If you are not certain of the definition, look it up and write the page number where it can be found in the text. The chapter organizer includes page references to the terms. There is also a complete glossary at the end of the text.

Constants . ( ) Equation . ( ) Expression . ( ) Formula . ( ) Knowns . ( ) Unknown . ( ) Variables . ( )

Do you eat at McDonald's. Have you ever thought which country can boast it has the most business per location? Of the 118 countries in which McDonald's does business, Russia serves 850,000 dinners annually per location. This is more than twice the store traffic of other markets. We could calculate volume in other markets as follows:

GLOBAL

$$\frac{1}{2} \times 850,000 = 425,000$$

Martin Thomas Photography/Alamy

As Burgers Boom in Russia, McDonald's Touts Discipline

To Maximize Potential, Chain Rations Growth; Trimming Wait Lines

By JANET ADAMY

Khamzat Khasbulatov

MOSCOW—At lunch time on a recent day here, Khamzat Khasbulatov sat in the world's second-busiest McDonald's and watched as dozens of people lined up at its 26 cash registers.

"I have too many customers," said Mr. Khasbulatov, chief executive of McDonald's Russia, as workers scrambled to assemble Big Macs and stuff french fries into red cartons.

Of the 118 countries where McDonald's Corp. does business, none can boast more activity than Russia. On average, each location serves about 850,000 diners annually—more than twice the store traffic in McDonald's other markets.

That has presented the world's largest restaurant chain with an unusual dilemma. Russia, with its burgeoning middle-class and consumer appetites

for all things American, is a jewel in the McDonald's system. But the company is being prudent about expansion here—due partly to Russia's famous bureaucracy and partly to the chain's own philosophical shift.

Aggressive growth plans at McDonald's backfired badly in the past. During the 1990s, the company was fixated on adding restaurants throughout the chain—as many as 2,500 stores a year. But by 2000, the condition of its existing locations, as well as the appeal of certain menu items, deteriorated. Two years later, the company's flawed expansion strategy was hammering its profits and stock price.

Learning Unit 5–1 explains how to solve for unknowns in equations. In Learning Unit 5–2 you learn how to solve for unknowns in word problems. When you complete these learning units, you will not have to memorize as many formulas to solve business and personal math applications. Also, with the increasing use of computer software, a basic working knowledge of solving for the unknown has become necessary.

Learning Unit 5–1: Solving Equations for the Unknown

LO 1

The Rose Smith letter below is based on a true story. Note how Rose states that the blueprint aids, the lesson on repetition, and the chapter organizers were important factors in the successful completion of her business math course.

Rose Smith
15 Locust Street
Lynn, MA 01915

Dear Professor Slater,

Thank you for helping me get through your Business Math class. When I first started, my math anxiety level was real high. I felt I had no head for numbers. When you told us we would be covering the chapter on solving equations, I'll never forget how I started to shake. I started to panic. I felt I could never solve a word problem. I thought I was having an algebra attack.

Now that it's over (90 on the chapter on unknowns), I'd like to tell you what worked for me so you might pass this on to other students. It was your blueprint aids. Drawing boxes helped me to think things out. They were a tool that helped me more clearly understand how to dissect each word problem. They didn't solve the problem for me, but gave me the direction I needed. Repetition was the key to my success. At first I got them all wrong but after the third time, things started to click. I felt more confident. Your chapter organizers at the end of the chapter were great. Thanks for your patience – your repetition breeds success – now students are asking me to help them solve a word problem. Can you believe it!

Best,

Rose

Rose Smith

Many of you are familiar with the terms *variables* and *constants*. If you are planning to prepare for your retirement by saving only what you can afford each year, your saving is a *variable;* if you plan to save the same amount each year, your saving is a *constant*. Now you can also say that you cannot buy clothes by size because of the many variables involved. This unit explains the importance of mathematical variables and constants when solving equations.

Basic Equation-Solving Procedures

When you go to a shopping mall does your purchase(s) depend upon price, who you are shopping with, time of year, or just impulse buying?

From the *Wall Street Journal* heading "Less Shopping = Fewer Malls" may mean you will have fewer new malls in which to shop due to the economy. But no explanation is given as to how the equation has changed. The definition of an equation which follows may suggest to you what is meant by the equation.

Do you know the difference between a mathematical expression, equation, and formula? A mathematical **expression** is a meaningful combination of numbers and letters called *terms*. Operational signs (such as $+$ or $-$) within the expression connect the terms to show a relationship between them. For example, $6 + 2$ or $6A - 4A$ are mathematical expressions. An **equation** is a mathematical statement with an equal sign showing that a mathematical expression on the left equals the mathematical expression on the right. An equation has

Less Shopping = Fewer Malls

Construction of New Centers Slows Along With Economy; 'We're Not Going to Build'

an equal sign; an expression does not have an equal sign. A **formula** is an equation that expresses in symbols a general fact, rule, or principle. Formulas are shortcuts for expressing a word concept. For example, in Chapter 10 you will learn that the formula for simple interest is Interest (I) = Principal (P) × Rate (R) × Time (T). This means that when you see $I = P \times R \times T$, you recognize the simple interest formula. Now let's study basic equations.

As a mathematical statement of equality, equations show that two numbers or groups of numbers are equal. For example, $6 + 4 = 10$ shows the equality of an equation. Equations also use letters as symbols that represent one or more numbers. These symbols, usually a letter of the alphabet, are **variables** that stand for a number. We can use a variable even though we may not know what it represents. For example, $A + 2 = 6$. The variable A represents the number or **unknown** (4 in this example) for which we are solving. We distinguish variables from numbers, which have a fixed value. Numbers such as 3 or -7 are **constants** or **knowns,** whereas A and $3A$ (this means 3 times the variable A) are variables. So we can now say that variables and constants are *terms of mathematical expressions.*

Usually in solving for the unknown, we place variable(s) on the left side of the equation and constants on the right. The following rules for variables and constants are important.

VARIABLES AND CONSTANTS RULES
1. If no number is in front of a letter, it is a 1: $B = 1B$; $C = 1C$.
2. If no sign is in front of a letter or number, it is a +: $C = +C$; $4 = +4$.

You should be aware that in solving equations, the meaning of the symbols $+$, $-$, $\times$, and $\div$ has not changed. However, some variations occur. For example, you can also write $A \times B$ (A times B) as $A \cdot B$, $A(B)$, or AB. Also, A divided by B is the same as A/B. Remember that to solve an equation, you must find a number that can replace the unknown in the equation and make it a true statement. Now let's take a moment to look at how we can change verbal statements into variables.

Assume Dick Hersh, an employee of Nike, is 50 years old. Let's assign Dick Hersh's changing age to the symbol A. The symbol A is a variable.

Verbal statement	Variable A (age)
Dick's age 8 years ago	$A - 8$
Dick's age 8 years from today	$A + 8$
Four times Dick's age	$4A$
One-fifth Dick's age	$A/5$

FIGURE	5.1

Equality in equations

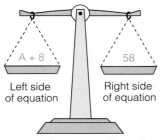

Left side of equation   Right side of equation

Dick's age in 8 years will equal 58.

To visualize how equations work, think of the old-fashioned balancing scale shown in Figure 5.1. The pole of the scale is the equals sign. The two sides of the equation are the two pans of the scale. In the left pan or left side of the equation, we have $A + 8$; in the right pan or right side of the equation, we have 58. To solve for the unknown (Dick's present age), we isolate or place the unknown (variable) on the left side and the numbers on the right. We will do this soon. For now, remember that to keep an equation (or scale) in balance, we must perform mathematical operations (addition, subtraction, multiplication, and division) to *both* sides of the equation.

SOLVING FOR THE UNKNOWN RULE
Whatever you do to one side of an equation, you must do to the other side.

How to Solve for Unknowns in Equations

This section presents seven drill situations and the rules that will guide you in solving for unknowns in these situations. We begin with two basic rules—the opposite process rule and the equation equality rule.

OPPOSITE PROCESS RULE

If an equation indicates a process such as addition, subtraction, multiplication, or division, solve for the unknown or variable by using the opposite process. For example, if the equation process is addition, solve for the unknown by using subtraction.

EQUATION EQUALITY RULE

You can add the same quantity or number to both sides of the equation and subtract the same quantity or number from both sides of the equation without affecting the equality of the equation. You can also divide or multiply both sides of the equation by the same quantity or number *(except zero)* without affecting the equality of the equation.

To check your answer(s), substitute your answer(s) for the letter(s) in the equation. The sum of the left side should equal the sum of the right side.

LO 2

Drill Situation 1: Subtracting Same Number from Both Sides of Equation

Example	**Mechanical steps**	**Explanation**
$A + 8 = 58$	$A + 8 = 58$	8 is subtracted from *both* sides of equation to isolate variable A on the left.
Dick's age A plus 8 equals 58.	$\underline{ -8 \quad -8}$	
	$A = \boxed{50}$	

Check

$50 + 8 = 58$

$58 = 58$

Note: Since the equation process used *addition,* we use the opposite process rule and solve for variable A with *subtraction.* We also use the equation equality rule when we subtract the same quantity from both sides of the equation.

Drill Situation 2: Adding Same Number to Both Sides of Equation

Example	**Mechanical steps**	**Explanation**
$B - 50 = 80$	$B - 50 = 80$	50 is added to *both* sides to isolate variable B on the left.
Some number B less 50 equals 80.	$\underline{ +50 \quad +50}$	
	$B = \boxed{130}$	**Check**

Check

$130 - 50 = 80$

$80 = 80$

Note: Since the equation process used *subtraction,* we use the opposite process rule and solve for variable B with *addition.* We also use the equation equality rule when we add the same quantity to both sides of the equation.

Drill Situation 3: Dividing Both Sides of Equation by Same Number

Example	**Mechanical steps**	**Explanation**
$7G = 35$	$7G = 35$	By dividing both sides by 7, G equals 5.
Some number G times 7 equals 35.	$\dfrac{7G}{7} = \dfrac{35}{7}$	
	$G = \boxed{5}$	**Check**

Check

$7(5) = 35$

$35 = 35$

Note: Since the equation process used *multiplication,* we use the opposite process rule and solve for variable G with *division.* We also use the equation equality rule when we divide both sides of the equation by the same quantity.

Drill Situation 4: Multiplying Both Sides of Equation by Same Number

Example	Mechanical steps	Explanation
$\dfrac{V}{5} = 70$	$\dfrac{V}{5} = 70$	By multiplying both sides by 5, V is equal to 350.
Some number V divided by 5 equals 70.	$5\left(\dfrac{V}{5}\right) = 70(5)$ $V = \boxed{350}$	**Check** $\dfrac{350}{5} = 70$ $70 = 70$

Note: Since the equation process used *division,* we use the opposite process rule and solve for variable V with *multiplication.* We also use the equation equality rule when we multiply both sides of the equation by the same quantity.

Drill Situation 5: Equation That Uses Subtraction and Multiplication to Solve for Unknown

MULTIPLE PROCESSES RULE
When solving for an unknown that involves more than one process, do the addition and subtraction before the multiplication and division.

Example	Mechanical steps	Explanation
$\dfrac{H}{4} + 2 = 5$	$\dfrac{H}{4} + 2 = 5$	1. Move constant to right side by subtracting 2 from both sides.
When we divide unknown H by 4 and add the result to 2, the answer is 5.	$\begin{array}{rcl} \dfrac{H}{4} + 2 &=& 5 \\[4pt] -2 & & -2 \\[4pt] \dfrac{H}{4} &=& 3 \end{array}$ $4\left(\dfrac{H}{4}\right) = 4(3)$ $H = \boxed{12}$	2. To isolate H, which is divided by 4, we do the opposite process and multiply 4 times *both* sides of the equation.
		Check $\dfrac{12}{4} + 2 = 5$ $3 + 2 = 5$ $5 = 5$

Drill Situation 6: Using Parentheses in Solving for Unknown

PARENTHESES RULE
When equations contain parentheses (which indicate grouping together), you solve for the unknown by first multiplying each item inside the parentheses by the number or letter just outside the parentheses. Then you continue to solve for the unknown with the opposite process used in the equation. Do the additions and subtractions first; then the multiplications and divisions.

Example

$5(P - 4) = 20$

The unknown P
less 4, multiplied
by 5 equals 20.

Mechanical steps

$5(P - 4) = 20$

$5P - 20 = 20$

$\underline{+ 20 \qquad +20}$

$\dfrac{\cancel{5}P}{\cancel{5}} = \dfrac{40}{5}$

$P = 8$

Explanation

1. Parentheses tell us that
   everything inside parentheses is multiplied by 5.
   Multiply 5 by P and 5
   by -4.

2. Add 20 to both sides to
   isolate $5P$ on left.

3. To remove 5 in front of P,
   divide both sides by 5 to
   result in P equals 8.

Check

$5(8 - 4) = 20$

$5(4) = 20$

$20 = 20$

Drill Situation 7: Combining Like Unknowns

LIKE UNKNOWNS RULE
To solve equations with like unkowns, you first combine the unknowns and then solve with the opposite process used in the equation.

Example

$4A + A = 20$

Mechanical steps

$4A + A = 20$

$\dfrac{\cancel{5}A}{\cancel{5}} = \dfrac{20}{5}$

$A = 4$

Explanation

To solve this equation: $4A +
1A = 5A$. Thus, $5A = 20$. To
solve for A, divide both sides
by 5, leaving A equals 4.

Before you go to Learning Unit 5–2, let's check your understanding of this unit.

LU 5–1	PRACTICE QUIZ

Complete this **Practice Quiz**
to see how you are doing.

1. Write equations for the following (use the letter Q as the variable). Do not solve for the
    unknown.
    a. Nine less than one-half a number is fourteen.
    b. Eight times the sum of a number and thirty-one is fifty.
    c. Ten decreased by twice a number is two.
    d. Eight times a number less two equals twenty-one.
    e. The sum of four times a number and two is fifteen.
    f. If twice a number is decreased by eight, the difference is four.

2. Solve the following:
    a. $B + 24 = 60$ b. $D + 3D = 240$ c. $12B = 144$
    d. $\dfrac{B}{6} = 50$ e. $\dfrac{B}{4} + 4 = 16$ f. $3(B - 8) = 18$

Solutions with Step-by-Step
Help on DVD

✓ Solutions

1. a. $\dfrac{1}{2}Q - 9 = 14$ b. $8(Q + 31) = 50$ c. $10 - 2Q = 2$

    d. $8Q - 2 = 21$ e. $4Q + 2 = 15$ f. $2Q - 8 = 4$

2. a. $B + 24 = -60$ b. $\dfrac{\cancel{4}D}{\cancel{4}} = \dfrac{240}{4}$ c. $\dfrac{\cancel{12}B}{\cancel{12}} = \dfrac{144}{12}$

    $\underline{-24 \qquad -24}$ $D = 60$ $B = 12$

    $B = 36$

d. $\cancel{6}\left(\dfrac{B}{\cancel{6}}\right) = 50(6)$

$\qquad\qquad B = \boxed{300}$

e. $\dfrac{B}{4} + 4 = 16$

$\qquad\quad \underline{-4 \qquad -4}$

$\qquad\quad \dfrac{B}{4} = 12$

$\qquad\quad \cancel{4}\left(\dfrac{B}{\cancel{4}}\right) = 12(4)$

$\qquad\qquad B = \boxed{48}$

f. $3(B - 8) = 18$

$\qquad 3B - 24 = 18$

$\qquad \underline{ + 24 \quad +24}$

$\qquad \dfrac{\cancel{3}B}{\cancel{3}} = \dfrac{42}{3}$

$\qquad\qquad B = \boxed{14}$

LU 5–1a EXTRA PRACTICE QUIZ WITH WORKED-OUT SOLUTIONS

Need more practice? Try this **Extra Practice Quiz** (check figures in Chapter Organizer, p. 126). Worked-out Solutions can be found in Appendix B at end of text.

1. Write equations for the following (use the letter *Q* as the variable). Do not solve for the unknown.

   a. Eight less than one-half a number is sixteen.
   b. Twelve times the sum of a number and forty-one is 1,200.
   c. Seven decreased by twice a number is one.
   d. Four times a number less two equals twenty-four.
   e. The sum of three times a number and three is nineteen.
   f. If twice a number is decreased by six, the difference is five.

2. Solve the following:

   a. $B + 14 = 70$
   b. $D + 4D = 250$
   c. $11B = 121$
   d. $\dfrac{B}{8} = 90$
   e. $\dfrac{B}{2} + 2 = 16$
   f. $3(B - 6) = 18$

Learning Unit 5–2: Solving Word Problems for the Unknown

LO 1

When you buy a candy bar such as a Snickers, you should turn the candy bar over and carefully read the ingredients and calories contained on the back of the candy bar wrapper. For example, on the back of the Snickers wrapper you will read that there are "170 calories per piece." You could misread this to mean that the entire Snickers bar has 170 calories. However, look closer and you will see that the Snickers bar is divided into three pieces, so if you eat the entire bar, instead of consuming 170 calories, you will consume 510 calories. Making errors like this could result in a weight gain that you cannot explain.

$\dfrac{1}{3}S = 170 \text{ calories}$

$\cancel{3}\left(\dfrac{1}{\cancel{3}}S\right) = 170 \times 3$

$S = \boxed{510} \text{ calories per bar}$

In this unit, we use blueprint aids in six different situations to help you solve for unknowns. Be patient and *persistent*. Remember that the more problems you work, the easier the process becomes. Do not panic! Repetition is the key. Study the five steps that follow. They will help you solve for unknowns in word problems.

SOLVING WORD PROBLEMS FOR UNKNOWNS
Step 1. Carefully read the entire problem. You may have to read it several times.
Step 2. Ask yourself: "What is the problem looking for?"
Step 3. When you are sure what the problem is asking, let a variable represent the unknown. If the problem has more than one unknown, represent the second unknown in terms of the same variable. For example, if the problem has two unknowns, Y is one unknown. The second unknown is 4Y—4 times the first unknown.
Step 4. Visualize the relationship between unknowns and variables. Then set up an equation to solve for unknown(s).
Step 5. Check your result to see if it is accurate.

Word Problem Situation 1: Number Problems From the *Wall Street Journal* clipping "Why Dora the Explorer Can't Come to Your Kid's Birthday Party" you can see the price of costumes could be affected. If we assume the price of a Dora costume has dropped in price $40 to $150, what was the price of the original Dora costume?

Why Dora the Explorer Can't Come To Your Kid's Birthday Party

* * *

The Issue Is Trademark Infringement; Invite SpongeBob, Get SquishyGuy

BY KATHERINE ROSMAN

In planning birthday parties for their children, parents are facing stumbling blocks that include trademark infringement.

For children's parties, many companies around the country provide costumed characters popular with kids—characters like Dora the Explorer, Bob the Builder and Hannah Montana. In recent years, corporations that own the rights to some of the more popular characters, companies that include Marvel Entertainment Inc., Scholastic Inc., and HIT Entertainment, have sent cease-and-desist letters, threatened lawsuits and in some cases received settlements from companies that market unauthorized character impersonators.

The threats rattle the costume industry. Some companies hire lawyers to advise them on how to stay out of trouble and remain in business. Others are now commissioning costumes that only slightly resemble characters owned by media companies. They have names like "Big Red Tickle Monster," instead of Elmo, and "Explorer Girl with Backpack," rather than Dora.

Dora the Explorer

Nickelodeon/Everett Collection

Blueprint aid

LO 2

Unknown(s)	Variable(s)	Relationship*
Original Dora rental price	D	D − $40 = New price

*This column will help you visualize the equation before setting up the actual equation.

Mechanical steps

$$D - 40 = \$150$$
$$\underline{+ 40 \quad + 40}$$
$$D \quad = \boxed{\$190}$$

CHAPTER ORGANIZER AND REFERENCE GUIDE

Solving for unknowns from basic equations	Mechanical steps to solve unknowns	Key point(s)
Situation 6: Using parentheses in solving for unknown, pp. 117–118	$$6(A - 5) = 12$$ $$6A - 30 = 12$$ $$\underline{+ 30 \quad + 30}$$ $$\frac{6A}{6} = \frac{42}{6}$$ $$A = \boxed{7}$$	Parentheses indicate multiplication. Multiply 6 times A and 6 times -5. Result is $6A - 30$ on left side of the equation. Now add 30 to both sides to isolate $6A$ on left. To remove 6 in front of A, divide both sides by 6, to result in A equal to 7. Note that when deleting parentheses, we did not have to multiply the right side.
Situation 7: Combining like unknowns, p. 118	$$6A + 2A = 64$$ $$\frac{8A}{8} = \frac{64}{8}$$ $$A = \boxed{8}$$	$6A + 2A$ combine to $8A$. To solve for A, we divide both sides by 8.

Solving for unknowns from word problems	Blueprint aid	Mechanical steps to solve unknown with check
Situation 1: Number problems, p. 120 **U.S. Air reduced its airfare to California by $60. The sale price was $95. What was the original price?**	<table><tr><td>**Unknown(s)**</td><td>**Variable(s)**</td><td>**Relationship**</td></tr><tr><td>Original price</td><td>P</td><td>$P - \$60 =$ Sale price Sale price = $95</td></tr></table>	$$P - \$60 = \$\ 95$$ $$\underline{+ 60 \quad + 60}$$ $$P = \boxed{\$155}$$ **Check** $$\$155 - \$60 = \$95$$ $$\$95 = \$95$$
Situation 2: Finding the whole when part is known, p. 121 **K. McCarthy spends ⅛ of her budget for school. What is the total budget if school costs $5,000?**	<table><tr><td>**Unknown(s)**</td><td>**Variable(s)**</td><td>**Relationship**</td></tr><tr><td>Total budget</td><td>B</td><td>⅛B School = $5,000</td></tr></table>	$$\frac{1}{8}B = \$5,000$$ $$8\left(\frac{B}{8}\right) = \$5,000(8)$$ $$B = \boxed{\$40,000}$$ **Check** $$\frac{1}{8}(\$40,000) = \$5,000$$ $$\$5,000 = \$5,000$$
Situation 3: Difference problems, p. 121 **Moe sold 8 times as many suitcases as Bill. The difference in their sales is 280 suitcases. How many suitcases did each sell?**	<table><tr><td>**Unknown(s)**</td><td>**Variable(s)**</td><td>**Relationship**</td></tr><tr><td>Suitcases sold: Moe Bill</td><td> 8S S</td><td> 8S $\underline{-\ S}$ 280 suitcases</td></tr></table>	$$8S - S = 280 \text{ (Bill)}$$ $$\frac{7S}{7} = \frac{280}{7}$$ $$S = \boxed{40} \text{ (Bill)}$$ $$8(40) = \boxed{320} \text{ (Moe)}$$ **Check** $$320 - 40 = 280$$ $$280 = 280$$
Situation 4: Calculating unit sales, p. 121 **Moe sold 8 times as many suitcases as Bill. Together they sold a total of 360. How many did each sell?**	<table><tr><td>**Unknown(s)**</td><td>**Variable(s)**</td><td>**Relationship**</td></tr><tr><td>Suitcases sold: Moe Bill</td><td> 8S S</td><td> 8S $\underline{+\ S}$ 360 suitcases</td></tr></table>	$$8S + S = 280$$ $$\frac{9S}{9} = \frac{360}{9}$$ $$S = \boxed{40} \text{ (Bill)}$$ $$8(40) = \boxed{320} \text{ (Moe)}$$ **Check** $$320 + 40 = 360$$ $$360 = 360$$

(continues)

CHAPTER ORGANIZER AND REFERENCE GUIDE

Solving for unknowns from word problems	Blueprint aid	Mechanical steps to solve unknown with check
Situation 5: Calculating unit and dollar sales (cost per unit) when *total units not given*, p. 122 Blue Furniture Company ordered sleepers ($300) and nonsleepers ($200) that cost $8,000. Blue expects sleepers to outsell nonsleepers 2 to 1. How many units of each were ordered? What were dollar costs of each?	<table><tr><td>Unknown(s)</td><td>Variable(s)</td><td>Price</td><td>Relationship</td></tr><tr><td>Sleepers Nonsleepers</td><td>2N N</td><td>$300 200</td><td>600N +200N $8,000 total cost</td></tr></table>	$600N + 200N = 8,000$ $\dfrac{800N}{800} = \dfrac{8,000}{800}$ $N = 10$ (nonsleepers) $2N = 20$ (sleepers) **Check** $10 \times \$200 = \$2,000$ $20 \times \$300 = \underline{\ 6,000}$ $= \$8,000$
Situation 6: Calculating unit and dollar sales (cost per unit) when *total units given*, p. 122 Blue Furniture Company ordered 30 sofas (sleepers and nonsleepers) that cost $8,000. The wholesale unit cost was $300 for the sleepers and $200 for the nonsleepers. How many units of each were ordered? What were dollar costs of each?	<table><tr><td>Unknown(s)</td><td>Variable(s)</td><td>Price</td><td>Relationship</td></tr><tr><td>*Unit costs* Sleepers Nonsleepers</td><td>S 30 − S</td><td>$300 200</td><td>300S +200(30 − S) $ 8,000 total cost</td></tr></table> *Note:* When the total units are given, the higher-priced item (sleepers) is assigned to the variable first. This makes the mechanical steps easier to complete.	$300S + 200(30 - S) = 8,000$ $300S + 6,000 - 200S = 8,000$ $100S + 6,000 = 8,000$ $\underline{\quad - 6,000 \qquad\qquad - 6,000}$ $\dfrac{100S}{100} = \dfrac{2,000}{100}$ $S = 20$ Nonsleepers $= 30 - 20$ $= 10$ **Check** $20(\$300) + 10(\$200) = \$8,000$ $\$6,000 + \ \$2,000 = \$8,000$ $\$8,000 = \$8,000$
KEY TERMS	Constants, *p. 115* Formula, *p. 115* Equation, *p. 114* Knowns, *p. 115* Expression, *p. 114* Unknown, *p. 115*	Variables, *p. 115*

CHECK FIGURES FOR EXTRA PRACTICE QUIZZES WITH PAGE REFERENCES. (WORKED-OUT SOLUTIONS IN APPENDIX B.)	LU 5–1a (p. 119)
	1. A. $Q/2 - 8 = 16$ B. $12(Q + 41) = 1,200$
	   C. $7 - 2Q = 1$ D. $4Q - 2 = 24$
	   E. $3Q + 3 = 19$ F. $2Q - 6 = 5$
	2. A. 56 B. 50 C. 11
	   D. 720 E. 496 F. 12
		LU 5–2a (p. 124)
		1. $P = \$190$
		2. $S = \$49,000$
		3. Morse 7; Micro 56
		4. Cara 120; Susie 240
		5. Meatball 72; cheese 216; Meatball = $504;
		   cheese = $1,296
		6. Meatball $504; cheese $1,296

Critical Thinking Discussion Questions

1. Explain the difference between a variable and a constant. What would you consider your monthly car payment—a variable or a constant?

2. How does the opposite process rule help solve for the variable in an equation? If a Mercedes costs 3 times as much as a Saab, how could the opposite process rule be used? The selling price of the Mercedes is $60,000.

3. What is the difference between Word Problem Situations 5 and 6 in Learning Unit 5–2? Show why the more expensive item in Word Problem Situation 6 is assigned to the variable first.

Check figures for odd-numbered problems in Appendix C   Name _____   Date _____

DRILL PROBLEMS (First of Three Sets)

Solve the unknown from the following equations:

5–1. $E - 20 = 110$ **5–2.** $B + 110 = 400$ **5–3.** $Q + 100 = 400$ **5–4.** $Q - 60 = 850$

5–5. $5Y = 75$ **5–6.** $\dfrac{P}{6} = 92$ **5–7.** $8Y = 96$ **5–8.** $\dfrac{N}{16} = 5$

5–9. $4(P - 9) = 64$ **5–10.** $3(P - 3) = 27$

WORD PROBLEMS (First of Three Sets)

5–11. Kathy and Jeanne are elementary school teachers. Jeanne works for Marquez Charter School in Pacific Palisades, California, where class size reduction is a goal for 2009. Kathy works for a noncharter school where funds do not allow for class size reduction policies. Kathy's fifth-grade class has 1.5 times as many students as Jeanne's. If there are a total of 60 students, how many students does Jeanne's class have? How many students does Kathy's class have?

5–12. In 1955 an antique car that originally cost \$3,668 is valued today at \$62,125 if in excellent condition, which is $1\frac{3}{4}$ times as much as a car in very nice condition—if you can find an owner willing to part with one for any price. What would be the value of the car in very nice condition?

5–13. Joe Sullivan and Hugh Kee sell cars for a Ford dealer. Over the past year, they sold 300 cars. Joe sells 5 times as many cars as Hugh. How many cars did each sell?

5–14. Nanda Yueh and Lane Zuriff sell homes for ERA Realty. Over the past 6 months they sold 120 homes. Nanda sold 3 times as many homes as Lane. How many homes did each sell?

5–15. Dots sells T-shirts ($2) and shorts ($4). In April, total sales were $600. People bought 4 times as many T-shirts as shorts. How many T-shirts and shorts did Dots sell? Check your answer.

5–16. Dots sells 250 T-shirts ($2) and shorts ($4). In April, total sales were $600. How many T-shirts and shorts did Dots sell? Check your answer. *Hint:* Let S = Shorts.

DRILL PROBLEMS (Second of Three Sets)

5–17. $7B = 490$

5–18. $7(A - 5) = 63$

5–19. $\dfrac{N}{9} = 7$

5–20. $18(C - 3) = 162$

5–21. $9Y - 10 = 53$

5–22. $7B + 5 = 26$

WORD PROBLEMS (Second of Three Sets)

5–23. On a flight from Boston to San Diego, American reduced its Internet price by $190.00. The sale price was $420.99. What was the original price?

5–24. Jill, an employee at Old Navy, budgets $\frac{1}{5}$ of her yearly salary for clothing. Jill's total clothing bill for the year is $8,000. What is her yearly salary?

5–25. Bill's Roast Beef sells 5 times as many sandwiches as Pete's Deli. The difference between their sales is 360 sandwiches. How many sandwiches did each sell?

5–26. The count of discouraged unemployed workers rose to 503,000, $2\frac{1}{2}$ times as many as in the previous year. How many discouraged unemployed workers were there in the previous year?

5–27. A local Computer City sells batteries ($3) and small boxes of pens ($5). In August, total sales were $960. Customers bought 5 times as many batteries as boxes of pens. How many of each did Computer City sell? Check your answer.

5–28. Staples sells boxes of pens ($10) and rubber bands ($4). Leona ordered a total of 24 cartons for $210. How many boxes of each did Leona order? Check your answer. *Hint:* Let P = Pens.

DRILL PROBLEMS (Third of Three Sets)

5–29. $A + 90 - 15 = \quad 210$

5–30. $5Y + 15(Y + 1) = \quad 35$

5–31. $3M + 20 = \quad 2M + 80$

5–32. $20(C - 50) = 19{,}000$

WORD PROBLEMS (Third of Three Sets)

5–33. In 2008, FDNY, New York City Fire Department, had 221 fire houses with 11,275 full-time uniformed firefighters. During 2008, they responded to a total of 473,335 incidents. The top five engine companies responded to an average of 5,254 calls. Engine 75 had a total of 18 calls in one 24-hour shift. They responded to five times as many medical emergencies as they did structural fires. How many structural fires did they respond to in that 24-hour shift?

5–34. At General Electric, shift 1 produced 4 times as much as shift 2. General Electric's total production for July was 5,500 jet engines. What was the output for each shift?

5–35. Ivy Corporation gave 84 people a bonus. If Ivy had given 2 more people bonuses, Ivy would have rewarded $\frac{2}{3}$ of the workforce. How large is Ivy's workforce?

5–36. Jim Murray and Phyllis Lowe received a total of $50,000 from a deceased relative's estate. They decided to put $10,000 in a trust for their nephew and divide the remainder. Phyllis received $\frac{3}{4}$ of the remainder; Jim received $\frac{1}{4}$. How much did Jim and Phyllis receive?

5–37. The first shift of GME Corporation produced $1\frac{1}{2}$ times as many lanterns as the second shift. GME produced 5,600 lanterns in November. How many lanterns did GME produce on each shift?

5–38. Wal-Mart sells thermometers ($2) and hot-water bottles ($6). In December, Wal-Mart's total sales were $1,200. Customers bought 7 times as many thermometers as hot-water bottles. How many of each did Wal-Mart sell? Check your answer.

5–39. Ace Hardware sells boxes of wrenches ($100) and hammers ($300). Howard ordered 40 boxes of wrenches and hammers for $8,400. How many boxes of each are in the order? Check your answer.

5–40. Kent Christy is organizing a fundraiser for the pool he manages. He bought ice-cream cones ($.75) and ice-cream sandwiches ($1.00) to sell. His total bill was $225. **(a)** If he ordered twice the number of ice-cream cones than ice-cream sandwiches, how many of each did he buy? **(b)** What did he spend for ice-cream cones? **(c)** What did he spend for ice-cream sandwiches?

5–41. Bessy has 6 times as much money as Bob, but when each earns $6, Bessy will have 3 times as much money as Bob. How much does each have before and after earning the $6?

 SUMMARY PRACTICE TEST

1. Delta reduced its round-trip ticket price from Portland to Boston by $140. The sale price was $401.90. What was the original price? *(p. 120)*

2. David Role is an employee of Google. He budgets $\frac{1}{7}$ of his salary for clothing. If Dave's total clothing for the year is $12,000, what is his yearly salary? *(p. 121)*

3. A local Best Buy sells 8 times as many iPods as Sears. The difference between their sales is 490 iPods. How many iPods did each sell? *(p. 121)*

4. Working at Staples, Jill Reese and Abby Lee sold a total of 1,200 calculators. Jill sold 5 times as many calculators as Abby. How many did each sell? *(p. 121)*

5. Target sells sets of pots ($30) and dishes ($20) at the local store. On the July 4 weekend, Target's total sales were $2,600. People bought 6 times as many pots as dishes. How many of each did Target sell? Check your answer. *(p. 122)*

6. A local Dominos sold a total of 1,600 small pizzas ($9) and pasta dinners ($13) during the Super Bowl. How many of each did Dominos sell if total sales were $15,600? Check your answer. *(p. 122)*

one-fourth of the local workforce.

But UVA provides Charlottesville with more than employment. The faculty's research, especially in biotechnology, often results in private spinoff companies, such as former professor Martin Chapman's Indoor Biotechnologies, which develops allergen-detecting products. And UVA produces fine employees, too. Graduates "provide good intellectual talent," says Michael Latsko, chief talent officer for SNL Financial, a global financial-research firm headquartered in Charlottesville.

The city is a two-hour drive from Washington, D.C., and three hours from the Norfolk naval base. This proximity helped it draw in the U.S. Army National Ground Intelligence Center, which employs 750 people in a variety of fields, including engineering and foreign affairs. Next year the center will add 800 to 1,600 jobs.

Big, stable employers plus the UVA student body add up to paying customers for the small businesses that give Charlottesville its spunk. An eclectic mix of more than 150 shops, galleries and restaurants line the historic downtown pedestrian mall.

For example, one-year-old Siips Wine and Champagne Bar has already become a hot spot with its ballroom-dancing and tango nights. Just a block away, Sharon Nichols opened her Dog and Horse Lovers Boutique a year earlier. She chose Charlottesville for her dream store because it's a "vibrant city surrounded by horse country."

STACY RAPACON

5 ATHENS
SOUTHERN COMFORT

It's nicknamed the Classic City for both its name and its neoclassical architecture, but Athens, Ga., is anything but old-fashioned. Although Southern charm clings to streets lined with Greek Revival mansions and Victorian-era storefronts, the air is charged with change.

The University of Georgia, for which Athens was created as a home, is in

Behind the Numbers

THE MAKING OF THE TOP 10

Below are some key numbers we used to choose our Best Cities for 2009. But they're only a fraction of the factors we considered. Our process is based on the work of Kevin Stolarick, of the Martin Prosperity Institute, a think tank that studies economic prosperity. Stolarick came up with a formula that identifies cities with stable employment, even in tough times. "We found cities that are independent of the national trends—places that may slow down but still keep adding jobs," Stolarick says.

Based on the formula, we looked for places with a professional, high-quality workforce that will help generate new jobs and businesses once the recession ends.

Stolarick also included in the formula a measurement of the "creative class," which comes from his work with Richard Florida, academic director of the Martin Institute and author of *The Rise of the Creative Class.* Creative-class workers—scientists, engineers, educators, writers, artists, entertainers and others—inject both economic and cultural vitality into a city and help make it a vibrant place to live.

We whittled the list of candidates to ten cities based on the numbers and our preliminary reporting. Then we traveled to most of the cities to interview business and community leaders. Our rankings factor in both the data and the results of our travels.

Metro area*	Population	Unemployment rate	Income growth†	Cost of living index#	Median household income‡	Percentage of workforce in creative class
Huntsville, Ala.	395,645	6.8%	12.5%	83.1	$50,647	40%
Albuquerque, N.M.	845,913	6.3	7.5	88.5	45,325	30
Washington, D.C.	5,358,130	5.9	13.0	102.1	83,200	44
Charlottesville, Va.	194,391	5.7	9.4	96.4	53,398	38
Athens, Ga.	189,264	6.8	15.6	88.9	40,774	32
Olympia, Wash.	245,181	8.3	8.6	112.4	57,773	35
Austin, Tex.	1,652,602	6.2	7.6	87.1	56,746	36
Madison, Wis.	561,505	6.4	8.0	86.6	59,709	35
Flagstaff, Ariz.	128,558	6.6	15.0	100.2	49,633	28
Raleigh, N.C.	1,088,765	8.6	2.4	86.7	58,111	36

*Represents the metropolitan statistical area. †Reflects household-income growth from 2004 to 2008. #National average equals 100. ‡As of 2007. SOURCES: Bureau of Labor Statistics, City-Data.com, Martin Prosperity Institute, U.S. Census Bureau.

large part responsible for that energy. Athens has 110,000 residents, almost a third of whom are students. The university is the city's largest employer.

Though the economy in much of the state is in crisis—half of Georgia's counties are reporting unemployment of 10% or higher, and the rate has jumped to 9.1% in Atlanta—the unemployment rate in Athens is 6.8%.

In addition to the university, Athens boasts a hub of regional medical services and has an unexpected manufacturing base. Athens Regional Medical Center, St. Mary's Health Care System and Landmark Hospital, a long-term acute-care facility, provide health care and jobs not only for the community but also for nearby

counties. International manufacturing companies, such as Carrier and DuPont, have operations in Athens.

Hospitality is another driver of the economy, and the only sector to have shown employment growth in 2009. Tourism and conventions add to the pot, but the big show is football season, when the Bulldogs come out to play.

The city offers an impressively eclectic variety of entertainment. As the birthplace of the B-52s, R.E.M. and Widespread Panic, Athens serves up music from rock and blues to alt-country. Boutiques and restaurants keep the downtown streets buzzing. Loft space and apartments sit above the hum, adding life after the last note of the night fades away. **JESSICA ANDERSON**

From Kiplinger's Personal Finance, July 2009, p. 73.

BUSINESS MATH ISSUE

The formula used in the study is based on wrong assumptions.

1. List the key points of the article and information to support your position.
2. Write a group defense of your position using math calculations to support your view.

Finding Online Homework Help for Kids

We Seek an Answer To a Pizza Problem; Ignored by Dr. Math

By PEGGY EDERSHEIM KALB

With school in full swing, many kids are shouldering hours of nightly homework. When students are stumped, they can turn to their (sometimes clueless) parents or head to a flurry of online homework help sites.

CRANKY CONSUMER

We looked around for sites appropriate for our sixth-grade tester. And we wanted help solving this geometry problem: what is a better buy? A square pizza measuring 8 inches by 8 inches that costs $10 or a round pizza with a 9-inch diameter that also costs $10?

Our first site was thebeehive. org. Created by the not-for-profit One Economy Corp. as a tool to help low-income families, the site offers easy access to information on a wide range of topics. By clicking on "school" on the home page (none of the other topics looked at all relevant), we got right to homework help. The section is divided into elementary-, middle- and high-school help.

Our answer was just a few clicks away. "Math" in the high-school section took us to Webmath.com, which offered a coherent explanation of how to do the problem along with a "circle calculator" on which to do the arithmetic. We went to "geometry problem solver," then to "geometry-circles," and there was the formula; we plugged in the information we

Christoph Hitz

find an online calculator—but it has a wealth of formulas, as well as answers to commonly asked questions (ours included). The "Frequently Asked Questions" list included everything from "What years are leap years?" "How do I find the day of the week for any date?" "How do I find a calendar for any year?" to "What is a prime number?" To those questions, the site offers explanations along with sample problems and their solutions.

For less common questions, the site offers "Ask Dr. Math," where new questions are fielded. We did try asking Dr. Math the pizza math question, but we weren't surprised that we never heard back—the site warns that if the answer is among the most commonly asked questions, and an applicable answer is already available, Dr. Math probably won't respond. We also tried a logic problem but didn't hear back on that one either. Turns out, Dr. Math is manned by volunteers who love math; if there is a volunteer who finds your problem interesting, or feels

with everything from how to calculate your age in dog years, to an "airport calculator," which calculates distances and bearing between U.S. airports, are some very useful tools, including one that helped us calculate the area of our circular pizza. Our one complaint? We found the multicolored shapes and numbers which jump around on the already-busy Web page a little distracting, but our tester liked them.

Getting our math question answered by a "live" person at sites that offer personalized tutoring, however, was more complicated. At Anytimetutor.com, we never did figure out how to take advantage of the "one free math session" offered on the home page, even though we tried a few times. (There was no response to our email requests for the free session either). We gave up and forked over our credit-card number. The cost: $1 per email question to be answered in up to 12 hours, $2 for an answer in up to four hours, $2.25 for one hour and $2.50 for live help

was offline the first time we checked. Eventually, we were able to IM with the "Live Support" person who explained the system, and we emailed our question late in the afternoon. Our question was answered at 4:37 the next morning; the solution was written out but it wasn't explained in a way that really helped our tester.

Next up was VistaTutor. com, a Bangladesh-based tutoring site. The company, started by entrepreneur K. Ganesh, provides a team of tutors in 31 subjects, 24 hours a day. The price averages $100 per month for unlimited tutoring, with an introductory month at $50. But we were offered one month for $25 in an email the company sent us the day after our free trial.

Still, signing up for the free trial wasn't smooth sailing. We got a hard sell from the "academic coordinator": he tried to persuade us to sign up for the service before we tried it, offering us a discount—that was already on the Web site—if we signed up immediately. When we said we wanted him to solve our math problem first, he tried solving it and got it wrong. Finally, he passed us to a tutor. (John Stuppy, president of TutorVista, regretted that had happened, but pointed out that the "academic coordinators" are sales people, not tutors, and that he was probably just trying to fill in at a busy time.)

Internet Projects: See text Web site (www.mhhe.com/slater10e) and The Business Math Internet Resource Guide.

Classroom Notes

6

PERCENTS AND THEIR APPLICATIONS

The Jeep Patriot, above, is only 66% domestic—as defined by the U.S. government's standards—while the Toyota Sequoia, seen below, is 80%.

Wall Street Journal © 2009

Jeff Haynes/AFP/Getty Images

LU 6–1: Conversions

1. Convert decimals to percents (including rounding percents), percents to decimals, and fractions to percents (pp. 138–141).

2. Convert percents to fractions (p. 141).

LU 6–2: Application of Percents—Portion Formula

1. List and define the key elements of the portion formula (p. 143).

2. Solve for one unknown of the portion formula when the other two key elements are given (pp. 143–147).

3. Calculate the rate of percent increases and decreases (pp. 147–149).

VOCABULARY PREVIEW

Here are the key terms in this chapter. When you finish the chapter, if you feel you know the term, place a checkmark within the parentheses following the term. If you are not certain of the definition, look it up and write the page number where it can be found in the text. The chapter organizer includes page references to the terms. There is also a complete glossary at the end of the text.

Base . ( ) Percent decrease . ( ) Percent increase . ( ) Percents . ( ) Portion . ( ) Rate . ( )

Did you know that 70% of Internet users in China are thirty years of age or younger? This fact is from the *Wall Street Journal* clipping "Youthful Target." Note in the *Wall Street Journal* clipping how percents are used to express various decreases and increases between two or more numbers, or to determine a decrease or increase. Note in the *Wall Street Journal* clip "Popped Bubbles" Coca-Cola has 42.7% market share.

To understand percents, you should first understand the conversion relationship between decimals, percents, and fractions as explained in Learning Unit 6–1. Then, in Learning Unit 6–2, you will be ready to apply percents to personal and business events.

GLOBAL

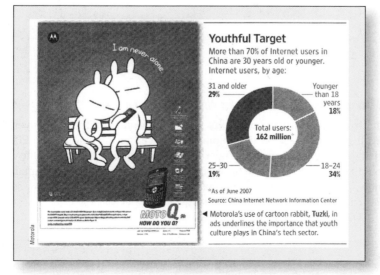

Youthful Target
More than 70% of Internet users in China are 30 years old or younger. Internet users, by age:

- 31 and older **29%**
- Younger than 18 years **18%**
- 18–24 **34%**
- 25–30 **19%**

Total users: **162 million***

*As of June 2007
Source: China Internet Network Information Center

◄ Motorola's use of cartoon rabbit, **Tuzki**, in ads underlines the importance that youth culture plays in China's tech sector.

Wall Street Journal © 2007

Popped Bubbles
Major soda companies hold the largest carbonated drinks, but some smaller

Company	Market share in 2008
1. Coca-Cola	42.7%
2. PepsiCo	30.8
3. Dr Pepper Snapple	15.3
4. Cott	4.7
5. National Beverage	2.6
6. Hansen Natural	0.8
7. Red Bull	0.7
8. Big Red	0.4
9. Rockstar	0.4
10. Private label and other	1.6

Source: Beverage Digest

Wall Street Journal © 2008

Learning Unit 6–1: Conversions

LO 1

When we described parts of a whole in previous chapters, we used fractions and decimals. Percents also describe parts of a whole. The word *percent* means per 100. The percent symbol (%) indicates hundredths (division by 100). **Percents** are the result of expressing numbers as part of 100.

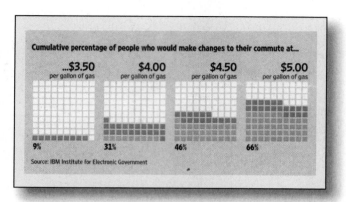

Percents can provide some revealing information. The *Wall Street Journal* clipping "Cumulative Percentage of People Who Would Make Changes to Their Commute at . . ." shows that if gas were to reach $5.00 per gallon, 66% would change their daily commuting routine.

Let's return to the M&M's® example from earlier chapters. In Table 6.1, we use our bag of 55 M&M's® to show how fractions, decimals, and percents can refer to the same parts of a whole. For example, the bag of 55 M&M's® contains 18 yellow M&M's®. As you can see in Table 6.1, the 18 candies in the bag of 55 can be expressed as a fraction ($\frac{18}{55}$), decimal (.33), and percent (32.73%). If you visit the M&M's® website, you will see that the standard is 11 yellow M&M's®. The clipping (in margin) "What Colors Come in Your Bag?" shows an M&M's® Milk Chocolate Candies Color Chart.

Wall Street Journal © 2008

In this unit we discuss converting decimals to percents (including rounding percents), percents to decimals, fractions to percents, and percents to fractions. You will see when you study converting fractions to percents why you should first learn how to convert decimals to percents.

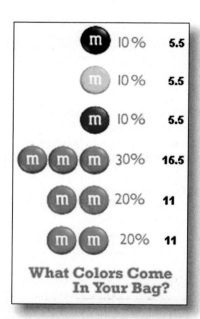

What Colors Come In Your Bag?

Information adapted from http://us.mms.com/ us/about/products/milkchocolate/

TABLE	6.1	Analyzing a bag of M&M's®

Color	Fraction	Decimal (hundredth)	Percent (hundredth)
Yellow	$\frac{18}{55}$	.33	32.73%
Red	$\frac{10}{55}$	.18	18.18
Blue	$\frac{9}{55}$	.16	16.36
Orange	$\frac{7}{55}$	.13	12.73
Brown	$\frac{6}{55}$	.11	10.91
Green	$\frac{5}{55}$	.09	9.09
Total	$\frac{55}{55} = 1$	1.00	100.00%

Converting Decimals to Percents

The *Wall Street Journal* clip "Tax Facts" shows that in 2007 the payers thought that it would be all right to cheat on the amount they owed on income tax. In 2007, 5% thought it was all right to cheat as much as possible. If the clipping had stated the 5% as a decimal (.05), could you give its equivalent in percent? The decimal .05 in decimal fraction is $\frac{5}{100}$. As you know, percents are the result of expressing numbers as part of 100, so 5% = $\frac{5}{100}$. You can now conclude that .05 = $\frac{5}{100}$ = 5%.

The steps for converting decimals to percents are as follows:

TAX FACTS

How do you feel about tax cheating? Here are results of a recent survey, done for the IRS Oversight Board by an outside private firm, asking: How much do you think is an acceptable amount to cheat on your income taxes?

	2007	2005	2003
As much as possible	5%	3%	5%
A little here and there	8	7	12
Not at all	84	88	81

Note: The percentages don't add up to 100%. The others either said they don't know or didn't respond.
Source: IRS Oversight Board 2007 Taxpayer Attitude Survey

CONVERTING DECIMALS TO PERCENTS

Step 1. Move the decimal point two places to the right. You are multiplying by 100. If necessary, add zeros. This rule is also used for whole numbers and mixed decimals.

Step 2. Add a percent symbol at the end of the number.

EXAMPLES

$$.66 = .66. = \boxed{66\%}$$ $$.8 = .80. = \boxed{80\%}$$ $$8 = 8.00. = \boxed{800\%}$$

Add 1 zero to make two places.   Add 2 zeros to make two places.

$$.425 = .42.5 = \boxed{42.5\%}$$ $$.007 = .00.7 = \boxed{.7\%}$$ $$2.51 = 2.51. = \boxed{251\%}$$

Caution: One percent means 1 out of every 100. Since .7% is less than 1%, it means $\frac{7}{10}$ of 1%—a very small amount. Less than 1% is less than .01. To show a number less than 1%, you must use more than two decimal places and add 2 zeros. Example: .7% = .007.

Rounding Percents

When necessary, percents should be rounded. Rounding percents is similar to rounding whole numbers. Use the following steps to round percents:

ROUNDING PERCENTS
Step 1. When you convert from a fraction or decimal, be sure your answer is in percent before rounding.
Step 2. Identify the specific digit. If the digit to the right of the identified digit is 5 or greater, round up the identified digit.
Step 3. Delete digits to right of the identified digit.

For example, Table 6.1 (p. 138) shows that the 18 yellow M&M's® rounded to the nearest hundredth percent is 32.73% of the bag of 55 M&M's®. Let's look at how we arrived at this figure.

When using a calculator, you press $\boxed{18} \boxed{\div} \boxed{55} \boxed{\%}$. This allows you to go right to percent, avoiding the decimal step.

Step 1. $\dfrac{18}{55} = .3272727 = 32.72727\%$ Note that the number is in percent! Identify the hundredth percent digit.

Step 2. 32.73727% Digit to the right of the identified digit is greater than 5, so the identified digit is increased by 1.

Step 3. $\boxed{32.73\%}$ Delete digits to the right of the identified digit.

Converting Percents to Decimals

Note in the following *Wall Street Journal* clip "Still a Small Bite" that Apple Computer has only a .4% share of the personal-computer market in China.

GLOBAL

Associated Press

Apple employees answer questions from customers following the opening of the company's first store in China.

Still a Small Bite

Apple has a tiny share of China's personal-computer market—0.4% as of first quarter of 2008—but hopes to increase it by opening stores. Here's a look at the rest.

In the paragraph and steps that follow, you will learn how to convert percents to decimals. The example below the steps using 5% comes from the clipping "Tax Facts" (p. 138). As previously indicated, the example using .4% comes from the clipping "Still a Small Bite."

To convert percents to decimals, you reverse the process used to convert decimals to percents. In our earlier discussion on converting decimals to percents (p. 138), we asked if the 5% in the "Tax Facts" clipping had been in decimals and not percent, could you convert the decimals to the 5%? Once again, the definition of percent states that $5\% = \frac{5}{100}$. The fraction $\frac{5}{100}$ can be written in decimal form as .05. You can conclude that $5\% = \frac{5}{100} = .05$. Now you can see this procedure in the following conversion steps:

CONVERTING PERCENTS TO DECIMALS

Step 1. Drop the percent symbol.

Step 2. Move the decimal point two places to the left. You are dividing by 100. If necessary, add zeros.

EXAMPLES

Note that when a percent is less than 1%, the decimal conversion has at least two leading zeros before the number .004.

$.4\% = .00.4 = \boxed{.004}$ $2\% = .02. = \boxed{.02}$ $66\% = .66. = \boxed{.66}$

Add 2 zeros to make two places.   Add 1 zero to make two places.

$54.5\% = .54.5 = \boxed{.545}$ $824.4\% = 8.24.4 = \boxed{8.244}$

Now we must explain how to change fractional percents such as $\frac{1}{5}\%$ to a decimal. Remember that fractional percents are values less than 1%. For example, $\frac{1}{5}\%$ is $\frac{1}{5}$ of 1%. Fractional percents can appear singly or in combination with whole numbers. To convert them to decimals, use the following steps:

CONVERTING FRACTIONAL PERCENTS TO DECIMALS

Step 1. Convert a single fractional percent to its decimal equivalent by dividing the numerator by the denominator. If necessary, round the answer.

Step 2. If a fractional percent is combined with a whole number (mixed fractional percent), convert the fractional percent first. Then combine the whole number and the fractional percent.

Step 3. Drop the percent symbol; move the decimal point two places to the left (this divides the number by 100).

EXAMPLES

$\frac{1}{5}\% = .20\% = .00.20 = \boxed{.0020}$ Think of $7\frac{3}{4}\%$ as

$\frac{1}{4}\% = .25\% = .00.25 = \boxed{.0025}$ $7\% = \quad .07$

$7\frac{3}{4}\% = 7.75\% = .07.75 = \boxed{.0775}$ $+ \frac{3}{4}\% = \quad + .0075$

$6\frac{1}{2}\% = 6.5\% = .06.5 = \boxed{.065}$ $7\frac{3}{4}\% = \quad .0775$

Converting Fractions to Percents

When fractions have denominators of 100, the numerator becomes the percent. Other fractions must be first converted to decimals; then the decimals are converted to percents.

CONVERTING FRACTIONS TO PERCENTS
Step 1. Divide the numerator by the denominator to convert the fraction to a decimal.
Step 2. Move the decimal point two places to the right; add the percent symbol.

EXAMPLES

$$\frac{3}{4} = .75 = .75. = \boxed{75\%} \qquad \frac{1}{5} = .20 = .20. = \boxed{20\%} \qquad \frac{1}{20} = .05 = .05. = \boxed{5\%}$$

LO 2

Converting Percents to Fractions

Using the definition of percent, you can write any percent as a fraction whose denominator is 100. Thus, when we convert a percent to a fraction, we drop the percent symbol and write the number over 100, which is the same as multiplying the number by $\frac{1}{100}$. This method of multiplying by $\frac{1}{100}$ is also used for fractional percents.

CONVERTING A WHOLE PERCENT (OR A FRACTIONAL PERCENT) TO A FRACTION
Step 1. Drop the percent symbol.
Step 2. Multiply the number by $\frac{1}{100}$.
Step 3. Reduce to lowest terms.

EXAMPLES

$$76\% = 76 \times \frac{1}{100} = \frac{76}{100} = \boxed{\frac{19}{25}} \qquad \frac{1}{8}\% = \frac{1}{8} \times \frac{1}{100} = \boxed{\frac{1}{800}}$$

$$156\% = 156 \times \frac{1}{100} = \frac{156}{100} = 1\frac{56}{100} = \boxed{1\frac{14}{25}}$$

Sometimes a percent contains a whole number and a fraction such as $12\frac{1}{2}\%$ or 22.5%. Extra steps are needed to write a mixed or decimal percent as a simplified fraction.

CONVERTING A MIXED OR DECIMAL PERCENT TO A FRACTION
Step 1. Drop the percent symbol.
Step 2. Change the mixed percent to an improper fraction.
Step 3. Multiply the number by $\frac{1}{100}$.
Step 4. Reduce to lowest terms.
Note: If you have a mixed or decimal percent, change the decimal portion to fractional equivalent and continue with Steps 1 to 4.

EXAMPLES $$12\frac{1}{2}\% = \frac{25}{2} \times \frac{1}{100} = \frac{25}{200} = \boxed{\frac{1}{8}}$$

$$12.5\% = 12\frac{1}{2}\% = \frac{25}{2} \times \frac{1}{100} = \frac{25}{200} = \boxed{\frac{1}{8}}$$

$$22.5\% = 22\frac{1}{2}\% = \frac{45}{2} \times \frac{1}{100} = \frac{45}{200} = \boxed{\frac{9}{40}}$$

It's time to check your understanding of Learning Unit 6–1.

$ MONEY TIPS

Nearly half, 47%, of adult Americans have no life-insurance coverage. Even though this is an unpleasant topic to think about, consider the impact on the loved ones you leave behind if they have to come up with funeral costs for you while they are going through the grieving process.

LU 6-1	PRACTICE QUIZ

Complete this **Practice Quiz** to see how you are doing.

Convert to percents (round to the nearest tenth percent as needed):

1. .6666 _____ **2.** .832 _____

3. .004 _____ **4.** 8.94444 _____

Convert to decimals (remember, decimals representing less than 1% will have at least 2 leading zeros before the number):

5. $\frac{1}{4}$% _____ **6.** $6\frac{3}{4}$% _____

7. 87% _____ **8.** 810.9% _____

Convert to percents (round to the nearest hundredth percent):

9. $\frac{1}{7}$ _____ **10.** $\frac{2}{9}$ _____

Convert to fractions (remember, if it is a mixed number, first convert to an improper fraction):

11. 19% _____ **12.** $71\frac{1}{2}$% _____ **13.** 130% _____

14. $\frac{1}{2}$% _____ **15.** 19.9% _____

 Solutions with Step-by-Step Help on DVD

✓ Solutions

1. .66.66 = 66.7%

2. .83.2 = 83.2%

3. .00.4 = .4%

4. 8.94.444 = 894.4%

5. $\frac{1}{4}$% = .25% = .0025

6. $6\frac{3}{4}$% = 6.75% = .0675

7. 87% = .87. = .87

8. 810.9% = 8.10.9 = 8.109

9. $\frac{1}{7}$ = .14.285 = 14.29%

10. $\frac{2}{9}$ = .22.2$\bar{2}$ = 22.22%

11. 19% = 19 × $\frac{1}{100}$ = $\frac{19}{100}$

12. $71\frac{1}{2}$% = $\frac{143}{2}$ × $\frac{1}{100}$ = $\frac{143}{200}$

13. 130% = 130 × $\frac{1}{100}$ = $\frac{130}{100}$ = $1\frac{30}{100}$ = $1\frac{3}{10}$

14. $\frac{1}{2}$% = $\frac{1}{2}$ × $\frac{1}{100}$ = $\frac{1}{200}$

15. $19\frac{9}{10}$% = $\frac{199}{10}$ × $\frac{1}{100}$ = $\frac{199}{1,000}$

LU 6-1a	EXTRA PRACTICE QUIZ WITH WORKED-OUT SOLUTIONS

Need more practice? Try this **Extra Practice Quiz** (check figures in Chapter Organizer, p. 155). Worked-out Solutions can be found in Appendix B at end of text.

Convert to percents (round to the nearest tenth percent as needed):

1. .4444 **2.** .782

3. .006 **4.** 7.93333

Convert to decimals (remember, decimals representing less than 1% will have at least 2 leading zeros before the number):

5. $\frac{1}{5}$% **6.** $7\frac{4}{5}$%

7. 92% **8.** 765.8%

Convert to percents (round to the nearest hundredth percent):

9. $\frac{1}{3}$ **10.** $\frac{3}{7}$

Convert to fractions (remember, if it is a mixed number, first convert to an improper fraction):

11. 17%   **12.** $82\frac{1}{4}\%$ **13.** 150%

14. $\frac{1}{4}\%$ **15.** 17.8%

Learning Unit 6–2: Application of Percents—Portion Formula

LO 1

The bag of M&M's® we have been studying contains Milk Chocolate M&M's®. M&M/Mars also makes Peanut M&M's® and some other types of M&M's®. To study the application of percents to problems involving M&M's®, we make two key assumptions:

1. Total sales of Milk Chocolate M&M's®, Peanut M&M's®, and other M&M's® chocolate candies are $400,000.

2. Eighty percent of M&M's® sales are Milk Chocolate M&M's®. This leaves the Peanut and other M&M's® chocolate candies with 20% of sales (100% − 80%).

80% M&M's®		20% M&M's®		100%
Milk Chocolate M&M's®	+	Peanut and other chocolate candies	=	Total sales ($400,000)

Before we begin, you must understand the meaning of three terms—*base, rate,* and *portion.* These terms are the key elements in solving percent problems.

- **Base (*B*).** The **base** is the beginning whole quantity or value (100%) with which you will compare some other quantity or value. Often the problems give the base after the word *of.* For example, the whole (total) sales of M&M's®—Milk Chocolate M&M's, Peanut, and other M&M's® chocolate candies—are $400,000.

- **Rate (*R*).** The **rate** is a percent, decimal, or fraction that indicates the part of the base that you must calculate. The percent symbol often helps you identify the rate. For example, Milk Chocolate M&M's® currently account for 80% of sales. So the rate is 80%. Remember that 80% is also $\frac{4}{5}$, or .80.

- **Portion (*P*).** The **portion** is the amount or part that results from the base multiplied by the rate. For example, total sales of M&M's® are $400,000 (base); $400,000 times .80 (rate) equals $320,000 (portion), or the sales of Milk Chocolate M&M's®. *A key point to remember is that portion is a number and not a percent. In fact, the portion can be larger than the base if the rate is greater than 100%.*

Solving Percents with the Portion Formula

LO 2

In problems involving portion, base, and rate, we give two of these elements. You must find the third element. Remember the following key formula:

Portion (*P*) = Base (*B*) × Rate (*R*)

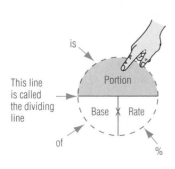

To help you solve for the portion, base, and rate, this unit shows pie charts. The shaded area in each pie chart indicates the element that you must solve for. For example, since we shaded *portion* in the pie chart at the left, you must solve for portion. To use the pie charts, put your finger on the shaded area (in this case portion). The formula that remains tells you what to do. So in the pie chart at the left, you solve the problem by multiplying base by the rate. Note the circle around the pie chart is broken since we want to emphasize that portion can be larger than base if rate is greater than 100%. The horizontal line in the pie chart is called the dividing line, and we will use it when we solve for base or rate.

The following example summarizes the concept of base, rate, and portion. Assume that you received a small bonus check of $100. This is a gross amount—your company did not withhold any taxes. You will have to pay 20% in taxes.

Base: 100%—whole. Usually given after the word *of*—but not always.	Rate: Usually expressed as a percent but could also be a decimal or fraction.	Portion: A number—not a percent and not the whole.
$100 bonus check	20% taxes	$20 taxes

First decide what you are looking for. You want to know how much you must pay in taxes—the portion. How do you get the portion? From the portion formula Portion (P) = Base (B) × Rate (R), you know that you must multiply the base ($100) by the rate (20%). When you do this, you get $100 × .20 = $20. So you must pay $20 in taxes.

Let's try our first word problem by taking a closer look at the M&M's® example to see how we arrived at the $320,000 sales of Milk Chocolate M&M's® given earlier. We will be using blueprint aids to help dissect and solve each word problem.

Solving for Portion

The Word Problem Sales of Milk Chocolate M&M's® are 80% of the total M&M's® sales. Total M&M's® sales are $400,000. What are the sales of Milk Chocolate M&M's®?

The facts	Solving for?	Steps to take	Key points
Milk Chocolate M&M's® sales: 80%. Total M&M's® sales: $400,000.	Sales of Milk Chocolate M&M's®.	Identify key elements. Base: $400,000. Rate: .80. Portion: ? Portion = Base × Rate.	Amount or part of beginning — Portion (?) — Base ($400,000) × Rate (.80) — Beginning whole quantity (often after "of") — Percent symbol or word (here we put into decimal) — Portion and rate must relate to same piece of base.

Steps to solving problem

1. Set up the formula.   Portion = Base × Rate

2. Calculate portion (sales of Milk $P = \$400{,}000 \times .80$
   Chocolate M&M's®).

                                                          $P = \$320{,}000$

In the first column of the blueprint aid, we gather the facts. In the second column, we state that we are looking for sales of Milk Chocolate M&M's®. In the third column, we identify each key element and the formula needed to solve the problem. Review the pie chart in the fourth column. Note that the portion and rate must relate to the same piece of the base. In this word problem, we can see from the solution below the blueprint aid that sales of Milk Chocolate M&M's® are $320,000. The $320,000 does indeed represent 80% of the base. Note here that the portion ($320,000) is less than the base of $400,000 since the rate is less than 100%.

Now let's work another word problem that solves for the portion.

The Word Problem Sales of Milk Chocolate M&M's® are 80% of the total M&M's® sales. Total M&M's® sales are $400,000. What are the sales of Peanut and other M&M's® chocolate candies?

The facts	Solving for?	Steps to take	Key points
Milk Chocolate M&M's® sales: 80%. *Total M&M's® sales: $400,000.*	Sales of Peanut and other M&M's® chocolate candies.	Identify key elements. *Base: $400,000.* *Rate: .20 (100% − 80%).* *Portion: ?* Portion = Base × Rate.	If 80% of sales are Milk Chocolate M&M's, then 20% are Peanut and other M&M's® chocolate candies. Portion (?) Base × Rate ($400,000) (.20) Portion and rate must relate to same piece of base.

Steps to solving problem

1. Set up the formula.   Portion = Base × Rate

2. Calculate portion (sale of Peanut and other $P = \$400,000 \times .20$
   M&M's® chocolate candies).
   $P = \$80,000$

In the previous blueprint aid, note that we must use a rate that agrees with the portion so the portion and rate refer to the same piece of the base. Thus, if 80% of sales are Milk Chocolate M&M's®, 20% must be Peanut and other M&M's® chocolate candies (100% − 80% = 20%). So we use a rate of .20.

In Step 2, we multiplied $400,000 × .20 to get a portion of $80,000. This portion represents the part of the sales that were *not* Milk Chocolate M&M's®. Note that the rate of .20 and the portion of $80,000 relate to the same piece of the base—$80,000 is 20% of $400,000. Also note that the portion ($80,000) is less than the base ($400,000) since the rate is less than 100%.

Take a moment to review the two blueprint aids in this section. Be sure you understand why the rate in the first blueprint aid was 80% and the rate in the second blueprint aid was 20%.

Solving for Rate

The Word Problem Sales of Milk Chocolate M&M's® are $320,000. Total M&M's® sales are $400,000. What is the percent of Milk Chocolate M&M's® sales compared to total M&M's® sales?

The facts	Solving for?	Steps to take	Key points
Milk Chocolate M&M's® sales: $320,000. *Total M&M's® sales: $400,000.*	Percent of Milk Chocolate M&M's® sales to total M&M's® sales.	Identify key elements. *Base: $400,000.* *Rate: ?* *Portion: $320,000* $\text{Rate} = \dfrac{\text{Portion}}{\text{Base}}$	Since portion is less than base, the rate must be less than 100% Portion ($320,000) Base × Rate ($400,000) (?) Portion and rate must relate to the same piece of base.

Steps to solving problem

1. Set up the formula. $\text{Rate} = \dfrac{\text{Portion}}{\text{Base}}$

2. Calculate rate (percent of Milk $R = \dfrac{\$320,000}{\$400,000}$
   Chocolate M&M's® sales).
   $R = 80\%$

Note that in this word problem, the rate of 80% and the portion of $320,000 refer to the same piece of the base.

The Word Problem Sales of Milk Chocolate M&M's® are $320,000. Total sales of Milk Chocolate M&M's, Peanut, and other M&M's® chocolate candies are $400,000. What percent of Peanut and other M&M's® chocolate candies are sold compared to total M&M's® sales?

The facts	Solving for?	Steps to take	Key points
Milk Chocolate M&M's® sales: $320,000. Total M&M's® sales: $400,000.	Percent of Peanut and other M&M's® chocolate candies sales compared to total M&M's® sales.	Identify key elements. Base: $400,000. Rate: ? Portion: $80,000 ($400,000 − $320,000). Rate = $\dfrac{\text{Portion}}{\text{Base}}$	Represents sales of Peanut and other M&M's® chocolate candies Portion ($80,000) Base × Rate ($400,000) (?) When portion becomes $80,000, the portion and rate now relate to same piece of base.

Steps to solving problem

1. Set up the formula.

$$\text{Rate} = \frac{\text{Portion}}{\text{Base}}$$

2. Calculate rate.

$$R = \frac{\$80,000}{\$400,000}\quad (\$400,000 - \$320,000)$$

$$R = \boxed{20\%}$$

The word problem asks for the rate of candy sales that are *not* Milk Chocolate M&M's. Thus, $400,000 of total candy sales less sales of Milk Chocolate M&M's® ($320,000) allows us to arrive at sales of Peanut and other M&M's® chocolate candies ($80,000). The $80,000 portion represents 20% of total candy sales. The $80,000 portion and 20% rate refer to the same piece of the $400,000 base. Compare this blueprint aid with the blueprint aid for the previous word problem. Ask yourself why in the previous word problem the rate was 80% and in this word problem the rate is 20%. In both word problems, the portion was less than the base since the rate was less than 100%.

Now we go on to calculate the base. Remember to read the word problem carefully so that you match the rate and portion to the same piece of the base.

Solving for Base

The Word Problem Sales of Peanut and other M&M's® chocolate candies are 20% of total M&M's® sales. Sales of Milk Chocolate M&M's® are $320,000. What are the total sales of all M&M's®?

The facts	Solving for?	Steps to take	Key points
Peanut and other M&M's® chocolate candies sales: 20%. Milk Chocolate M&M's® sales: $320,000.	Total M&M's® sales.	Identify key elements. Base: ? Rate: .80 (100% − 20%) Portion: $320,000 Base = $\dfrac{\text{Portion}}{\text{Rate}}$	Portion ($320,000) Base × Rate (?) (.80) (100% − 20%) Portion ($320,000) and rate (.80) do relate to the same piece of base.

Steps to solving problem

1. Set up the formula.

$$\text{Base} = \frac{\text{Portion}}{\text{Rate}}$$

2. Calculate the base.

$$B = \frac{\$320,000}{.80} \longleftarrow \$320,000 \text{ is } 80\% \text{ of base}$$

$$B = \boxed{\$400,000}$$

Note that we could not use 20% for the rate. The $320,000 of Milk Chocolate M&M's®
represents 80% (100% − 20%) of the total sales of M&M's®. We use 80% so that the portion and rate refer to same piece of the base. Remember that the portion ($320,000) is less
than the base ($400,000) since the rate is less than 100%.

LO 3

Calculating Percent Increases and Decreases

The following *Wall Street Journal* clipping, "Winter Could Test Energy Math," states that
heating oil could face increases of between 50% and 100%. Using this clipping, let's look
at how to calculate percent increases and decreases.

Wall Street Journal © 2008

Rate of Percent Increase

Assume: Home heating oil increases from $3.00 to $4.50 per gallon.

$$\text{Rate} = \frac{\text{Portion}}{\text{Base}} \quad \begin{matrix} \longleftarrow \text{Difference between old and new oil price} \\ \longleftarrow \text{Old oil price} \end{matrix}$$

$$R = \frac{\$1.50\,(\$4.50 - \$3.00)}{\$3.00}$$

$$R = \boxed{50\%}$$

Let's prove the 50% with a pie chart.

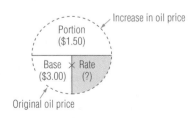

The formula for calculating oil's **percent increase** is as follows:

Percent increase

$$
\text{Percent of increase } (R) \text{ (50\%)} = \frac{\text{Amount of increase } (P) \text{ (\$1.50)}}{\text{Original oil price } (B) \text{ (\$3.00)}}
$$

Now let's look at how to calculate the math for a decrease in oil prices from $3.00 to $2.70.

Rate of Percent Decrease

Assume: Home heating oil per gallon drops from $3.00 per gallon to $2.70 per gallon.

$$
\text{Rate} = \frac{\text{Portion}}{\text{Base}} \quad \begin{array}{l} \leftarrow \text{Difference between old and new oil price} \\ \leftarrow \text{Old oil price amount} \end{array}
$$

$$
R = \frac{\$.30\,(\$3.00 - \$2.70)}{\$3.00}
$$

$$
R = \boxed{10\%}
$$

Let's prove the 10% with a pie chart.

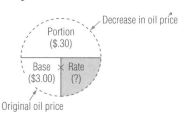

The formula for calculating oil **percent decrease** is as follows:

Percent decrease

$$
\text{Percent of decrease } (R) \text{ (10\%)} = \frac{\text{Amount of decrease } (P) \text{ (\$.30)}}{\text{Original oil price } (B) \text{ (\$3.00)}}
$$

In conclusion, the following steps can be used to calculate percent increases and decreases:

CALCULATING PERCENT INCREASES AND DECREASES

Step 1. Find the difference between amounts (such as oil costs).

Step 2. Divide Step 1 by the original amount (the base): $R = P \div B$. Be sure to express your answer in percent.

Before concluding this chapter, we will show how to calculate a percent increase and decrease using M&M's® (Figure 6.1).

FIGURE 6.1

Bag of 18.40-ounce M&M's®

Additional Examples Using M&M's

The Word Problem Sheila Leary went to her local supermarket and bought the bag of M&M's® shown in Figure 6.1 (p. 148). The bag gave its weight as 18.40 ounces, which was 15% more than a regular 1-pound bag of M&M's®. Sheila, who is a careful shopper, wanted to check and see if she was actually getting a 15% increase. Let's help Sheila dissect and solve this problem.

The facts	Solving for?	Steps to take	Key points
New bag of M&M's®: 18.40 oz. 15% increase in weight. *Original bag of M&M's®:* 16 oz. (1 lb.)	Checking percent increase of 15%.	Identify key elements. Base: 16 oz. Rate: ? Portion: 2.40 oz. $\left(\begin{array}{r} 18.40 \text{ oz.} \\ -\ 16.00 \\ \hline 2.40 \text{ oz.} \end{array}\right)$ Rate $= \dfrac{\text{Portion}}{\text{Base}}$	Difference between base and new weight Portion (2.40 oz.) Base × Rate (16 oz.) (?) Original amount sold

Steps to solving problem

1. Set up the formula.

$$\text{Rate} = \frac{\text{Portion}}{\text{Base}}$$

2. Calculate the rate.

$$R = \frac{2.40 \text{ oz.}}{16.00 \text{ oz.}} \begin{array}{l} \leftarrow \text{Difference between base and new weight.} \\ \leftarrow \text{Old weight equals 100\%.} \end{array}$$

$$R = 15\% \text{ increase}$$

The new weight of the bag of M&M's® is really 115% of the old weight:

$$\begin{array}{rcl} 16.00 \text{ oz.} & = & 100\% \\ +\ 2.40 & = & +\ 15 \\ \hline 18.40 \text{ oz.} & = & 115\% & = 1.15 \end{array}$$

We can check this by looking at the following pie chart:

Portion = Base × Rate

18.40 oz. = 16 oz. × 1.15

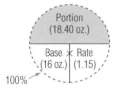

Portion (18.40 oz.)

Base × Rate (16 oz.) (1.15)

100%

Why is the portion greater than the base? Remember that the portion can be larger than the base only if the rate is greater than 100%. Note how the portion and rate relate to the same piece of the base—18.40 oz. is 115% of the base (16 oz.).

Let's see what could happen if M&M/Mars has an increase in its price of sugar. This is an additional example to reinforce the concept of percent decrease.

The Word Problem The increase in the price of sugar caused the M&M/Mars company to decrease the weight of each 1-pound bag of M&M's® to 12 ounces. What is the rate of percent decrease?

The facts	Solving for?	Steps to take	Key points
16-oz. bag of M&M's®: reduced to 12 oz.	Rate of percent decrease.	Identify key elements. Base: 16 oz. Rate: ? Portion: 4 oz. (16 oz. − 12 oz.) Rate $= \dfrac{\text{Portion}}{\text{Base}}$	Amount of decrease Portion (4 oz.) Base × Rate (16 oz.) (?) Old base 100%

Steps to solving problem

1. Set up the formula.

$$\text{Rate} = \frac{\text{Portion}}{\text{Base}}$$

2. Calculate the rate.

$$R = \frac{4 \text{ oz.}}{16.00 \text{ oz.}}$$

$$R = 25\% \text{ decrease}$$

The new weight of the bag of M&M's® is 75% of the old weight:

$$
\begin{array}{rcr}
16 \text{ oz.} & = & 100\% \\
- \ 4 & & - \ 25 \\
\hline
12 \text{ oz.} & = & 75\%
\end{array}
$$

We can check this by looking at the following pie chart:

Portion = Base × Rate

12 oz. = 16 oz. × .75

Note that the portion is smaller than the base because the rate is less than 100%. Also note how the portion and rate relate to the same piece of the base—12 ounces is 75% of the base (16 oz.).

After your study of Learning Unit 6–2, you should be ready for the Practice Quiz.

LU 6–2 PRACTICE QUIZ

Complete this Practice Quiz to see how you are doing.

Solve for portion:

1. 38% of 900.

2. 60% of $9,000.

Solve for rate (round to nearest tenth percent as needed):

3. 430 is _____ % of 5,000.

4. 200 is _____ % of 700.

Solve for base (round to the nearest tenth as needed):

5. 55 is 40% of _____.

6. 900 is $4\frac{1}{2}\%$ of _____.

Solve the following (blueprint aids are shown in the solution; you might want to try some on scrap paper):

7. Five out of 25 students in Professor Ford's class received an A grade. What percent of the class *did not* receive the A grade?

8. Abby Biernet has yet to receive 60% of her lobster order. Abby received 80 lobsters to date. What was her original order?

9. Assume in 2009, Dunkin' Donuts Company had $300,000 in doughnut sales. In 2010, sales were up 40%. What are Dunkin' Donuts sales for 2010?

10. The price of an Apple computer dropped from $1,600 to $1,200. What was the percent decrease?

11. In 1982, a ticket to the Boston Celtics cost $14. In 2010, a ticket cost $50. What is the percent increase to the nearest hundredth percent?

Solutions with Step-by-Step Help on DVD

✓ Solutions

1. $342 = 900 \times .38$
   $(P) = (B) \times (R)$

2. $\$5,400 = \$9,000 \times .60$
   $(P) \ = \ (B) \ \times (R)$

3. $\dfrac{(P)430}{(B)5,000} = .086 = 8.6\% \ (R)$

4. $\dfrac{(P)200}{(B)700} = .2857 = 28.6\% \ (R)$

5. $\dfrac{(P)55}{(R).40} = 137.5 \ (B)$

6. $\dfrac{(P)900}{(R).045} = 20,000 \ (B)$

7. Percent of Professor Ford's class that did not receive an A grade:

The facts	Solving for?	Steps to take	Key points
5 As. 25 in class.	Percent that did not receive A.	Identify key elements. *Base:* 25 *Rate:* ? *Portion:* 20 (25 − 5). Rate $= \dfrac{\text{Portion}}{\text{Base}}$	Portion (20) Base (25) × Rate (?) The whole Portion and rate must relate to same piece of base.

Steps to solving problem

1. Set up the formula. $\text{Rate} = \dfrac{\text{Portion}}{\text{Base}}$

2. Calculate the base rate. $R = \dfrac{20}{25}$

   $R = 80\%$

8. Abby Biernet's original order:

The facts	Solving for?	Steps to take	Key points
60% of the order not in. 80 lobsters received.	Total order of lobsters.	Identify key elements. *Base:* ? *Rate:* .40 (100% − 60%) *Portion:* 80. Base $= \dfrac{\text{Portion}}{\text{Rate}}$	Portion (80) Base (?) × Rate (.40) 80 lobsters represent 40% of the order Portion and rate must relate to same piece of base.

Steps to solving problem

1. Set up the formula. $\text{Base} = \dfrac{\text{Portion}}{\text{Rate}}$

2. Calculate the base rate. $B = \dfrac{80}{.40}$ ← 80 lobsters is 40% of base.

   $B = 200$ lobsters

9. Dunkin' Donuts Company sales for 2010:

The facts	Solving for?	Steps to take	Key points
2009: $300,000 sales. *2010:* Sales up 40% from 2009.	Sales for 2010.	Identify key elements. *Base:* $300,000. *Rate:* 1.40. Old year 100% New year +40 140% *Portion:* ? Portion = Base × Rate.	2010 sales Portion (?) Base ($300,000) × Rate (1.40) 2009 sales When rate is greater than 100%, portion will be larger than base.

Steps to solving problem

1. Set up the formula.   Portion = Base × Rate
2. Calculate the portion. $P = \$300,000 \times 1.40$
                                          $P = \$420,000$

10. Percent decrease in Apple computer price:

The facts	Solving for?	Steps to take	Key points
Apple computer was $1,600; now, $1,200.	Percent decrease in price.	Identify key elements. *Base:* $1,600. *Rate:* ? *Portion:* $400 ($1,600 − $1,200). $Rate = \dfrac{Portion}{Base}$	Difference in price Portion ($400) Base ($1,600) × Rate (?) Original price

Steps to solving problem

1. Set up the formula. $Rate = \dfrac{Portion}{Base}$

2. Calculate the rate. $R = \dfrac{\$400}{\$1,600}$
                                          $R = 25\%$

11. Percent increase in Boston Celtics ticket:

Pat Greenhouse/Boston Globe/Landov

The facts	Solving for?	Steps to take	Key points
$14 ticket (old). $50 ticket (new).	Percent increase in price.	Identify key elements. *Base:* $14 *Rate:* ? *Portion:* $36 ($50 − $14) $Rate = \dfrac{Portion}{Base}$	Difference in price Portion ($36) Base ($14) × Rate (?) Original price When portion is greater than base, rate will be greater than 100%.

Steps to solving problem

1. Set up the formula. $Rate = \dfrac{Portion}{Base}$

2. Calculate the rate. $R = \dfrac{\$36}{\$14}$
                                          $R = 2.5714 = 257.14\%$

END-OF-CHAPTER PROBLEMS   connect™ (plus+)   www.mhhe.com/slater10e

Check figures for odd-numbered problems in Appendix C   Name _____ Date _____

DRILL PROBLEMS

Convert the following decimals to percents:

6–1. .66   **6–2.** .943   **6–3.** .8

6–4. 8.00   **6–5.** 3.561   **6–6.** 6.006

Convert the following percents to decimals:

6–7. 9%   **6–8.** 16%   **6–9.** $64\frac{3}{10}\%$

6–10. 75.9%   **6–11.** 119%   **6–12.** 89%

Convert the following fractions to percents (round to the nearest tenth percent as needed):

6–13. $\frac{1}{12}$ **6–14.** $\frac{1}{400}$

6–15. $\frac{7}{8}$ **6–16.** $\frac{11}{12}$

Convert the following to fractions and reduce to the lowest terms:

6–17. 4%   **6–18.** $18\frac{1}{2}\%$

6–19. $31\frac{2}{3}\%$ **6–20.** $61\frac{1}{2}\%$

6–21. 6.75%   **6–22.** 182%

Solve for the portion (round to the nearest hundredth as needed):

6–23. 7% of 150   **6–24.** 125% of 4,320   **6–25.** 25% of 410

6–26. 119% of 128.9   **6–27.** 17.4% of 900   **6–28.** 11.2% of 85

6–29. $12\frac{1}{2}\%$ of 919   **6–30.** 45% of 300

6–31. 18% of 90   **6–32.** 30% of 2,000

Solve for the base (round to the nearest hundredth as needed):

6–33. 170 is 120% of _____   **6–34.** 36 is .75% of _____

6–35. 50 is .5% of _____   **6–36.** 10,800 is 90% of _____

6–37. 800 is $4\frac{1}{2}\%$ of _____

Solve for rate (round to the nearest tenth percent as needed):

6–38. _____ of 80 is 50   **6–39.** _____ of 85 is 92

6–40. _____ of 250 is 65   **6–41.** 110 is _____ of 100

6–42. .09 is _____ of 2.25   **6–43.** 16 is _____ of 4

Solve the following problems. Be sure to show your work. Round to the nearest hundredth or hundredth percent as needed:

6–44. What is 180% of 310?

6–45. 66% of 90 is what?

6–46. 40% of what number is 20?

6–47. 770 is 70% of what number?

6–48. 4 is what percent of 90?

6–49. What percent of 150 is 60?

Complete the following table:

Product	Selling price 2008	Selling price 2009	Amount of decrease or increase	Percent change (to nearest hundredth percent as needed)
6–50. Hamilton watch	$650	$500		
6–51. College textbook	$100	$120		

WORD PROBLEMS (First of Four Sets)

6–52. At a local Dunkin' Donuts, a survey showed that out of 1,200 customers eating lunch, 240 ordered coffee with their meal. What percent of customers ordered coffee?

6–53. What percent of customers in Problem 6–52 did not order coffee?

6–54. In August 2008, gas was selling for $4.07 a gallon. The price of a gallon of regular unleaded dropped to $3.52 on September 11, 2008. What was the percent decrease? Round to the nearest hundredth percent.

6–55. Wally Chin, the owner of an ExxonMobil station, bought a used Ford pickup truck, paying $2,000 as a down payment. He still owes 80% of the selling price. What was the selling price of the truck?

6–56. Maria Fay bought 4 Dunlop tires at a local Goodyear store. The salesperson told her that her mileage would increase by 8%. Before this purchase, Maria was getting 24 mpg. What should her mileage be with the new tires to the nearest hundredth?

6–57. Jeff Rowe went to Best Buy and bought a Canon digital camera. The purchase price was $400. Jeff made a down payment of 40%. How much was Jeff's down payment?

6–58. Assume that in the year 2010, 800,000 people attended the Christmas Eve celebration at Walt Disney World. If in 2011, attendance for the Christmas Eve celebration is expected to increase by 35%. What is the total number of people expected at Walt Disney World for this event?

6–59. Pete Smith found in his attic a Woody Woodpecker watch in its original box. It had a price tag on it for $4.50. The watch was made in 1949. Pete brought the watch to an antiques dealer and sold it for $35. What was the percent of increase in price? Round to the nearest hundredth percent.

6–60. Christie's Auction sold a painting for $24,500. It charges all buyers a 15% premium of the final bid price. How much did the bidder pay Christie's?

WORD PROBLEMS (Second of Four Sets)

6–61. Out of 9,000 college students surveyed, 540 responded that they do not eat breakfast. What percent of the students do not eat breakfast?

6–62. What percent of college students in Problem 6–61 eat breakfast?

6–63. Alice Hall made a $3,000 down payment on a new Ford Explorer wagon. She still owes 90% of the selling price. What was the selling price of the wagon?

6–64. Rainfall for January in Fiji averages 12″ according to *World Travel Guide*. This year it rained 5% less. How many inches (to the nearest tenth) did it rain this year?

6–65. Jim and Alice Lange, employees at Walmart, have put themselves on a strict budget. Their goal at year's end is to buy a boat for $15,000 in cash. Their budget includes the following:

40% food and lodging   20% entertainment   10% educational

Jim earns $1,900 per month and Alice earns $2,400 per month. After one year, will Alice and Jim have enough cash to buy the boat?

6–66. The price of a Fossil watch dropped from $49.95 to $30.00. What was the percent decrease in price? Round to the nearest hundredth percent.

6–67. The Museum of Science in Boston estimated that 64% of all visitors came from within the state. On Saturday, 2,500 people attended the museum. How many attended the museum from out of state?

6–68. Staples pays George Nagovsky an annual salary of $36,000. Today, George's boss informs him that he will receive a $4,600 raise. What percent of George's old salary is the $4,600 raise? Round to the nearest tenth percent.

6–69. In 2010, a local Dairy Queen had $550,000 in sales. In 2011, Dairy Queen's sales were up 35%. What were Dairy Queen's sales in 2011?

6–70. Blue Valley College has 600 female students. This is 60% of the total student body. How many students attend Blue Valley College?

6–71. Dr. Grossman was reviewing his total accounts receivable. This month, credit customers paid $44,000, which represented 20% of all receivables (what customers owe) due. What was Dr. Grossman's total accounts receivable?

6–72. Massachusetts has a 5% sales tax. Timothy bought a Toro lawn mower and paid $20 sales tax. What was the cost of the lawn mower before the tax?

6–73. The price of an antique doll increased from $600 to $800. What was the percent of increase? Round to the nearest tenth percent.

6–74. A local Borders bookstore ordered 80 marketing books but received 60 books. What percent of the order was missing?

WORD PROBLEMS (Third of Four Sets)

6–75. At a Christie's auction, the auctioneer estimated that 40% of the audience was from within the state. Eight hundred people attended the auction. How many out-of-state people attended?

6–76. Due to increased mailing costs, the new rate will cost publishers $50 million; this is 12.5% more than they paid the previous year. How much did it cost publishers last year? Round to the nearest hundreds.

6–77. In 2011, Jim Goodman, an employee at Walgreens, earned $45,900, an increase of 17.5% over the previous year. What were Jim's earnings in 2010? Round to the nearest cent.

6–78. If the number of mortgage applications declined by 7% to 1,625,415, what had been the previous year's number of applications?

6–79. In 2011, the price of a business math text rose to $150. This is 8% more than the 2010 price. What was the old selling price? Round to the nearest cent.

6–80. Web Consultants, Inc., pays Alice Rose an annual salary of $48,000. Today, Alice's boss informs her that she will receive a $6,400 raise. What percent of Alice's old salary is the $6,400 raise? Round to the nearest tenth percent.

6–81. Earl Miller, a lawyer, charges Lee's Plumbing, his client, 25% of what he can collect for Lee from customers whose accounts are past due. The attorney also charges, in addition to the 25%, a flat fee of $50 per customer. This month, Earl collected $7,000 from 3 of Lee's past-due customers. What is the total fee due to Earl?

6–82. A local Petco ordered 100 dog calendars but received 60. What percent of the order was missing?

6–83. Blockbuster Video uses MasterCard. MasterCard charges $2\frac{1}{2}\%$ on net deposits (credit slips less returns). Blockbuster made a net deposit of $4,100 for charge sales. How much did MasterCard charge Blockbuster?

6–84. In 2010, Internet Access had $800,000 in sales. In 2011, Internet Access sales were up 45%. What are the sales for 2011?

WORD PROBLEMS (Fourth of Four Sets)

6–85. Saab Corporation raised the base price of its popular 900 series by $1,200 to $33,500. What was the percent increase? Round to the nearest tenth percent.

6–86. The sales tax rate is 8%. If Jim bought a new Buick and paid a sales tax of $1,920, what was the cost of the Buick before the tax?

6–87. Puthina Unge bought a new Compaq computer system on sale for $1,800. It was advertised as 30% off the regular price. What was the original price of the computer? Round to the nearest dollar.

6–88. John O'Sullivan has just completed his first year in business. His records show that he spent the following in advertising:

Newspaper $600   Radio $650   Yellow Pages $700   Local flyers $400

What percent of John's advertising was spent on the Yellow Pages? Round to the nearest hundredth percent.

6–89. Jay Miller sold his ski house at Attitash Mountain in New Hampshire for $35,000. This sale represented a loss of 15% off the original price. What was the original price Jay paid for the ski house? Round your answer to the nearest dollar.

6–90. Out of 4,000 colleges surveyed, 60% reported that SAT scores were not used as a high consideration in viewing their applications. How many schools view the SAT as important in screening applicants?

6–91. If refinishing your basement at a cost of $45,404 would add $18,270 to the resale value of your home, what percent of your cost is recouped? Round to the nearest percent.

6–92. A major airline laid off 4,000 pilots and flight attendants. If this was a 12.5% reduction in the workforce, what was the size of the workforce after the layoffs?

6–93. Assume 450,000 people line up on the streets to see the Macy's Thanksgiving Parade in 2010. If attendance is expected to increase 30%, what will be the number of people lined up on the street to see the 2011 parade?

CHALLENGE PROBLEMS

6–94. Kyle Drummond works as an auto mechanic. He just finished a job taking 3.25 hours of labor at $60 per hour. The parts he used totaled $55. If there is a 120% markup on parts, what was the customer charged?

6–95. A local Dunkin' Donuts shop reported that its sales have increased exactly 22% per year for the last 2 years. This year's sales were $82,500. What were Dunkin' Donuts sales 2 years ago? Round each year's sales to the nearest dollar.

SUMMARY PRACTICE TEST

Convert the following decimals to percents. *(p. 139)*

1. .921   **2.** .4   **3.** 15.88   **4.** 8.00

Convert the following percents to decimals. *(p. 140)*

5. 42%   **6.** 7.98%   **7.** 400%   **8.** $\frac{1}{4}$%

Convert the following fractions to percents. Round to the nearest tenth percent. *(p. 141)*

9. $\frac{1}{6}$ **10.** $\frac{1}{3}$

Convert the following percents to fractions and reduce to the lowest terms as needed. *(p. 141)*

11. $19\frac{3}{8}$%   **12.** 6.2%

Solve the following problems for portion, base, or rate:

13. An Arby's franchise has a net income before taxes of $900,000. The company's treasurer estimates that 40% of the company's net income will go to federal and state taxes. How much will the Arby's franchise have left? *(p. 144)*

14. Domino's projects a year-end net income of $699,000. The net income represents 30% of its annual sales. What are Domino's projected annual sales? *(p. 146)*

15. Target ordered 400 iPods. When Target received the order, 100 iPods were missing. What percent of the order did Target receive? *(p. 145)*

16. Matthew Song, an employee at Putnam Investments, receives an annual salary of $120,000. Today his boss informed him that he would receive a $3,200 raise. What percent of his old salary is the $3,200 raise? Round to the nearest hundredth percent. *(p. 145)*

17. The price of a Delta airline ticket from Los Angeles to Boston increased to $440. This is a 15% increase. What was the old fare? Round to the nearest cent. *(p. 146)*

18. Scupper Grace earns a gross pay of $900 per week at Office Depot. Scupper's payroll deductions are 29%. What is Scupper's take-home pay? *(p. 144)*

19. Mia Wong is reviewing the total accounts receivable of Wong's department store. Credit customers paid $90,000 this month. This represents 60% of all receivables due. What is Mia's total accounts receivable? *(p. 146)*

LOWDOWN

What You Need to Know About Your Credit Score

It's the key to many of life's major purchases.

BY JESSICA ANDERSON

1. LEARN THE COMBINATION.

The three-digit number that is your credit score predicts how likely you are to repay a loan, based on information in your credit report. The two major criteria, which account for up to two-thirds of your score, are your payment history and your outstanding debt. You should pay at least the minimum amount due each month—on time. The amount of debt relative to your credit limit is your credit utilization; it's best to keep it below 25%. How long you've had credit counts, too, and authorized-user accounts can help you build credit even if you're not the one paying the bills. (FICO reversed an earlier decision to drop authorized-user accounts.) Among other factors affecting your score are the number of inquiries on your account and your mix of credit.

2. ALL CREDIT SCORES ARE NOT CREATED EQUAL. The FICO

score, which ranges from 300 to 850, is the only one you need to know. It's the basis for at least 75% of

mortgage decisions, and 90% of the largest banks rely on it. The credit-monitoring bureaus have created others, such as the Vantage-Score, but few lenders use them.

3. ONE SCORE, THREE VERSIONS.

You actually have three FICO scores, one with each of the major credit bureaus: Equifax, Experian and TransUnion. Lenders often contract exclusively with one bureau, which in turn will give them a price break when they buy scores. Ask your lender which bureau it uses—you could get a leg up. Mortgage lenders are the exception: They obtain all three scores and have to resolve the differences among them. The crudest method, says Craig Watts, public affairs director for FICO, is for a lender to kick out the top and bottom scores and consider only the middle number.

4. HOW TO GET A TWOFER. The

cheapest way to get your FICO score is to order one along with your request for

a free annual credit report from Equifax (go to www .annualcreditreport.com); it'll cost you $8. Your FICO score and credit report from Equifax and TransUnion are available at myFICO .com, but you'll pay $15.95 each. Of the three bureaus, Equifax is the only one that will sell you a credit report and FICO score from its main Web site ($15.95). For TransUnion FICO scores, go to www.transunioncs.com ($14.95). As of mid February, Experian had stopped selling FICO credit scores to consumers.

5. GARBAGE IN, GARBAGE OUT.

The credit bureaus are obligated to report correctly only what lenders report to them. So if an error affecting your score originates with your lender, complaining to the credit bureau

probably won't help and could be a waste of time— the bureaus typically have 30 to 45 days to respond to a complaint. If you think a mistake has been made, contact your lender immediately. And keep an eye on your credit report. An annual checkup using your free credit report should suffice, unless you're shopping for a large loan.

6. YOU CAN SCORE *TOO* HIGH.

A score of 820 to 830 could make you seem unprofitable, says John Ulzheimer, president of consumer education at Credit.com. "Culprits" are usually at least in their forties, with long credit histories and little or no outstanding debt. You won't be turned down, but you may not receive new offers. "The sweet spot is 750 to 800," says Ulzheimer. ■

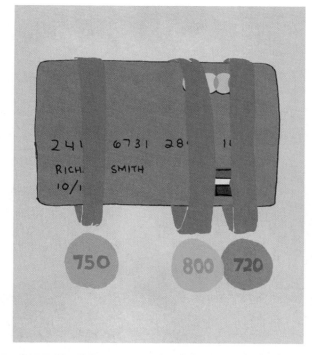

From Kiplinger's Personal Finance, August 2009, p. 69.

BUSINESS MATH ISSUE

FICO scores should be used less by banks in loan decisions.

1. List the key points of the article and information to support your position.
2. Write a group defense of your position using math calculations to support your view.

PROJECT A

Calculate the actual cost of a bathroom remodel that was not recovered. Prove your answer.

Payback Time

Selected remodeling projects with average estimated percentage of costs recovered when home is sold.

PROJECT	COST	AMOUNT RECOUPED
Deck addition (wood) Build a 16-by-20-foot deck, including a built-in bench, planter, stairs and rail system	$10,347	85.4%
Siding replacement Replace 1,250 square feet with new vinyl siding, including trim	$9,910	83.2%
Minor kitchen remodel Includes new laminated countertops and fronts for 30 linear feet of cabinetry, oven, cooktop, sink and faucet, flooring	$21,185	83%
Window replacement – wood Replace 10 3-by-5-foot double-hung windows with new insulated windows	$11,384	81.2%
Bathroom remodel Includes new tub and tiling, solid-surface counter and sink, recessed medicine cabinet, vinyl wallpaper	$15,789	78.3%
Basement remodel Includes a 5-by-8-foot bathroom and a wet bar with under-counter refrigerator	$59,435	75.1%
Two-story addition A 24-by-16-foot wing including family room with prefabricated fireplace and a bedroom with full bath	$139,297	73.9%
Master suite addition A 24-by-16-foot bedroom with walk-in closet and bathroom with shower and raised whirlpool tub	$98,863	69%
Sunroom addition Build a 200-square-foot room with 10 large skylights, casement windows with movable shades and quarry tile floor	$69,817	59.1%
Home office remodel Convert a 12-by-12-foot room with custom cabinetry including 20 linear feet of laminated desktop, computer workstation, wall storage and rewiring for computer, telephone and other electronics	$27,193	57%

Source: Remodeling 2007 Cost vs. Value Report. Cost data from HomeTech Information Systems; includes labor. Recoup values are based on a 2007 survey of 2,700 members of the National Association of Realtors. Data for 60 cities can be downloaded free from www.costvsvalue.com

PROJECT B

Calculate the percent change of stores for each chain as of 12/31/08. Round to nearest hundredth percent.

Slicing Away

Two of the three big pizza chains lost U.S. outlets last year; in contrast, burger giant McDonald's grew

Chain	Stores as of 12/31/08	Stores as of 12/31/07
Pizza Hut	6,103	6,144
Domino's	5,086*	5,155
Papa John's	2,792	2,760
McDonald's	13,918	13,862

*Nine-month figures as of Sept. 30, 2008   Sources: company reports

Internet Projects: See text Web site (www.mhhe.com/slater10e) and The Business Math Internet Resource Guide.

FIGURE   7.1

Bookstore invoice showing a
trade discount

Invoice No.: 5582

McGraw-Hill/Irwin Publishing Co.
1333 Burr Ridge Parkway
Burr Ridge, Illinois 60527

Date: July 8, 2010
Ship: Two-day UPS
Terms: 2/10, n/30

Sold to: North Shore Community College Bookstore
1 Ferncroft Road
Danvers, MA 01923

Description	Unit list price	Total amount
50 Financial Management—Block/Hirt	$95.66	$4,783.00
10 Introduction to Business—Nichols	89.50	895.00
Total List Price		$5,678.00
Less: Trade Discount 25%		−1,419.50
Net Price		$4,258.50
Plus: Prepaid Shipping Charge		125.00
Total Invoice Amount		$4,383.50

---

amount is given in percent. This is the **trade discount rate,** which is a percent off the list price that retailers can deduct. The following formula for calculating a trade discount amount gives the numbers from the Figure 7.1 invoice in parentheses:

TRADE DISCOUNT AMOUNT FORMULA

Trade discount amount = List price × Trade discount rate
($1,419.50)   ($5,678.00)   (25%)

The price that the retailer (bookstore) pays the manufacturer (publisher) or wholesaler is the **net price.** The following formula for calculating the net price gives the numbers from the Figure 7.1 invoice in parentheses:

NET PRICE FORMULA

Net price   =   List price   −   Trade discount amount
($4,258.50)   ($5,678.00)   ($1,419.50)

Frequently, manufacturers and wholesalers issue catalogs to retailers containing list prices of the seller's merchandise and the available trade discounts. To reduce printing costs when prices change, these sellers usually update the catalogs with new *discount sheets.* The discount sheet also gives the seller the flexibility of offering different trade discounts to different classes of retailers. For example, some retailers buy in quantity and service the products. They may receive a larger discount than the retailer who wants the manufacturer to service the products. Sellers may also give discounts to meet a competitor's price, to attract new retailers, and to reward the retailers who buy product-line products. Sometimes the ability of the retailer to negotiate with the seller determines the trade discount amount.

Retailers cannot take trade discounts on freight, returned goods, sales tax, and so on. Trade discounts may be single discounts or a chain of discounts. Before we discuss single trade discounts, let's study freight terms.

Freight Terms

If you think in 2007 Federal Express had the largest market share you would be wrong. The *Wall Street Journal* clip "Thin Slice" at left in margin shows the leader is UPS with 49.6% of the express package market.

The most common **freight terms** are *FOB shipping point* and *FOB destination.* These terms determine how the freight will be paid. The key words in the terms are *shipping point* and *destination.*

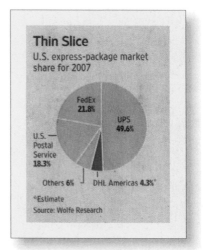

Thin Slice

U.S. express-package market share for 2007

FedEx 21.8%
UPS 49.6%
U.S. Postal Service 18.3%
Others 6%
DHL Americas 4.3%*

*Estimate
Source: Wolfe Research

Wall Street Journal © 2008

Frances Roberts/Alamy

FOB shipping point means free on board at shipping point; that is, the buyer pays the freight cost of getting the goods to the place of business.

For example, assume that IBM in San Diego bought goods from Argo Suppliers in Boston. Argo ships the goods FOB Boston by plane. IBM takes title to the goods when the aircraft in Boston receives the goods, so IBM pays the freight from Boston to San Diego. Frequently, the seller (Argo) prepays the freight and adds the amount to the buyer's (IBM) invoice. When paying the invoice, the buyer takes the cash discount off the net price and adds the freight cost. FOB shipping point can be illustrated as follows:

FOB shipping point (Boston)

LO 2

FOB destination means the seller pays the freight cost until it reaches the buyer's place of business. If Argo ships its goods to IBM FOB destination or FOB San Diego, the title to the goods remains with Argo. Then it is Argo's responsibility to pay the freight from Boston to IBM's place of business in San Diego. FOB destination can be illustrated as follows:

FOB destination (San Diego)

The following *Wall Street Journal* clipping "Stung by Soaring Transport Costs, Factories Bring Jobs Home Again" reveals how the costs of shipping have risen.

GLOBAL

OIL SHOCKER

Stung by Soaring Transport Costs, Factories Bring Jobs Home Again

BY TIMOTHY AEPPEL

The rising cost of shipping everything from industrial-pump parts to lawn-mower batteries to living-room sofas is forcing some manufacturers to bring production back to North America and freeze plans to send even more work overseas.

"My cost of getting a shipping container here from China just keeps going up—and I don't see any end in sight," says Claude Hayes, president of the retail heating division at DESA LLC. He says that cost has jumped about 15%, to about $5,300, since January and is set to increase again next month to $5,600.

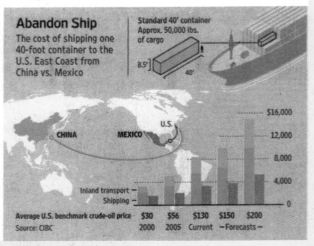

Wall Street Journal © 2008

Now you are ready for the discussion on single trade discounts.

Single Trade Discount

In the introduction to this unit, we showed how to use the trade discount amount formula and the net price formula to calculate the McGraw-Hill/Irwin Publishing Company textbook sale to the North Shore Community College Bookstore. Since McGraw-Hill/Irwin gave the bookstore only one trade discount, it is a **single trade discount.** In the following word problem, we use the formulas to solve another example of a single trade discount. Again, we will use a blueprint aid to help dissect and solve the word problem.

The Word Problem The list price of a Macintosh computer is $2,700. The manufacturer offers dealers a 40% trade discount. What are the trade discount amount and the net price?

The facts	Solving for?	Steps to take	Key points
List price: $2,700. Trade discount rate: 40%.	Trade discount amount. Net price.	Trade discount amount = List price × Trade discount rate. Net price = List price − Trade discount amount.	Trade discount amount — Portion (?) Base ($2,700) × Rate (.40) — List price Trade discount rate

Steps to solving problem

1. Calculate the trade discount amount. $2,700 × .40 = $1,080

2. Calculate the net price. $2,700 − $1,080 = **$1,620**

Now let's learn how to check the dealers' net price of $1,620 with an alternate procedure using a complement.

How to Calculate the Net Price Using Complement of Trade Discount Rate

The **complement** of a trade discount rate is the difference between the discount rate and 100%. The following steps show you how to use the complement of a trade discount rate:

CALCULATING NET PRICE USING COMPLEMENT OF TRADE DISCOUNT RATE
Step 1. To find the complement, subtract the single discount rate from 100%.
Step 2. Multiply the list price times the complement (from step 1).

Think of a complement of any given percent (decimal) as the result of subtracting the percent from 100%.

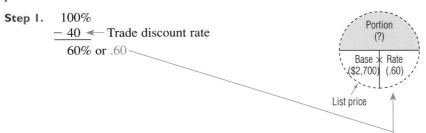

Step 1.   100%
            − 40 ← Trade discount rate
            60% or .60

The complement means that we are spending 60 cents per dollar because we save 40 cents per dollar. Since we planned to spend $2,700, we multiply .60 by $2,700 to get a net price of $1,620.

Step 2. **$1,620** = $2,700 × .60

Note how the portion ($1,620) and rate (.60) relate to the same piece of the base ($2,700). The portion ($1,620) is smaller than the base, since the rate is less than 100%.

Be aware that some people prefer to use the trade discount amount formula and the net price formula to find the net price. Other people prefer to use the complement of the trade discount rate to find the net price. The result is always the same.

Finding List Price When You Know Net Price and Trade Discount Rate

LO 3

The following formula has many useful applications:

CALCULATING LIST PRICE WHEN NET PRICE AND TRADE DISCOUNT RATE ARE KNOWN
List price = $\dfrac{\text{Net price}}{\text{Complement of trade discount rate}}$

Next, let's see how to dissect and solve a word problem calculating list price.

The Word Problem A Macintosh computer has a $1,620 net price and a 40% trade discount. What is its list price?

The facts	Solving for?	Steps to take	Key points
Net price: $1,620. Trade discount rate: 40%.	List price.	List price = $\dfrac{\text{Net price}}{\text{Complement of trade discount rate}}$	Net price — Portion ($1,620) — Base (?) × Rate (.60) — List price — 100% −40%

Steps to solving problem

1. Calculate the complement of the trade discount.

    $\begin{array}{r} 100\% \\ -\ 40 \\ \hline 60\% = .60 \end{array}$

2. Calculate the list price.

    $\dfrac{\$1,620}{.60} = \boxed{\$2,700}$

Note that the portion ($1,620) and rate (.60) relate to the same piece of the base.

Let's return to the McGraw-Hill/Irwin invoice in Figure 7.1 (p. 173) and calculate the list price using the formula for finding list price when net price and trade discount rate are known. The net price of the textbooks is $4,258.50. The complement of the trade discount rate is 100% − 25% = 75% = .75. Dividing the net price $4,258.50 by the complement .75 equals $5,678.00, the list price shown in the McGraw-Hill/Irwin invoice. We can show this as follows:

$$\frac{\$4,258.50}{.75} = \$5,678.00, \text{ the list price}$$

Chain Discounts

LO 4

Frequently, manufacturers want greater flexibility in setting trade discounts for different classes of customers, seasonal trends, promotional activities, and so on. To gain this flexibility, some sellers give **chain** or **series discounts**—trade discounts in a series of two or more successive discounts.

Sellers list chain discounts as a group, for example, 20/15/10. Let's look at how Mick Company arrives at the net price of office equipment with a 20/15/10 chain discount.

EXAMPLE   The list price of the office equipment is $15,000. The chain discount is 20/15/10. The long way to calculate the net price is as follows:

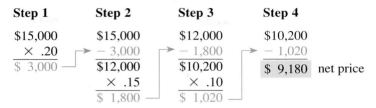

Step 1	Step 2	Step 3	Step 4
$15,000	$15,000	$12,000	$10,200
× .20	− 3,000	− 1,800	− 1,020
$ 3,000	$12,000	$10,200	$ 9,180 net price
	× .15	× .10	
	$ 1,800	$ 1,020	

Never add the 20/15/10 together

Note how we multiply the percent (in decimal) times the new balance after we subtract the previous trade discount amount. For example, in Step 3, we change the last discount, 10%, to decimal form and multiply times $10,200. Remember that each percent is multiplied by a successively *smaller* base. You could write the 20/15/10 discount rate in any order and still arrive at the same net price. Thus, you would get the $9,180 net price if the discount were 10/15/20 or 15/20/10. However, sellers usually give the larger discounts first. *Never try to shorten this step process by adding the discounts.* Your net price will be incorrect because, when done properly, each percent is calculated on a different base.

Net Price Equivalent Rate

In the example above, you could also find the $9,180 net price with the **net price equivalent rate**—a shortcut method. Let's see how to use this rate to calculate net price.

CALCULATING NET PRICE USING NET PRICE EQUIVALENT RATE
Step 1. Subtract each chain discount rate from 100% (find the complement) and convert each percent to a decimal.
Step 2. Multiply the decimals. Do not round off decimals, since this number is the net price equivalent rate.
Step 3. Multiply the list price times the net price equivalent rate (Step 2).

The following word problem with its blueprint aid illustrates how to use the net price equivalent rate method.

The Word Problem   The list price of office equipment is $15,000. The chain discount is 20/15/10. What is the net price?

The facts	Solving for?	Steps to take	Key points
List price: $15,000. Chain discount: 20/15/10	Net price.	Net price equivalent rate. Net price = List price 　　　　× Net price 　　　　equivalent rate.	Do not round net price equivalent rate.

Steps to solving problem

1. Calculate the complement of each rate and convert each percent to a decimal.

100%	100%	100%
− 20	− 15	− 10
80%	85%	90%
↓	↓	↓
.8	.85	.9

2. Calculate the net price equivalent rate. (Do not round.)

   .8 × .85 × .9 = .612   Net price equivalent rate
   For each $1, you are spending about 61 cents.

3. Calculate the net price (actual cost to buyer).

   $15,000 × .612 = **$9,180**

Next we see how to calculate the trade discount amount with a simpler method.

In the previous word problem, we could calculate the trade discount amount as follows:

$15,000 ← List price
− 9,180 ← Net price
$ 5,820 ← Trade discount amount

Single Equivalent Discount Rate

You can use another method to find the trade discount by using the **single equivalent discount rate.**

CALCULATING TRADE DISCOUNT AMOUNT USING SINGLE EQUIVALENT DISCOUNT RATE
Step 1. Subtract the net price equivalent rate from 1. This is the single equivalent discount rate.
Step 2. Multiply the list price times the single equivalent discount rate. This is the trade discount amount.

Let's now do the calculations.

Step 1.   1.000 ← If you are using a calculator, just press 1.
      − .612
       .388 ← This is the single equivalent discount rate.

Step 2. $15,000 × .388 = **$5,820** → This is the trade discount amount.

Remember that when we use the net price equivalent rate, the buyer of the office equipment pays $.612 on each $1 of list price. Now with the single equivalent discount rate, we can say that the buyer saves $.388 on each $1 of list price. The .388 is the single equivalent discount rate for the 20/15/10 chain discount. Note how we use the .388 single equivalent discount rate as if it were the only discount.

It's time to try the Practice Quiz.

LU 7–1   **PRACTICE QUIZ**

Complete this **Practice Quiz** to see how you are doing.[1]

1. The list price of a dining room set with a 40% trade discount is $12,000. What are the trade discount amount and net price (use complement method for net price)?
2. The net price of a video system with a 30% trade discount is $1,400. What is the list price?
3. Lamps Outlet bought a shipment of lamps from a wholesaler. The total list price was $12,000 with a 5/10/25 chain discount. Calculate the net price and trade discount amount. (Use the net price equivalent rate and single equivalent discount rate in your calculation.)

 Solutions with Step-by-Step Help on DVD

✓ **Solutions**

1. Dining room set trade discount amount and net price:

The facts	Solving for?	Steps to take	Key points
List price: $12,000. Trade discount rate: 40%.	Trade discount amount. Net price.	Trade discount amount = List price × Trade discount rate. Net price = List price × Complement of trade discount rate.	Trade discount amount Portion (?) Base ($12,000) × Rate (.40) List price Trade discount rate

[1]For all three problems we will show blueprint aids. You might want to draw them on scrap paper.

Steps to solving problem

1. Calculate the trade discount. $12,000 × .40 = **$4,800** Trade discount amount

2. Calculate the net price. $12,000 × .60 = **$7,200** (100% − 40% = 60%)

2.   Video system list price:

The facts	Solving for?	Steps to take	Key points
Net price: $1,400. Trade discount rate: 30%.	List price.	List price = $\dfrac{\text{Net price}}{\text{Complement of trade discount}}$	Net price Portion ($1,400) Base × Rate (?) (.70) List price 100% −30%

Steps to solving problem

1. Calculate the complement of trade discount.   100%
− 30
70% = .70

2. Calculate the list price. $\dfrac{\$1,400}{.70}$ = **$2,000**

3.   Lamps Outlet's net price and trade discount amount:

The facts	Solving for?	Steps to take	Key points
List price: $12,000. Chain discount: 5/10/25.	Net price. Trade discount amount.	Net price = List price × Net price equivalent rate. Trade discount amount = List price × Single equivalent discount rate.	Do not round off net price equivalent rate or single equivalent discount rate.

Steps to solving problem

1. Calculate the complement of each chain discount.

   100%   100%   100%
− 5   − 10   − 25
95%   90%   75%

2. Calculate the net price equivalent rate.   .95 × .90 × .75 = .64125

3. Calculate the net price. $12,000 × .64125 = **$7,695**

4. Calculate the single equivalent discount rate.   1.00000
− .64125
.35875

5. Calculate the trade discount amount. $12,000 × .35875 = **$4,305**

LU 7–1a   EXTRA PRACTICE QUIZ WITH WORKED-OUT SOLUTIONS

Need more practice? Try this **Extra Practice Quiz** (check figures in Chapter Organizer, p. 191). Worked-out Solutions can be found in Appendix B at end of text.

1. The list price of a dining room set with a 30% trade discount is $16,000. What are the trade discount amount and net price (use complement method for net price)?

2. The net price of a video system with a 20% trade discount is $400. What is the list price?

3. Lamps Outlet bought a shipment of lamps from a wholesaler. The total list price was $14,000 with a 4/8/20 chain discount. Calculate the net price and trade discount amount. (Use the net price equivalent rate and single equivalent discount rate in your calculation.)

Learning Unit 7–2: Cash Discounts, Credit Terms, and Partial Payments

LO 1

To introduce this learning unit, we will use the New Hampshire Propane Company invoice that follows. The invoice shows that if you pay your bill early, you will receive a 19-cent discount. Every penny counts.

Sean Clayton/The Image Works

New Hampshire Propane Company				
Date	**Description**	**Qty.**	**Price**	**Total**
	Previous Balance			**$0.00**
06/24/10	PROPANE	3.60	$3.40	$12.24

Invoice No. 004433L	**Totals this invoice:** $12.24
	AMOUNT DUE: $12.24
Invoice Date 6/26/10	**Prompt Pay Discount:** $0.19
	Net Amount Due if RECEIVED by 07/10/10: $12.05

Due Date	7/26/10

Now let's study cash discounts.

Cash Discounts

In the New Hampshire Propane Company invoice, we receive a cash discount of 19 cents. This amount is determined by the **terms of the sale,** which can include the credit period, cash discount, discount period, and freight terms.

Buyers can often benefit from buying on credit. The time period that sellers give buyers to pay their invoices is the **credit period.** Frequently, buyers can sell the goods bought during this credit period. Then, at the end of the credit period, buyers can pay sellers with the funds from the sales of the goods. When buyers can do this, they can use the consumer's money to pay the invoice instead of their money.

> A cash discount is for prompt payment. A trade discount is not.

Sellers can also offer a cash discount, or reduction from the invoice price, if buyers pay the invoice within a specified time. This time period is the **discount period,** which is part of the total credit period. Sellers offer this cash discount because they can use the dollars to better advantage sooner than later. Buyers who are not short of cash like cash discounts because the goods will cost them less and, as a result, provide an opportunity for larger profits.

> Trade discounts should be taken before cash discounts.

Remember that buyers do not take cash discounts on freight, returned goods, sales tax, and trade discounts. Buyers take cash discounts on the *net price* of the invoice. Before we discuss how to calculate cash discounts, let's look at some aids that will help you calculate credit **due dates** and **end of credit periods.**

Aids in Calculating Credit Due Dates

Sellers usually give credit for 30, 60, or 90 days. Not all months of the year have 30 days. So you must count the credit days from the date of the invoice. The trick is to remember the number of days in each month. You can choose one of the following three options to help you do this.

> Years divisible by 4 are leap years. Leap years occur in 2012 and 2016.

Option 1: Days-in-a-Month Rule You may already know this rule. Remember that every 4 years is a leap year.

> Thirty days has September, April, June, and November; all the rest have 31 except February has 28, and 29 in leap years.

Option 2: Knuckle Months Some people like to use the knuckles on their hands to remember which months have 30 or 31 days. Note in the following diagram that each knuckle represents a month with 31 days. The short months are in between the knuckles.

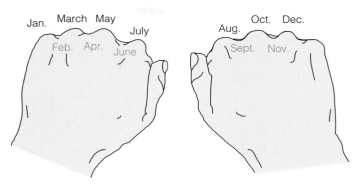

31 days: Jan., March, May, July, Aug., Oct., Dec.

Option 3: Days-in-a-Year Calendar The days-in-a-year calendar (excluding leap year) is another tool to help you calculate dates for discount and credit periods (Table 7.1, p. 182). For example, let's use Table 7.1 to calculate 90 days from August 12.

EXAMPLE   By Table 7.1: August 12 =   224 days
                                      + 90
                                      ─────
                                       314 days

Search for day 314 in Table 7.1. You will find that day 314 is November 10. In this example, we stayed within the same year. Now let's try an example in which we overlap from year to year.

EXAMPLE   What date is 80 days after December 5?
    Table 7.1 shows that December 5 is 339 days from the beginning of the year. Subtracting 339 from 365 (the end of the year) tells us that we have used up 26 days by the end of the year. This leaves 54 days in the new year. Go back in the table and start with the beginning of the year and search for 54 (80 − 26) days. The 54th day is February 23.

By table	**Without use of table**
365 days in year	December 31
− 339 days until December 5	− December 5
26 days used in year	26
	+ 31 days in January
80 days from December 5	57
− 26 days used in year	+ 23 due date (February 23)
54 days in new year or	80 total days
February 23	

When you know how to calculate credit due dates, you can understand the common business terms sellers offer buyers involving discounts and credit periods. Remember that discount and credit terms vary from one seller to another.

Common Credit Terms Offered by Sellers

The common credit terms sellers offer buyers include *ordinary dating, receipt of goods (ROG),* and *end of month (EOM).* In this section we examine these credit terms. To determine the due dates, we used the exact days-in-a-year calendar (Table 7.1, p. 182).

Ordinary Dating

Today, businesses frequently use the **ordinary dating** method. It gives the buyer a cash discount period that begins with the invoice date. The credit terms of two common ordinary dating methods are 2/10, n/30 and 2/10, 1/15, n/30.

2/10, n/30 Ordinary Dating Method The 2/10, n/30 is read as "two ten, net thirty." Buyers can take a 2% cash discount off the gross amount of the invoice if they pay the bill within 10 days from the invoice date. If buyers miss the discount period, the net amount—without a

TABLE	7.1	Exact days-in-a-year calendar (excluding leap year)*

Day of month	31 Jan.	28 Feb.	31 Mar.	30 Apr.	31 May	30 June	31 July	31 Aug.	30 Sept.	31 Oct.	30 Nov.	31 Dec.
1	1	32	60	91	121	152	182	213	244	274	305	335
2	2	33	61	92	122	153	183	214	245	275	306	336
3	3	34	62	93	123	154	184	215	246	276	307	337
4	4	35	63	94	124	155	185	216	247	277	308	338
5	5	36	64	95	125	156	186	217	248	278	309	339
6	6	37	65	96	126	157	187	218	249	279	310	340
7	7	38	66	97	127	158	188	219	250	280	311	341
8	8	39	67	98	128	159	189	220	251	281	312	342
9	9	40	68	99	129	160	190	221	252	282	313	343
10	10	41	69	100	130	161	191	222	253	283	314	344
11	11	42	70	101	131	162	192	223	254	284	315	345
12	12	43	71	102	132	163	193	224	255	285	316	346
13	13	44	72	103	133	164	194	225	256	286	317	347
14	14	45	73	104	134	165	195	226	257	287	318	348
15	15	46	74	105	135	166	196	227	258	288	319	349
16	16	47	75	106	136	167	197	228	259	289	320	350
17	17	48	76	107	137	168	198	229	260	290	321	351
18	18	49	77	108	138	169	199	230	261	291	322	352
19	19	50	78	109	139	170	200	231	262	292	323	353
20	20	51	79	110	140	171	201	232	263	293	324	354
21	21	52	80	111	141	172	202	233	264	294	325	355
22	22	53	81	112	142	173	203	234	265	295	326	356
23	23	54	82	113	143	174	204	235	266	296	327	357
24	24	55	83	114	144	175	205	236	267	297	328	358
25	25	56	84	115	145	176	206	237	268	298	329	359
26	26	57	85	116	146	177	207	238	269	299	330	360
27	27	58	86	117	147	178	208	239	270	300	331	361
28	28	59	87	118	148	179	209	240	271	301	332	362
29	29	—	88	119	149	180	210	241	272	302	333	363
30	30	—	89	120	150	181	211	242	273	303	334	364
31	31	—	90	—	151	—	212	243	—	304	—	365

*Often referred to as a Julian calendar.

discount—is due between day 11 and day 30. *Freight, returned goods, sales tax, and trade discounts must be subtracted from the gross before calculating a cash discount.*

EXAMPLE $400 invoice dated July 5: terms 2/10, n/30; no freight; paid on July 11.

Step 1. Calculate end of 2% discount period:

July   5 date of invoice
+ 10 days

July 15 end of 2% discount period

Step 2. Calculate end of credit period:

July 5 by Table 7.1

186 days

+ 30

216 days

Search in Table 7.1 for 216 → August 4 → end of credit period

Step 3. Calculate payment on July 11:

.02 × $400 = $8 cash discount

$400 − $8 = $392 paid

> *Note:* A 2% cash discount means that you save 2 cents on the dollar and pay 98 cents on the dollar. Thus, $.98 × $400 = $392.

The following time line illustrates the 2/10, n/30 ordinary dating method beginning and ending dates of the above example:

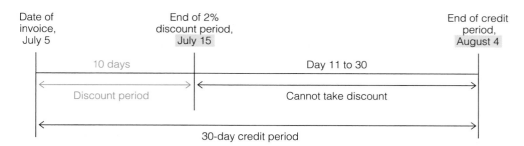

2/10, 1/15, n/30 Ordinary Dating Method The 2/10, 1/15, n/30 is read "two ten, one fifteen, net thirty." The seller will give buyers a 2% (2 cents on the dollar) cash discount if they pay within 10 days of the invoice date. If buyers pay between day 11 and day 15 from the date of the invoice, they can save 1 cent on the dollar. If buyers do not pay on day 15, the net or full amount is due 30 days from the invoice date.

EXAMPLE $600 invoice dated May 8; $100 of freight included in invoice price; paid on May 22. Terms 2/10, 1/15, n/30.

Step 1. Calculate the end of the 2% discount period:

May   8 date of invoice

+ 10 days

May 18 end of 2% discount period

Step 2. Calculate end of 1% discount period:

May 18 end of 2% discount period

+   5 days

May 23 end of 1% discount period

Step 3. Calculate end of credit period:

May 8 by Table 7.1

128 days

+ 30

158 days

Search in Table 7.1 for 158 → June 7 → end of credit period

Step 4. Calculate payment on May 22 (14 days after date of invoice):

$600 invoice

− 100 freight

$500

× .01

$5.00

$500 − $5.00 + $100 freight = $595

> A 1% discount means we pay $.99 on the dollar or $500 × $.99 = $495 + $100 freight = $595.
>
> *Note:* Freight is added back since no cash discount is taken on freight.

The following time line illustrates the 2/10, 1/15, n/30 ordinary dating method beginning and ending dates of the above example:

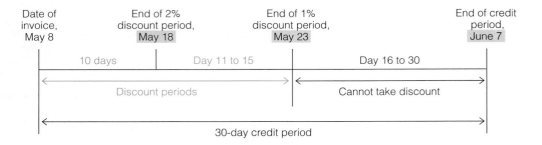

Receipt of Goods (ROG)

3/10, n/30 ROG With the **receipt of goods (ROG),** the cash discount period begins when buyer receives goods, *not* the invoice date. Industry often uses the ROG terms when buyers cannot expect delivery until a long time after they place the order. Buyers can take a 3% discount within 10 days *after* receipt of goods. Full amount is due between day 11 and day 30 if cash discount period is missed.

EXAMPLE $900 invoice dated May 9; no freight or returned goods; the goods were received on July 8; terms 3/10, n/30 ROG; payment made on July 20.

Step 1. Calculate the end of the 3% discount period:

> July   8 date goods arrive
> $\underline{+\ 10}$ days
> July 18 end of 3% discount period

Step 2. Calculate the end of the credit period:

Search in Table 7.1 for 219 → August 7 → end of credit period

Step 3. Calculate payment on July 20:

Missed discount period and paid net or full amount of $900.

The following time line illustrates 3/10, n/30 ROG beginning and ending dates of the above example:

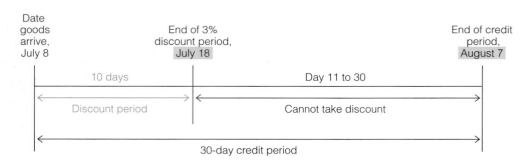

LU 7–2a EXTRA PRACTICE QUIZ WITH WORKED-OUT SOLUTIONS

Need more practice? Try this **Extra Practice Quiz** (check figures in Chapter Organizer, p. 191). Worked-out Solutions can be found in Appendix B at end of text.

Complete the following table:

	Date of invoice	Date goods received	Terms	Last day of discount period*	End of credit period
1.	July 8		2/10, n/30		
2.	February 24	June 12	3/10, n/30 ROG		
3.	May 12		4/10, 1/30, n/60		
4.	April 14		2/10 EOM		
5.	April 27		2/10 EOM		

*If more than one discount, assume date of last discount.

6. Metro Corporation sent Vasko Corporation an invoice for equipment with a $9,000 list price. Metro dated the invoice June 29. Terms were 2/10 EOM. Vasko receives a 30% trade discount and paid the discount on August 9. What was the cost of equipment for Vasko?

7. Complete amount to be credited and balance outstanding:

Amount of invoice: $700
Terms: 2/10, 1/15, n/30
Date of invoice: September 28
Paid October 3: $600

CHAPTER ORGANIZER AND REFERENCE GUIDE

Topic	Key point, procedure, formula	Example(s) to illustrate situation
Trade discount amount, p. 173	$\text{Trade discount amount} = \text{List price} \times \text{Trade discount rate}$	$600 list price 30% trade discount rate Trade discount amount = $600 × .30 = $180
Calculating net price, p. 173	$\text{Net price} = \text{List price} - \text{Trade discount amount}$ or $\text{List price} \times \text{Complement of trade discount price}$	$600 list price 30% trade discount rate Net price = $600 × .70 = $420 　1.00 　− .30 　　.70
Freight, p. 174	FOB shipping point—buyer pays freight. FOB destination—seller pays freight.	Moose Company of New York sells equipment to Agee Company of Oregon. Terms of shipping are FOB New York. Agee pays cost of freight since terms are FOB shipping point.
Calculating list price when net price and trade discount rate are known, p. 176	$\text{List price} = \dfrac{\text{Net price}}{\text{Complement of trade discount rate}}$	40% trade discount rate Net price, $120 $\dfrac{\$120}{.60} = \$200$ list price (1.00 − .40)

(continues)

CHAPTER ORGANIZER AND REFERENCE GUIDE

Topic	Key point, procedure, formula	Example(s) to illustrate situation
Chain discounts, p. 176	Successively lower base.	5/10 on a $100 list item $\begin{array}{ll} \$\ 100 & \$\ 95 \\ \times\ .05 & \times\ .10 \\ \hline \$\ 5.00 & \$9.50 \end{array}$ (running balance) $\begin{array}{l} \$95.00 \\ -\ 9.50 \\ \hline \boxed{\$85.50} \end{array}$ net price
Net price equivalent rate, p. 177	$\dfrac{\text{Actual cost}}{\text{to buyer}} = \dfrac{\text{List}}{\text{price}} \times \dfrac{\text{Net price}}{\text{equivalent rate}}$ Take complement of each chain discount and multiply—do not round. $\dfrac{\text{Trade discount}}{\text{amount}} = \dfrac{\text{List}}{\text{price}} - \dfrac{\text{Actual cost}}{\text{to buyer}}$	Given: 5/10 on $1,000 list price Take complement: $.95 \times .90 = .855$ (net price equivalent) $\$1,000 \times .855 = \boxed{\$855}$ (actual cost or net price) $\begin{array}{l} \$1,000 \\ -\ \ \ 855 \\ \hline \boxed{\$\ \ 145} \end{array}$ trade discount amount
Single equivalent discount rate, p. 178	$\dfrac{\text{Trade discount}}{\text{amount}} = \dfrac{\text{List}}{\text{price}} \times \dfrac{1-\text{Net price}}{\text{equivalent rate}}$	See preceding example for facts: $1 - .855 = .145$ $.145 \times \$1,000 = \boxed{\$145}$
Cash discounts, p. 180	Cash discounts, due to prompt payment, are not taken on freight, returns, etc.	Gross $1,000 (includes freight) Freight $25 Terms, 2/10, n/30 Returns $25 Purchased: Sept. 9; paid Sept. 15 Cash discount = $950 × .02 = $\boxed{\$19}$
Calculating due dates, p. 180	*Option 1:* Thirty days has September, April, June, and November; all the rest have 31 except February has 28, and 29 in leap years. *Option 2:* Knuckles—31-day month; in between knuckles are short months. *Option 3:* Days-in-a-year table.	Invoice $500 on March 5; terms 2/10, n/30 March 5 *End of discount* + 10 *period:* ———————→ March 15 *End of credit* March 5 = 64 days *period by* + 30 *Table 7.1:* ———————→ 94 days Search in Table 7.1 April 4
Common terms of sale **a. Ordinary dating, p. 181**	Discount period begins from date of invoice. Credit period ends 20 days from the end of the discount period unless otherwise stipulated; example, 2/10, n/60—the credit period ends 50 days from end of discount period.	Invoice $600 (freight of $100 included in price) dated March 8; payment on March 16; 3/10, n/30. March 8 *End of discount* + 10 *period:* ———————→ March 18 *End of credit* March 8 = 67 days *period by* + 30 *Table 7.1:* ———————→ 97 days Search in Table 7.1 April 7 *If paid on March 16:* $.97 \times \$500 = \$485$ $\underline{+\ 100}$ freight $\boxed{\$585}$

(continues)

CHAPTER ORGANIZER AND REFERENCE GUIDE

Topic	Key point, procedure, formula	Example(s) to illustrate situation
b. Receipt of goods (ROG), p. 184	Discount period begins when goods are received. Credit period ends 20 days from end of discount period.	4/10, n/30, ROG. $600 invoice; no freight; dated August 5; goods received October 2, payment made October 20. $\begin{aligned} &\text{October} \quad 2 \\ &\text{End of discount} \qquad + \ 10 \\ &\text{period:} \longrightarrow \boxed{\text{October 12}} \end{aligned}$ End of October 2 = 275 credit period + 30 by Table 7.1: $\longrightarrow$ 305 $\downarrow$ Search in Table 7.1 $\boxed{\text{November 1}}$ *Payment on October 20:* No discount, pay $\boxed{\$600}$
c. End of month (EOM), p. 185	On or before 25th of the month, discount period is 10 days after month following sale. After 25th of the month, an additional month is gained.	$1,000 invoice dated May 12; no freight or returns; terms 2/10 EOM. End of discount period $\rightarrow$ $\boxed{\text{June 10}}$ End of credit period $\rightarrow$ $\boxed{\text{June 30}}$
Partial payments, p. 187	$\text{Amount credited} = \dfrac{\text{Partial payment}}{1 - \text{Discount rate}}$	$200 invoice, terms 2/10, n/30, dated March 2, paid $100 on March 5. $\dfrac{\$100}{1 - .02} = \dfrac{\$100}{.98} = \boxed{\$102.04}$

KEY TERMS	Cash discount, *p. 172*
	Chain discounts, *p. 176*
	Complement, *p. 175*
	Credit period, *p. 180*
	Discount period, *p. 180*
	Due dates, *p. 180*
	End of credit period, *p. 180*
	End of month (EOM), *p. 185*
	FOB destination, *p. 174*
		FOB shipping point, *p. 174*
		Freight terms, *p. 173*
		Invoice, *p. 172*
		List price, *p. 172*
		Net price, *p. 173*
		Net price equivalent rate,
		  p. 177
		Ordinary dating, *p. 181*
		Receipt of goods (ROG), *p. 184* Series discounts, *p. 176*
		Single equivalent discount
		  rate, *p. 178*
		Single trade discount, *p. 175*
		Terms of the sale, *p. 180*
		Trade discount, *p. 172*
		Trade discount amount, *p. 172*
		Trade discount rate, *p. 173*

CHECK FIGURES FOR EXTRA PRACTICE QUIZZES WITH PAGE REFERENCES. (WORKED-OUT SOLUTIONS IN APPENDIX B)	LU 7–1a (p. 179) **1.** $4,800 TD; $11,200 NP **2.** $500 **3.** $9,891.84 NP; TD $4,108.16	LU 7–2a (p. 189) **1.** July 18; Aug. 7 **2.** June 22; July 12 **3.** June 11; July 11 **4.** May 10; May 30 **5.** June 10; June 30 **6.** $6,174 **7.** a) $612.24 b) $87.76

Critical Thinking Discussion Questions

1. What is the net price? June Long bought a jacket from a catalog company. She took her trade discount off the original price plus freight. What is wrong with June's approach? Who would benefit from June's approach—the buyer or the seller?

2. How do you calculate the list price when the net price and trade discount rate are known? A publisher tells the bookstore its net price of a book along with a suggested trade discount of 20%. The bookstore uses a 25% discount rate. Is this ethical when textbook prices are rising?

3. If Jordan Furniture ships furniture FOB shipping point, what does that mean? Does this mean you get a cash discount?

4. What are the steps to calculate the net price equivalent rate? Why is the net price equivalent rate *not* rounded?

(cont. on next page)

5. What are the steps to calculate the single equivalent discount rate? Is this rate off the list or net price? Explain why this calculation of a single equivalent discount rate may not always be needed.

6. What is the difference between a discount and credit period? Are all cash discounts taken before trade discounts? Agree or disagree? Why?

7. Explain the following credit terms of sale:
   a. 2/10, n/30.
   b. 3/10, n/30 ROG.
   c. 1/10 EOM (on or before 25th of month).
   d. 1/10 EOM (after 25th of month).

8. Explain how to calculate a partial payment. Whom does a partial payment favor—the buyer or the seller?

END-OF-CHAPTER PROBLEMS Mc Graw Hill **connect** (plus+) www.mhhe.com/slater10e

Check figures for odd-numbered problems in Appendix C

Name _____ Date _____

DRILL PROBLEMS

For all problems, round your final answer to the nearest cent. Do not round net price equivalent rates or single equivalent discount rates.

Complete the following:

Item	List price	Chain discount	Net price equivalent rate (in decimals)	Single equivalent discount rate (in decimals)	Trade discount	Net price
7–1. Verizon Blackberry	$299	4/1				
7–2. Panasonic DVD player	$199	8/4/3				
7–3. IBM scanner	$269	7/3/1				

Complete the following:

Item	List price	Chain discount	Net price	Trade discount
7–4. Trotter treadmill	$3,000	9/4		
7–5. Maytag dishwasher	$450	8/5/6		
7–6. Hewlett-Packard scanner	$320	3/5/9		
7–7. Land Rover roofrack	$1,850	12/9/6		

7–8. Which of the following companies, A or B, gives a higher discount? Use the single equivalent discount rate to make your choice (convert your equivalent rate to the nearest hundredth percent).

Company A	Company B
8/10/15/3	10/6/16/5

Complete the following:

	Invoice	Dates when goods received	Terms	Last day* of discount period	Final day bill is due (end of credit period)
7–9.	June 18		1/10, n/30		
7–10.	Nov. 27		2/10 EOM		
7–11.	May 15	June 5	3/10, n/30, ROG		
7–12.	April 10		2/10, 1/30, n/60		
7–13.	June 12		3/10 EOM		
7–14.	Jan. 10	Feb. 3 (no leap year)	4/10, n/30, ROG		

*If more than one discount, assume date of last discount.

Complete the following by calculating the cash discount and net amount paid:

	Gross amount of invoice (freight charge already included)	Freight charge	Date of invoice	Terms of invoice	Date of payment	Cash discount	Net amount paid
7–15.	$7,000	$100	4/8	2/10, n/60	4/15		
7–16.	$600	None	8/1	3/10, 2/15, n/30	8/13		
7–17.	$200	None	11/13	1/10 EOM	12/3		
7–18.	$500	$100	11/29	1/10 EOM	1/4		

Complete the following:

	Amount of invoice	Terms	Invoice date	Actual partial payment made	Date of partial payment	Amount of payment to be credited	Balance outstanding
7–19.	$700	2/10, n/60	5/6	$400	5/15		
7–20.	$600	4/10, n/60	7/5	$400	7/14		

WORD PROBLEMS (Round to Nearest Cent as Needed)

7–21. The list price of an orange dial Luminox watch is $650. Katz Jewelers receives a trade discount of 30%. Find the trade discount amount and the net price.

7–22. A model NASCAR race car lists for $79.99 with a trade discount of 40%. What is the net price of the car?

7–23. Lucky you! You went to couponcabin.com and found a 20% off coupon to your significant other's favorite store. Armed with that coupon, you went to the store only to find a storewide sale offering 10% off everything in the store. In addition, your credit card has a special offer that allows you to save 10% if you use your credit card for all purchases that day. Using your credit card, what will you pay before tax for the $155 gift you found? Use the single equivalent discount to calculate how much you save and then calculate your final price.

7–24. Levin Furniture buys a living room set with a $4,000 list price and a 55% trade discount. Freight (FOB shipping point) of $50 is not part of the list price. What is the delivered price (including freight) of the living room set, assuming a cash discount of 2/10, n/30, ROG? The invoice had an April 8 date. Levin received the goods on April 19 and paid the invoice on April 25.

7–25. A manufacturer of skateboards offered a 5/2/1 chain discount to many customers. Bob's Sporting Goods ordered 20 skateboards for a total $625 list price. What was the net price of the skateboards? What was the trade discount amount?

7–26. Home Depot wants to buy a new line of fertilizers. Manufacturer A offers a 21/13 chain discount. Manufacturer B offers a 26/8 chain discount. Both manufacturers have the same list price. What manufacturer should Home Depot buy from?

7–27. Maplewood Supply received a $5,250 invoice dated 4/15/06. The $5,250 included $250 freight. Terms were 4/10, 3/30, n/60. **(a)** If Maplewood pays the invoice on April 27, what will it pay? **(b)** If Maplewood pays the invoice on May 21, what will it pay?

7–28. A local Sports Authority ordered 50 pairs of tennis shoes from Nike Corporation. The shoes were priced at $85 for each pair with the following terms: 4/10, 2/30, n/60. The invoice was dated October 15. Sports Authority sent in a payment on October 28. What should have been the amount of the check?

7–29. Macy of New York sold LeeCo. of Chicago office equipment with a $6,000 list price. Sale terms were 3/10, n/30 FOB New York. Macy agreed to prepay the $30 freight. LeeCo. pays the invoice within the discount period. What does LeeCo. pay Macy?

7–30. Royal Furniture bought a sofa for $800. The sofa had a $1,400 list price. What was the trade discount rate Royal received? Round to the nearest hundredth percent.

7–31. Amazon.com paid a $6,000 net price for textbooks. The publisher offered a 30% trade discount. What was the publisher's list price? Round to the nearest cent.

7–32. Bally Manufacturing sent Intel Corporation an invoice for machinery with a $14,000 list price. Bally dated the invoice July 23 with 2/10 EOM terms. Intel receives a 40% trade discount. Intel pays the invoice on August 5. What does Intel pay Bally?

7–33. On August 1, Intel Corporation (Problem 7–32) returns $100 of the machinery due to defects. What does Intel pay Bally on August 5? Round to nearest cent.

7–34. Stacy's Dress Shop received a $1,050 invoice dated July 8 with 2/10, 1/15, n/60 terms. On July 22, Stacy's sent a $242 partial payment. What credit should Stacy's receive? What is Stacy's outstanding balance?

7–35. On March 11, Jangles Corporation received a $20,000 invoice dated March 8. Cash discount terms were 4/10, n/30. On March 15, Jangles sent an $8,000 partial payment. What credit should Jangles receive? What is Jangles' outstanding balance?

ADDITIONAL SET OF WORD PROBLEMS

7–36. MONEY Magazine published an article titled "Take the bite out of dental costs." This article recommends a few tips for saving money at the dentist: 1. get a dentist who is part of your insurance plan, 2. join a non-insurance related discount club, 3. choose your treatment wisely—there is more than one way to treat a dental problem, 4. be flexible—if the treatment is not urgent, consider waiting until next year so you can make a financial plan, 5. Negotiate—politely, and 6. brush up—take care of your teeth by brushing and flossing twice daily. If you negotiated successfully with your dentist on the cost of a treatment and she is willing to provide you 3/15, n/30 terms, what amount will be credited to your balance if you make a partial payment of $150 within the discount period?

7–37. Borders.com paid a $79.99 net price for each calculus textbook. The publisher offered a 20% trade discount. What was the publisher's list price?

7–38. HomeOffice.com buys a computer from Compaq Corporation. The computer has a $1,200 list price with a 30% trade discount. What is the trade discount amount? What is the net price of the computer? Freight charges are FOB destination.

7–39. Vail Ski Shop received a $1,201 invoice dated July 8 with 2/10, 1/15, n/60 terms. On July 22, Vail sent a $485 partial payment. What credit should Vail receive? What is Vail's outstanding balance?

7–40. True Value received an invoice dated 4/15/02. The invoice had a $5,500 balance that included $300 freight. Terms were 4/10, 3/30, n/60. True Value pays the invoice on April 29. What amount does True Value pay?

7–41. Baker's Financial Planners purchased seven new computers for $850 each. It received a 15% discount because it purchased more than five and an additional 6% discount because it took immediate delivery. Terms of payment were 2/10, n/30. Baker's pays the bill within the cash discount period. How much should the check be? Round to the nearest cent.

7–42. On May 14, Talbots of Boston sold Forrest of Los Angeles $7,000 of fine clothes. Terms were 2/10 EOM FOB Boston. Talbots agreed to prepay the $80 freight. If Forrest pays the invoice on June 8, what will Forrest pay? If Forrest pays on June 20, what will Forrest pay?

7–43. Sam's Ski Boards.com offers 5/4/1 chain discounts to many of its customers. The Ski Hut ordered 20 ski boards with a total list price of $1,200. What is the net price of the ski boards? What was the trade discount amount? Round to the nearest cent.

7–44. Majestic Manufacturing sold Jordans Furniture a living room set for an $8,500 list price with 35% trade discount. The $100 freight (FOB shipping point) was not part of the list price. Terms were 3/10, n/30 ROG. The invoice date was May 30. Jordans received the goods on July 18 and paid the invoice on July 20. What was the final price (include cost of freight) of the living room set?

7–45. Boeing Truck Company received an invoice showing 8 tires at $110 each, 12 tires at $160 each, and 15 tires at $180 each. Shipping terms are FOB shipping point. Freight is $400; trade discount is 10/5; and a cash discount of 2/10, n/30 is offered. Assuming Boeing paid within the discount period, what did Boeing pay?

7–46. Verizon offers to sell cellular phones listing for $99.99 with a chain discount of 15/10/5. Cellular Company offers to sell its cellular phones that list at $102.99 with a chain discount of 25/5. If Irene is to buy 6 phones, how much could she save if she buys from the lower-priced company?

7–47. Bryant Manufacture sells its furniture to wholesalers and retailers. It offers to wholesalers a chain discount of 15/10/5 and to retailers a chain discount of 15/10. If a sofa lists for $500, how much would the wholesaler and retailer pay?

CHALLENGE PROBLEMS

7–48. The nonprofit dog adoption organization, Wags are Us, is purchasing dog food from their local pet store for $335. Because the organization is a nonprofit, the store is offering Wags are Us a trade discount of 35% at 5/15 EOM. If Wags are Us purchases the dog food on June 28, when is the end of its discount period and credit period? What will *Wags are Us* owe if the organization pays before the end of the discount period?

7–49. On March 30, Century Television received an invoice dated March 28 from ACME Manufacturing for 50 televisions at a cost of $125 each. Century received a 10/4/2 chain discount. Shipping terms were FOB shipping point. ACME prepaid the $70 freight. Terms were 2/10 EOM. When Century received the goods, 3 sets were defective. Century returned these sets to ACME. On April 8, Century sent a $150 partial payment. Century will pay the balance on May 6. What is Century's final payment on May 6? Assume no taxes.

Complete the following: *(pp. 173, 176)*

	Item	List price	Single trade discount	Net price
1.	Apple iPod	$350	5%	
2.	Palm Pilot		10%	$190

Calculate the net price and trade discount (use net price equivalent rate and single equivalent discount rate) for the following: *(pp. 176–178)*

	Item	List price	Chain discount	Net price	Trade discount
3.	Sony HD flat-screen TV	$899	5/4		

4. From the following, what is the last date for each discount period and credit period? *(p. 180)*

	Date of invoice	Terms	End of discount period	End of credit period
a.	Nov. 4	2/10, n/30		
b.	Oct. 3, 2009	3/10, n/30 ROG (Goods received March 10, 2010)		
c.	May 2	2/10 EOM		
d.	Nov. 28	2/10 EOM		

5. Best Buy buys an iPod from a wholesaler with a $300 list price and a 5% trade discount. What is the trade discount amount? What is the net price of the iPod? *(p. 173)*

6. Jordan's of Boston sold Lee Company of New York computer equipment with a $7,000 list price. Sale terms were 4/10, n/30 FOB Boston. Jordan's agreed to prepay the $400 freight. Lee pays the invoice within the discount period. What does Lee pay Jordan's? *(pp. 173, 180)*

7. Julie Ring wants to buy a new line of Tonka trucks for her shop. Manufacturer A offers a 14/8 chain discount. Manufacturer B offers a 15/7 chain discount. Both manufacturers have the same list price. Which manufacturer should Julie buy from? *(p. 177)*

8. Office.com received a $8,000 invoice dated April 10. Terms were 2/10, 1/15, n/60. On April 14, Office.com sent an $1,900 partial payment. What credit should Office.com receive? What is Office.com's outstanding balance? Round to the nearest cent. *(p. 187)*

9. Logan Company received from Furniture.com an invoice dated September 29. Terms were 1/10 EOM. List price on the invoice was $8,000 (freight not included). Logan receives a 8/7 chain discount. Freight charges are Logan's responsibility, but Furniture.com agreed to prepay the $300 freight. Logan pays the invoice on November 7. What does Logan Company pay Furniture.com? *(pp. 177, 185)*

WAL-MART'S PROGRAM HAS SPURRED COMPETITORS TO MEET ITS ROCK-BOTTOM PRICES.

SAVE BIG ON PRESCRIPTIONS

Do your drugs cost too much? Find out how to get well for less. BY JESSICA L. ANDERSON

WHEN ORDERING YOUR prescriptions, it helps to think jeans. You could buy a designer pair for, say, $200. But if the fit is right, $50 Gap jeans would do just as well and cost a lot less.

Likewise, if you're a savvy shopper, you'll compare drug prices and choose the medication that fits you best and costs the least. Nobody but you will know the difference.

Go generic. Switching to generic drugs could save you up to 80% per prescription. Thanks to a tidal wave of brand-name drugs losing patent protection—among them popular medications such as cholesterol-reducing Zocor, antihypertensive Toprol-XL and antidepressant Zoloft—more generics are available than ever before, and chances are your medication is among them. Kristin Begley, of benefits consultant Hewitt Associates, says that $60 billion worth of brand-name drugs are coming off patent in the next three years.

If your medication hasn't gone generic yet, you're not out of luck. Ask your doctor if there is a similar generic drug in the same therapeutic class. The most common conditions—high cholesterol, depression, allergies and diabetes—all have generics available, says Ron Fontanetta, a principal at benefits-consulting firm Towers Perrin. "It's the single best way to save money."

Because generics cost less on the retail side, employers typically offer better coverage for them, too. Company plans that still use co-payments commonly charge $10, $20 or $40 for prescriptions, with generics the least expensive, preferred brands (on the plan's approved, or formulary, list) in the middle and non-preferred brands the most expensive. By switching from a nonpreferred brand to a generic, you could save $30 in a snap.

The push for transparency in health-care costs has led many employers to switch from co-pays to co-insurance, meaning that the insurer pays a percentage of a drug's cost—typically 80%—and you pick up the rest. Lipitor, a widely used cholesterol reducer, costs $82 for a 30-day supply at Drugstore.com, so you'd pay $16.40. But for a similar generic drug that costs $28, you'd pay just $5.60, saving you an additional 66%.

Some companies up the ante by adding extra incentives to make the switch, such as offering tiered co-insurance rates—say, 80% for generic drugs but just 50% for brand-name medicines. Reducing the co-insurance on Lipitor from 80% to 50% makes using a generic drug even more attractive. Begley says she is starting to see "coupon" programs in which companies foot the whole bill for a few months after an employee makes the switch.

If you still need an incentive, here it is: generic drugs for $4. Wal-Mart and its warehouse retailer, Sam's Club, started the ball rolling in 2006, offering 30-day supplies of some drugs for just $4. The program has expanded to more than 360 medications. Rival Target has a $4-drug program that includes 315 medications; Walgreens offers 90-day supplies of some 300 generics for $12.99.

Costco jumped on the $4 bandwagon early on, but it dropped that approach and switched to a program of 100 pills for $10 because of lost revenue. One regional grocery chain, Giant Eagle, now offers 400 generic drugs for $4. Meijer, another regional chain, offers seven common antibiotics free. Missing in action? Big names CVS and Rite Aid.

Meds by mail. More than half the money spent on drugs today goes toward treating chronic conditions,

From Kiplinger's Personal Finance, May 2008, p. 71.

BUSINESS MATH ISSUE

Generic drugs should never be bought online.

1. List the key points of the article and information to support your position.
2. Write a group defense of your position using math calculations to support your view.

PROJECT A
Do you agree with minimum pricing?
Define your position.

State Law Targets 'Minimum Pricing'

BY JOSEPH PEREIRA

In a move that could lead to lower prices for consumers across the country, Maryland has passed a law that prohibits manufacturers from requiring retailers to charge minimum prices for their goods.

The law, which takes effect Oct. 1, takes aim at agreements that many manufacturers have been forcing on retailers, requiring them to charge minimum prices on certain products. The practice has surged since a controversial 2007 U.S. Supreme Court ruling that no longer makes such agreements automatically illegal under federal antitrust law.

Under the new state law, retailers doing business in Maryland—as well as state officials—can sue manufacturers that impose minimum-pricing agreements. The law also covers transactions in which consumers in Maryland buy goods on the Internet, even when the retailer is based out of state. That could potentially affect manufacturers throughout the country.

Minimum-pricing agreements keep retail profit margins higher, which in turn keeps retailers from pressuring manufacturers to lower the wholesale prices they pay for those goods. Suppliers also think that eliminating pricing competition can help retailers spend more money promoting their products to consumers. But certain retailers—particularly online ones—that attract customers because of low prices say the agreements stifle competition and gouge consumers.

Maryland's legislation is one of a series of recent initiatives aimed at circumventing the Supreme Court decision. A congressional subcommittee is scheduled to hold a hearing today in which several opponents of minimum-pricing agreements are expected to testify, including **eBay** Inc. and Federal Trade Commissioner Pamela Jones Harbour.

Hearings are expected next month in the U.S. Senate on a bill called the Discount Pricing Consumer Protection Act. Introduced by Sen. Herb Kohl (D., Wis.), it is aimed at circumventing the Supreme

Court's ruling and making minimum-pricing agreements between manufacturers and retailers illegal under federal law once again.

In a 5-4 decision, a majority of Supreme Court justices said such agreements, which previously had been illegal, must be reviewed on a case-by-case basis—a leniency that legal experts say has emboldened manufacturers over the past two years to require retailers to enter into the agreements.

"Today there are an estimated 5,000

Maryland stores can now sue manufacturers that impose minimum-pricing agreements.

companies that have implemented minimum-pricing policies, much of it happening in the wake of the Supreme Court decision," said Christopher S. Finnerty, a Boston attorney who advises manufacturers on pricing issues.

Charles Shafer, a University of Baltimore law professor and president of the Maryland Consumer Rights Coalition, said: "The Supreme Court has basically abandoned the consumer, and now the states and the federal government are finding they have to step into the breach."

One company with a minimum-pricing policy is **Kolcraft Enterprises** Inc., a Chicago-based supplier of bassinets and strollers sold by **Wal-Mart Stores** Inc. According to a copy of a pricing agreement obtained by The Wall Street Journal, Kol-

craft requires retailers to charge a minimum price of $159.99 for its Contours Classique 3-in-1 Bassinet. Wal-Mart's price is $169.88. The price dictated by Kolcraft for its Options Tandem Stroller is $219.99; Wal-Mart charges $219.98.

The agreement states that the policy is intended, among other things, "to protect all Kolcraft and Kolcraft-licensed brands from diminution." Kolcraft also sells products under the Sealy and Jeep brands. Eileen Lysaught, Kolcraft's general counsel and vice-president of operations, declined to comment, as did Wal-Mart.

The Maryland bill won the support of the Maryland Retailers Association, whose members include Wal-Mart, **Target** Corp. and **Sears Holdings** Corp. Wal-Mart did not take a position on the Maryland bill. But Rhoda M. Washington, Wal-Mart's regional senior manager for state and local government relations, says, "Wal-Mart customers expect competitive, reasonable prices, and the Maryland legislature is seeking to ensure that we can deliver on that promise." Target and Sears declined to comment.

The association's president, Tom Saquella, said high-end retailers initially expressed reservations about the bill, while mass merchandisers favored it. But eventually "we got a majority" supporting it, he said. "Basically our merchants don't want manufacturers telling us what we can sell our merchandise at."

Maryland already has an antitrust law that bans price fixing. But because Maryland is one of a number of states where federal-court interpretations take precedent over state law, the Supreme Court's ruling essentially nullified state law. By creating a new law that explicitly bans all minimum-pricing agreements between manufacturers and retailers, state legal experts say, Maryland is now able to preempt the high-court ruling. Legal experts say more than 30 other states that filed briefs with the Supreme Court could join Maryland in enacting such a law.

"We're making it clear to the judges in this state that Maryland was not adopting
Please turn to page D6

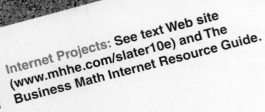

Internet Projects: See text Web site
(www.mhhe.com/slater10e) and The
Business Math Internet Resource Guide.

Video Case

FedEx is well-known for its small package delivery business, which successfully transports millions of small packages worldwide daily. FedEx is also the number 1 provider of expedited freight shipments transporting 3,500 to 5,000 express skid shipments a night. The planning and coordination required to ship this volume of large or heavy shipments is a challenge for the logistics side of the freight business.

In order to qualify as freight, a package must weigh at least 151 pounds. It must be palletized, stackable, forklift-friendly, and shrink-wrapped or banded for stability. The uniform cargo footprint can be no larger than 16 square feet and no taller than 70 inches with a maximum weight for a standard freight package of 2,200 pounds. These requirements are necessary to meet the specific center of gravity and weight-limit qualifications required by each aircraft.

FedEx's cutting-edge tracking technology and logistic capabilities allow them to guarantee pickup and subsequent delivery times within a three- to four-hour time span. This core attribute paved the way for FedEx Custom Critical—the fastest, 24/7, door-to-door, same-day delivery of urgent freight, valuable items and hazardous goods service available. Utilizing a service fleet of ground-expedited transportation vehicles equipped with satellite monitoring systems as well as an array of air options provides the quick turnaround time demanded. In most cases packages are picked up within 90 minutes from the customer's call and delivered within 15 minutes of the scheduled delivery time.

FedEx continues to strive to meet and beat customer expectations through its array of package and freight delivery systems. With a history that officially began operations on April 17, 1973, with 14 small aircraft, FedEx has come a long way...baby.

PROBLEM 1

The video discusses the requirements of a package to qualify as freight. A package must weigh at least 151 pounds. It must be palletized, stackable, forklift-friendly and shrink-wrapped or banded for stability. The uniform cargo footprint can be no larger than 16 square feet and no taller than 70 inches with a maximum weight for a standard freight package of 2,200 pounds. If you are shipping 6,751 pounds of stackable 8 foot square items with a value of $33,150, does your shipment qualify as freight? If so, how many freight packages would you need? Calculate the actual pounds for each freight package.

PROBLEM 2

The video discusses the logistics involved in some of FedEx's service offerings. FedEx ships FOB destination because the seller pays the freight. If there is damage to a domestic freight shipment, FedEx will provide up to $50 per pound insurance on new items or $0.50 per pound on used items up to $100,000. Is the shipment of new items discussed in problem 1 fully covered? Will you need to buy additional coverage? Why or why not?

PROBLEM 3

In the December 9, 2008, New York Times article, "FedEx Lowers 2009 Earnings Forecast," FedEx said it expected to earn an average of $4.13 a share for the fiscal year ending in May, down from its original estimate of an average of $5.00 a share. Analysts were predicting that the company would earn $5.15 a share, according to Thomson Reuters. What percent reduction is the company's new estimate from the original estimate in earnings per share? What percent reduction in earnings per share is there between the original estimate and the analysts' predictions? Round to the nearest tenth percent.

PROBLEM 4

The Wall Street Journal reported on September 19, 2008, that FedEx Corp., in response to a 22% decline in net income for its first fiscal quarter, "will raise prices in January, cut capital spending, park aircraft, freeze most hiring and trim employees' hours." FedEx announced on March 2, 2009, an average increase of 6.9% for U.S. services to help offset a reduction in business effective immediately. If a FedEx First Overnight package costs $67.41 for a 1 pound package to ship today, what did it cost to ship before the increase? Round to the nearest cent.

PROBLEM 5

On January 5, 2009, UPS posted their new rates. UPS ground rates have increased an average of 5.9%. Air and international services have increased an average of 4.9%. UPS Next Day Air costs $42.81 for a 1 pound package. This reflects an increase of 4.9%. What was the cost to ship this package before the air increase? Round to the nearest cent. Comparing against data in problem 4, what is the difference in price between UPS and FedEx to ship a 1 pound package overnight? Would you choose FedEx or UPS to ship your package? Why?

PROBLEM 6

Despite an historical "no layoff" policy, FedEx laid off 900 employees in the early part of 2009 as reported the February 9, 2009, Memphis Business Journal. If FedEx (FDX), headquartered in Memphis, Tennessee, has 233,457 U.S. employees, what percent were laid off in February? Round to the nearest tenth percent.

MARKUPS AND MARKDOWNS

Shopping Around

Cash-strapped shoppers are continuing to crowd cheap-and-chic Zara stores, like this one in Madrid, owned by Inditex, a Spanish fashion retailer. Inditex is now challenging Gap's rank as the world's biggest specialty clothing vendor by revenue.

	Inditex	Gap
Annual sales	$14.1 billion	$14.5 billion
Number of stores	4,264	3,100
Number of countries	73	6
Biggest brand	Zara	Gap
Number of other brands	6	3
Based in	Arteixo, Spain	San Francisco
First store opened	1975	1969
First foreign store	1989 Oporto, Portugal	1987 London

Source: the companies

The Wall Street Journal © 2009

Aly Song/Reuters/Landov

LU 8–1: Markups[1] Based on Cost (100%)

1. Calculate dollar markup and percent markup on cost (p. 205).
2. Calculate selling price when you know the cost and percent markup on cost (p. 206).
3. Calculate cost when dollar markup and percent markup on cost are known (p. 207).
4. Calculate cost when you know the selling price and percent markup on cost (p. 207).

LU 8–2: Markups Based on Selling Price (100%)

1. Calculate dollar markup and percent markup on selling price (p. 210).
2. Calculate selling price when dollar markup and percent markup on selling price are known (p. 210).
3. Calculate selling price when cost and percent markup on selling price are known (p. 211).
4. Calculate cost when selling price and percent markup on selling price are known (p. 212).
5. Convert from percent markup on cost to percent markup on selling price and vice versa (p. 212).

LU 8–3: Markdowns and Perishables

1. Calculate markdowns; compare markdowns and markups (p. 215).

VOCABULARY PREVIEW

Here are key terms in this chapter. After completing the chapter, if you know the term, place a checkmark in the parenthesis. If you don't know the term, look it up and put the page number where it can be found.

Cost . ( ) **Dollar markdown** . ( ) **Dollar markup** . ( ) **Gross profit** . ( ) **Margin** . ( ) **Markdowns** . ( ) **Markup** . ( ) **Net profit (net income)** . ( ) **Operating expenses (overhead)** . ( ) **Percent markup on cost** . ( ) **Percent markup on selling price** . ( ) **Selling price** . ( )

Are you one of the many shoppers who shop at the Gap? If you read the *Wall Street Journal* clip, "Gap to Merge Brands Into Single Stores," (p. 204) you will see that your shopping experience will change. Gap plans to have kids, baby, maternity body, and adult merchandise in one store. They also plan to cut inventory and cost by this new strategy.

Before we study the two pricing methods available to Gap (percent markup on cost and percent markup on selling price), we must know the following terms:

- **Selling price.** The price retailers charge consumers. The total selling price of all the goods sold by a retailer (like Gap) represents the retailer's total sales.

- **Cost.** The price retailers pay to a manufacturer or supplier to bring the goods into the store.

- **Markup, margin, or gross profit.** These three terms refer to the difference between the cost of bringing the goods into the store and the selling price of the goods.

[1]Some texts use the term *markon* (selling price minus cost).

Paul Sakuma/AP Photo

Gap to Merge Brands Into Single Stores

Gap Inc. plans to close a handful of small stand-alone GapBody, Gap-Kids and babyGap stores to test a strategy of consolidating Gap brand offerings in its namesake stores and reducing its square footage.

"It's been clear to us by doing the numbers and talking to customers in our stores, having kids, baby, maternity, body, and adult in the same box makes sense," Chief Executive Glenn Murphy said at a conference hosted by Piper Jaffray Cos. in New York.

The consolidation was one example Mr. Murphy used to illustrate the San Francisco-based apparel retailer's new real-estate strategy, which involves figuring out which of its 3,100 stores to reposition, relocate, remodel and "right size."

For the retail strategy in general, he said, "we probably won't see much of a benefit in 2008, but in 2009 going forward..."

By combining a 10,000-square-foot Gap adult and body store with a 5,000-square-foot kids-only store, Gap could save $225,000 a year in rent alone, he said.

The "sweetspot" for Gap stores is 6,000 to 10,000 square feet and for Old Navy, 14,000 to 16,000 square feet, he said.

Gap has been struggling with sluggish sales across all its brands and has been trying to boost earnings by cutting inventory and costs.

Wall Street Journal © 2008

- **Operating expenses or overhead.** The regular expenses of doing business such as wages, rent, utilities, insurance, and advertising.
- **Net profit or net incomes.** The profit remaining after subtracting the cost of bringing the goods into the store and the operating expenses from the sale of the goods (including any returns or adjustments). This is called the *breakeven* point.

From these definitions, we can conclude that *markup* represents the amount that retailers must add to the cost of the goods to cover their operating expenses and make a profit.[2]

Let's assume Gap plans to sell hooded fleece jackets for $23 that cost them $18.

Basic selling price formula

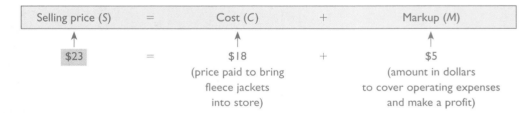

Selling price (S)	=	Cost (C)	+	Markup (M)
$23	=	$18	+	$5
		(price paid to bring fleece jackets into store)		(amount in dollars to cover operating expenses and make a profit)

In the Gap example, the markup is a dollar amount, or a **dollar markup.** Markup is also expressed in percent. When expressing markup in percent, retailers can choose a percent based on *cost* (Learning Unit 8–1) or a percent based on *selling price* (Learning Unit 8–2).

When you go out to dinner at a salad bar, you might be amazed to discover how much certain foods are marked up. For example, at one restaurant, potatoes are marked up 62.5% and shrimp are marked up 75%. Now let's look at how to calculate markup percents.

Learning Unit 8–1: Markups Based on Cost (100%)

In Chapter 6 you were introduced to the portion formula, which we used to solve percent problems. We also used the portion formula in Chapter 7 to solve problems involving trade and cash discounts. In this unit you will see how we use the basic selling price formula and the portion formula to solve percent markup situations based on cost. We will be using blueprint aids to show how to dissect and solve all word problems in this chapter.

---

[2]In this chapter, we concentrate on the markup of retailers. Manufacturers and suppliers also use markup to determine selling price.

Many manufacturers mark up goods on cost because manufacturers can get cost information more easily than sales information. Since retailers have the choice of using percent markup on cost or selling price, in this unit we assume Gap has chosen percent markup on cost. In Learning Unit 8–2 we show how Gap would determine markup if it decided to use percent markup on selling price.

Businesses that use **percent markup on cost** recognize that cost is 100%. This 100% represents the base of the portion formula. All situations in this unit use cost as 100%.

To calculate percent markup on cost, we will use the hooded fleece jacket sold by Gap and begin with the basic selling price formula given in the chapter introduction. When we know the dollar markup, we can use the portion formula to find the percent markup on cost.

Markup expressed in dollars:

Selling price ($23) = Cost ($18) + Markup ($5)

Markup expressed as a percent markup on cost:

Cost	100.00%
+ Markup	+ 27.78
= Selling price	127.78%

> Cost is 100%—the base. Dollar markup is the portion, and percent markup on cost is the rate.

In Situation 1 (below) we show why Gap has a 27.78% markup based on cost by presenting the hooded fleece jacket as a word problem. We solve the problem with the blueprint aid used in earlier chapters. In the second column, however, you will see footnotes after two numbers. These refer to the steps we use below the blueprint aid to solve the problem. Throughout the chapter, the numbers that we are solving for are in red. Remember that cost is the base for this unit.

LO 1

Situation 1: Calculating Dollar Markup and Percent Markup on Cost

Dollar markup is calculated with the basic selling price formula $S = C + M$. When you know the cost and selling price of goods, reverse the formula to $M = S - C$. Subtract the cost from the selling price, and you have the dollar markup.

The percent markup on cost is calculated with the portion formula. For Situation 1 the *portion* (P) is the dollar markup, which you know from the selling price formula. In this unit the *rate* (R) is always the percent markup on cost and the *base* (B) is always the cost (100%). To find the percent markup on cost (R), use the portion formula $R = \frac{P}{B}$ and divide the dollar markup (P) by the cost (B). Convert your answer to a percent and round if necessary.

Now we will look at the Gap example to see how to calculate the 27.78% markup on cost.

The Word Problem The Gap pays $18 for a hooded fleece jacket, which the store plans to sell for $23. What is Gap's dollar markup? What is the percent markup on cost (round to the nearest hundredth percent)?

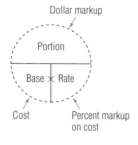
Dollar markup
Portion
Base × Rate
Cost   Percent markup
on cost

The facts	Solving for?	Steps to take	Key points
Hooded fleece jacket cost: $18. Hooded fleece jacket selling price: $23.	% $ C 100.00% $18 + M 27.78² 5¹ = S 127.78% $23 ¹Dollar markup. ²Percent markup on cost.	$\dfrac{\text{Dollar}}{\text{markup}} = \dfrac{\text{Selling}}{\text{price}} - \text{Cost}.$ $\dfrac{\text{Percent}}{\text{markup on cost}} = \dfrac{\text{Dollar markup}}{\text{Cost}}$	Dollar markup Portion ($5) Base ($18) × Rate (?) Cost

Steps to solving problem

1. Calculate the dollar markup.   Dollar markup = Selling price − Cost

$5   = $23   − $18

2. Calculate the percent markup on cost.   Percent markup on cost = $\dfrac{\text{Dollar markup}}{\text{Cost}}$

$$= \frac{\$5}{\$18} = 27.78\%$$

In the check note how we calculate the cost when we know the dollar markup and percent markup on cost.

Check

$$\text{Cost } (B) = \frac{\text{Dollar markup } (P)}{\text{Percent markup on cost } (R)}$$

$$= \frac{\$5}{.2778} = \$18$$

LO 2

Situation 2: Calculating Selling Price When You Know Cost and Percent Markup on Cost

Now let's look at Mel's Furniture where we calculate Mel's dollar markup and selling price.

The Word Problem Mel's Furniture bought a lamp that cost $100. To make Mel's desired profit, he needs a 65% markup on cost. What is Mel's dollar markup? What is his selling price?

The facts	Solving for?	Steps to take	Key points
Lamp cost: $100. Markup on cost: 65%.	% $ C 100% $100 + M 65 65² = S 165% $165¹ ¹Dollar markup. ²Selling price.	$S = \text{Cost} \times \left(1 + \begin{array}{c}\text{Percent}\\ \text{markup}\\ \text{on cost}\end{array}\right)$ $M = S - C.$	Selling price Portion (?) Base × Rate ($100) (1.65) Cost 100% +65%

Steps to solving problem

1. Calculate the selling price.

$$\underset{(P)}{\text{Selling price}} = \underset{(B)}{\text{Cost}} \times (1 + \underset{(R)}{\text{Percent markup on cost}}) = \$100 \times 1.65 = \$165$$

2. Calculate the dollar markup. $M = S - C$

$$\$65 = \$165 - \$100$$

LO 3

Situation 3: Calculating Cost When You Know Selling Price and Percent Markup on Cost

The Word Problem Jill Sport, owner of Sports, Inc., sells tennis rackets for $50. To make her desired profit, Jill needs a 40% markup on cost. What do the tennis rackets cost Jill? What is the dollar markup?

The facts	Solving for?			Steps to take	Key points
Selling price: $50.

Markup on cost: 40%. | | % | $ | $Cost = \dfrac{Selling\ price}{Percent}$ | Selling price |
	C	100%	$35.71[1]	$1 + markup\ on\ cost$	Portion ($50)
	+ M	40	14.29[2]		
	= S	140%	$50.00	$M = S - C.$	Base × Rate (?) (1.40)
	[1]Cost. [2]Dollar markup.				Cost 100% +40%

LO 4

Steps to solving problem

1. Calculate the cost.

$$S = C + M$$

$$\$50.00 = C + .40C \longleftarrow \text{This means 40\% times cost. } C \text{ is the}$$

$$\frac{\$50.00}{1.40} = \frac{1.40C}{1.40} \qquad \text{same as } 1C. \text{ Adding } .40C \text{ to } 1C$$
$$\text{gives the percent markup on cost of}$$
$$\boxed{\$35.71} = C \qquad 1.40C \text{ in decimal.}$$

2. Calculate the dollar markup.

$$M = S - C$$
$$M = \$50.00 - \$35.71$$
$$M = \boxed{\$14.29}$$

Now try the following Practice Quiz to check your understanding of this unit.

LU 8–1   PRACTICE QUIZ

Solve the following situations (markups based on cost):

1. Irene Westing bought a desk for $400 from an office supply house. She plans to sell the desk for $600. What is Irene's dollar markup? What is her percent markup on cost? Check your answer.

2. Suki Komar bought dolls for her toy store that cost $12 each. To make her desired profit, Suki must mark up each doll 35% on cost. What is the dollar markup? What is the selling price of each doll? Check your answer.

3. Jay Lyman sells calculators. His competitor sells a new calculator line for $14 each. Jay needs a 40% markup on cost to make his desired profit, and he must meet price competition. At what cost can Jay afford to bring these calculators into the store? What is the dollar markup? Check your answer.

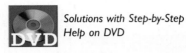

Solutions with Step-by-Step Help on DVD

✓ Solutions

1. Irene's dollar markup and percent markup on cost:

The facts	Solving for?	Steps to take	Key points
Desk cost: $400. Desk selling price: $600.	% $ C 100% $400 + M 50² 200¹ = S 150% $600 ¹Dollar markup. ²Percent markup on cost.	Dollar markup = Selling price − Cost. Percent markup on cost = Dollar markup / Cost	Dollar markup Portion ($200) Base × Rate ($400) (?) Cost

Steps to solving problem

1. Calculate the dollar markup.

Dollar markup = Selling price − Cost

$200 = $600 − $400

2. Calculate the percent markup on cost.

Percent markup on cost = $\dfrac{\text{Dollar markup}}{\text{Cost}}$

$= \dfrac{\$200}{\$400} = 50\%$

$$\text{Cost } (B) = \frac{\text{Dollar markup } (P)}{\text{Percent markup on cost } (R)}$$

$$= \frac{\$200}{.50} = \$400$$

2. Dollar markup and selling price of doll:

The facts	Solving for?	Steps to take	Key points
Doll cost: $12 each. Markup on cost: 35%.	% $ C 100% $12.00 + M 35 4.20² = S 135% $16.20¹ ¹Dollar markup. ²Selling price.	S = Cost × (1 + Percent markup on cost) M = S − C.	Selling price Portion (?) Base × Rate ($12) (1.35) Cost 100% +35%

Steps to solving problem

1. Calculate the dollar markup.   S = $16.20

Selling price = Cost × (1 + Percent markup on cost) = $12.00 × 1.35 = $16.20
     (P)   (B)   (R)

2. Calculate the selling price.   M = S − C

M = $16.20 − $12.00

M = $4.20

3. Cost and dollar markup:

The facts	Solving for?	Steps to take	Key points
Selling price: $14. Markup on cost: 40%.	% $ C 100% $10¹ + M 40 4² = S 140% $14 ¹Cost. ²Dollar markup.	$Cost = \dfrac{Selling\ price}{Percent}$ $\dfrac{}{1 + markup\ on\ cost}$ $M = S - C.$	Selling price Portion ($14) Base × Rate (?) (1.40) Cost 100% +40%

Steps to solving problem

1. Calculate the cost.

$$Cost\ (B) = \frac{Selling\ price\ (P)}{1 + Percent\ markup\ on\ cost\ (R)} = \frac{\$14}{1.40} = \$10$$

2. Calculate the dollar markup.

$$M = S - C$$
$$M = \$14 - \$10$$
$$M = \$4$$

LU 8–1a   EXTRA PRACTICE QUIZ WITH WORKED-OUT SOLUTIONS

Need more practice? Try this **Extra Practice Quiz** (check figures in Chapter Organizer, p. 221). Worked-out Solutions can be found in Appendix B at end of text.

Solve the following situations (markups based on cost):

1. Irene Westing bought a desk for $800 from an office supply house. She plans to sell the desk for $1,200. What is Irene's dollar markup? What is her percent markup on cost? Check your answer.

2. Suki Komar bought dolls for her toy store that cost $14 each. To make her desired profit, Suki must mark up each doll 38% on cost. What is the selling price? What is the dollar markup of each doll? Check your answer.

3. Jay Lyman sells calculators. His competitor sells a new calculator line for $16 each. Jay needs a 42% markup on cost to make his desired profit, and he must meet price competition. At what cost can Jay afford to bring these calculators into the store? What is the dollar markup? Check your answer.

Learning Unit 8–2: Markups Based on Selling Price (100%)

Many retailers mark up their goods on the selling price since sales information is easier to get than cost information. These retailers use retail prices in their inventory and report their expenses as a percent of sales.

Businesses that mark up their goods on selling price recognize that selling price is 100%. We begin this unit by assuming Gap has decided to use percent markup based on selling price. We repeat Gap's selling price formula expressed in dollars.

Markup expressed in dollars:

Selling price ($23) = Cost ($18) + Markup ($5)

Markup expressed as **percent markup on selling price:**

Cost	78.26%
+ Markup	+ 21.74
= Selling price	100.00%

Selling price is 100%—the base. Dollar markup is the portion, and percent markup on selling price is the rate.

Tony Anderson/Getty Images

In Situation 1 (below) we show why Gap has a 21.74% markup based on selling price. In the last unit, markups were on *cost*. In this unit, markups are on *selling price*.

LO 1

Situation 1: Calculating Dollar Markup and Percent Markup on Selling Price

The dollar markup is calculated with the selling price formula used in Situation 1, Learning Unit 8–1: $M = S - C$. To find the percent markup on selling price, use the portion formula $R = \frac{P}{B}$, where rate (the percent markup on selling price) is found by dividing the portion (dollar markup) by the base (selling price). Note that when solving for percent markup on cost in Situation 1, Learning Unit 8–1, you divided the dollar markup by the cost.

The Word Problem   The cost to Gap for a hooded fleece jacket is $18; the store then plans to sell them for $23. What is Gap's dollar markup? What is its percent markup on selling price? (Round to the nearest hundredth percent.)

The facts	Solving for?	Steps to take	Key points
Hooded fleece jacket cost: $18. Hooded fleece jacket price: $23.		%	$ | C	78.26%	$18 | + M	21.74%[2]	$5[1] | = S	100.00%	$23 | [1]Dollar markup. [2]Percent markup on selling price.	$\dfrac{\text{Dollar}}{\text{markup}} = \dfrac{\text{Selling}}{\text{price}} - \text{Cost.}$ $\dfrac{\text{Percent}}{\text{markup on selling price}} = \dfrac{\text{Dollar markup}}{\text{Selling price}}$	Dollar markup Portion ($5) Base × Rate ($23) (?) Selling price

Steps to solving problem

1. Calculate the dollar markup.

$$\text{Dollar markup} = \text{Selling price} - \text{Cost}$$
$$\$5 = \$23 - \$18$$

2. Calculate the percent markup on selling price.

$$\dfrac{\text{Percent markup}}{\text{on selling price}} = \dfrac{\text{Dollar markup}}{\text{Selling price}}$$
$$= \dfrac{\$5}{\$23} = 21.74\%$$

You can check the percent markup on selling price with the portion formula by dividing the dollar markup (P) by the percent markup on selling price (R).

Check

$$\text{Selling price (B)} = \dfrac{\text{Dollar markup (P)}}{\text{Percent markup on selling price (R)}}$$

$$= \dfrac{\$5}{.2174} = \$23$$

LO 2

Situation 2: Calculating Selling Price When You Know Cost and Percent Markup on Selling Price

The Word Problem Mel's Furniture bought a lamp that cost $100. To make Mel's desired profit, he needs a 65% markup on selling price. What are Mel's selling price and his dollar markup?

The facts	Solving for?	Steps to take	Key points
Lamp cost: $100. Markup on selling price: 65%.	% $ C 35% $100.00 + M 65 185.71² = S 100% $285.71¹ ¹Selling price. ²Dollar markup.	$S = C + M.$ or $S = \dfrac{Cost}{1 - \text{Percent markup on selling price}}$	

Steps to solving problem

1. Calculate the selling price.

$$\text{Selling price } (B) = \frac{\text{Cost } (P)}{1 - \text{Percent markup on selling price } (R)}$$

$$= \frac{\$100.00}{1 - .65} = \frac{\$100.00}{.35} = \boxed{\$285.72}$$

2. Calculate the dollar markup.

$$M = S - C$$
$$\boxed{\$185.71} = \$285.71 - \$100.00$$

LO 3

Situation 3: Calculating Cost When You Know Selling Price and Percent Markup on Selling Price

The Word Problem Jill Sport, owner of Sports, Inc., sells tennis rackets for $50. To make her desired profit, Jill needs a 40% markup on the selling price. What is the dollar markup? What do the tennis rackets cost Jill?

The facts	Solving for?	Steps to take	Key points
Selling price: $50. Markup on selling price: 40%.	% $ C 60% $30¹ + M 40 20² = S 100% $50 ¹Dollar markup. ²Cost.	$S = C + M.$ or $\text{Cost} = \text{Selling price} \times \left(1 - \dfrac{\text{Percent markup}}{\text{on selling price}}\right)$	

Steps to solving problem

1. Calculate the cost.

$$\boxed{\underset{(P)}{\text{Cost}} = \underset{(B)}{\underset{\text{price}}{\text{Selling}}} \times \left(1 - \underset{(R)}{\underset{\text{on selling price}}{\text{Percent markup}}}\right)} = \$50 \times .60 = \boxed{\$30}$$

$$(1.00 - .40)$$

2. Calculate the dollar markup.

$$M = S - C$$
$$M = \$50 - \$30$$
$$M = \$20$$

LO 4

To check your cost, use the portion formula Cost (P) = Selling price (B) × (100% selling price − Percent markup on selling price) (R).

In Table 8.1, we compare percent markup on cost with percent markup on retail (selling price). This table is a summary of the answers we calculated from the word problems in Learning Units 8–1 and 8–2. The word problems in the units were the same except in Learning Unit 8–1, we assumed markups were on cost, while in Learning Unit 8–2, markups were on selling price. Note that in Situation 1, the dollar markup is the same $5, but the percent markup is different.

Let's now look at how to convert from percent markup on cost to percent markup on selling price and vice versa. We will use Situation 1 from Table 8.1.

LO 5

Formula for Converting Percent Markup on Cost to Percent Markup on Selling Price

To convert percent markup on cost to percent markup on selling price:

$$\frac{.2778}{1 + .2778} = \boxed{21.74\%}$$

$$\boxed{\frac{\text{Percent markup on cost}}{1 + \text{Percent markup on cost}}}$$

TABLE 8.1

Comparison of markup on cost versus markup on selling price

Markup based on cost— Learning Unit 8–1	Markup based on selling price— Learning Unit 8–2
Situation 1: Calculating dollar amount of markup and percent markup on cost.	*Situation 1: Calculating dollar amount of markup and percent markup on selling price.*
Hooded fleece jacket cost, $18.	Hooded fleece jacket cost, $18.
Hooded fleece jacket selling price, $23.	Hooded fleece jacket selling price, $23.
$M = S - C$	$M = S - C$
$M = \$23 - \$18 = \boxed{\$5}$ markup (p. 205)	$M = \$23 - \$18 = \boxed{\$5}$ markup (p. 210)
$M \div C = \$5 \div \$18 = 27.78\%$	$M \div S = \$5 \div \$23 = 21.74\%$
Situation 2: Calculating selling price on cost.	*Situation 2: Calculating selling price on selling price.*
Lamp cost, $100. 65% markup on cost	Lamp cost, $100. 65% markup on selling price
$S = C \times (1 + \text{Percent markup on cost})$	$S = C \div (1 - \text{Percent markup on selling price})$
$S = \$100 \times 1.65 = \boxed{\$165}$ (p. 206)	$S = \$100.00 \div .35$
	$(100\% - 65\% = 35\% = .35)$
$(100\% + 65\% = 165\% = 1.65)$	$S = \boxed{\$285.71}$ (p. 210)
Situation 3: Calculating cost on cost.	*Situation 3: Calculating cost on selling price.*
Tennis racket selling price, $50. 40% markup on cost	Tennis racket selling price, $50. 40% markup on selling price
$C = S \div (1 + \text{Percent markup on cost})$	$C = S \times (1 - \text{Percent markup on selling price})$
$C = \$50.00 \div 1.40$	$C = \$50 \times .60 = \boxed{\$30}$ (p. 211)
$(100\% + 40\% = 140\% = 1.40)$	
$C = \boxed{\$35.71}$ (p. 207)	$(100\% - 40\% = 60\% = .60)$

Formula for Converting Percent Markup on Selling Price to Percent Markup on Cost

To convert percent markup on selling price to percent markup on cost:

Percent markup on selling price
1 − Percent markup on selling price

$$\frac{.2174}{1 - .2174} = \boxed{27.78\%}$$

Key point: A 21.74% markup on selling price or a 27.78% markup on cost results in same dollar markup of $5.

Now let's test your knowledge of Learning Unit 8–2.

LU 8–2	**PRACTICE QUIZ**

*Complete this **Practice Quiz** to see how you are doing.*

Solve the following situations (markups based on selling price). Note numbers 1, 2, and 3 are parallel problems to those in Practice Quiz 8–1.

1. Irene Westing bought a desk for $400 from an office supply house. She plans to sell the desk for $600. What is Irene's dollar markup? What is her percent markup on selling price (round to the nearest tenth percent)? Check your answer. Selling price will be slightly off due to rounding.

2. Suki Komar bought dolls for her toy store that cost $12 each. To make her desired profit, Suki must mark up each doll 35% on the selling price. What is the selling price of each doll? What is the dollar markup? Check your answer.

3. Jay Lyman sells calculators. His competitor sells a new calculator line for $14 each. Jay needs a 40% markup on the selling price to make his desired profit, and he must meet price competition. What is Jay's dollar markup? At what cost can Jay afford to bring these calculators into the store? Check your answer.

4. Dan Flow sells wrenches for $10 that cost $6. What is Dan's percent markup at cost? Round to the nearest tenth percent. What is Dan's percent markup on selling price? Check your answer.

Solutions with Step-by-Step Help on DVD

✓ Solutions

1. Irene's dollar markup and percent markup on selling price:

The facts	Solving for?	Steps to take	Key points
Desk cost: $400. Desk selling price: $600.			

Solving for?:

	%	$
C	66.7%	$400
+ M	33.3[2]	200[1]
= S	100%	$600

[1]Dollar markup.
[2]Percent markup on selling price.

Steps to take:

$$\frac{\text{Dollar}}{\text{markup}} = \frac{\text{Selling}}{\text{price}} - \text{Cost}$$

$$\frac{\text{Percent markup on selling price}} = \frac{\text{Dollar markup}}{\text{Selling price}}$$

Key points: Markup, Portion ($200), Base ($600) × Rate (?), Selling price

Steps to solving problem

1. Calculate the dollar markup.

Dollar markup = Selling price − Cost

$$\boxed{\$200} = \$600 - \$400$$

2. Calculate the percent markup on selling price.

$$\frac{\text{Percent markup}}{\text{on selling price}} = \frac{\text{Dollar markup}}{\text{Selling price}}$$

$$= \frac{\$200}{\$600} = \boxed{33.3\%}$$

Check

$$\text{Selling price } (B) = \frac{\text{Dollar markup } (P)}{\text{Percent markup on selling price } (R)}$$

$$= \frac{\$200}{.333} = \$600.60*$$

*(not exactly $600 due to rounding)

2.   Selling price of doll and dollar markup:

The facts	Solving for?	Steps to take	Key points
Doll cost: $12 each. Markup on selling price: 35%.	% $ C 65% $12.00 + M 35 6.46² = S 100% $18.46¹ ¹Selling price. ²Dollar markup.	S = C + M or $S = \dfrac{\text{Cost}}{1 - \begin{array}{l}\text{Percent markup} \\ \text{on selling price}\end{array}}$	Cost Portion ($12) Base × Rate (?) (.65) Selling price 100% −35%

Steps to solving problem

1. Calculate the selling price.

$$\text{Selling price } (B) = \frac{\text{Cost } (P)}{1 - \text{Percent markup on selling price } (R)} = \frac{\$12.00}{.65} = \boxed{\$18.46}$$

2. Calculate the dollar markup.
$$M = S - C$$
$$\boxed{\$6.46} = \$18.46 - \$12.00$$

3.   Dollar markup and cost:

The facts	Solving for?	Steps to take	Key points
Selling price: $14. Markup on selling price: 40%.	% $ C 60% $ 8.40¹ + M 40 5.60² = S 100% $14.00 ¹Dollar markup. ²Cost.	S = C + M or $\text{Cost} = \text{Selling price} \times \left(1 - \begin{array}{l}\text{Percent markup} \\ \text{on selling price}\end{array}\right)$	Cost Portion (?) Base × Rate ($14) (.60) Selling price 100% −40%

Steps to solving problem

1. Calculate the cost.

$$\underset{(P)}{\text{Cost}} = \underset{(B)}{\text{Selling price}} \times (1 - \underset{(R)}{\text{Percent markup on selling price}}) = \$14.00 \times .60 = \boxed{\$8.40}$$

$$(1.00 - .40)$$

2. Calculate the dollar markup. $M = S - C$

$$M = \$14 - \$8.40$$

$$M = \boxed{\$5.60}$$

4.   Cost = $\dfrac{\$4}{\$6}$ = **66.7%** $\dfrac{.40}{1 - .40} = \dfrac{.40}{.60} = \dfrac{2}{3} = 66.7\%$

   Selling price = $\dfrac{\$4}{\$10}$ = **40%** $\dfrac{.667}{1 + .667} = \dfrac{.667}{1.667} = 40\%$ (due to rounding)

LU 8–2a	EXTRA PRACTICE QUIZ WITH WORKED-OUT SOLUTIONS

Need more practice? Try this **Extra Practice Quiz** (check figures in Chapter Organizer, p. 221). Worked-out Solutions can be found in Appendix B at end of text.

Solve the following situations (markups based on selling price).

1. Irene Westing bought a desk for $800 from an office supply house. She plans to sell the desk for $1,200. What is Irene's dollar markup? What is her percent markup on selling price (round to the nearest tenth percent)? Check your answer. Selling price will be slightly off due to rounding.

2. Suki Komar bought dolls for her toy store that cost $14 each. To make her desired profit, Suki must mark up each doll 38% on selling price. What is the selling price of each doll? What is the dollar markup? Check your answer.

3. Jay Lyman sells calculators. His competitor sells a new calculator line for $16 each. Jay needs a 42% markup on the selling price to make his desired profit, and he must meet price competition. At what cost can Jay afford to bring these calculators into the store? What is Jay's dollar markup? Check your answer.

4. Dan Flow sells wrenches for $12 that cost $7. What is Dan's percent markup at cost? Round to the nearest tenth percent. What is Dan's percent markup on selling price? Check your answer.

Learning Unit 8–3: Markdowns

© Blend Images/Alamy

Have you ever wondered how your local retail store determines a typical markdown on clothing? The following *Wall Street Journal* clipping "Sale Rack Shuffle" explains the typical markdown money arrangement between a clothing vendor and a retailer. Evidently, the retailer does not always take the entire financial loss when a piece of clothing is marked down until it sells.

Sale Rack Shuffle

How a typical markdown-money arrangement between a clothing vendor and a retailer works:

1. Vendor makes dress at cost of **$50**
2. Sells to retailer at wholesale price of **$80**
3. Retailer marks up dress to **$200**
4. Dress gets marked down after 8 to 12 weeks (starting at 25% off) **$150**
5. The dress gets marked down again until it sells; the retailer and the vendor negotiate how to share the cost of the markdown.

Wall Street Journal © 2005

This learning unit focuses your attention on how to calculate markdowns.

Markdowns

Markdowns are reductions from the original selling price caused by seasonal changes, special promotions, style changes, and so on. We calculate the markdown percent as follows:

$$\text{Markdown percent} = \frac{\text{Dollar markdown}}{\text{Selling price (original)}}$$

Let's look at the following Kmart example:

Dollar markdown

Portion
($7.20)

Base × Rate
($18)   (?)

Original selling price

EXAMPLE   Kmart marked down an $18 video to $10.80. Calculate the **dollar markdown** and the markdown percent.

$18.00 Original selling price
− 10.80 Sale price
  $ 7.20 Markdown

$$\frac{\text{Dollar markdown, } \$7.20}{\text{Selling price (original), } \$18.00} = \boxed{40\%}$$

Calculating a Series of Markdowns and Markups

Often the final selling price is the result of a series of markdowns (and possibly a markup in between markdowns). We calculate additional markdowns on the previous selling price. Note in the following example how we calculate markdown on selling price after we add a markup.

EXAMPLE   Jones Department Store paid its supplier $400 for a TV. On January 10, Jones marked the TV up 60% on selling price. As a special promotion, Jones marked the TV down 30% on February 8 and another 20% on February 28. No one purchased the TV, so Jones marked it up 10% on March 11. What was the selling price of the TV on March 11?

January 10: Selling price = Cost   + Markup

$$S = \$400 \quad + .60S$$
$$- .60S \qquad\qquad - .60S$$

$$\frac{.40S}{.40} = \frac{\$400}{.40}$$
$$S = \$1,000$$

Check
$$S = \frac{\text{Cost}}{1 - \text{Percent markup on selling price}}$$

$$S = \frac{\$400}{1 - .60} = \frac{\$400}{.40} = \$1,000$$

February 8
markdown:
   100%
− 30
  70% → .70 × $1,000 = $700 selling price

February 28
additional markdown:
   100%
− 20
  80% → .80 × $700 = $560

March 11
additional markup:
   100%
+ 10
110% → 1.10 × $560 = $616

It's time to try the Practice Quiz.

| LU 8–3 | PRACTICE QUIZ |

Complete this **Practice Quiz**
to see how you are doing.

Solutions with Step-by-Step
Help on DVD

1. Sunshine Music Shop bought a stereo for $600 and marked it up 40% on selling price. To promote customer interest, Sunshine marked the stereo down 10% for one week. Since business was slow, Sunshine marked the stereo down an additional 5%. After a week, Sunshine marked the stereo up 2%. What is the new selling price of the stereo to the nearest cent? What is the markdown percent based on the original selling price to the nearest hundredth percent?

✓ **Solutions**

1. $$S = \frac{\text{Cost}}{1 - \text{Percent markup on selling price}}$$

$$S = \frac{\$600}{1 - .40} = \frac{\$600}{.60} = \$1,000$$

First markdown: $.90 \times \$1,000 = \$900$ selling price
Second markdown: $.95 \times \$900\ \ = \$855$ selling price
Markup: $1.02 \times \$855\ \ = \boxed{\$872.10}$ final selling price

$\$1,000 - \$872.10 = \dfrac{\$127.90}{\$1,000} = \boxed{12.79\%}$

LU 8–3a EXTRA PRACTICE QUIZ WITH WORKED-OUT SOLUTIONS

Need more practice? Try this **Extra Practice Quiz** (check figures in Chapter Organizer, p. 221). Worked-out Solutions can be found in Appendix B at end of text.

1. Sunshine Music Shop bought a stereo for $800 and marked it up 30% on selling price. To promote customer interest, Sunshine marked the stereo down 10% for one week. Since business was slow, Sunshine marked the stereo down an additional 5%. After a week, Sunshine marked the stereo up 2%. What is the new selling price of the stereo to the nearest cent? What is the markdown percent based on the original selling price to the nearest hundredth percent?

Classroom Notes

CHAPTER ORGANIZER AND REFERENCE GUIDE

Topic	Key point, procedure, formula	Example(s) to illustrate situation
Markups based on cost: Cost is 100% (base), p. 205	Selling price (S) = Cost (C) + Markup (M)	$400 = $300 + 100 $S\ \ =\ C\ +\ M$
Percent markup on cost, p. 206 **Cost, p. 206**	$\dfrac{\text{Dollar markup (portion)}}{\text{Cost (base)}} = \dfrac{\text{Percent markup}}{\text{on cost (rate)}}$ $C = \dfrac{\text{Dollar markup}}{\text{Percent markup on cost}}$	$\dfrac{\$100}{\$300} = \dfrac{1}{3} = 33\dfrac{1}{3}\%$ $\dfrac{\$100}{.33} = \$303$ Off slightly due to rounding
Calculating selling price, p. 207	$S = \text{Cost} \times (1 + \text{Percent markup on cost})$	Cost, $6; percent markup on cost, 20% $S = \$6 + .20(\$6)$ **Check** $S = \$6 + \$1.20$ $S = \boxed{\$7.20}$ $\boxed{\$6 \times 1.20 = \$7.20}$
Calculating cost, p. 208	$\text{Cost} = \dfrac{\text{Selling price}}{1 + \text{Percent markup on cost}}$	$S = \$100; M = 70\%$ of cost $\qquad S = C + M$ $\$100 = C + .70C$ $\quad\left(\begin{array}{l}\text{Remember,}\\ C = 1.00C\end{array}\right)$ $\$100 = 1.7C$ $\dfrac{\$100}{1.7} = C$ **Check** $\boxed{\$58.82} = C$ $\boxed{\dfrac{\$100}{1 + .70} = \$58.82}$
Markups based on selling price: selling price is 100% (Base), p. 211	Dollar markup = Selling price − Cost	$M = S - C$ $\boxed{\$600} = \$1,000 - \$400$
Percent markup on selling price, p. 212 **Selling price, p. 212**	$\dfrac{\text{Dollar markup (portion)}}{\text{Selling price (base)}} = \dfrac{\text{Percent markup}}{\text{selling price (rate)}}$ $S = \dfrac{\text{Dollar markup}}{\text{Percent markup on selling price}}$	$\dfrac{\$600}{\$1,000} = \boxed{60\%}$ $\dfrac{\$600}{.60} = \boxed{\$1,000}$
Calculating selling price, p. 213	$\text{Selling price} = \dfrac{\text{Cost}}{1 - \dfrac{\text{Percent markup}}{\text{on selling price}}}$	Cost, $400; percent markup on S, 60% $S = C + M$ $S = \$400 + .60S$ $S - .60S = \$400 + .60S - .60S$ $\dfrac{.40S}{.40} = \dfrac{\$400}{.40}$ $\boxed{S = \$1,000}$ Check → $\boxed{\dfrac{\$400}{1 - .60} = \dfrac{\$400}{.40} = \$1,000}$

(continues)

CHAPTER ORGANIZER AND REFERENCE GUIDE

Topic	Key point, procedure, formula	Example(s) to illustrate situation
Calculating cost, p. 214	$S = C + M$ **Check** $\text{Cost} = \dfrac{\text{Selling}}{\text{price}} \times \left(1 - \dfrac{\text{Percent markup}}{\text{on selling price}}\right)$	$\$1,000 = C + 60\%(\$1,000)$ $\$1,000 = C + \$600$ $\boxed{\$400} = C$ **Check** $\longrightarrow$ $\boxed{\begin{array}{l}\$1,000 \times (1 - .60)\\ \$1,000 \times .40 = \$400\end{array}}$
Conversion of markup percent, p. 215	Percent markup Percent markup on cost to on selling price $\boxed{\dfrac{\text{Percent markup on cost}}{1 + \text{Percent markup on cost}}}$ Percent markup Percent markup on selling price to on cost $\boxed{\dfrac{\text{Percent markup on selling price}}{1 - \text{Percent markup on selling price}}}$	*Round to nearest percent:* 54% markup on cost $\longrightarrow$ $\boxed{35\%}$ markup on selling price $\boxed{\dfrac{.54}{1 + .54} = \dfrac{.54}{1.54} = 35\%}$ 35% markup on $\longrightarrow$ $\boxed{54\%}$ markup selling price on cost $\boxed{\dfrac{.35}{1 - .35} = \dfrac{.35}{.65} = 54\%}$
Markdowns, p. 216	$\text{Markdown percent} = \dfrac{\text{Dollar markdown}}{\text{Selling price (original)}}$	$\$40$ selling price 10% markdown $\$40 \times .10 = \$4$ markdown $\dfrac{\$4}{\$40} = \boxed{10\%}$

KEY TERMS	Cost, *p. 204*
	Dollar markdown, *p. 218*
	Dollar markup, *p. 205*
	Gross profit, *p. 203*
	Margin, *p. 204*
		Markdowns, *p. 218*
		Markup, *p. 204*
		Net profit (net income), *p. 204*
		Operating expenses
		  (overhead), *p. 204*
			Percent markup on cost, *p. 205*
			Percent markup on
			  selling price, *p. 211*
			Selling price, *p. 204*

CHECK FIGURES FOR EXTRA PRACTICE QUIZZES WITH PAGE REFERENCES. (WORKED-OUT SOLUTIONS IN APPENDIX B)	LU 8–1a (p. 211) **1.** $400; 50% **2.** $5.32; $19.32 **3.** $11.27; $4.73	LU 8–2a (p. 217) **1.** $400; 33.3% **2.** $22.58; $8.58 **3.** $6.72; $9.28 **4.** 71.4%; 41.7%	LU 8–3a (p. 218) **1.** $996.69; 12.79%

Critical Thinking Discussion Questions

1. Assuming markups are based on cost, explain how the portion formula could be used to calculate cost, selling price, dollar markup, and percent markup on cost. Pick a company and explain why it would mark goods up on cost rather than on selling price.

2. Assuming markups are based on selling price, explain how the portion formula could be used to calculate cost, selling price, dollar markup, and percent markup on selling price. Pick a company and explain why it would mark up goods on selling price rather than on cost.

3. What is the formula to convert percent markup on selling price to percent markup on cost? How could you explain that a 40% markup on selling price, which is a 66.7% markup on cost, would result in the same dollar markup?

4. Explain how to calculate markdowns. Do you think stores should run one-day-only markdown sales? Would it be better to offer the best price "all the time"?

Check figures for odd-numbered problems in Appendix C   Name _____   Date _____

DRILL PROBLEMS

Assume markups in Problems 8–1 to 8–6 are based on cost. Find the dollar markup and selling price for the following problems. Round answers to the nearest cent.

	Item	Cost	Markup percent	Dollar markup	Selling price
8–1.	HP Paulson Laptop	$700	30%		
8–2.	Hamilton khaki multi-touch watch	$400	40%		

Solve for cost (round to the nearest cent):

8–3. Selling price of office furniture at Staples, $6,000

Percent markup on cost, 40%

Actual cost?

8–4. Selling price of lumber at Home Depot, $4,000

Percent markup on cost, 30%

Actual cost?

Complete the following:

	Cost	Selling price	Dollar markup	Percent markup on cost*
8–5.	$15.10	$22.00	?	?
8–6.	?	?	$4.70	102.17%

*Round to the nearest hundredth percent.

Assume markups in Problems 8–7 to 8–12 are based on selling price. Find the dollar markup and cost (round answers to the nearest cent):

	Item	Selling price	Markup percent	Dollar markup	Cost
8–7.	Sony LCD TV	$1,000	45%		
8–8.	IBM scanner	$80	30%		

Solve for the selling price (round to the nearest cent):

8–9. Selling price of a complete set of pots and pans at Walmart?

40% markup on selling price

Cost, actual, $66.50

8–10. Selling price of a dining room set at Macy's?

55% markup on selling price

Cost, actual, $800

Complete the following:

	Cost	Selling price	Dollar markup	Percent markup on selling price (round to nearest tenth percent)
8–11.	$14.80	$49.00	?	?
8–12.	?	?	$4	20%

By conversion of the markup formula, solve the following (round to the nearest whole percent as needed):

	Percent markup on cost	**Percent markup on selling price**
8–13.	12.4%	?
8–14.	?	13%

Complete the following:

8–15. Calculate the final selling price to the nearest cent and markdown percent to the nearest hundredth percent:

Original selling price	First markdown	Second markdown	Markup	Final markdown
$5,000	20%	10%	12%	5%

4. Sports Authority marks up New Balance sneakers $30 and sells them for $109. Markup is on cost. What are the cost and percent markup to the nearest hundredth percent? *(p. 205)*

5. The Shoe Outlet bought boots for $60 and marks up the boots 55% on the selling price. What is the selling price of the boots? Round to the nearest cent. *(p. 211)*

6. Office Max sells a desk for $450 and marks up the desk 35% on the selling price. What did the desk cost Office Max? Round to the nearest cent. *(p. 211)*

7. Zales sells diamonds for $1,100 that cost $800. What is Zales's percent markup on selling price? Round to the nearest hundredth percent. Check the selling price. *(p. 211)*

8. Earl Miller, a customer of J. Crew, will pay $400 for a new jacket. J. Crew has a 60% markup on selling price. What is the most that J. Crew can pay for this jacket? *(p. 211)*

9. Home Liquidators mark up its merchandise 35% on cost. What is the company's equivalent markup on selling price? Round to the nearest tenth percent. *(p. 213)*

Wear it once and request a **REFUND**?

I have a friend who habitually buys expensive clothes, wears them once to a fancy party, then reattaches all the tags and returns them to the store, as if unused, for a refund. What do you think about this?

As I see it, anyone who "buys" products with the intention of using them and then returning them is stealing that one-time use from the store. Sadly, I hear from friends in retail that this practice is quite common—and not confined to apparel. It has led many stores to accept returns only for store credit, not a refund. So who gets hurt in the end? All the other customers.

My sisters and I are shareholders in a closely held firm founded by our late father and now run by our brother. We suspect that he is charging some personal

MONEY & ETHICS
by Knight Kiplinger

living expenses (such as nonprofessional travel and entertainment) to the business, which diminishes its profitability and our dividends. What should we do?

If true, it is not only unethical but illegal, and it could get your business into trouble with the IRS. Ask your brother about it, raising your concerns in a courteous way that presumes nothing. If you are not satisfied, exercise your shareholder right to examine the books and commission a professional audit.

Have a money-and-ethics question you'd like answered in this column? Write editor in chief Knight Kiplinger at ethics@kiplinger.com.

From *Kiplinger's,* October 2007, p. 20.

WHAT'S THE DEAL? | These loans help homeowners turn their equity into cash.

More seniors tap their homes for **INCOME**

MORE OLDER Americans wanting to take advantage of the rise in home prices over the past decade without having to move are considering a reverse mortgage to tap their equity. About 150,000 homeowners will apply for one this year—twice last year's number, reports the National Reverse Mortgage Lenders Association.

With a reverse mortgage, you receive tax-free cash instead of making payments. Your debt increases rather than decreases, but you do not have to repay it until you move. If you die, your estate settles up. Payout options include a line of credit

or fixed monthly payments for life or a specific period. You must be 62 to qualify.

The most common type is the federally insured home-equity conversion mortgage, which is subject to the Federal Housing Administration's loan limits ($362,790 for high-cost urban areas, $200,160 elsewhere), but you will get only a percentage of that. The exact amount depends on your locale, your age, your equity in your home and the interest rate.

For now, high up-front fees make reverse mortgages useful mainly for people who plan to stay in their homes for more than a few years and have few other assets.

STOCK TO WATCH
Perfect **DIVIDEND** stream

For low-risk income and nice growth, try a pipeline. **Magellan Midstream Partners, LP,** one of the largest operators in the U.S., with 8,500 miles of conduits for gasoline and other refined fuels, has a perfect record. Since the partnership went public in 2001, Magellan (don't confuse it with the fund) has raised dividends every quarter. Today's rate of 63 cents gives you a yield of 6%-plus. The shares have risen steadily.

IN THE PIPELINE

Magellan Midstream Partners, LP
SYMBOL: MMP
PRICE: $40
DISTRIBUTIONS PER SHARE:
2006: $2.34
2007: $1.25
Data to August 20.

SITTING PRETTY: Americans who are age 62 and older hold a total of $4.3 trillion of equity in their homes.

BUSINESS MATH ISSUE

Retail stores should always charge customers a fee for returned goods

1. List the key points of the article and information to support your position.
2. Write a group defense of your position using math calculations to support your view.

PROJECT A

Based on the economic downturn of 2009 and 2010, have Macy's strategies worked?

Check it out on the Web and report back.

Macy's to Bring FAO Schwarz Into Its Stores

By Vanessa O'Connell

IN AN EFFORT to attract more shoppers, **Macy's** Inc. is expected to announce Friday plans to open FAO Schwarz toy boutiques in all 685 Macy's stores that carry children's clothing.

As many as 275 of Macy's 812 locations, including those in downtown Minneapolis, Union Square in San Francisco and Dadeland Mall in Miami, will get the toy boutiques by fall, in time for the holiday shopping season. The rest will open in 2009 and 2010.

Under the deal, FAO Schwarz will lease the floor space and pay Macy's an undisclosed percentage of sales as rent.

The venture is part of a broader trend in which big retailers are teaming up with specialty merchants to create stores within stores. With foot traffic down at many malls, department stores and other big chains are scrambling to give shoppers more reasons to step inside. For their smaller partners, such deals provide a chance to reach new customers with less financial risk than opening independent outlets.

J.C. Penney Co. is trying to attract younger shoppers with upscale Sephora cosmetic and fragrance shops in its stores. Over the past two years, it has in-

stalled them in 72 J.C. Penney locations and is working with Sephora—a unit of Paris-based **LVMH Moët Hennessy Louis Vuitton** SA—to roll them out in more than 300 of its 1,074 stores by 2010. Penney staffs the in-store shops and owns the Sephora merchandise.

Lord & Taylor, a unit of **NRDC Equity Partners**, plans to open Fortunoff jewelry-and-watch boutiques in all 47 of its stores in February. NRDC, a big retail developer, acquired the 21-store Fortunoff chain in March.

Along with its potential advantages, however, the strategy poses the risk of tarnishing the specialty retailer's more-exclusive brand. Penney says that is why it doesn't cut prices in its Sephora shops, even when it offers discounts elsewhere in its stores.

At FAO Schwarz, "We spent a lot of time thinking about the risk" before concluding that the Macy's rollout would broaden the store's image and help counter the perception that all of its toys are expensive, said Chief Executive Edward Schmults. "At a time of economic weakness, to be able to roll out this many stores at one time is just tremendous," he added. "Macy's is where Mom is shopping."

Macy's opened an **FAO Schwarz boutique** in Chicago as a test in November.

Macy's Chief Executive Terry J. Lundgren said the deal "will drive store traffic, particularly to our children's departments," which traditionally have had lower sales per square foot than other departments.

In a test over the past seven months, a 5,300-square-foot FAO Schwarz boutique at Macy's cavernous State Street store in Chicago produced a "ripple effect" of higher sales in children's apparel and accessories, he said.

For FAO Schwarz, the arrangement is a way to raise its profile. At its peak in the late 1990s, the fabled toy retailer had 40 stores. But

after running into financial trouble, it closed 18 stores in 2002 and sold the rest to Right Start Co., which filed for bankruptcy protection in 2003 and closed the remaining FAO Schwarz stores.

In 2004, hedge fund **D.E. Shaw** & Co. bought and reopened FAO Schwarz's flagship Fifth Avenue store in New York and a second location at Caesar's Palace in Las Vegas, as well as the retailer's catalog and Internet-sales businesses. D.E. Shaw is currently seeking to expand the 145-year-old brand.

The FAO Schwarz deal is part of a push by Cincinnati-based Ma-

cy's to differentiate its stores from the competition. It recently struck agreements with celebrities and well-known designers, including Martha Stewart, Donald Trump and Tommy Hilfiger, for exclusive merchandise.

Macy's has struggled to integrate the 400 department stores it acquired in its 2005 purchase of May Department Stores. Earlier this week, it reported a $59 million loss for the first quarter ended May 3, because of restructuring costs and a decline in sales. Sales in the period fell 2.9% to $5.75 billion.

Macy's plans to play up the FAO Schwarz connection in its fourth-quarter marketing campaign, according to Peter Sachse, its chief marketing officer. The chain hasn't had a year-round toy department in its stores for many years, according to spokesman Jim Sluzewski.

The new boutiques will include FAO Schwarz's private-label toys as well as independent brands such as Alex crafts and Lionel trains. FAO Schwarz toys will eventually be sold on the Macy's Web site, but Mr. Lundgren said there wasn't a timetable for online sales.

—Rachel Dodes contributed to this article

Internet Projects: See text Web site (www.mhhe.com/slater10e) and The Business Math Internet Resource Guide.

Video Case

Noodles & Company is a rapidly expanding restaurant in the "quick-casual" dining world. Close attention to detail through effective and efficient operations management is the core attribute that enables Noodles & Company to provide hot, fresh food in a timely manner. With time a scarce resource for many, Noodles & Company has found a way to satisfy the time-hungry niche market by providing high-quality food quickly.

Management spends much time analyzing business processes and functions to ensure customers receive a premium food experience. Noodles & Company plans the customers' experience from the moment they enter the restaurant to the moment they leave. Operations goals require each customer to have his or her meal within five minutes of placing an order.

Once the order is taken through the guest interaction point of purchase (30 seconds), the order is sent to the kitchen technologically. Through the division of tasks, every function of

the kitchen is made as efficient as possible. The line is set up with previously portioned meats and vegetables that flow in the same flow process each dish requires. Stations have a "job aid" providing the appropriate weight and ingredients for each dish. The preheated pan is critical to throughput and operational efficiency. With the help of 30,000 BTU burners, each dish gets through the sauté line in 3.5 minutes. An additional 30 seconds is used at the garnish station and the meal is served to the customer within 5 minutes.

Just-in-time inventory maintains that only what is needed is prepared. First-in first-out (FIFO) inventory method ensures the freshest ingredients. Food preparation is conducted throughout the day to ensure freshness. Focusing on every element from entry to exit allows Noodles & Company to deliver on the company's promise of quick, fresh, customized food served in a no-tip welcoming setting.

PROBLEM 1

The video discusses the extensive planning required to meet the operational goals for serving high-quality foods quickly. The goal of 5 minutes from order-taking to serving each meal is critical to maintaining Noodles & Company's promise to the customer of high-quality food served quickly. If a meal needs to be remade due to a processing error, what percent increase is this additional 3.5 minutes?

PROBLEM 2

In a June 17, 2009, press release, Noodles & Company says it was named one of the top three restaurants in America by a national magazine for the second time in six months. *Parents* magazine placed Noodles & Company third on its top 10 list of Best Fast-Casual Family Restaurants. In 2004, Noodles & Company decided to offer franchises for a $35,000 up-front fee and 5% of their annual revenue. Units average more than $1 million in annual sales. As a franchisee, how much revenue must be submitted to Noodles & Company with annual sales of $989,675?

PROBLEM 3

A May 20, 2009, Noodles & Company press release mentions there are more than 205 locations in 18 states. If they expect to grow by 17% in 2009, what is the expected number of restaurants they plan to open? Round to the nearest whole number.

PROBLEM 4

The Noodles & Company location in Parker, Colorado, sells its Pad Thai for $4.25 for a small, $5.25 for a regular with an additional $2.00 for protein for either size. If Noodles & Company is making a 300% markup based on the cost on their food, what is the cost for a small size Pad Thai with protein? Round to the nearest cent.

PROBLEM 5

As noted in the video, Noodles & Company has a no-tip policy. This helps to streamline operations while keeping the focus of employees on their tasks at hand. In problem 4 above, what would you save on a meal of a large Pad Thai with protein if you typically tip 20%? How much would you save if you brought your family of four with each meal averaging $6.50?

PROBLEM 6

In problem 4 above, the markup based on cost was 300%. What is the corresponding markup based on selling price?

PROBLEM 7

If a regular Pad Thai with protein costs $11.50 in Annapolis, Maryland, how much more are you paying in Maryland than in Parker, CO (see problem 4)? What percent is this difference? Round to the nearest percent.

A Word Problem Approach—Chapters 6, 7, 8

1. Assume Kellogg's produced 715,000 boxes of Corn Flakes this year. This was 110% of the annual production last year. What was last year's annual production? *(p. •••)*

2. A new Sony camcorder has a list price of $420. The trade discount is 10/20 with terms of 2/10, n/30. If a retailer pays the invoice within the discount period, what is the amount the retailer must pay? *(p. •••)*

3. JCPenney sells loafers with a markup of $40. If the markup is 30% on cost, what did the loafers cost JCPenney? Round to the nearest dollar. *(p. •••)*

4. Aster Computers received from Ring Manufacturers an invoice dated August 28 with terms 2/10 EOM. The list price of the invoice is $3,000 (freight not included). Ring offers Aster a 9/8/2 trade chain discount. Terms of freight are FOB shipping point, but Ring prepays the $150 freight. Assume Aster pays the invoice on October 9. How much will Ring receive? *(p. •••)*

5. Runners World marks up its Nike jogging shoes 25% on selling price. The Nike shoe sells for $65. How much did the store pay for them? *(p. •••)*

6. Ivan Rone sells antique sleds. He knows that the most he can get for a sled is $350. Ivan needs a 35% markup on cost. Since Ivan is going to an antiques show, he wants to know the maximum he can offer a dealer for an antique sled. *(p. •••)*

Disney Plans To Reduce Staff At Theme Parks

BY PETER SANDERS

Walt Disney Co. said Wednesday it will restructure its domestic theme-park operations, including an unspecified number of layoffs, amid languishing attendance and sharply reduced operating income.

The announcement came less than two weeks after a deadline to accept voluntary buyouts that the company offered to about 600 executives in its Parks and Resorts division. Disney officials declined to say how many executives took a voluntary buyout, but said the number was "satisfactory."

Wall Street Journal © 2009

Gene Duncan/AP Photo

LU 9–1: Calculating Various Types of Employees' Gross Pay

1. Define, compare, and contrast weekly, biweekly, semimonthly, and monthly pay periods *(p. 236).*

2. Calculate gross pay with overtime on the basis of time *(p. 237).*

3. Calculate gross pay for piecework, differential pay schedule, straight commission with draw, variable commission scale, and salary plus commission *(pp. 237–239).*

LU 9–2: Computing Payroll Deductions for Employees' Pay; Employers' Responsibilities

1. Prepare and explain the parts of a payroll register *(pp. 240–243).*

2. Explain and calculate federal and state unemployment taxes *(p. 243).*

VOCABULARY PREVIEW

Here are key terms in this chapter. After completing the chapter, if you know the term, place a checkmark in the parenthesis. If you don't know the term, look it up and put the page number where it can be found.

Biweekly . ( ) **Deductions** . ( ) **Differential pay schedule** . ( ) **Draw** . ( ) **Employee's Withholding Allowance Certificate (W-4)** . ( ) **Fair Labor Standards Act** . ( ) **Federal income tax withholding (FIT)** . ( ) **Federal Insurance Contribution Act (FICA)** . ( ) **Federal Unemployment Tax Act (FUTA)** . ( ) **Gross pay** . ( ) **Medicare** . ( ) **Monthly** . ( ) **Net pay** . ( ) **Overrides** . ( ) **Overtime** . ( ) **Payroll register** . ( ) **Percentage method** . ( ) **Semimonthly** . ( ) **Social Security** . ( ) **State income tax (SIT)** . ( ) **State Unemployment Tax Act (SUTA)** . ( ) **Straight commission** . ( ) **Variable commission scale** . ( ) **W-4** . ( ) **Weekly** . ( )

Wal-Mart to Pay Millions in Fees

Associated Press

Wal-Mart Stores Inc. has been ordered to pay $36.4 million in fees and expenses to attorneys representing Pennsylvania employees who won a class-action award for working off the clock.

The award, including fees and interest, now totals $187.6 million. The suit involved 187,000 current and former employees who worked at Wal-Mart and Sam's Club from March 1998 through May 2006.

A Philadelphia jury last year rejected Wal-Mart's claim that some people chose to work through breaks or that a few minutes of extra work was insignificant.

The plaintiffs initially won a $78.5 million class-action award for lost wages. Most of the group qualified for a share of an additional $62.3 million in damages under a state law invoked when a company withholds pay without cause for more than 30 days.

Jason Janik/Bloomberg News/Landov

The *Wall Street Journal* clipping "Wal-Mart to Pay Millions in Fees" shows how the company was penalized for not paying employees who worked through breaks or who put in a few minutes of extra work off the clock.

This chapter discusses (1) the type of pay people work for, (2) how employers calculate paychecks and deductions, and (3) what employers must report and pay in taxes.

Learning Unit 9–1: Calculating Various Types of Employees' Gross Pay

LO 1

Logan Company manufactures dolls of all shapes and sizes. These dolls are sold worldwide. We study Logan Company in this unit because of the variety of methods Logan uses to pay its employees.

Companies usually pay employees **weekly, biweekly, semimonthly,** or **monthly.** How often employers pay employees can affect how employees manage their money. Some employees prefer a weekly paycheck that spreads the inflow of money. Employees who have monthly bills may find the twice-a-month or monthly paycheck more convenient. All employees would like more money to manage.

Let's assume you earn $50,000 per year. The following table shows what you would earn each pay period. Remember that 13 weeks equals one quarter. Four quarters or 52 weeks equals a year.

Salary paid	Period (based on a year)	Earnings for period (dollars)
Weekly	52 times (once a week)	$ 961.54 ($50,000 ÷ 52)
Biweekly	26 times (every two weeks)	$1,923.08 ($50,000 ÷ 26)
Semimonthly	24 times (twice a month)	$2,083.33 ($50,000 ÷ 24)
Monthly	12 times (once a month)	$4,166.67 ($50,000 ÷ 12)

Now let's look at some pay schedule situations and examples of how Logan Company calculates its payroll for employees of different pay status.

LO 2

Situation 1: Hourly Rate of Pay; Calculation of Overtime

The **Fair Labor Standards Act** sets minimum wage standards and overtime regulations for employees of companies covered by this federal law. The law provides that employees working for an hourly rate receive time-and-a-half pay for hours worked in excess of their regular 40-hour week. The current hourly minimum wage is $7.25 effective summer of 2009. Many managerial people, however, are exempt from the time-and-a-half pay for all hours in excess of a 40-hour week.

In addition to many managerial people being exempt from time-and-a-half pay for more than 40 hours, other workers may also be exempt. Note in the *Wall Street Journal* clipping "Golden Arches in China," McDonald's is raising wages in China amid tightening labor laws by China's government-backed union.

GLOBAL

Golden Arches in China

BEIJING—**McDonald's** Corp. is raising wages and adopting new uniforms, stepping up efforts to burnish its image as an employer in China amid tightening labor laws and scrutiny by China's government-backed trade union.

McDonald's said it will raise wages for its restaurant crews 12% to 56% above China's minimum-wage guidelines as of Sept. 1, a move that will affect about 45,000 full-time and part-time workers, including students. Full-time workers in the large southern city of Guangzhou, for example, will see their monthly wages rise 21% to 1,072 yuan ($142).

The change will average out to a 30% pay rise for all McDonald's frontline staff, said Jeffrey Schwartz, chief executive for China for McDonald's, based in Oak Brook, Ill.

Wages at McDonald's and its fast-food rival **Yum Brands** Inc., which runs the KFC and Pizza Hut chains, have been under increased scrutiny in China after the powerful All-China Federation of Trade Unions in April accused the fast-food giants of violating la-

815 restaurants currently, with plans for 100 new restaurants a year

50,000 crew workers employed

1990, first restaurant opens in Shenzhen

2% of company's global revenue generated in China

Olympic sponsor

80,000 to 120,000 new uniforms will be issued this year

Runs 46 food-processing plants

Source: the company

bor laws by underpaying part-time workers in Guangzhou.

Local authorities later absolved the companies of wrongdoing, but McDonald's, KFC and Pizza Hut received negative publicity in local media reports that focused especially on the issue of part-time workers, who weren't covered under the city's legal minimum wage of 7.50 yuan an hour.

Mr. Schwartz said the Guangzhou incident "expedited" the company's pay-rise program, which he said had been in the planning process

for a year. While the negative publicity didn't appear to affect sales, Mr. Schwartz said, "for me as an employer, I didn't want to be portrayed that way, because we're not that way."

Yum Brands, of Louisville, Ky., didn't respond yesterday to requests for comment.

While the American fast-food giants have been under particular scrutiny because of their size and high-profile brands, wage pressures in China in general have risen lately amid a sharp increase in the price of basic necessities.

Now we return to our Logan Company example. Logan Company is calculating the weekly pay of Ramon Valdez who works in its manufacturing division. For the first 40 hours Ramon works, Logan calculates his **gross pay** (earnings before **deductions**) as follows:

> Gross pay = Hours employee worked × Rate per hour

Ramon works more than 40 hours in a week. For every hour over his 40 hours, Ramon must be paid an **overtime** pay of at least 1.5 times his regular pay rate. The following formula is used to determine Ramon's overtime:

> Hourly overtime pay rate = Regular hourly pay rate × 1.5

Logan Company must include Ramon's overtime pay with his regular pay. To determine Ramon's gross pay, Logan uses the following formula:

> Gross pay = Earnings for 40 hours + Earnings at time-and-a-half rate (1.5)

We are now ready to calculate Ramon's gross pay from the following data:

EXAMPLE

Employee	M	T	W	Th	F	S	Total hours	Rate per hour
Ramon Valdez	13	$8\frac{1}{2}$	10	8	$11\frac{1}{4}$	$10\frac{3}{4}$	$61\frac{1}{2}$	$9

$$\begin{array}{r} 61\frac{1}{2} \text{ total hours} \\ -40 \text{ regular hours} \\ \hline 21\frac{1}{2} \text{ hours overtime}^{1} \end{array}$$ Time-and-a-half pay: $9 × 1.5 = $13.50

Gross pay = (40 hours × $9) + ($21\frac{1}{2}$ hours × $13.50)

= $360 + $290.25

= $650.25

Note that the $13.50 overtime rate came out even. However, throughout the text, *if an overtime rate is greater than two decimal places, do not round it. Round only the final answer. This gives greater accuracy.*

LO 3

Situation 2: Straight Piece Rate Pay

Some companies, especially manufacturers, pay workers according to how much they produce. Logan Company pays Ryan Foss for the number of dolls he produces in a week. This gives Ryan an incentive to make more money by producing more dolls. Ryan receives $.96 per doll, less any defective units. The following formula determines Ryan's gross pay:

> Gross pay = Number of units produced × Rate per unit

Companies may also pay a guaranteed hourly wage and use a piece rate as a bonus. However, Logan uses straight piece rate as wages for some of its employees. The *Wall Street Journal* article "Pay Scales Divide Factory" (p. 238) show the trend that has companies such as Goodyear Tire not providing all employees with the same pay packages.

---

[1]Some companies pay overtime for time over 8 hours in one day; Logan Company pays overtime for time over 40 hours per week.

Pay Scales Divide Factory

Issue Gets Touchy As More Firms Use Two-Tier System

By TIMOTHY AEPPEL

GADSDEN, Ala.—Few things better illustrate the diminished fortunes of the American factory worker than the emergence of "$13 workers" at **Goodyear Tire & Rubber** Co.

Jobs at the U.S.'s largest tire maker by revenue used to be coveted mainly because everyone from janitors to skilled machine operators could expect to eventually earn more than $20 an hour, with lush benefits.

That rich compensation is now slipping away. New workers hired under Goodyear's latest labor agreement earn just $13 an hour with fewer benefits for the first three years and many will likely never achieve the lofty pay packages of the past.

Wall Street Journal © 2008

EXAMPLE During the last week of April, Ryan Foss produced 900 dolls. Using the above formula, Logan Company paid Ryan $864.

$$\text{Gross pay} = 900 \text{ dolls} \times \$.96$$
$$= \boxed{\$864}$$

Situation 3: Differential Pay Schedule

Some of Logan's employees can earn more than the $.96 straight piece rate for every doll they produce. Logan Company has set up a **differential pay schedule** for these employees. The company determines the rate these employees make by the amount of units the employees produce at different levels of production.

EXAMPLE Logan Company pays Abby Rogers on the basis of the following schedule:

	Units produced	Amount per unit
First 50 →	1–50	$ .50
Next 100 →	51–150	.62
Next 50 →	151–200	.75
	Over 200	1.25

Last week Abby produced 300 dolls. What is Abby's gross pay?
Logan calculated Abby's gross pay as follows:

$$(50 \times \$.50) + (100 \times \$.62) + (50 \times \$.75) + (100 \times \$1.25)$$
$$\$25 \quad + \quad \$62 \quad + \quad \$37.50 \quad + \quad \$125 \quad = \boxed{\$249.50}$$

Now we will study some of the other types of employee commission payment plans.

Situation 4: Straight Commission with Draw

Companies frequently use **straight commission** to determine the pay of salespersons. This commission is usually a certain percentage of the amount the salesperson sells. An example of one group of companies ceasing to pay commissions is the rental-car companies.

Companies such as Logan Company allow some of its salespersons to draw against their commission at the beginning of each month. A **draw** is an advance on the salesperson's commission. Logan subtracts this advance later from the employee's commission earned based on sales. When the commission does not equal the draw, the salesperson owes Logan the difference between the draw and the commission.

EXAMPLE Logan Company pays Jackie Okamoto a straight commission of 15% on her net sales (net sales are total sales less sales returns). In May, Jackie had net sales of $56,000. Logan gave Jackie a $600 draw in May. What is Jackie's gross pay?
Logan calculated Jackie's commission minus her draw as follows:

$$\$56,000 \times .15 = \$8,400$$
$$- \ 600$$
$$\boxed{\$7,800}$$

Commission

Portion

Base × Rate

Net sales   Commission rate

Logan Company pays some people in the sales department on a variable commission scale. Let's look at this, assuming the employee had no draw.

Situation 5: Variable Commission Scale

A company with a **variable commission scale** uses different commission rates for different levels of net sales.

EXAMPLE Last month, Jane Ring's net sales were $160,000. What is Jane's gross pay based on the following schedule?

Up to $35,000   4%
Excess of $35,000 to $45,000   6%
Over $45,000   8%

Gross pay = ($35,000 × .04) + ($10,000 × .06) + ($115,000 × .08)

= $1,400   + $600   + $9,200

= $11,200

Situation 6: Salary Plus Commission

Logan Company pays Joe Roy a $3,000 monthly salary plus a 4% commission for sales over $20,000. Last month Joe's net sales were $50,000. Logan calculated Joe's gross monthly pay as follows:

Gross pay = Salary + (Commission × Sales over $20,000)

= $3,000 +   (.04 × $30,000)

= $3,000 + $1,200

= $4,200

Before you take the Practice Quiz, you should know that many managers today receive **overrides.** These managers receive a commission based on the net sales of the people they supervise.

LU 9–1   PRACTICE QUIZ

Complete this **Practice Quiz** to see how you are doing.

1. Jill Foster worked 52 hours in one week for Delta Airlines. Jill earns $10 per hour. What is Jill's gross pay, assuming overtime is at time-and-a-half?
2. Matt Long had $180,000 in sales for the month. Matt's commission rate is 9%, and he had a $3,500 draw. What was Matt's end-of-month commission?
3. Bob Meyers receives a $1,000 monthly salary. He also receives a variable commission on net sales based on the following schedule (commission doesn't begin until Bob earns $8,000 in net sales):

$8,000–$12,000   1%   Excess of $20,000 to $40,000   5%
Excess of $12,000 to $20,000 3%   More than $40,000   8%

Assume Bob earns $40,000 net sales for the month. What is his gross pay?

Solutions with Step-by-Step Help on DVD

✓ Solutions

1. 40 hours × $10.00 = $400.00
   12 hours × $15.00 = __180.00__ ($10.00 × 1.5 = $15.00)
                       $580.00
2. $180,000 × .09 = $16,200
                    − __3,500__
                      $12,700
3. Gross pay = $1,000 + ($4,000 × .01) + ($8,000 × .03) + ($20,000 × .05)
             = $1,000 + $40   + $240   + $1,000
             = $2,280

LU 9–1a   EXTRA PRACTICE QUIZ WITH WORKED-OUT SOLUTIONS

Need more practice? Try this **Extra Practice Quiz** (check figures in Chapter Organizer, p. 246). Worked-out Solutions can be found in Appendix B at end of text.

1. Jill Foster worked 54 hours in one week for Delta Airlines. Jill earns $12 per hour. What is Jill's gross pay, assuming overtime is at time-and-a-half?
2. Matt Long had $210,000 in sales for the month. Matt's commission rate is 8%, and he had a $4,000 draw. What was Matt's end-of-month commission?

3. Bob Myers receives a $1,200 monthly salary. He also receives a variable commission on net sales based on the following schedule (commission doesn't begin until Bob earns $9,000 in net sales).

$9,000 to $12,000	1%	Excess of $20,000 to $40,000	5%
Excess of $12,000 to $20,000	3%	More than $40,000	8%

Assume Bob earns $60,000 net sales for the month. What is his gross pay?

Learning Unit 9–2: Computing Payroll Deductions for Employees' Pay; Employers' Responsibilities

Did you know that Walmart is the largest employer in twenty-one states? Can you imagine the accounting involved to pay all these employees?

This unit begins by dissecting a paycheck. Then we give you an insight into the tax responsibilities of employers.

LO 1

Computing Payroll Deductions for Employees

Companies often record employee payroll information in a multicolumn form called a **payroll register.** The increased use of computers in business has made computerized registers a timesaver for many companies.

Glo Company uses a multicolumn payroll register. Below is Glo's partial payroll register showing the payroll information for Alice Rey during week 47. Let's check each column to see if Alice's take-home pay of $1,573.81 is correct. Note how the circled letters in the register correspond to the explanations that follow.

GLO COMPANY Payroll Register Week #47																
Employee name	Allow. & marital status	Cum. earn.	Sal. per week	**Earnings**			Cum. earn.	**FICA Taxable Earnings**		**Deductions**						
				Reg.	Ovt.	Gross		S.S.	Med.	**FICA**		FIT	SIT	Health ins.	Net pay	
										S.S.	Med.					
Rey, Alice	M-2	105,750	2,250	2,250	—	2,250	108,000	1,050	2,250	65.10	32.63	343.46	135	100	1,573.81	
	(A)	(B)	(C)		(D)		(E)	(F)	(G)	(H)	(I)	(J)	(K)	(L)	(M)	

Payroll Register Explanations

(A)—Allowance and marital status
(B), (C), (D)—Cumulative earnings before payroll, salaries, earnings
(E)—Cumulative earnings after payroll

When Alice was hired, she completed the **W-4 (Employee's Withholding Allowance Certificate)** form shown in Figure 9.1 stating that she is married and claims an allowance (exemption) of 2. Glo Company will need this information to calculate the federal income tax (J).

FIGURE 9.1

Employee's W-4 form

Form **W-4** Department of the Treasury Internal Revenue Service	**Employee's Withholding Allowance Certificate** ► For Privacy Act and Paperwork Reduction Act Notice, see reverse.

OMB No. 1545-0010
20**XX**

1 Type or print your first name and middle initial — Alice Last name — Rey 2 Your social security number — 021 36 9494

Home address (number and street or rural route) — 2 Roundy Road

3 ☐ Single ☒ Married ☐ Married, but withhold at higher Single rate. **Note:** If married, but legally separated, or spouse is a nonresident alien, check the Single box.

City or town, state, and ZIP code — Marblehead, MA 01945

4 If your last name differs from that on your social security card, check here and call 1-800-772-1213 for a new card . . . . . ► ☐

5 Total number of allowances you are claiming (from line G above or from the worksheets on page 2 if they apply) . **5** 2
6 Additional amount, if any, you want withheld from each paycheck . . . . **6** $
7 I claim exemption from withholding for 1995 and I certify that I meet **BOTH** of the following conditions for exemption:
 • Last year I had a right to a refund of **ALL** Federal income tax withheld because I had **NO** tax liability; **AND**
 • This year I expect a refund of **ALL** Federal income tax withheld because I expect to have **NO** tax liability.
 If you meet both conditions, enter "EXEMPT" here . . . . ► **7**
Under penalties of perjury, I certify that I am entitled to the number of withholding allowances claimed on this certificate or entitled to claim exempt status.

Employee's signature ► *Alice Rey* Date ► 1/1 , 20 XX

8 Employer's name and address (Employer: Complete 8 and 10 only if sending to the IRS) | 9 Office code (optional) | 10 Employer identification number

Cat. No. 10220Q

Before this pay period, Alice has earned $105,750 (47 weeks × $2,250 salary per week). Since Alice receives no overtime, her $2,250 salary per week represents her gross pay (pay before any deductions).

After this pay period, Alice has earned $108,000 ($105,750 + $2,250).

The **Federal Insurance Contribution Act (FICA)** funds the **Social Security** program. The program includes Old Age and Disability, Medicare, Survivor Benefits, and so on. The FICA tax requires separate reporting for Social Security and **Medicare.** We will use the following rates for Glo Company:

	Rate	Base
Social Security	6.20%	$106,800
Medicare	1.45	No base

These rates mean that Alice Rey will pay Social Security taxes on the first $106,800 she earns this year. After earning $106,800, Alice's wages will be exempt from Social Security. Note that Alice will be paying Medicare taxes on all wages since Medicare has no base cutoff.

Ⓕ,Ⓖ—Taxable earnings for Social Security and Medicare

To help keep Glo's record straight, the *taxable earnings column only shows what wages will be taxed. This amount is not the tax.* For example, in week 47, only $1,050 of Alice's salary will be taxable for Social Security.

$106,800 Social Security base
$\underline{- \ 105,750}$ Ⓑ
$ \ \ \ 1,050$

Ⓗ—Social Security

To calculate Alice's Social Security tax, we multiply $1,050 Ⓕ by 6.2%:

$1,050 × .062 = **$65.10**

Ⓘ—Medicare

Since Medicare has no base, Alice's entire weekly salary is taxed 1.45%, which is multiplied by $2,250.

$2,250 × .0145 = **$32.63**

Ⓙ—FIT

Using the W-4 form Alice completed, Glo deducts **federal income tax withholding (FIT).** The more allowances an employee claims, the less money Glo deducts from the employee's paycheck. Glo uses the percentage method to calculate FIT.[2]

The Percentage Method[3]

Today, since many companies do not want to store the tax tables, they use computers for their payroll. These companies use the **percentage method.** For this method we use Table 9.1 and Table 9.2 on page 242 from Circular E to calculate Alice's FIT.

Step 1. In Table 9.1, locate the weekly withholding for one allowance. Multiply this number by 2.

$70.19 × 2 = $140.38

Step 2. Subtract $140.38 in Step 1 from Alice's total pay.

$2,250.00
$\underline{- \ \ \ 140.38}$
$2,109.62

Step 3. In Table 9.2, locate the married person's weekly pay table. The $2,109.62 falls between $1,455 and $2,785. The tax is $179.80 plus 25% of the excess over $1,455.00.

$2,109.62
$\underline{- \ 1,455.00}$
$ \ \ \ 654.62

Tax $179.80 + .25 ($654.62)

$179.80 + $163.66 = **$343.46**

---

[2]The *Business Math Handbook* has a sample of the wage bracket method.

[3]An alternative method is called the wage bracket method that is shown in the *Business Math Handbook*.

TABLE 9.1

Percentage method income tax withholding table

Payroll Period	One Withholding Allowance
Weekly	$ 70.19
Biweekly	140.38
Semimonthly	152.08
Monthly	304.17
Quarterly	912.50
Semiannually	1,825.00
Annually	3,650.00
Daily or miscellaneous (each day of the payroll period)	14.04

TABLE 9.2   Percentage method income tax withholding taxes

TABLE 1—WEEKLY Payroll Period

(a) SINGLE person (including head of household)—

If the amount of wages (after subtracting withholding allowances) is: The amount of income tax to withhold is:

Not over $51 . . . . $0

Over—	But not over—		of excess over—
$51	—$200	. . . 10%	—$51
$200	—$681	. . . $14.90 plus 15%	—$200
$681	—$1,621	. . . $87.05 plus 25%	—$681
$1,621	—$3,338	. . . $322.05 plus 28%	—$1,621
$3,338	—$7,212	. . . $802.81 plus 33%	—$3,338
$7,212	. . . .	. . . $2,081.23 plus 35%	—$7,212

(b) MARRIED person—

If the amount of wages (after subtracting withholding allowances) is: The amount of income tax to withhold is:

Not over $154 . . . . $0

Over—	But not over—		of excess over—
$154	—$461	. . . 10%	—$154
$461	—$1,455	. . . $30.70 plus 15%	—$461
$1,455	—$2,785	. . . $179.80 plus 25%	—$1,455
$2,785	—$4,165	. . . $512.30 plus 28%	—$2,785
$4,165	—$7,321	. . . $898.70 plus 33%	—$4,165
$7,321	. . . .	. . . $1,940.18 plus 35%	—$7,321

TABLE 2—BIWEEKLY Payroll Period

(a) SINGLE person (including head of household)—

If the amount of wages (after subtracting withholding allowances) is: The amount of income tax to withhold is:

Not over $102 . . . . $0

Over—	But not over—		of excess over—
$102	—$400	. . . 10%	—$102
$400	—$1,362	. . . $29.80 plus 15%	—$400
$1,362	—$3,242	. . . $174.10 plus 25%	—$1,362
$3,242	—$6,677	. . . $644.10 plus 28%	—$3,242
$6,677	—$14,423	. . . $1,605.90 plus 33%	—$6,677
$14,423	. . . .	. . . $4,162.08 plus 35%	—$14,423

(b) MARRIED person—

If the amount of wages (after subtracting withholding allowances) is: The amount of income tax to withhold is:

Not over $308 . . . . $0

Over—	But not over—		of excess over—
$308	—$921	. . . 10%	—$308
$921	—$2,910	. . . $61.30 plus 15%	—$921
$2,910	—$5,569	. . . $359.65 plus 25%	—$2,910
$5,569	—$8,331	. . . $1,024.40 plus 28%	—$5,569
$8,331	—$14,642	. . . $1,797.76 plus 33%	—$8,331
$14,642	. . . .	. . . $3,880.39 plus 35%	—$14,642

TABLE 3—SEMIMONTHLY Payroll Period

(a) SINGLE person (including head of household)—

If the amount of wages (after subtracting withholding allowances) is: The amount of income tax to withhold is:

Not over $110 . . . . $0

Over—	But not over—		of excess over—
$110	—$433	. . . 10%	—$110
$433	—$1,475	. . . $32.30 plus 15%	—$433
$1,475	—$3,513	. . . $188.60 plus 25%	—$1,475
$3,513	—$7,233	. . . $698.10 plus 28%	—$3,513
$7,233	—$15,625	. . . $1,739.70 plus 33%	—$7,233
$15,625	. . . .	. . . $4,509.06 plus 35%	—$15,625

(b) MARRIED person—

If the amount of wages (after subtracting withholding allowances) is: The amount of income tax to withhold is:

Not over $333 . . . . $0

Over—	But not over—		of excess over—
$333	—$998	. . . 10%	—$333
$998	—$3,152	. . . $66.50 plus 15%	—$998
$3,152	—$6,033	. . . $389.60 plus 25%	—$3,152
$6,033	—$9,025	. . . $1,109.85 plus 28%	—$6,033
$9,025	—$15,863	. . . $1,947.61 plus 33%	—$9,025
$15,863	. . . .	. . . $4,204.15 plus 35%	—$15,863

TABLE 4—MONTHLY Payroll Period

(a) SINGLE person (including head of household)—

If the amount of wages (after subtracting withholding allowances) is: The amount of income tax to withhold is:

Not over $221 . . . . $0

Over—	But not over—		of excess over—
$221	—$867	. . . 10%	—$221
$867	—$2,950	. . . $64.60 plus 15%	—$867
$2,950	—$7,025	. . . $377.05 plus 25%	—$2,950
$7,025	—$14,467	. . . $1,395.80 plus 28%	—$7,025
$14,467	—$31,250	. . . $3,479.56 plus 33%	—$14,467
$31,250	. . . .	. . . $9,017.95 plus 35%	—$31,250

(b) MARRIED person—

If the amount of wages (after subtracting withholding allowances) is: The amount of income tax to withhold is:

Not over $667 . . . . $0

Over—	But not over—		of excess over—
$667	—$1,996	. . . 10%	—$667
$1,996	—$6,304	. . . $132.90 plus 15%	—$1,996
$6,304	—$12,067	. . . $779.10 plus 25%	—$6,304
$12,067	—$18,050	. . . $2,219.85 plus 28%	—$12,067
$18,050	—$31,725	. . . $3,895.09 plus 33%	—$18,050
$31,725	. . . .	. . . $8,407.84 plus 35%	—$31,725

Ⓚ—SIT

Ⓛ—Health insurance
Ⓜ—Net pay

We assume a 6% **state income tax (SIT)**.

$2,250 × .06 = $135.00

Alice contributes $100 per week for health insurance.
Alice's **net pay** is her gross pay less all deductions.

```
  $2,250.00  gross
 −    65.10  Social Security
 −    32.63  Medicare
 −   343.46  FIT
 −   135.00  SIT
 −   100.00  health insurance
 = $1,573.81 net pay
```

Employers' Responsibilities

In the first section of this unit, we saw that Alice contributed to Social Security and Medicare. Glo Company has the legal responsibility to match her contributions. Besides matching Social Security and Medicare, Glo must pay two important taxes that employees do not have to pay—federal and state unemployment taxes.

Federal Unemployment Tax Act (FUTA)

The federal government participates in a joint federal-state unemployment program to help unemployed workers. At this writing, employers pay the government a 6.2% **FUTA** tax on the first $7,000 paid to employees as wages during the calendar year. Any wages in excess of $7,000 per worker are exempt wages and are not taxed for FUTA. If the total cumulative amount the employer owes the government is less than $100, the employer can pay the liability yearly (end of January in the following calendar year). If the tax is greater than $100, the employer must pay it within a month after the quarter ends.

Companies involved in a state unemployment tax fund can usually take a 5.4% credit against their FUTA tax. *In reality, then, companies are paying .8% (.008) to the federal unemployment program.* In all our calculations, FUTA is .008.

RF/Corbis

LO 2

EXAMPLE   Assume a company had total wages of $19,000 in a calendar year. No employee earned more than $7,000 during the calendar year. The FUTA tax is .8% (6.2% minus the company's 5.4% credit for state unemployment tax). How much does the company pay in FUTA tax?

The company calculates its FUTA tax as follows:

```
   6.2% FUTA tax
 − 5.4% credit for SUTA tax
 =  .8% tax for FUTA
```

.008 × $19,000 = $152 FUTA tax due to federal government

State Unemployment Tax Act (SUTA)

The current **SUTA** tax in many states is 5.4% on the first $7,000 the employer pays an employee. Some states offer a merit rating system that results in a lower SUTA rate for companies with a stable employment period. The federal government still allows 5.4% credit on FUTA tax to companies entitled to the lower SUTA rate. Usually states also charge companies with a poor employment record a higher SUTA rate. However, these companies cannot take any more than the 5.4% credit against the 6.2% federal unemployment rate.

EXAMPLE   Assume a company has total wages of $20,000 and $4,000 of the wages are exempt from SUTA. What are the company's SUTA and FUTA taxes if the company's SUTA rate is 5.8% due to a poor employment record?

The exempt wages (over $7,000 earnings per worker) are not taxed for SUTA or FUTA. So the company owes the following SUTA and FUTA taxes:

```
  $20,000
 −   4,000 (exempt wages)
  $16,000 × .058 = $928  SUTA
```

Federal FUTA tax would then be:

$16,000 × .008 = $128

You can check your progress with the following Practice Quiz.

Complete this **Practice Quiz** to see how you are doing.

1. Calculate Social Security taxes, Medicare taxes, and FIT for Joy Royce. Joy's company pays her a monthly salary of $9,500. She is single and claims 1 deduction. Before this payroll, Joy's cumulative earnings were $103,300. (Social Security maximum is 6.2% on $106,800, and Medicare is 1.45%.) Calculate FIT by the percentage method.

2. Jim Brewer, owner of Arrow Company, has three employees who earn $300, $700, and $900 a week. Assume a state SUTA rate of 5.1%. What will Jim pay for state and federal unemployment taxes for the first quarter?

Solutions with Step-by-Step Help on DVD

✓ **Solutions**

1. **Social Security**   **Medicare**

$106,800 $9,500 × .0145 = $137.75
− 103,300
$ 3,500 × .062 = $217.00

FIT
Percentage method: $9,500.00
$304.17 × 1 =   − 304.17 (Table 9.1)
$9,195.83

$7,025 to $14,467 → $1,395.80 plus 28% of excess over $7,025
(Table 9.2)

$9,195.83
− 7,025.00
$2,170.83 × .28 = $ 607.83
+ 1,395.80
$2,003.63

2. 13 weeks × $300 = $ 3,900
13 weeks × $700 =   9,100 ($9,100 − $7,000) → $2,100 ⎫ Exempt wages
13 weeks × $900 = 11,700 ($11,700 − $7,000) → 4,700 ⎬ (not taxed for
$24,700 $6,800 ⎭ FUTA or SUTA)

$24,700 − $6,800 = $17,900 taxable wages   *Note:* FUTA remains at .008
SUTA = .051 × $17,900 = $912.90   whether SUTA rate is higher
FUTA = .008 × $17,900 = $143.20   or lower than standard.

Need more practice? Try this **Extra Practice Quiz** (check figures in Chapter Organizer, p. 246). Worked-out Solutions can be found in Appendix B at end of text.

1. Calculate Social Security taxes, Medicare taxes, and FIT for Joy Royce. Joy's company pays her a monthly salary of $10,000. She is single and claims 1 deduction. Before this payroll, Joy's cumulative earnings were $106,300. (Social Security maximum is 6.2% on $106,800, and Medicare is 1.45%.) Calculate FIT by the percentage method.

2. Jim Brewer, owner of Arrow Company, has three employees who earn $200, $800, and $950 a week. Assume a state SUTA rate of 5.1%. What will Jim pay for state and federal unemployment taxes for the first quarter?

CHAPTER ORGANIZER AND REFERENCE GUIDE

Topic	Key point, procedure, formula	Example(s) to illustrate situation
Gross pay, p. 237	$\text{Hours employee worked} \times \text{Rate per hour}$	$6.50 per hour at 36 hours Gross pay = 36 × $6.50 = $234
Overtime, p. 237	$\text{Gross earnings (pay)} = \text{Regular pay} + \text{Earnings at overtime rate } (1\tfrac{1}{2})$	$6 per hour; 42 hours Gross pay = (40 × $6) + (2 × $9) = $240 + $18 = $258
Straight piece rate, p. 237	$\text{Gross pay} = \text{Number of units produced} \times \text{Rate per unit}$	1,185 units; rate per unit, $.89 Gross pay = 1,185 × $.89 = $1,054.65
Differential pay schedule, p. 238	Rate on each item is related to the number of items produced.	1–500 at $.84; 501–1,000 at $.96; 900 units produced. Gross pay = (500 × $.84) + (400 × $.96) = $420 + $384 = $804
Straight commission, p. 238	Total sales × Commission rate Any draw would be subtracted from earnings.	$155,000 sales; 6% commission $155,000 × .06 = $9,300
Variable commission scale, p. 238	Sales at different levels pay different rates of commission.	Up to $5,000, 5%; $5,001 to $10,000, 8%; over $10,000, 10% Sold: $6,500 Solution: ($5,000 × .05) + ($1,500 × .08) = $250 + $120 = $370
Salary plus commission, p. 239	$\text{Regular wages (fixed)} + \text{Commissions earned}$	Base $400 per week + 2% on sales over $14,000 Actual sales: $16,000 $400 (base) + (.02 × $2,000) = $440
Payroll register, p. 240	Multicolumn form to record payroll. Married and paid weekly. (Table 9.2) Claims 1 allowance. FICA rates from chapter.	(see table below)
FICA, p. 241 **Social Security Medicare**	6.2% on $106,800 (S.S.) 1.45% (Med.)	If John earns $107,000, what did he contribute for the year to Social Security and Medicare? S.S.: $106,800 × .062 = $6,621.60 Med.: $107,000 × .0145 = $1,551.50
FIT calculation (percentage method), p. 241	*Facts:* Al Doe: Married Claims: 2 Paid weekly: $1,600	$1,600.00 − 140.38 ($70.19 × 2) Table 9.1 $1,459.62 By Table 9.2 $1,459.62 − 1,455.00 $ 4.62 $179.80 + .25($4.62) $179.80 + $1.16 = $180.96
State and federal unemployment, p. 243	Employer pays these taxes. Rates are 6.2% on $7,000 for federal and 5.4% for state on $7,000. 6.2% − 5.4% = .8% federal rate after credit. If state unemployment rate is higher than 5.4%, no additional credit is taken. If state unemployment rate is less than 5.4%, the full 5.4% credit can be taken for federal unemployment.	Cumulative pay before payroll, $6,400; this week's pay, $800. What are state and federal unemployment taxes for employer, assuming a 5.2% state unemployment rate? State → .052 × $600 = $31.20 Federal → .008 × $600 = $4.80 ($6,400 + $600 = $7,000 maximum)

Payroll register example:

Earnings	Deductions			Net pay
	FICA			
Gross	S.S.	Med.	FIT	
1,100	68.20	15.95	116.02	899.83

(continues)

CHAPTER ORGANIZER AND REFERENCE GUIDE

Topic	Key point, procedure, formula		Example(s) to illustrate situation

KEY TERMS	Biweekly, *p. 236*
	Deductions, *p. 237*
	Differential pay schedule, *p. 238*
	Draw, *p. 238*
	Employee's Withholding Allowance
	    Certificate (W-4), *p. 240*
	Fair Labor Standards Act, *p. 236*
	Federal income tax withholding
	    (FIT), *p. 241*
	Federal Insurance Contribution
	    Act (FICA), *p. 241*
		Federal Unemployment Tax Act
		    (FUTA), *p. 243*
		Gross pay, *p. 237*
		Medicare, *p. 241*
		Monthly, *p. 236*
		Net pay, *p. 243*
		Overrides, *p. 239*
		Overtime, *p. 237*
		Payroll register, *p. 240*
		Percentage method, *p. 241*
			Semimonthly, *p. 241*
			Social Security, *p. 241*
			State income tax (SIT), *p. 243*
			State Unemployment Tax Act
			    (SUTA), *p. 243*
			Straight commission, *p. 238*
			Variable commission
			    scale, *p. 238*
			W-4, *p. 240*
			Weekly, *p. 236*

CHECK FIGURES FOR EXTRA PRACTICE QUIZZES WITH PAGE REFERENCES. (WORKED-OUT SOLUTIONS IN APPENDIX B.)	LU 9–1a (p. 239) 1. $732 2. $12,800 3. $4,070		LU 9–2a (p. 244) 1. $31; 145; $2,143.63 2. $846.60; $132.80

Critical Thinking Discussion Questions

1. Explain the difference between biweekly and semimonthly. Explain what problems may develop if a retail store hires someone on straight commission to sell cosmetics.

2. Explain what each column of a payroll register records (p. 240) and how each number is calculated. Social Security tax is based on a specific rate and base; Medicare tax is based on a rate but no base. Do you think this is fair to all taxpayers?

3. What taxes are the responsibility of the employer? How can an employer benefit from a merit-rating system for state unemployment?

END-OF-CHAPTER PROBLEMS  connect™ (plus+) www.mhhe.com/slater10e

Check figures for odd-numbered problems in Appendix C

Name _____ Date _____

DRILL PROBLEMS

Complete the following table:

Employee	M	T	W	Th	F	Hours	Rate per hour	Gross pay
9–1. Tom Bradey	10	7	8	7	6		$7.39	
9–2. Kristina Shaw	5	9	10	8	8		$8.10	

Complete the following table (assume the overtime for each employee is a time-and-a-half rate after 40 hours):

Employee	M	T	W	Th	F	Sa	Total regular hours	Total overtime hours	Regular rate	Overtime rate	Gross earnings
9–3. Blue	12	9	9	9	9	3			$8.00		
9–4. Tagney	14	8	9	9	5	1			$7.60		

Calculate gross earnings:

Worker	Number of units produced	Rate per unit	Gross earnings
9–5. Lang	480	$3.50	
9–6. Swan	846	$ .58	

Calculate the gross earnings for each apple picker based on the following differential pay scale:

1–1,000: $.03 each   1,001–1,600: $.05 each   Over 1,600: $.07 each

Apple picker	Number of apples picked	Gross earnings
9–7. Ryan	1,600	
9–8. Rice	1,925	

Employee	Total sales	Commission rate	Draw	End-of-month commission received
9–9. Reese	$300,000	7%	$8,000	

Ron Company has the following commission schedule:

Commission rate	Sales
2%	Up to $80,000
3.5%	Excess of $80,000 to $100,000
4%	More than $100,000

Calculate the gross earnings of Ron Company's two employees:

Employee	Total sales	Gross earnings
9–10. Bill Moore	$ 70,000	
9–11. Ron Ear	$155,000	

Complete the following table, given that A Publishing Company pays its salespeople a weekly salary plus a 2% commission on all net sales over $5,000 (no commission on returned goods):

	Employee	Gross sales	Return	Net sales	Given quota	Commission sales	Commission rates	Total commission	Regular wage	Total wage
9–12.	Ring	$ 8,000	$ 25		$5,000		2%		$250	
9–13.	Porter	$12,000	$100		$5,000		2%		$250	

Calculate the Social Security and Medicare deductions for the following employees (assume a tax rate of 6.2% on $106,800 for Social Security and 1.45% for Medicare):

Employee	Cumulative earnings before this pay period	Pay amount this period	Social Security	Medicare
9–14. Lee	$105,800	$2,000		
9–15. Chin	$99,300	$8,000		
9–16. Davis	$600,000	$4,000		

Complete the following payroll register. Calculate FIT by the percentage method for this weekly period; Social Security and Medicare are the same rates as in the previous problems. No one will reach the maximum for FICA.

	Employee	Marital status	Allowances claimed	Gross pay	FIT	FICA S.S.	FICA Med.	Net pay
9–17.	Jim Day	M	2	$1,400				
9–18.	Ursula Lang	M	4	$1,900				

Personal Finance

>> **MONEY** // INSURANCE / ASK KIM

THIS COBRA SAVES LIVES

If you lose your job, you won't lose your health insurance. BY KIMBERLY LANKFORD

CAN YOU Translate, please?

WHO SHOULD TAKE IT?

You can't be rejected or charged more under COBRA because of your health, so it's a good deal for people with medical conditions who might otherwise have a tough time finding affordable insurance. But if you're healthy and live in a state with a competitive health-insurance market (which includes most states other than New York and New Jersey), you may find a better deal on your own. You can search for individual policies at Ehealthinsurance.com. ▪

WHAT IS COBRA?

The Consolidated Omnibus Budget Reconciliation Act is a federal law passed in 1986. It requires companies with 20 or more employees to continue offering health insurance at group rates to former employees and their family members after they're no longer eligible for the group—because of job loss or divorce, for example. Some states have similar rules for companies with fewer than 20 employees.

WHO QUALIFIES?

Former employees, spouses, former spouses and dependent children are eligible, regardless of their health. There are exceptions: You cannot get COBRA if your employer no longer offers health insurance to current employees. You're also out of luck if the company goes out of business. Federal employees are covered by a law similar to COBRA.

HOW LONG DOES IT LAST?

COBRA provides up to 18 months of coverage from the time you leave your job or drop to part-time status. The coverage lasts up to 36 months after you no longer qualify as a dependent on an employee's policy. That includes, for example, a child who reaches the cutoff age for coverage or a former spouse who gets a divorce from the employee.

HOW MUCH DOES IT COST?

Probably more than you expect. You have to pay the employee's and the employer's share of the premium—or an average of $12,680 for families this year—plus up to 2% in administrative costs. But legislation Congress passed earlier this year provides a 65% COBRA subsidy for up to nine months for people who lose their job between September 1, 2008, and December 31, 2009.

Slater's Business Math Scrapbook

Applying Your Skills

PROJECT A

Do you believe COBRA is the answer for laid-off workers?
Agree or disagree.

PROJECT B

Do you agree with the IRS ruling?

Stimulus Makes Cobra Coverage A Better Bet

Subsidy for Laid-Off Workers Eliminates Barrier That Kept Many Out of the Program

BY M.P. McQUEEN

Congress has just given a big assist to millions of jobless Americans facing a tough decision: Do they reach into their wallet to continue health insurance coverage with their old employer or not?

As part of the economic-stimulus package signed into law this week, the federal government will provide a nine-month subsidy covering 65% of the Cobra premium for people who qualify. Eligible workers who originally opted not to take Cobra but who now want the subsidized version have 60 days after they receive notice from their employers to sign up, says Richard G. Schwartz, a benefits lawyer in New York.

Fewer than one in 10 eligible workers recently opted for continuing insurance coverage in 2007 under Cobra, the federal law that allows many workers to continue group health insurance when they leave a job. The big reason: Cobra is expensive. Under the law, workers must pay the entire premium—plus a 2% administrative fee—even though employers typically picked up the lion's share of the cost. The average cost of Cobra coverage for a family is $13,000 a year—big money for someone who is unemployed.

The new legislation might help people like Chuck Fleming, 41 years old, of Aurora, Colo. His job in the legal department of Janus Capital Group Inc., a Denver-based financial-services company,

Uncoiling Cobra

The stimulus package makes it easier to afford extended health coverage after losing a job:

■ The law provides a federal subsidy for 65% of the premium for nine months for workers who qualify.

■ The subsidy applies to workers who lose their jobs between Sept. 1, 2008, and Dec. 31, 2009.

■ Workers who may have pre-existing conditions must maintain coverage to protect insurability.

IRS Deals FedEx a Setback On Classification of Workers

BY COREY DADE

The Internal Revenue Service has determined that the roughly 13,000 independent contractors for **FedEx** Corp.'s U.S. ground-delivery business in 2002 were, in fact, employees and assessed the company $319 million in back taxes and fines, according to a filing by the company with the Securities and Exchange Commission.

FedEx also said the IRS currently is investigating the status of contractors hired by the company between 2004 and 2006, raising the prospect of additional penalties. FedEx couldn't immediately say how many contractors were engaged in that span, but the work force currently stands at about 15,000.

The decision is the most significant blow to an embattled model whose low operating costs have been critical to the rapid growth of the FedEx Ground unit, in which the contractors are hired as drivers.

Separately, the SEC filing said FedEx received a grand jury subpoena from the Department of Justice for documents as part of a probe into possible price-fixing among air-freight forwarders. (Please see related article on Page A6A.)

The Memphis, Tenn., company, which posted $35.2 billion in revenue last year, has seen revenue from its ground-delivery business grow by a quarterly average of about 10% over the past five years. In that time, package volume in the unit has exploded 86%. On each delivery, FedEx Ground earns 23 cents more than heavily unionized rival United Parcel Service Inc.

FedEx says it will appeal the decision to the IRS in a process that could move to the federal courts and take years to resolve. FedEx wouldn't have to pay the penalty until its final challenge is denied.

Scores of current and former drivers and organized labor, which has targeted FedEx as ripe for unionization, have alleged that FedEx controls virtually every aspect of contractors' work, from the wearing of uniforms to delivery routes, and that they should be reclassified as employees and given benefits.

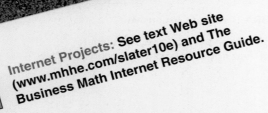

Internet Projects: See text Web site (www.mhhe.com/slater10e) and The Business Math Internet Resource Guide.

254

Video Case

Washburn International, founded in 1883, makes 80 models of instruments, both custom and for the mass market. Washburn is a privately held company with over 100 employees and annual sales of $48 million. This compares to its annual sales of $300,000 when Rudy Schlacher took over in 1976. When he acquired the company, about 250 guitars were produced per month; now 15,000 are produced each month.

The Washburn tradition of craftsmanship and innovation has withstood the tests of economics, brand competition, and fashion. Since its birth in Chicago, the name Washburn has been branded into the world's finest stringed instruments. To maintain quality, Washburn must have an excellent pool of qualified employees who are passionate about craftsmanship.

Washburn consolidated its four divisions in an expansive new 130,000 square foot plant in Mundelein, Illinois. The catalyst for consolidating operations in Mundelein was a chronic labor shortage in Elkhart and Chicago. The Mundelein plant was the ideal home for all Washburn operations because it had the necessary space, was cost effective, and gave Washburn access to a labor pool.

To grow profitably, Washburn must also sell its other products. To keep Washburn's 16 domestic salespeople tuned in to the full line, the company offers an override incentive. It is essential that to produce quality guitars, Washburn must keep recruiting dedicated, well-qualified, and team-oriented employees and provide them with profitable incentives.

PROBLEM 1

$120,000 was paid to 16 of Washburn's salespeople in override commissions. **(a)** What was the average amount paid to each salesperson? **(b)** What amount of the average sales commission will go toward the salesperson's Social Security tax? **(c)** What amount will go toward Medicare?

PROBLEM 2

Washburn is seeking a Sales and Marketing Coordinator with a bachelor's degree or equivalent experience, knowledgeable in Microsoft Office. This position pays $25,000 to $35,000, depending on experience. Assume a person is paid weekly and earns $32,500. Using the percentage method, what would be the taxes withheld for a married person who claims 3 exemptions?

PROBLEM 3

Guitarists hoping for a little country music magic in their playing can now buy an instrument carved out of oak pews from the former home of the Grand Ole Opry. Only 243 of the Ryman Limited Edition Acoustic Guitars are being made, each costing $6,250. Among the first customers were singers Vince Gill, Amy Grant, and Loretta Lynn, Ms. Lynn purchased two guitars. What would be the total revenue received by Washburn if all the guitars are sold?

PROBLEM 4

Under Washburn's old pay system, phone reps received a commission of 1.5% only on instruments they sold. Now the phone reps are paid an extra .75% commission on field sales made in their territory; the outside salespeople still get a commission up to 8%, freeing them to focus on introducing new products and holding in-store clinics. Assume sales were $65,500: **(a)** How much would phone reps receive? **(b)** How much would the outside salespeople receive?

PROBLEM 5

Washburn introduced the Limited Edition EA27 Gregg Allman Signature Series Festival guitar—only 500 guitars were produced with a selling price of $1,449.90. If Washburn's markup is 35% on selling price, what was Washburn's total cost for the 500 guitars?

PROBLEM 6

Retailers purchased $511 million worth of guitars from manufacturers—some 861,300 guitars—according to a study done by the National Association of Music Merchants. **(a)** What would be the average selling price of a guitar? **(b)** Based on the average selling price, if manufacturer's markup on cost is 40%, what would be the average cost?

PROBLEM 7

A Model NV 300 acoustic-electric guitar is being sold for a list price of $1,899.90, with a cash discount of 3/10, n/30. Sales tax is 7% and shipping is $30.40. How much is the final price if the cash discount period was met?

PROBLEM 8

A Model M3SWE mandolin has a list price of $1,299.90, with a chain discount of 5/3/2. **(a)** What would be the trade discount amount? **(b)** What would be the net price?

PROBLEM 9

A purchase was made of 2 Model J282DL six-string acoustic guitars at $799.90 each, with cases priced at $159.90, and 3 Model EA10 festival series acoustic-electric guitars at $729.90, with cases listed at $149.90. If sales tax is 6%, what is the total cost?

PROBLEM 10

Production of guitars has increased by what percent since Rudy Schlacher took over Washburn?

chapter
10   SIMPLE INTEREST

William West/AFP/Getty Images

Left Unpaid

Highest default rates over the past eight years for franchises with 50 or more SBA-backed loans

Franchise	Number of loans 2001–08	8-year default rate
Mr. Goodcents	55	55%
Philly Connection	63	51
Cottman Transmission	165	49
All Tune & Lube	81	47
Cornwell Quality Tools	55	42

Fiscal 2008* loan defaults at franchises with 50 or more SBA-backed loans

Franchise	Total loans 2001–08	Number of defaulted loans in '08	Franchise	Total loans 2001–08	Number of defaulted loans in '08
Quiznos	1,963	108	CiCi's Pizza	155	13
Cold Stone Creamery	763	75	Carvel Ice Cream	78	12
Subway	2,148	42	Domino's Pizza	242	11
Curves for Women	362	24	Dream Dinners	61	11
Planet Beach	230	22	Taco Del Mar	71	11
Aamco Transmission	169	15			

Source: U.S. Small Business Administration

*Year ended Sept. 30

Wall Street Journal © 2008

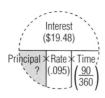

The following formula is used to calculate the principal of a loan:

$$Principal = \frac{Interest}{Rate \times Time}$$

Note how we illustrated this in the margin. The shaded area is what we are solving for. When solving for principal, rate, or time, you are dividing. Interest will be in the numerator, and the denominator will be the other two elements multiplied by each other.

Step 1. Set up the formula. $P = \dfrac{\$19.48}{.095 \times \dfrac{90}{360}}$

Step 2. When using a calculator, press

Step 2. Multiply the denominator.   .095 times 90 divided by 360 (do not round)

$P = \dfrac{\$19.48}{.02375}$

Step 3. When using a calculator, press

Step 3. Divide the numerator by the result of Step 2. $P = \$820.21$

Step 4. Check your answer. $\$19.48 = \$820.21 \times .095 \times \dfrac{90}{360}$

$\qquad\qquad\qquad\qquad (I)\qquad (P)\qquad (R)\qquad (T)$

Finding the Rate

EXAMPLE Tim Jarvis borrowed $820.21 from a bank. Tim's interest is $19.48 for 90 days. What rate of interest did Tim pay using the ordinary interest method?

The following formula is used to calculate the rate of interest:

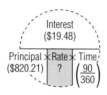

$$Rate = \frac{Interest}{Principal \times Time}$$

Step 1. Set up the formula. $R = \dfrac{\$19.48}{\$820.21 \times \dfrac{90}{360}}$

Step 2. Multiply the denominator. Do not round the answer. $R = \dfrac{\$19.48}{\$205.0525}$

Step 3. Divide the numerator by the result of Step 2. $R = 9.5\%$

Step 2. When using a calculator, press

Step 4. Check your answer. $\$19.48 = \$820.21 \times .095 \times \dfrac{90}{360}$

$\qquad\qquad\qquad\qquad (I)\qquad (P)\qquad (R)\qquad (T)$

Step 3. When using a calculator, press

Finding the Time

EXAMPLE Tim Jarvis borrowed $820.21 from a bank. Tim's interest is $19.48 at 9.5%. How much time does Tim have to repay the loan using the ordinary interest method?

The following formula is used to calculate time:

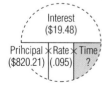

$$Time \text{ (in years)} = \frac{Interest}{Principal \times Rate}$$

$ MONEY TIPS

Be wary of using payday loans. A payday loan is a small, short-term *loan* that is intended to cover a borrower's expenses until his or her next payday. These services tend to keep you upside-down with your cash flow due to high interest rate charges encouraging repeat use.

Step 1. Set up the formula. $T = \dfrac{\$19.48}{\$820.21 \times .095}$

Step 2. Multiply the denominator. Do not round the answer. $T = \dfrac{\$19.48}{\$77.91995}$

Step 3. Divide the numerator by the result of Step 2. $T = .25$ years

Step 4. Convert years to days (assume 360 days). $.25 \times 360 = \boxed{90 \text{ days}}$

(continued on next page)

Step 5. Check your answer.

$$\$19.48 = \$820.21 \times .095 \times \frac{90}{360}$$

$$\quad\quad (I) \quad\quad\quad (P) \quad\quad (R) \quad\quad (T)$$

Before we go on to Learning Unit 10–3, let's check your understanding of this unit.

LU 10–2   PRACTICE QUIZ

Complete this **Practice Quiz** to see how you are doing.

Complete the following (assume 360 days):

	Principal	Interest rate	Time (days)	Simple interest
1.	?	5%	90 days	$8,000
2.	$7,000	?	220 days	350
3.	$1,000	8%	?	300

Solutions with Step-by-Step Help on DVD

✓ **Solutions**

1. $\dfrac{\$8,000}{.05 \times \dfrac{90}{360}} = \dfrac{\$8,000}{.0125} = \boxed{\$640,000}$ $P = \dfrac{I}{R \times T}$

2. $\dfrac{\$350}{\$7,000 \times \dfrac{220}{360}} = \dfrac{\$350}{\$4,277.7777} = \boxed{8.18\%}$ $R = \dfrac{I}{P \times T}$

(do not round)

3. $\dfrac{\$300}{\$1,000 \times .08} = \dfrac{\$300}{\$80} = 3.75 \times 360 = \boxed{1,350 \text{ days}}$ $T = \dfrac{I}{P \times R}$

LU 10–2a   EXTRA PRACTICE QUIZ WITH WORKED-OUT SOLUTIONS

Need more practice? Try this **Extra Practice Quiz** (check figures in Chapter Organizer, p. 265). Worked-out Solutions can be found in Appendix B at end of text.

Complete the following (assume 360 days):

	Principal	Interest rate	Time (days)	Simple interest
1.	?	4%	90 days	$9,000
2.	$6,000	?	180 days	280
3.	$900	6%	?	190

Learning Unit 10–3: U.S. Rule—Making Partial Note Payments before Due Date

Often a person may want to pay off a debt in more than one payment before the maturity date. The **U.S. Rule** allows the borrower to receive proper interest credits. This rule states that any partial loan payment first covers any interest that has built up. The remainder of the partial payment reduces the loan principal. Courts or legal proceedings generally use the U.S. Rule. The Supreme Court originated the U.S. Rule in the case of *Story* v. *Livingston*.

LO 1

EXAMPLE   Joe Mill owes $5,000 on an 11%, 90-day note. On day 50, Joe pays $600 on the note. On day 80, Joe makes an $800 additional payment. Assume a 360-day year. What is Joe's adjusted balance after day 50 and after day 80? What is the ending balance due?

To calculate $600 payment on day 50:

Step 1. Calculate interest on principal from date of loan to date of first principal payment. Round to nearest cent.

$I = P \times R \times T$

$I = \$5,000 \times .11 \times \dfrac{50}{360}$

$I = \$76.39$

Milos Jokic/Shutterstock

Step 2. Apply partial payment to interest due. Subtract remainder of payment from principal. This is the **adjusted balance** (principal).

$600.00 payment
− 76.39 interest
$523.61

$5,000.00 principal
−   523.61
$4,476.39 adjusted balance— principal

To calculate $800 payment on day 80:

Step 3. Calculate interest on adjusted balance that starts from previous payment date and goes to new payment date. Then apply Step 2.

Compute interest on $4,476.39 for 30 days (80 − 50)

$I = \$4{,}476.39 \times .11 \times \dfrac{30}{360}$

$I = \$41.03$

$800.00 payment
− 41.03 interest
$758.97

$4,476.39
− 758.97
$3,717.42 adjusted balance

$ MONEY TIPS

Make a partial payment only if the interest rate on the loan you are paying on is greater than the interest rate on your other loans or the rate you can earn on investing your money. Always use your money where it does the most for you.

Step 4. At maturity, calculate interest from last partial payment. *Add* this interest to adjusted balance.

Ten days are left on note since last payment.

$I = \$3{,}717.42 \times .11 \times \dfrac{10}{360}$

$I = \$11.36$

Balance owed = **$3,728.78** $\left(\begin{array}{r}\$3{,}717.42 \\ +\quad 11.36\end{array}\right)$

Note that when Joe makes two partial payments, Joe's total interest is $128.78 ($76.39 + $41.03 + $11.36). If Joe had repaid the entire loan after 90 days, his interest payment would have been $137.50—a total savings of $8.72.

Let's check your understanding of the last unit in this chapter.

LU 10–3 PRACTICE QUIZ

Complete this **Practice Quiz** to see how you are doing.

Solutions with Step-by-Step Help on DVD

Polly Flin borrowed $5,000 for 60 days at 8%. On day 10, Polly made a $600 partial payment. On day 40, Polly made a $1,900 partial payment. What is Polly's ending balance due under the U.S. Rule (assume a 360-day year)?

✓ **Solutions**

$\$5{,}000 \times .08 \times \dfrac{10}{360} = \$11.11$

$600.00
− 11.11
$588.89

$5,000.00
− 588.89
$4,411.11

$\$4{,}411.11 \times .08 \times \dfrac{30}{360} = \$29.41$

$1,900.00
−   29.41
$1,870.59

$4,411.11
− 1,870.59
$2,540.52

$\$2{,}540.52 \times .08 \times \dfrac{20}{360} = \$11.29$

$ 11.29
+ 2,450.52
$2,551.81

LU 10–3a EXTRA PRACTICE QUIZ WITH WORKED-OUT SOLUTIONS

Need more practice? Try this **Extra Practice Quiz** (check figures in Chapter Organizer, p. 265). Worked-out Solutions can be found in Appendix B at end of text.

Polly Flin borrowed $4,000 for 60 days at 4%. On day 15, Polly made a $700 partial payment. On day 40, Polly made a $2,000 partial payment. What is Polly's ending balance due under the U.S. Rule (assume a 360-day year)?

CHAPTER ORGANIZER AND REFERENCE GUIDE

Topic	Key point, procedure, formula	Example(s) to illustrate situation
Simple interest for months, p. 258	Interest = Principal × Rate × Time (I) (P) (R) (T)	$2,000 at 9% for 17 months $I = \$2,000 \times .09 \times \dfrac{17}{12}$ $I = \boxed{\$255}$
Exact interest, p. 259	$T = \dfrac{\text{Exact number of days}}{365}$ $I = P \times R \times T$	$1,000 at 10% from January 5 to February 20 $I = \$1,000 \times .10 \times \dfrac{46}{365}$ Feb. 20: 51 days Jan. 5: − 5 46 days $I = \boxed{\$12.60}$
Ordinary interest (Bankers Rule), p. 259	$T = \dfrac{\text{Exact number of days}}{360}$ $I = P \times R \times T$ Higher interest costs	$I = \$1,000 \times .10 \times \dfrac{46}{360}$ (51 − 5) $I = \boxed{\$12.78}$
Finding unknown in simple interest formula (use 360 days), p. 260	$I = P \times R \times T$	Use this example for illustrations of simple interest formula parts: $1,000 loan at 9%, 60 days $I = \$1,000 \times .09 \times \dfrac{60}{360} = \boxed{\$15}$
Finding the principal, p. 261	$P = \dfrac{I}{R \times T}$	$P = \dfrac{\$15}{.09 \times \dfrac{60}{360}} = \dfrac{\$15}{.015} = \boxed{\$1,000}$
Finding the rate, p. 261	$R = \dfrac{I}{P \times T}$	$R = \dfrac{\$15}{\$1,000 \times \dfrac{60}{360}} = \dfrac{\$15}{166.66666} = .09$ $= \boxed{9\%}$ *Note:* We did not round the denominator.
Finding the time, p. 261	$T = \dfrac{I}{P \times R}$ (in years) Multiply answer by 360 days to convert answer to days for ordinary interest.	$T = \dfrac{\$15}{\$1,000 \times .09} = \dfrac{\$15}{\$90} = .1666666$ $.1666666 \times 360 = 59.99 = \boxed{60 \text{ days}}$

(continues)

10–16. On September 12, Jody Jansen went to Sunshine Bank to borrow $2,300 at 9% interest. Jody plans to repay the loan on January 27. Assume the loan is on ordinary interest. What interest will Jody owe on January 27? What is the total amount Jody must repay at maturity?

10–17. Kelly O'Brien met Jody Jansen (Problem 10–16) at Sunshine Bank and suggested she consider the loan on exact interest. Recalculate the loan for Jody under this assumption. How much would she save in interest?

10–18. May 3, 2010, Leven Corp. negotiated a short-term loan of $685,000. The loan is due October 1, 2010, and carries a 6.86% interest rate. Use ordinary interest to calculate the interest. What is the total amount Leven would pay on the maturity date?

10–19. Gordon Rosel went to his bank to find out how long it will take for $1,200 to amount to $1,650 at 8% simple interest. Please solve Gordon's problem. Round time in years to the nearest tenth.

10–20. Bill Moore is buying a used Winnebago. His April monthly interest at 12% was $125. What was Bill's principal balance at the beginning of April? Use 360 days.

10–21. On April 5, 2010, Janeen Camoct took out an $8\frac{1}{2}$% loan for $20,000. The loan is due March 9, 2011. Use ordinary interest to calculate the interest. What total amount will Janeen pay on March 9, 2011?

10–22. Sabrina Bowers took out the same loan as Janeen (Problem 10–21). Sabrina's terms, however, are exact interest. What is Sabrina's difference in interest? What will she pay on March 9, 2011?

10–23. Max Wholesaler borrowed $2,000 on a 10%, 120-day note. After 45 days, Max paid $700 on the note. Thirty days later, Max paid an additional $630. What is the final balance due? Use the U.S. Rule to determine the total interest and ending balance due. Use ordinary interest.

ADDITIONAL SET OF WORD PROBLEMS

10–24. Lane French had a bad credit rating and went to a local cash center. He took out a $100 loan payable in two **weeks** at $115. What is the percent of interest paid on this loan? Do not round denominator before dividing.

10–25. Availability of state and federal disaster loans was the featured article in *The Enterprise Ledger* (AL) on March 14, 2007. Alabama Deputy Treasurer Anthony Leigh said the state program allows the state treasurer to place state funds in Alabama banks at 2 percent below the market interest rate. The bank then agrees to lend the funds to individuals or businesses for 2 percent below the normal charge, to help Alabama victims of disaster to secure emergency short-term loans. Laura Harden qualifies for an emergency loan. She will need $3,500 for 5 months and the local bank has an interest rate of $4\frac{3}{4}$ percent. **(a)** What would have been the maturity value of a non-emergency loan? **(b)** What will be the maturity value of the emergency loan? Round to the nearest cent.

10–26. On September 14, Jennifer Rick went to Park Bank to borrow $2,500 at $11\frac{3}{4}$% interest. Jennifer plans to repay the loan on January 27. Assume the loan is on ordinary interest. What interest will Jennifer owe on January 27? What is the total amount Jennifer must repay at maturity?

10–27. Steven Linden met Jennifer Rick (Problem 10–26) at Park Bank and suggested she consider the loan on exact interest. Recalculate the loan for Jennifer under this assumption.

10–28. Lance Lopes went to his bank to find out how long it will take for $1,000 to amount to $1,700 at 12% simple interest. Can you solve Lance's problem? Round time in years to the nearest tenth.

10–29. Margie Pagano is buying a car. Her June monthly interest at $12\frac{1}{2}$% was $195. What was Margie's principal balance at the beginning of June? Use 360 days. Do not round the denominator before dividing.

10–30. Shawn Bixby borrowed $17,000 on a 120-day, 12% note. After 65 days, Shawn paid $2,000 on the note. On day 89, Shawn paid an additional $4,000. What is the final balance due? Determine total interest and ending balance due by the U.S. Rule. Use ordinary interest.

10–31. Carol Miller went to Europe and forgot to pay her $740 mortgage payment on her New Hampshire ski house. For her 59 days overdue on her payment, the bank charged her a penalty of $15. What was the rate of interest charged by the bank? Round to the nearest hundredth percent (assume 360 days).

10–32. Abe Wolf bought a new kitchen set at Sears. Abe paid off the loan after 60 days with an interest charge of $9. If Sears charges 10% interest, what did Abe pay for the kitchen set (assume 360 days)?

10–33. Joy Kirby made a $300 loan to Robinson Landscaping at 11%. Robinson paid back the loan with interest of $6.60. How long in days was the loan outstanding (assume 360 days)? Check your answer.

10–34. Molly Ellen, bookkeeper for Keystone Company, forgot to send in the payroll taxes due on April 15. She sent the payment November 8. The IRS sent her a penalty charge of 8% simple interest on the unpaid taxes of $4,100. Calculate the penalty. (Remember that the government uses exact interest.)

10–35. Oakwood Plowing Company purchased two new plows for the upcoming winter. In 200 days, Oakwood must make a single payment of $23,200 to pay for the plows. As of today, Oakwood has $22,500. If Oakwood puts the money in a bank today, what rate of interest will it need to pay off the plows in 200 days (assume 360 days)?

10–36. You have the opportunity to purchase a used car in great condition for $14,500. A $2,000 down payment is required to receive 6% interest for 6 years. The car you currently own is in perfect working condition but you would like a change. Your spouse recommends using the $2,000 to remodel a bathroom in your home. The remodel is estimated to bring the value of your home up by $5,000. Determine the interest you will pay on the loan for the car. Considering the opportunity cost (value of the next best alternative forgone as the result of making a decision) for the $2,000, what should you do with the money?

10–37. Janet Foster bought a computer and printer at Computerland. The printer had a $600 list price with a $100 trade discount and 2/10, n/30 terms. The computer had a $1,600 list price with a 25% trade discount but no cash discount. On the computer, Computerland offered Janet the choice of (1) paying $50 per month for 17 months with the 18th payment paying the remainder of the balance or (2) paying 8% interest for 18 months in equal payments.

    a. Assume Janet could borrow the money for the printer at 8% to take advantage of the cash discount. How much would Janet save (assume 360 days)?

    b. On the computer, what is the difference in the final payment between choices 1 and 2?

 SUMMARY PRACTICE TEST

1. Lorna Hall's real estate tax of $2,010.88 was due on December 14, 2009. Lorna lost her job and could not pay her tax bill until February 27, 2010. The penalty for late payment is $6\frac{1}{2}\%$ ordinary interest. *(p. 259)*

    a. What is the penalty Lorna must pay?

    b. What is the total amount Lorna must pay on February 27?

2. Ann Hopkins borrowed $60,000 for her child's education. She must repay the loan at the end of 8 years in one payment with $5\frac{1}{2}\%$ interest. What is the maturity value Ann must repay? *(p. 258)*

3. On May 6, Jim Ryan borrowed $14,000 from Lane Bank at $7\frac{1}{2}\%$ interest. Jim plans to repay the loan on March 11. Assume the loan is on ordinary interest. How much will Jim repay on March 11? *(p. 259)*

4. Gail Ross met Jim Ryan (Problem 3) at Lane Bank. After talking with Jim, Gail decided she would like to consider the same loan on exact interest. Can you recalculate the loan for Gail under this assumption? *(p. 259)*

5. Claire Russell is buying a car. Her November monthly interest was $210 at $7\frac{3}{4}\%$ interest. What is Claire's principal balance (to the nearest dollar) at the beginning of November? Use 360 days. Do not round the denominator in your calculation. *(p. 261)*

6. Comet Lee borrowed $16,000 on a 6%, 90-day note. After 20 days, Comet paid $2,000 on the note. On day 50, Comet paid $4,000 on the note. What are the total interest and ending balance due by the U.S. Rule? Use ordinary interest. *(p. 262)*

Scams Exploit Hard Times

Prime targets are the unemployed and homeowners behind on their mortgages.

BY LAURA COHN

WHEN NANCY DIX RECEIVED A letter promising to help her prevent foreclosure on her home in Ansted, W.Va., she jumped at the chance. The letter, from an organization called Mortgage Rescue, said all she had to do to save her home was send the company a check for $921. So she did. Then she didn't hear anything—and got suspicious. The 67-year-old widow called the state attorney general's office, which referred her to Mountain State Justice, a nonprofit legal service. Turns out Mortgage Rescue was operating a scam, says Bren Pomponio, Dix's lawyer at Mountain State.

Fortunately, Dix hadn't signed over her deed when she sent the check—an additional layer of some similar scams. She never got her money back, but the legal service worked with her lender to keep her in her home. "Before you start sending money, talk to an attorney or a consumer group, or you'll be in the same mess I was in," Dix says.

Over the past five years, the FBI's mortgage-fraud caseload has jumped by

nearly 400%, to more than 2,100. The general rule still applies: If it sounds too good to be true, it is. If, for example, you receive a call from a firm that guarantees to stop a foreclosure but asks you not to contact your lender, it's a scam: Your lender is the only route to modifying your mortgage or preventing foreclosure. If you're having trouble making your payments, find a housing counselor approved by the U.S. Department of Housing and Urban Development at www.hud.gov.

Easy money. The sagging economy has inspired a number of schemes to watch for, from work-at-home ploys to tax and stimulus frauds (see "Ask Kim," May). Shady operators take advantage of economic hard times, says Edward Johnson, president of the Better Business Bureau of Metro Washington and Eastern Pennsylvania. "If you don't have a job and are having trouble keeping up with your mortgage, you will let your guard down."

If you're looking for quick cash, be on the alert for job-related scams, such as an ad

that promises you can earn money at home by stuffing envelopes—it's likely to be a pyramid scheme. You pay a fee upfront, and to make money you place ads and wait for people to respond and pay *you* a fee. Before you participate, ask the company to spell out, in writing, exactly what the job entails and whether you'll be on salary or commission. Also run the company's name by the BBB (www.bbb.org) and call the firm to make sure it's soliciting workers.

Another sneaky ploy involves bogus mystery-shopping firms that promise to pay shoppers to check out local stores. Scam operators may send out a letter with the company logo of an actual mystery-shopping service plus BBB certification, along with a check for several thousand dollars. The letter tells recipients to deposit the check, evaluate a money-wiring service,

and then wire part of the money back to the firm to test the service—often within seven days. The check bounces after you've wired the money back.

Now that credit is harder to get, the Federal Deposit Insurance Corp. has reported a jump in "advance-fee loan" scams. Someone calls you and says that if you simply pay a fee of $500 or $1,000 upfront, you'll be guaranteed a loan. But you never get the money.

Finally, watch out for "phishing" scams. You get a phony e-mail from a trusted institution that asks for your Social Security number or other information that could be used to tap into your financial accounts (see "Lowdown," on page 79). One prevalent scheme is an e-mail promising you a tax refund from the IRS—except the IRS never e-mails taxpayers. Phony Bank of America and Citibank messages are also common. ∎

■ EARN MONEY AT HOME BY STUFFING ENVELOPES? IT COULD BE A PYRAMID SCHEME.

BUSINESS MATH ISSUE

You should never take out a loan online.

1. List the key points of the article and information to support your position.
2. Write a group defense of your position using math calculations to support your view.

PROJECT A

Check-cashing shops should be outlawed. Agree or disagree and support your answer.

Alternative Way to Pay Utility Bills Draws Fire

Use of Check-Cashing Shops, Critics Say, Exposes Customers To Lure of High-Interest Loans

By REBECCA SMITH

RETIRED HIGH-SCHOOL math teacher Cynthia Elgar often pays her bills online, but when she got a disconnection notice from her Phoenix electric utility, Arizona Public Service, she realized a payment had gone awry somehow. In the past, she would have scooted over to a nearby utility office to make the late payment.

But the utility has shut down most of its neighborhood offices and relies on a network of retail stores and check-cashing facilities to receive in-person payments. APS directed Ms. Elgar to a Cash & More storefront in Phoenix. There, she waited along with fellow customers engaged in transactions such as cashing checks and getting short-term, high-interest "payday loans"—a business that consumer advocates say often preys on low-income people in dire financial straits.

"Why APS needs to use this sort of place to accept payments, I don't know," she says.

It is an experience that is increasingly common for utility customers. Across the U.S., utilities have shut down scores of customer-service centers in recent years and turned to retail outlets to take payments, in order to save money. Many of these locations are check-cashing centers, which cater to mainly low-income customers who don't use traditional banks, providing services such as loans and wire transfers on a fee basis.

The trend has sparked criticism from utility customers, regulators and consumer advocates. Customers say they miss the local centers where they were able to get personal service, such as arranging special payment plans. And some are simply uncomfortable going to check-cashing facilities.

But perhaps of greatest concern is that check-cashing facilities may be using utilities to build foot traffic, so they can steer consumers into expensive and addictive loan products that can carry annual interest rates in excess of 400%. At least one operator of check-cashing centers says that a number of customers who come in to pay utility bills also wind up taking out a payday loan, which is a short-term loan tied to the borrower's next paycheck.

Wall Street Journal © 2007

PROJECT B

Go to the Web and find the latest student default rates.

Student Loans: Default Rates Are Soaring

As Job Market Tightens, Graduates Are Squeezed; The 'Forbearance' Option

BY ANNE MARIE CHAKER

Defaults on student loans are skyrocketing amid a weak job market for graduates and steadily rising tuition costs.

According to new numbers from the U.S. Department of Education, default rates for federally guaranteed student loans are expected to reach 6.9% for fiscal year 2007. That's up from 4.6% two years earlier and would be the highest rate since 1998.

The situation is mirrored in the smaller private student-loan market. In 2008, **SLM** Corp. also known as Sallie Mae, wrote off 3.4% of its private loans that were already considered troubled, according to its latest annual report—more than double the figure in 2006. Student Loan Corp., a unit of **Citigroup** Inc., wrote off 2.3% of those loans in 2008, compared with 1.5% a year earlier.

"The volume of people in trouble is definitely increasing," says Deanne Loonin, a staff attorney at the Boston-based National Consumer Law Center who counsels low-income consumers on student loans and other debt issues.

Lenders say they are hearing more pleas for help as the unemployment rate worsens and debt levels soar among graduates.

Sarah Kostecki, a 24-year-old sales associate in New York, graduated last year from DePaul University with a major in international studies and $87,000 in debt, translating to monthly payments of $685, the vast majority of which are private loans.

Getting Relief

Here are some options for student borrowers who find themselves in trouble:

- **Forbearance.** This allows borrowers to put payments on hold, though they are on the hook for the interest that accrues.

- **Interest-only payments.** Borrowers can defer other payments until a later date.

- **Increase the borrowing period.** Allows borrowers to lower their monthly payments.

Wall Street Journal © 2009

Internet Projects: See text Web site (www.mhhe.com/slater10e) and The Business Math Internet Resource Guide.

chapter
11

PROMISSORY NOTES, SIMPLE DISCOUNT NOTES, AND THE DISCOUNT PROCESS

Ethan Miller/Getty Images

A Short Sale May Not Mean You're Home Free

By RUTH SIMON

Financially troubled borrowers may think that foreclosure or a short sale of their home means their mortgage woes are over.

Not necessarily.

Some homeowners are finding that when they sell their homes for less than the outstanding mortgages—a so-called short sale—standing mortgages—a so-called short sale—their mortgage companies are going after them for some or all of the difference. Mortgage companies are also sometimes taking legal action to recover unpaid amounts after a foreclosure is completed.

In a growing number of cases, holders of mortgages or home-equity loans are requiring borrowers in short sales to sign a promissory note, which is a written promise to pay back a loan or debt. Real-estate agents and attorneys say they have seen an increase in requests for promissory notes as mortgage companies look to short sales as an alternative to foreclosure.

In many states, lenders have always had the right to pursue former homeowners for unpaid mortgage debt. Yet until recently, most borrowers who ran into trouble were able to refinance or sell their homes and pay off their loans. Now, falling home prices are widening the gap between home values and mortgage balances, and the number of homeowners who can't make their mortgage payments is rising as the economy has weakened. More than 3.8 million homes will be lost in 2009 and 2010 because borrowers can't make their mortgage payments, according to forecasts from Moody's Economy.com.

LU 11–1: Structure of Promissory Notes; the Simple Discount Note

1. Differentiate between interest-bearing and noninterest-bearing notes *(pp. 278–279)*.

2. Calculate bank discount and proceeds for simple discount notes *(p. 279)*.

3. Calculate and compare the interest, maturity value, proceeds, and effective rate of a simple interest note with a simple discount note *(p. 279)*.

4. Explain and calculate the effective rate for a Treasury bill *(p. 280)*.

LU 11–2: Discounting an Interest-Bearing Note before Maturity

1. Calculate the maturity value, bank discount, and proceeds of discounting an interest-bearing note before maturity *(p. 281)*.

2. Identify and complete the four steps of the discounting process *(p. 281)*.

VOCABULARY PREVIEW

Here are key terms in this chapter. After completing the chapter, if you know the term, place a checkmark in the parenthesis. If you don't know the term, look it up and put the page number where it can be found.

Bank discount . ( ) **Bank discount rate** . ( ) **Contingent liability** . ( ) **Discounting a note** . ( ) **Discount period** . ( ) **Effective rate** . ( ) **Face value** . ( ) **Interest-bearing note** . ( ) **Maker** . ( ) **Maturity date** . ( ) **Maturity value (MV)** . ( ) **Noninterest-bearing note** . ( ) **Payee** . ( ) **Proceeds** . ( ) **Promissory note** . ( ) **Simple discount note** . ( ) **Treasury bill** . ( )

Goodyear to Tap Credit Due to Money-Fund Woes

BY JOHN KELL

Goodyear Tire & Rubber Co. will draw $600 million from its credit lines because of an inability to access some U.S. cash investments, more than half of which are held in a troubled money-market fund.

The company also said finalization of a trust to handle current and future retirees' health benefits is at hand, allowing Goodyear to remove $1.2 billion in liabilities from its balance sheet.

Goodyear said it will use the $600 million to support seasonal needs and enhance cash liquidity. The amount covers $360 million locked in the Reserve Primary Fund, the money-market mutual fund that "broke the buck" last week. Its net asset value dipped to 97 cents a share last week as a result of **Lehman Brothers Holdings** Inc.'s bankruptcy filing, marking the first time since 1994 that a money-market fund broke the buck.

Redemptions from the fund have been suspended, prompting Goodyear to make the credit-line drawdown. The company added that its other U.S. cash investments remain accessible.

Goodyear has faced continuing pressure, driven by the slumping U.S. economy that is causing customers to delay or skip new-car purchases and auto makers to subsequently ratchet back production. Goodyear's stock has been in a free fall, falling about 45% in the past four months amid concerns over raw-material prices and slowing car production.

Eric Glenn/Alamy

The *Wall Street Journal* clip "Goodyear to Tap Credit Due to Money-Fund Woes" shows the financial crises facing Goodyear. Goodyear will have to draw $600 million from its credit line.

This chapter begins with a discussion of the structure of promissory notes and simple discount notes. We also look at the application of discounting with Treasury bills. The chapter concludes with an explanation of how to calculate the discounting of promissory notes.

Learning Unit 11–1: Structure of Promissory Notes; the Simple Discount Note

Although businesses frequently sign promissory notes, customers also sign promissory notes. For example, some student loans may require the signing of promissory notes. Appliance stores often ask customers to sign a promissory note when they buy large appliances on credit. In this unit, promissory notes usually involve interest payments.

LO 1

Structure of Promissory Notes

To borrow money, you must find a lender (a bank or a company selling goods on credit). You must also be willing to pay for the use of the money. In Chapter 10 you learned that interest is the cost of borrowing money for periods of time.

Money lenders usually require that borrowers sign a **promissory note.** (See chapter opener regarding promissory notes and real estate.) This note states that the borrower will repay a certain sum at a fixed time in the future. The note often includes the charge for the use of the money, or the rate of interest. Figure 11.1 shows a sample promissory note with its terms identified and defined. Take a moment to look at each term.

In this section you will learn the difference between interest-bearing notes and non-interest-bearing notes.

Interest-Bearing versus Noninterest-Bearing Notes

A promissory note can be interest bearing or noninterest bearing. To be **interest bearing,** the note must state the rate of interest. Since the promissory note in Figure 11.1 states that its interest is 9%, it is an interest-bearing note. When the note matures, Regal Corporation "will pay back the original amount (**face value**) borrowed plus interest. The simple interest formula (also known as the interest formula) and the maturity value formula from Chapter 10 are used for this transaction."

$$\text{Interest} = \text{Face value (principal)} \times \text{Rate} \times \text{Time}$$
$$\text{Maturity value} = \text{Face value (principal)} + \text{Interest}$$

FIGURE 11.1

Interest-bearing promissory note

a. **Face value:** Amount of money borrowed—$10,000. The face value is also the principal of the note.
b. **Term:** Length of time that the money is borrowed—60 days.
c. **Date:** The date that the note is issued—October 2, 2010.
d. **Payee:** The company extending the credit—G.J. Equipment Company.
e. **Rate:** The annual rate for the cost of borrowing the money—9%.
f. **Maker:** The company issuing the note and borrowing the money—Regal Corporation.
g. **Maturity date:** The date the principal and interest rate are due—December 1, 2010.

If you sign a **noninterest-bearing** promissory note for $10,000, you pay back $10,000 at maturity. The maturity value of a noninterest-bearing note is the same as its face value. Usually, noninterest-bearing notes occur for short time periods under special conditions. For example, money borrowed from a relative could be secured by a noninterest-bearing promissory note.

LO 2

Simple Discount Note

The total amount due at the end of the loan, or the **maturity value (MV),** is the sum of the face value (principal) and interest. Some banks deduct the loan interest in advance. When banks do this, the note is a **simple discount note.**

In the simple discount note, the **bank discount** is the interest that banks deduct in advance and the **bank discount rate** is the percent of interest. The amount that the borrower receives after the bank deducts its discount from the loan's maturity value is the note's **proceeds.** Sometimes we refer to simple discount notes as noninterest-bearing notes. Remember, however, that borrowers *do* pay interest on these notes.

In the example that follows, Pete Runnels has the choice of a note with a simple interest rate (Chapter 10) or a note with a simple discount rate (Chapter 11). Table 11.1 provides a summary of the calculations made in the example and gives the key points that you should remember. Now let's study the example, and then you can review Table 11.1.

EXAMPLE Pete Runnels has a choice of two different notes that both have a face value (principal) of $14,000 for 60 days. One note has a simple interest rate of 8%, while the other note has a simple discount rate of 8%. For each type of note, calculate **(a)** interest owed, **(b)** maturity value, **(c)** proceeds, and **(d)** effective rate.

LO 3

Simple interest note—Chapter 10	Simple discount note—Chapter 11
Interest	**Interest**
a. $I =$ Face value (principal) $\times R \times T$	**a.** $I =$ Face value (principal) $\times R \times T$
$I = \$14,000 \times .08 \times \dfrac{60}{360}$	$I = \$14,000 \times .08 \times \dfrac{60}{360}$
$I = \$186.67$	$I = \$186.67$
Maturity value	**Maturity value**
b. $MV =$ Face value $+$ Interest	**b.** $MV =$ Face value
$MV = \$14,000 + \$186.67$	$MV = \$14,000$
$MV = \$14,186.67$	
Proceeds	**Proceeds**
c. Proceeds $=$ Face value	**c.** Proceeds $= MV -$ Bank discount
$= \$14,000$	$= \$14,000 - \$186.67$
	$= \$13,813.33$
Effective rate	**Effective rate**
d. Rate $= \dfrac{\text{Interest}}{\text{Proceeds} \times \text{Time}}$	**d.** Rate $= \dfrac{\text{Interest}}{\text{Proceeds} \times \text{Time}}$
$= \dfrac{\$186.67}{\$14,000 \times \dfrac{60}{360}}$	$= \dfrac{\$186.67}{\$13,813.33 \times \dfrac{60}{360}}$
$= 8\%$	$= 8.11\%$

TABLE 11.1

Comparison of simple interest note and simple discount note (Calculations from the Pete Runnels example)

Simple interest note (Chapter 10)	Simple discount note (Chapter 11)
1. A promissory note for a loan with a term of usually less than 1 year. *Example:* 60 days.	1. A promissory note for a loan with a term of usually less than 1 year. *Example:* 60 days.
2. Paid back by one payment at maturity. Face value equals actual amount (or principal) of loan (this is not maturity value).	2. Paid back by one payment at maturity. Face value equals maturity value (what will be repaid).
3. Interest computed on face value or what is actually borrowed. *Example:* $186.67.	3. Interest computed on maturity value or what will be repaid and not on actual amount borrowed. *Example:* $186.67.
4. Maturity value = Face value + Interest. *Example:* $14,186.67.	4. Maturity value = Face value. *Example:* $14,000.
5. Borrower receives the face value. *Example:* $14,000.	5. Borrower receives proceeds = Face value − Bank discount. *Example:* $13,813.33.
6. Effective rate (true rate is same as rate stated on note). *Example:* 8%.	6. Effective rate is higher since interest was deducted in advance. *Example:* 8.11%.
7. Used frequently instead of the simple discount note. *Example:* 8%.	7. Not used as much now because in 1969 congressional legislation required that the true rate of interest be revealed. Still used where legislation does not apply, such as personal loans.

Note that the interest of $186.67 is the same for the simple interest note and the simple discount note. The maturity value of the simple discount note is the same as the face value. In the simple discount note, interest is deducted in advance, so the proceeds are less than the face value. Note that the **effective rate** for a simple discount note is higher than the stated rate, since the bank calculated the rate on the face of the note and not on what Pete received.

LO 4

Application of Discounting—Treasury Bills

When the government needs money, it sells Treasury bills. A **Treasury bill** is a loan to the federal government for 28 days (4 weeks), 91 days (13 weeks), or 1 year. Note that the *Wall Street Journal* clipping "Full Slate of Treasury Sales" announces a new sale.

Treasury bills can be bought over the phone or on the government Web site. The purchase price (or proceeds) of a Treasury bill is the value of the Treasury bill less the discount. For example, if you buy a $10,000, 13-week Treasury bill at 8%, you pay $9,800 since you have not yet earned your interest ($10,000 × .08 × $\frac{13}{52}$ = $200). At maturity— 13 weeks—the government pays you $10,000. You calculate your effective yield (8.16% rounded to the nearest hundredth percent) as follows:

$$($10,000 - $200) \longrightarrow \frac{$200}{$9,800 \times \frac{13}{52}} = 8.16\% \text{ effective rate}$$

Now it's time to try the Practice Quiz and check your progress.

LU 11–1 PRACTICE QUIZ

Complete this **Practice Quiz** to see how you are doing.

1. Warren Ford borrowed $12,000 on a noninterest-bearing, simple discount, $9\frac{1}{2}$%, 60-day note. Assume ordinary interest. What are **(a)** the maturity value, **(b)** the bank's discount, **(c)** Warren's proceeds, and **(d)** the effective rate to the nearest hundredth percent?

2. Jane Long buys a $10,000, 13-week Treasury bill at 6%. What is her effective rate? Round to the nearest hundredth percent.

Solutions with Step-by-Step Help on DVD

✓ Solutions

1. **a.** Maturity value = Face value = $12,000
   b. Bank discount = MV × Bank discount rate × Time
   $$= $12,000 \times .095 \times \frac{60}{360}$$
   $$= $190$$
   c. Proceeds = MV − Bank discount
   $$= $12,000 - $190$$
   $$= $11,810$$
   d. Effective rate = $\frac{\text{Interest}}{\text{Proceeds} \times \text{Time}}$
   $$= \frac{$190}{$11,810 \times \frac{60}{360}}$$
   $$= $9.65\%$$

2. $10,000 \times .06 \times \frac{13}{52} = 150 interest
   $$\frac{$150}{$9,850 \times \frac{13}{52}} = 6.09\%$$

LU 11–1a EXTRA PRACTICE QUIZ WITH WORKED-OUT SOLUTIONS

Need more practice? Try this **Extra Practice Quiz** (check figures in Chapter Organizer, p. 284). Worked-out Solutions can be found in Appendix B at end of text.

1. Warren Ford borrowed $14,000 on a noninterest-bearing, simple discount, $4\frac{1}{2}$%, 60-day note. Assume ordinary interest. What are **(a)** the maturity value, **(b)** the bank's discount, **(c)** Warren's proceeds, and **(d)** the effective rate to the nearest hundredth percent?

2. Jane Long buys a $10,000 13-week Treasury bill at 4%. What is her effective rate? Round to the nearest hundredth percent.

END-OF-CHAPTER PROBLEMS Mc Graw Hill **connect** (plus+) www.mhhe.com/slater10e

Check figures for odd-numbered problems in Appendix C   Name _____ Date _____

DRILL PROBLEMS

Complete the following table for these simple discount notes. Use the ordinary interest method.

	Amount due at maturity	Discount rate	Time	Bank discount	Proceeds
11–1.	$14,000	$3\frac{3}{4}\%$	280 days		
11–2.	$20,000	$6\frac{1}{4}\%$	180 days		

Calculate the discount period for the bank to wait to receive its money:

	Date of note	Length of note	Date note discounted	Discount period
11–3.	April 12	45 days	May 2	
11–4.	March 7	120 days	June 8	

Solve for maturity value, discount period, bank discount, and proceeds (assume for Problems 11–5 and 11–6 a bank discount rate of 9%).

	Face value (principal)	Rate of interest	Length of note	Maturity value	Date of note	Date note discounted	Discount period	Bank discount	Proceeds
11–5.	$50,000	11%	95 days		June 10	July 18			
11–6.	$25,000	9%	60 days		June 8	July 10			

11–7. Calculate the effective rate of interest (to the nearest hundredth percent) of the following Treasury bill.
Given: $10,000 Treasury bill, 4% for 13 weeks.

WORD PROBLEMS

Use ordinary interest as needed.

11–8. Megan Green is interested in taking out a personal loan for $1,500. However, last year an identity theft scam left her with poor credit. Since then she has learned about the perils of identity theft from personal experience as well as from a variety of sources, including the August 18, 2009, article "Avoiding the Identity Theft Underworld" on www.forbes.com. Because of the resulting poor credit score due to the identity theft and the fact that she is providing no collateral, the bank is going to charge her a fee of 2% of her loan amount as well as take out the interest upfront. The bank is offering her 15% APR for six months. Calculate the effective interest rate.

11–9. Bill Blank signed an $8,000 note at Citizen's Bank. Citizen's charges a $6\frac{1}{2}\%$ discount rate. If the loan is for 300 days, find **(a)** the proceeds and **(b)** the effective rate charged by the bank (to the nearest tenth percent).

11–10. On January 18, 2007, *BusinessWeek* reported yields on Treasury bills. Bruce Martin purchased a $10,000 13-week Treasury bill at $9,881.25. **(a)** What was the amount of interest? **(b)** What was the effective rate of interest? Round to the nearest hundredth percent.

11–11. On September 5, Sheffield Company discounted at Sunshine Bank a $9,000 (maturity value), 120-day note dated June 5. Sunshine's discount rate was 9%. What proceeds did Sheffield Company receive?

11–12. The Treasury Department auctioned $21 billion in three-month bills in denominations of ten thousand dollars at a discount rate of 4.965%. What would be the effective rate of interest? Round your answer to the nearest hundredth percent.

11–13. Annika Scholten bought a $10,000, 13-week Treasury bill at 5%. What is her effective rate? Round to the nearest hundredth percent.

11–14. Ron Prentice bought goods from Shelly Katz. On May 8, Shelly gave Ron a time extension on his bill by accepting a $3,000, 8%, 180-day note. On August 16, Shelly discounted the note at Roseville Bank at 9%. What proceeds does Shelly Katz receive?

11–15. Rex Corporation accepted a $5,000, 8%, 120-day note dated August 8 from Regis Company in settlement of a past bill. On October 11, Rex discounted the note at Park Bank at 9%. What are the note's maturity value, discount period, and bank discount? What proceeds does Rex receive?

11–16. On May 12, Scott Rinse accepted an $8,000, 12%, 90-day note for a time extension of a bill for goods bought by Ron Prentice. On June 12, Scott discounted the note at Able Bank at 10%. What proceeds does Scott receive?

11–17. Hafers, an electrical supply company, sold $4,800 of equipment to Jim Coates Wiring, Inc. Coates signed a promissory note May 12 with 4.5% interest. The due date was August 10. Short of funds, Hafers contacted Charter One Bank on July 20; the bank agreed to take over the note at a 6.2% discount. What proceeds will Hafers receive?

CHALLENGE PROBLEMS

11–18. On March 30, Wade Thompson accepted a nine-month $32,250 promissory note at 7% interest from one of his clients to pay for some carpentry work he had completed. On April 27, he sold the note to Hammond Bank at 9.5% interest. What were his proceeds?

11–19. Tina Mier must pay a $2,000 furniture bill. A finance company will loan Tina $2,000 for 8 months at a 9% discount rate. The finance company told Tina that if she wants to receive exactly $2,000, she must borrow more than $2,000. The finance company gave Tina the following formula:

$$\text{What to ask for} = \frac{\text{Amount in cash to be received}}{1 - (\text{Discount} \times \text{Time of loan})}$$

Calculate Tina's loan request and the effective rate of interest to nearest hundredth percent.

SUMMARY PRACTICE TEST

1. On December 12, Lowell Corporation accepted a $160,000, 120-day, noninterest-bearing note from Able.com. What is the maturity value of the note? *(p. 278)*

2. The face value of a simple discount note is $17,000. The discount is 4% for 160 days. Calculate the following. *(p. 278)*

   a. Amount of interest charged for each note.

   b. Amount borrower would receive.

   c. Amount payee would receive at maturity.

   d. Effective rate (to the nearest tenth percent).

3. On July 14, Gracie Paul accepted a $60,000, 6%, 160-day note from Mike Lang. On November 12, Gracie discounted the note at Lend Bank at 7%. What proceeds did Gracie receive? *(p. 281)*

4. Lee.com accepted a $70,000, $6\frac{3}{4}$%, 120-day note on July 26. Lee discounts the note on October 28 at LB Bank at 6%. What proceeds did Lee receive? *(p. 281)*

5. The owner of Lease.com signed a $60,000 note at Reese Bank. Reese charges a $7\frac{1}{4}$% discount rate. If the loan is for 210 days, find **(a)** the proceeds and **(b)** the effective rate charged by the bank (to the nearest tenth percent). *(p. 282)*

6. Sam Slater buys a $10,000, 13-week Treasury bill at $5\frac{1}{2}$%. What is the effective rate? Round to the nearest hundredth percent. *(p. 280)*

Note: **A complete set of plastic overlays showing the concepts of compound interest and present value is found in Chapter 13.**

LU 12–1: Compound Interest (Future Value)—The Big Picture

1. Compare simple interest with compound interest *(pp. 293–294).*

2. Calculate the compound amount and interest manually and by table lookup *(pp. 295–298).*

3. Explain and compute the effective rate (APY) *(p. 298).*

LU 12–2: Present Value—The Big Picture

1. Compare present value (PV) with compound interest (FV) *(p. 300).*

2. Compute present value by table lookup *(pp. 301–303).*

3. Check the present value answer by compounding *(p. 303).*

VOCABULARY PREVIEW

Here are key terms in this chapter. After completing the chapter, if you know the term, place a checkmark in the parenthesis. If you don't know the term, look it up and put the page number where it can be found.

Annual percentage yield (APY) . ( ) Compound amount . ( ) Compounded annually . ( ) Compounded daily . ( ) Compounded monthly . ( ) Compounded quarterly . ( ) Compounded semiannually . ( ) Compounding . ( ) Compound interest . ( ) Effective rate . ( ) Future value (FV) . ( ) Nominal rate . ( ) Number of periods . ( ) Present value (PV) . ( ) Rate for each period . ( )

So when should you start saving for retirement? The *Kiplinger* clip "The Magic of Compounding" shows that if you wait 10 years (Age 22 to Age 32) to invest $100 a month at 8% you can lose $255,824 ($450,478 − $194,654).

In this chapter we look at the power of compounding—interest paid on earned interest. Let's begin by studying Learning Unit 12–1, which shows you how to calculate compound interest.

Learning Unit 12–1: Compound Interest (Future Value)—The Big Picture

So far we have discussed only simple interest, which is interest on the principal alone. Simple interest is either paid at the end of the loan period or deducted in advance. From the chapter introduction, you know that interest can also be compounded.

Compounding involves the calculation of interest periodically over the life of the loan (or investment). After each calculation, the interest is added to the principal. Future calculations are on the adjusted principal (old principal plus interest). **Compound interest,** then, is the interest on the principal plus the interest of prior periods. **Future value (FV),** or the **compound amount,** is the final amount of the loan or investment at the end of the last period. In the beginning of this unit, do not be concerned with how to calculate compounding but try to understand the meaning of compounding.

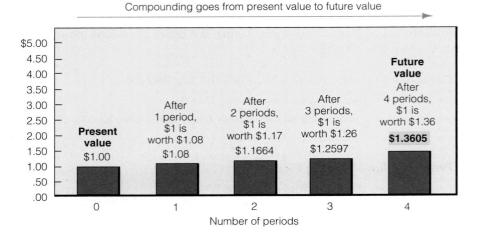

FIGURE	12.1

Future value of $1 at 8% for four periods

Check out the plastic overlays that appear within Chapter 13 to review these concepts.

Figure 12.1 shows how $1 will grow if it is calculated for 4 years at 8% annually. This means that the interest is calculated on the balance once a year. In Figure 12.1, we start with $1, which is the **present value (PV).** After year 1, the dollar with interest is worth $1.08. At the end of year 2, the dollar is worth $1.17. By the end of year 4, the dollar is worth $1.36 . Note how we start with the present and look to see what the dollar will be worth in the future. *Compounding goes from present value to future value.*

Before you learn how to calculate compound interest and compare it to simple interest, you must understand the terms that follow. These terms are also used in Chapter 13.

• **Compounded annually:** Interest calculated on the balance once a year.

• **Compounded semiannually:** Interest calculated on the balance every 6 months or every $\frac{1}{2}$ year.

• **Compounded quarterly:** Interest calculated on the balance every 3 months or every $\frac{1}{4}$ year.

• **Compounded monthly:** Interest calculated on the balance each month.

• **Compounded daily:** Interest calculated on the balance each day.

• **Number of periods:**[1] Number of years multiplied by the number of times the interest is compounded per year. For example, if you compound $1 for 4 years at 8% annually, semiannually, or quarterly, the following periods will result:

  Annually: 4 years × 1 = 4 periods

  Semiannually: 4 years × 2 = 8 periods

  Quarterly: 4 years × 4 = 16 periods

• **Rate for each period:**[2] Annual interest rate divided by the number of times the interest is compounded per year. Compounding changes the interest rate for annual, semiannual, and quarterly periods as follows:

  Annually: 8% ÷ 1 = 8%

  Semiannually: 8% ÷ 2 = 4%

  Quarterly: 8% ÷ 4 = 2%

Note that both the number of periods (4) and the rate (8%) for the annual example did not change. You will see later that rate and periods (not years) will always change unless interest is compounded yearly.

Now you are ready to learn the difference between simple interest and compound interest.

LO	1

Simple versus Compound Interest

Did you know that money invested at 6% will double in 12 years? The following *Wall Street Journal* clipping "Confused by Investing?" shows how to calculate the number of years it takes for your investment to double.

---

[1]Periods are often expressed with the letter *N* for number of periods.

[2]Rate is often expressed with the letter *i* for interest.

Confused by Investing?

If there's something about your investment portfolio that doesn't seem to add up, maybe you should check your math.

Lots of folks are perplexed by the mathematics of investing, so I thought a refresher course might help. Here's a look at some key concepts:

■ **10 Plus 10 is 21**

Imagine you invest $100, which earns 10% this year and 10% next. How much have you made? If you answered 21%, go to the head of the class.

Here's how the math works. This year's 10% gain turns your $100 into $110. Next year, you also earn 10%, but you start the year with $110. Result? You earn $11, boosting your wealth to $121.

Thus, your portfolio has earned a *cumulative* 21% return over two years, but the *annualized* return is just 10%. The fact that 21% is more, than double 10% can be attributed to the effect of investment compounding, the way that you earn money each year not only on your original investment, but also on earnings from prior years that you've reinvested.

■ **The Rule of 72**

To get a feel for compounding, try the rule of 72. What's that? If you divide a particular annual return into 72, you'll find out how many years it will take to double your money. Thus, at 10% a year, an investment will double in value in a tad over seven years.

The following three situations of Bill Smith will clarify the difference between simple interest and compound interest.

Situation 1: Calculating Simple Interest and Maturity Value

EXAMPLE   Bill Smith deposited $80 in a savings account for 4 years at an annual interest rate of 8%. What is Bill's simple interest?

To calculate simple interest, we use the following simple interest formula:

$$\text{Interest } (I) = \text{Principal } (P) \times \text{Rate } (R) \times \text{Time } (T)$$

$$\$25.60 = \$80 \times .08 \times 4$$

In 4 years Bill receives a total of $105.60 ($80.00 + $25.60)—principal plus simple interest.

Now let's look at the interest Bill would earn if the bank compounded Bill's interest on his savings.

Situation 2: Calculating Compound Amount and Interest without Tables[3]

You can use the following steps to calculate the compound amount and the interest manually:

CALCULATING COMPOUND AMOUNT AND INTEREST MANUALLY

Step 1. Calculate the simple interest and add it to the principal. Use this total to figure next year's interest.

Step 2. Repeat for the total number of periods.

Step 3. Compound amount − Principal = Compound interest.

EXAMPLE   Bill Smith deposited $80 in a savings account for 4 years at an annual compounded rate of 8%. What are Bill's compound amount and interest?

The following shows how the compounded rate affects Bill's interest:

	Year 1	Year 2	Year 3	Year 4
	$80.00	$86.40	$ 93.31	$100.77
	× .08	× .08	× .08	× .08
Interest	$ 6.40	$ 6.91	$ 7.46	$ 8.06
Beginning balance	+ 80.00	+ 86.40	+ 93.31	+ 100.77
Amount at year-end	$86.40	$93.31	$100.77	$108.83

[3]For simplicity of presentation, round each calculation to nearest cent before continuing the compounding process. The compound amount will be off by 1 cent.

Note that the beginning year 2 interest is the result of the interest of year 1 added to the principal. At the end of each interest period, we add on the period's interest. This interest becomes part of the principal we use for the calculation of the next period's interest. We can determine Bill's compound interest as follows:[4]

Compound amount	$108.83	
Principal	− 80.00	*Note:* In Situation 1 the interest was $25.60.
Compound interest	$ 28.83	

We could have used the following simplified process to calculate the compound amount and interest:

Year 1	**Year 2**	**Year 3**	**Year 4**
$80.00	$86.40	$ 93.31	$100.77
× 1.08	× 1.08	× 1.08	× 1.08
$86.40	$93.31	$100.77	$108.83 [5] ← Future value

When using this simplification, you do not have to add the new interest to the previous balance. Remember that compounding results in higher interest than simple interest. Compounding is the *sum* of principal and interest multiplied by the interest rate we use to calculate interest for the next period. So, 1.08 above is 108%, with 100% as the base and 8% as the interest.

LO 2

Situation 3: Calculating Compound Amount by Table Lookup

To calculate the compound amount with a future value table, use the following steps:

CALCULATING COMPOUND AMOUNT BY TABLE LOOKUP

Step 1. Find the periods: Years multiplied by number of times interest is compounded in 1 year.

Step 2. Find the rate: Annual rate divided by number of times interest is compounded in 1 year.

Step 3. Go down the Period column of the table to the number of periods desired; look across the row to find the rate. At the intersection of the two columns is the table factor for the compound amount of $1.

Step 4. Multiply the table factor by the amount of the loan. This gives the compound amount.

Four Periods
No. of times
compounded × No. of years
in 1 year
   1   ×   4

In Situation 2, Bill deposited $80 into a savings account for 4 years at an interest rate of 8% compounded annually. Bill heard that he could calculate the compound amount and interest by using tables. In Situation 3, Bill learns how to do this. Again, Bill wants to know the value of $80 in 4 years at 8%. He begins by using Table 12.1 (p. 297).

Looking at Table 12.1, Bill goes down the Period column to period 4, then across the row to the 8% column. At the intersection, Bill sees the number 1.3605. The marginal notes show how Bill arrived at the periods and rate. The 1.3605 table number means that $1 compounded at this rate will increase in value in 4 years to about $1.36. Do you recognize the $1.36? Figure 12.1 showed how $1 grew to $1.36. Since Bill wants to know the value of $80, he multiplies the dollar amount by the table factor as follows:

$$\$80.00 \ \times \ 1.3605 \ = \ \boxed{\$108.84}$$

Principal × Table factor = Compound amount (future value)

8% Rate
8% rate = $\dfrac{8\%}{1}$ → Annual rate
→ No. of times
compounded
in 1 year

Figure 12.2 (p. 297) illustrates this compounding procedure. We can say that compounding is a future value (FV) since we are looking into the future. Thus,

$108.84 − $80.00 = $28.84 interest for 4 years at 8%
compounded annually on $80.00

Now let's look at two examples that illustrate compounding more than once a year.

---

[4]The formula for compounding is $A = P(1 + i)^N$, where A equals compound amount, P equals the principal, i equals interest per period, and N equals number of periods. The calculator sequence would be as follows for Bill Smith: 1 [+] .08 [y^x] 4 × 80 [=] 108.84. A Financial Calculator Guide booklet is available that shows how to operate HP 10BII and TI BA II Plus.

[5]Off 1 cent due to rounding.

RF/Corbis

LO 1

From Figure 12.4, you can see that the present value of $1 is .7350. Remember that the $1 is only worth 74 cents if you wait 4 periods to receive it. This is one reason why so many athletes get such big contracts—much of the money is paid in later years when it is not worth as much.

Relationship of Compounding (FV) to Present Value (PV)—The Bill Smith Example Continued

In Learning Unit 12–1, our consideration of compounding started in the *present* ($80) and looked to find the *future* amount of $108.84. Present value (PV) starts with the *future* and tries to calculate its worth in the *present* ($80). For example, in Figure 12.5, we assume Bill Smith knew that in 4 years he wanted to buy a bike that cost $108.84 (future). Bill's bank pays 8% interest compounded annually. How much money must Bill put in the bank *today* (present) to have $108.84 in 4 years? To work from the future to the present, we can use a present value (PV) table. In the next section you will learn how to use this table.

FIGURE 12.5

Present value

Present value starts with the future and looks to the present

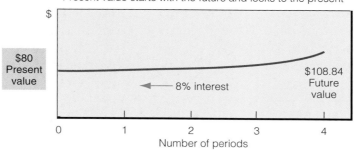

How to Use a Present Value (PV) Table[7]

To calculate present value with a present value table, use the following steps:

LO 2

CALCULATING PRESENT VALUE BY TABLE LOOKUP
Step 1. Find the periods: Years multiplied by number of times interest is compounded in 1 year.
Step 2. Find the rate: Annual rate divided by numbers of times interest is compounded in 1 year.
Step 3. Go down the Period column of the table to the number of periods desired; look across the row to find the rate. At the intersection of the two columns is the table factor for the compound value of $1.
Step 4. Multiply the table factor times the future value. This gives the present value.

Periods

4 × 1 = 4

No. of years   No. of times compounded in 1 year

Table 12.3 (p. 302) is a present value (PV) table that tells you what $1 is worth today at different interest rates. To continue our Bill Smith example, go down the Period column in Table 12.3 to 4. Then go across to the 8% column. At 8% for 4 periods, we see a table factor of .7350. This means that $1 in the future is worth approximately 74 cents today. If Bill invested 74 cents today at 8% for 4 periods, Bill would have $1.

Since Bill knows the bike will cost $108.84 in the future, he completes the following calculation:

$108.84 × .7350 = $80.00

This means that $108.84 in today's dollars is worth $80.00. Now let's check this.

[7]The formula for present value is $PV = \dfrac{A}{(1 + i)^N}$, where A equals future amount (compound amount), N equals number of compounding periods, and i equals interest rate per compounding period. The calculator sequence for Bill Smith would be as follows: 1 [+] .08 [y^x] 4 [=] [M+] 108.84 [÷] [MR] [=] 80.03.

TABLE **12.3** Present value of $1 at end period

Period	1%	1½%	2%	3%	4%	5%	6%	7%	8%	9%	10%
1	.9901	.9852	.9804	.9709	.9615	.9524	.9434	.9346	.9259	.9174	.9091
2	.9803	.9707	.9612	.9426	.9246	.9070	.8900	.8734	.8573	.8417	.8264
3	.9706	.9563	.9423	.9151	.8890	.8638	.8396	.8163	.7938	.7722	.7513
4	.9610	.9422	.9238	.8885	.8548	.8227	.7921	.7629	.7350	.7084	.6830
5	.9515	.9283	.9057	.8626	.8219	.7835	.7473	.7130	.6806	.6499	.6209
6	.9420	.9145	.8880	.8375	.7903	.7462	.7050	.6663	.6302	.5963	.5645
7	.9327	.9010	.8706	.8131	.7599	.7107	.6651	.6227	.5835	.5470	.5132
8	.9235	.8877	.8535	.7894	.7307	.6768	.6274	.5820	.5403	.5019	.4665
9	.9143	.8746	.8368	.7664	.7026	.6446	.5919	.5439	.5002	.4604	.4241
10	.9053	.8617	.8203	.7441	.6756	.6139	.5584	.5083	.4632	.4224	.3855
11	.8963	.8489	.8043	.7224	.6496	.5847	.5268	.4751	.4289	.3875	.3505
12	.8874	.8364	.7885	.7014	.6246	.5568	.4970	.4440	.3971	.3555	.3186
13	.8787	.8240	.7730	.6810	.6006	.5303	.4688	.4150	.3677	.3262	.2897
14	.8700	.8119	.7579	.6611	.5775	.5051	.4423	.3878	.3405	.2992	.2633
15	.8613	.7999	.7430	.6419	.5553	.4810	.4173	.3624	.3152	.2745	.2394
16	.8528	.7880	.7284	.6232	.5339	.4581	.3936	.3387	.2919	.2519	.2176
17	.8444	.7764	.7142	.6050	.5134	.4363	.3714	.3166	.2703	.2311	.1978
18	.8360	.7649	.7002	.5874	.4936	.4155	.3503	.2959	.2502	.2120	.1799
19	.8277	.7536	.6864	.5703	.4746	.3957	.3305	.2765	.2317	.1945	.1635
20	.8195	.7425	.6730	.5537	.4564	.3769	.3118	.2584	.2145	.1784	.1486
21	.8114	.7315	.6598	.5375	.4388	.3589	.2942	.2415	.1987	.1637	.1351
22	.8034	.7207	.6468	.5219	.4220	.3418	.2775	.2257	.1839	.1502	.1228
23	.7954	.7100	.6342	.5067	.4057	.3256	.2618	.2109	.1703	.1378	.1117
24	.7876	.6995	.6217	.4919	.3901	.3101	.2470	.1971	.1577	.1264	.1015
25	.7798	.6892	.6095	.4776	.3751	.2953	.2330	.1842	.1460	.1160	.0923
26	.7720	.6790	.5976	.4637	.3607	.2812	.2198	.1722	.1352	.1064	.0839
27	.7644	.6690	.5859	.4502	.3468	.2678	.2074	.1609	.1252	.0976	.0763
28	.7568	.6591	.5744	.4371	.3335	.2551	.1956	.1504	.1159	.0895	.0693
29	.7493	.6494	.5631	.4243	.3207	.2429	.1846	.1406	.1073	.0822	.0630
30	.7419	.6398	.5521	.4120	.3083	.2314	.1741	.1314	.0994	.0754	.0573
35	.7059	.5939	.5000	.3554	.2534	.1813	.1301	.0937	.0676	.0490	.0356
40	.6717	.5513	.4529	.3066	.2083	.1420	.0972	.0668	.0460	.0318	.0221

Note: For more detailed tables, see your booklet, the *Business Math Handbook*.

Comparing Compound Interest (FV) Table 12.1 with Present Value (PV) Table 12.3

We know from our calculations that Bill needs to invest $80 for 4 years at 8% compound interest annually to buy his bike. We can check this by going back to Table 12.1 and comparing it with Table 12.3. Let's do this now.

LO 3

Compound value Table 12.1				Present value Table 12.3			
Table 12.1	Present value		Future value	Table 12.3	Future value		Present value
1.3605	×	$80.00	= $108.84	.7350	×	$108.84	= $80.00
(4 per., 8%)				(4 per., 8%)			
We know the present dollar amount and find what the dollar amount is worth in the future.				We know the future dollar amount and find what the dollar amount is worth in the present.			

FIGURE 12.6

Present value

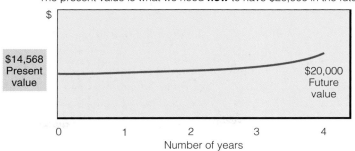

The present value is what we need ***now*** to have $20,000 in the future

$14,568 Present value

$20,000 Future value

Number of years

Note that the table factor for compounding is over 1 (1.3605) and the table factor for present value is less than 1 (.7350). The compound value table starts with the present and goes to the future. The present value table starts with the future and goes to the present.

Let's look at another example before trying the Practice Quiz.

EXAMPLE   Rene Weaver needs $20,000 for college in 4 years. She can earn 8% compounded quarterly at her bank. How much must Rene deposit at the beginning of the year to have $20,000 in 4 years?

Remember that in this example the bank compounds the interest *quarterly*. Let's first determine the period and rate on a quarterly basis:

$$\text{Periods} = 4 \times 4 \text{ years} = 16 \text{ periods} \qquad \text{Rate} = \frac{8\%}{4} = 2\%$$

Now we go to Table 12.3 and find 16 under the Period column. We then move across to the 2% column and find the .7284 table factor.

$$\$20,000 \times .7284 = \boxed{\$14,568}$$

(future value)   (present value)

We illustrate this in Figure 12.6.

We can check the $14,568 present value by using the compound value Table 12.1:

16 periods, 2% column = 1.3728 × $14,568 = $19,998.95[8]

Let's test your understanding of this unit with the Practice Quiz.

LU 12–2 | PRACTICE QUIZ

Complete this **Practice Quiz** to see how you are doing.

Use the present value Table 12.3 to complete:

Future amount desired	Length of time	Rate compounded	Table period	Rate used	PV factor	PV amount
1. $ 7,000	6 years	6% semiannually	_____	_____	_____	_____
2. $15,000	20 years	10% annually	_____	_____	_____	_____

3. Bill Blum needs $20,000 6 years from today to attend V.P.R. Tech. How much must Bill put in the bank today (12% quarterly) to reach his goal?

4. Bob Fry wants to buy his grandson a Ford Taurus in 4 years. The cost of a car will be $24,000. Assuming a bank rate of 8% compounded quarterly, how much must Bob put in the bank today?

Solutions with Step-by-Step Help on DVD

✓ Solutions

1.	12 periods (6 years × 2)	3% (6% ÷ 2)	.7014	$4,909.80 ($7,000 × .7014)
2.	20 periods (20 years × 1)	10% (10% ÷ 1)	.1486	$2,229.00 ($15,000 × .1486)

3.   6 years × 4 = 24 periods $\frac{12\%}{4} = 3\%$ .4919 × $20,000 = $9,838

4.   4 × 4 years = 16 periods $\frac{8\%}{4} = 2\%$ .7284 × $24,000 = $17,481.60

[8]Not quite $20,000 due to rounding of table factors.

LU 12–2a EXTRA PRACTICE QUIZ WITH WORKED-OUT SOLUTIONS

Need more practice? Try this **Extra Practice Quiz** (check figures in Chapter Organizer, p. 305). Worked-out Solutions can be found in Appendix B at end of text.

Use the *Business Math Handbook* to complete:

Future amount desired	Length of time	Rate compounded	Table period	Rate used	PV factor	PV amount
1. $ 9,000	7 years	5% semiannually	_____	_____	_____	_____
2. $20,000	20 years	4% annually	_____	_____	_____	_____

3. Bill Blum needs $40,000 6 years from today to attend V.P.R. Tech. How much must Bill put in the bank today (8% quarterly) to reach his goal?

4. Bob Fry wants to buy his grandson a Ford Taurus in 4 years. The cost of a car will be $28,000. Assuming a bank rate of 4% compounded quarterly, how much must Bob put in the bank today?

CHAPTER ORGANIZER AND REFERENCE GUIDE

Topic	Key point, procedure, formula	Example(s) to illustrate situation
Calculating compound amount without tables (future value), * p. 293	Determine new amount by multiplying rate times new balance (that includes interest added on). Start in present and look to future. $$\text{Compound interest} = \text{Compound amount} - \text{Principal}$$ PV ⟶ FV (Compounding)	$100 in savings account, compounded annually for 2 years at 8%: $100 × 1.08 = $108; $108 × 1.08 = $116.64 (future value)
Calculating compound amount (future value) by table lookup, p. 296	$$\text{Periods} = \frac{\text{Number of times compounded per year}} \times \text{Years of loan}$$ $$\text{Rate} = \frac{\text{Annual rate}}{\text{Number of times compounded per year}}$$ Multiply table factor (intersection of period and rate) times amount of principal.	*Example:* $2,000 @ 12% 5 years compounded quarterly: Periods = 4 × 5 years = 20 Rate = $\frac{12\%}{4}$ = 3% 20 periods, 3% = 1.8061 (table factor) $2,000 × 1.8061 = $3,612.20 (future value)
Effective rate (APY), p. 298	$$\text{Effective rate (APY)} = \frac{\text{Interest for 1 year}}{\text{Principal}}$$ or Rate can be seen in Table 12.1 factor.	$1,000 at 10% compounded semiannually for 1 year. By Table 12.1: 2 periods, 5% 1.1025 means at end of year investor has earned 110.25% of original principal. Thus the interest is 10.25%. $1,000 × 1.1025 = $1,102.50 − 1,000.00 = $ 102.50 $\frac{\$102.50}{\$1,000}$ = 10.25% effective rate (APY)
Calculating present value (PV) with table lookup, † p. 301	Start with future and calculate worth in the present. Periods and rate computed like in compound interest. PV ⟵ FV (Present value) Find periods and rate. Multiply table factor (intersection of period and rate) times amount of loan.	*Example:* Want $3,612.20 after 5 years with rate of 12% compounded quarterly: Periods = 4 × 5 = 20; % = 3% By Table 12.3: 20 periods, 3% = .5537 $3,612.20 × .5537 = $2,000.08 Invested today will yield desired amount in future

*$A = P(1 + i)^N$.

†$\frac{A}{(1 + i)^N}$ if table not used.

(continues)

CHAPTER ORGANIZER AND REFERENCE GUIDE

Topic	Key point, procedure, formula		Example(s) to illustrate situation	
KEY TERMS	Annual percentage yield (APY), p. 298 Compound amount, p. 293 Compounded annually, p. 294 Compounded daily, pp. 294, 299 Compounded monthly, p. 294	Compounded quarterly, p. 294 Compounded semiannually, p. 294 Compounding, p. 293 Compound interest, p. 293 Effective rate, p. 298	Future value (FV), p. 293 Nominal rate, p. 298 Number of periods, p. 294 Present value (PV), p. 294 Rate for each period, p. 294	
CHECK FIGURES FOR EXTRA PRACTICE QUIZZES WITH PAGE REFERENCES. (WORKED-OUT SOLUTIONS IN APPENDIX B.)	LU 12–1a (p. 300) 1. 4 periods; Int. = $41.22; $541.21 2. $541.21 3. $9,609.60 4. 6.14% 5. $2,429.64		LU 12–2a (p. 304) 1. $6,369.30 2. $9,128 3. $24,868 4. $23,878.40	

Critical Thinking Discussion Questions

1. Explain how periods and rates are calculated in compounding problems. Compare simple interest to compound interest.

2. What are the steps to calculate the compound amount by table? Why is the compound table factor greater than $1?

3. What is the effective rate (APY)? Why can the effective rate be seen directly from the table factor?

4. Explain the difference between compounding and present value. Why is the present value table factor less than $1?

Classroom Notes

Check figures for odd-numbered problems in Appendix C.   Name _____ Date _____

DRILL PROBLEMS

Complete the following without using Table 12.1 (round to the nearest cent for each calculation) and then check by Table 12.1 (check will be off due to rounding).

	Principal	Time (years)	Rate of compound interest	Compounded	Periods	Rate	Total amount	Total interest
12–1.	$1,600	2	6%	Semiannually				

Complete the following using compound future value Table 12.1:

	Time	Principal	Rate	Compounded	Amount	Interest
12–2.	12 years	$15,000	$3\frac{1}{2}\%$	Annually		
12–3.	6 months	$10,000	8%	Quarterly		
12–4.	3 years	$2,000	12%	Semiannually		

Calculate the effective rate (APY) of interest for 1 year.

12–5. Principal: $15,500
Interest rate: 12%
Compounded quarterly
Effective rate (APY):

12–6. Using Table 12.2, calculate what $700 would grow to at $6\frac{1}{2}\%$ per year compounded daily for 7 years.

Complete the following using present value of Table 12.3 or *Business Math Handbook* Table.

	Amount desired at end of period	Length of time	Rate	Compounded	On PV Table 12.3 Period used	Rate used	PV factor used	PV of amount desired at end of period
12–7.	$6,000	8 years	3%	Semiannually				
12–8.	$8,900	4 years	6%	Monthly				
12–9.	$17,600	7 years	12%	Quarterly				

12–10. $20,000   20 years   8%   Annually

12–11. Check your answer in Problem 12–9 by the compound value Table 12.1. The answer will be off due to rounding.

WORD PROBLEMS

12–12. Greg Lawrence anticipates he will need approximately $218,000 in 15 years to cover his 3-year-old daughter's college bills for a 4-year degree. How much would he have to invest today, at an interest rate of 8 percent compounded semiannually?

12–13. Lynn Ally, owner of a local Subway shop, loaned $40,000 to Pete Hall to help him open a Subway franchise. Pete plans to repay Lynn at the end of 8 years with 6% interest compounded semiannually. How much will Lynn receive at the end of 8 years?

12–14. Molly Hamilton deposited $50,000 at Bank of America at 8% interest compounded quarterly. What is the effective rate (APY) to the nearest hundredth percent?

12–15. Melvin Indecision has difficulty deciding whether to put his savings in Mystic Bank or Four Rivers Bank. Mystic offers 10% interest compounded semiannually. Four Rivers offers 8% interest compounded quarterly. Melvin has $10,000 to invest. He expects to withdraw the money at the end of 4 years. Which bank gives Melvin the better deal? Check your answer.

12–16. Lee Holmes deposited $15,000 in a new savings account at 9% interest compounded semiannually. At the beginning of year 4, Lee deposits an additional $40,000 at 9% interest compounded semiannually. At the end of 6 years, what is the balance in Lee's account?

12–17. Lee Wills loaned Audrey Chin $16,000 to open Snip Its Hair Salon. After 6 years, Audrey will repay Lee with 8% interest compounded quarterly. How much will Lee receive at the end of 6 years?

12–18. Morningstar.com is a useful personal and business investment site with in-depth detail on personal financial planning. After reading a March 19, 2009, article, "Preparing a Portfolio for Retirement," Arlene Supple, 47 years old, is evaluating her retirement portfolio. She paid her house off in anticipation of an early retirement. In addition, she has invested wisely in her company's 401k, a Roth IRA, municipal bonds, and certificates of deposit. She has amassed $287,000 in her diversified portfolio. Today, she has the opportunity to deposit her money at 4.0% compounded quarterly. If she retires at 54 years old, how much will her investment be worth?

12–19. John Roe, an employee of the Gap, loans $3,000 to another employee at the store. He will be repaid at the end of 4 years with interest at 6% compounded quarterly. How much will John be repaid?

12–20. In the aftermath of the mortgage crisis, Kyle and Mary Ellis from Las Vegas, NV, are considering remodeling their home. They originally wanted to sell their home and move to another area, but news from the *Las Vegas Sun* continues to show a decline in real estate values. Their plan now is to improve their home's curb appeal as well as update the interior. They estimate the cost will be $65,000. How much must they invest today at 6% interest compounded quarterly in order to have the money they need to remodel in 10 years?

12–21. Security National Bank is quoting 1-year certificates of deposit with an interest rate of 5% compounded semiannually. Joe Saver purchased a $5,000 CD. What is the CD's effective rate (APY) to the nearest hundredth percent? Use tables in the *Business Math Handbook*.

12–22. Jim Ryan, an owner of a Burger King restaurant, assumes that his restaurant will need a new roof in 7 years. He estimates the roof will cost him $9,000 at that time. What amount should Jim invest today at 6% compounded quarterly to be able to pay for the roof? Check your answer.

12–23. Tony Ring wants to attend Northeast College. He will need $60,000 4 years from today. Assume Tony's bank pays 12% interest compounded semiannually. What must Tony deposit today so he will have $60,000 in 4 years?

12–24. Could you check your answer (to the nearest dollar) in Problem 12–23 by using the compound value Table 12.1? The answer will be slightly off due to rounding.

12–25. Pete Air wants to buy a used Jeep in 5 years. He estimates the Jeep will cost $15,000. Assume Pete invests $10,000 now at 12% interest compounded semiannually. Will Pete have enough money to buy his Jeep at the end of 5 years?

12–26. Lance Jackson deposited $5,000 at Basil Bank at 9% interest compounded daily. What is Lance's investment at the end of 4 years?

12–27. Paul Havlik promised his grandson Jamie that he would give him $6,000 8 years from today for graduating from high school. Assume money is worth 6% interest compounded semiannually. What is the present value of this $6,000?

12–28. Earl Ezekiel wants to retire in San Diego when he is 65 years old. Earl is now 50. He believes he will need $300,000 to retire comfortably. To date, Earl has set aside no retirement money. Assume Earl gets 6% interest compounded semiannually. How much must Earl invest today to meet his $300,000 goal?

12–29. Jackie Rich would like to buy a $19,000 Toyota hybrid car in 4 years. Jackie wants to put the money aside now. Jackie's bank offers 8% interest compounded semiannually. How much must Jackie invest today?

12–30. John Smith saw the following advertisement. Could you show him how $88.77 was calculated?

| 9-Month CD | **6.05**%
Annual*
Percentage
Yield |

*As of January 31, 200X, and subject to change. Interest on the 9-month CD is credited on the maturity date and is not compounded. For example, a $2,000, 9-month CD on deposit for an interest rate of 6.00% (6.05% APY) will earn $88.77 at maturity. Withdrawals prior to maturity require the consent of the bank and are subject to a substantial penalty. There is $500 minimum deposit for IRA, SEP IRA, and Keogh CDs (except for 9-month CD for which the minimum deposit is $1,000). There is $1,000 minimum deposit for all personal CDs (except for 9-month CD for which the minimum deposit is $2,000). Offer not valid on jumbo CDs.

CHALLENGE PROBLEMS

12–31. Linda Roy received a $200,000 inheritance after taxes from her parents. She invested it at 4% interest compounded quarterly for 3 years. A year later, she sold one of her rental properties for $210,000 and invested that money at 3% compounded semi-annually for 2 years. Both of the investments have matured. She is hoping to have at least $500,000 in 7 years compounded annually at 2% interest so she can move to Hawaii. Will she meet her goal?

12–32. You are the financial planner for Johnson Controls. Assume last year's profits were $700,000. The board of directors decided to forgo dividends to stockholders and retire high-interest outstanding bonds that were issued 5 years ago at a face value of $1,250,000. You have been asked to invest the profits in a bank. The board must know how much money you will need from the profits earned to retire the bonds in 10 years. Bank A pays 6% compounded quarterly, and Bank B pays $6\frac{1}{2}$% compounded annually. Which bank would you recommend, and how much of the company's profit should be placed in the bank? If you recommended that the remaining money not be distributed to stockholders but be placed in Bank B, how much would the remaining money be worth in 10 years? Use tables in the *Business Math Handbook.** Round final answer to nearest dollar.

*Check glossary for unfamiliar terms.

SUMMARY PRACTICE TEST

1. Lorna Ray, owner of a Starbucks franchise, loaned $40,000 to Lee Reese to help him open a new flower shop online. Lee plans to repay Lorna at the end of 5 years with 4% interest compounded semiannually. How much will Lorna receive at the end of 5 years? *(p. 295)*

2. Joe Beary wants to attend Riverside College. Eight years from today he will need $50,000. If Joe's bank pays 6% interest compounded semiannually, what must Joe deposit today to have $50,000 in 8 years? *(p. 301)*

3. Shelley Katz deposited $30,000 in a savings account at 5% interest compounded semiannually. At the beginning of year 4, Shelley deposits an additional $80,000 at 5% interest compounded semiannually. At the end of 6 years, what is the balance in Shelley's account? *(p. 295)*

4. Earl Miller, owner of a Papa Gino's franchise, wants to buy a new delivery truck in 6 years. He estimates the truck will cost $30,000. If Earl invests $20,000 now at 5% interest compounded semiannually, will Earl have enough money to buy his delivery truck at the end of 6 years? *(pp. 295, 301)*

5. Minnie Rose deposited $16,000 in Street Bank at 6% interest compounded quarterly. What was the effective rate (APY)? Round to the nearest hundredth percent. *(p. 298)*

6. Lou Ling, owner of Lou's Lube, estimates that he will need $70,000 for new equipment in 7 years. Lou decided to put aside money today so it will be available in 7 years. Reel Bank offers Lou 6% interest compounded quarterly. How much must Lou invest to have $70,000 in 7 years? *(p. 301)*

7. Bernie Long wants to retire to California when she is 60 years of age. Bernie is now 40. She believes that she will need $900,000 to retire comfortably. To date, Bernie has set aside no retirement money. If Bernie gets 8% compounded semiannually, how much must Bernie invest today to meet her $900,000 goal? *(p. 301)*

8. Jim Jones deposited $19,000 in a savings account at 7% interest compounded daily. At the end of 6 years, what is the balance in Jim's account? *(p. 294)*

Personal Finance

✦ KipTip

How to Find a Better Bank

SMALL BANKS, CREDIT UNIONS AND ONLINE banks are hungry for your business, so they're beating big banks on fees and rates.

Community bank. Go to the Web site of the Independent Community Bankers of America (www.icba.org) and click on "community bank locator."

Credit union. Click on "locate a credit union" at the Credit Union National Association's site (www.creditunion.coop). You may be eligible to join one where you work or live, or because a family member belongs. Some credit unions have other entrees to membership. For example, you can become a member of the Pentagon Federal Credit Union if you join the National Military Family Association for a one-time $20 membership fee.

Online bank. Start at Bankrate.com, which lists the latest interest rates and offers. Click on the "compare rates" tab to find banks with above-average yields. If you find a deal at an online bank that you're not familiar with, make sure the institution is covered by FDIC insurance. Run the bank's name through the agency's Bank Find database (www2.fdic.gov/idasp/main_bankfind.asp).

the accompanying debit card.

Capital One, the credit-card issuer, has been expanding into banking and is offering incentives to attract customers. Recently, you could sign up to earn double rewards on checking accounts. Ira J. Furman, a 65-year-old lawyer in Freeport, N.Y., was already a customer of Capital One. But after receiving a call from the bank, he signed up for a rewards checking account, and he registered his wife, Carole, who will be eligible for a total of 5,000 points for opening a new account and using the bank for direct deposit. In

From Kiplinger's Personal Finance, August 2009, p. 46.

addition, Capital One customers earn rewards for using their debit card, for paying bills online and for making withdrawals. "The rewards-program incentive is, for me, the cherry on top," Furman says.

Savings accounts. If you're looking for a safe parking place for your cash, certificates of deposit are a better deal than money-market funds or Treasury securities. You can earn 2% on a six-month CD at Corus Bank in Illinois (www.corusbank.com) with a $10,000 deposit, or 1.93% at Nexity Bank in Alabama (www.nexity.com) with only a $1,000 deposit. If you commit your funds for a year, you can earn 2.49% at Ally Bank (www.ally.com) with no minimum deposit. Credit unions offer rates on a $10,000, one-year CD that are 0.7 point higher, on average, than bank rates, according to Datatrac.

Loans. Community banks, such as Liberty Bank, compete with credit unions for auto-loan business, so their rates are similar. "Larger institutions charge higher rates because they are not competing for this business," says Dale Blachford, of Liberty Bank.

At banks, car-loan interest rates average 7.04% for 60 months and 7.31% for 36 months, according to Bankrate .com. Liberty charges customers with good credit 5.95% for loans of all lengths. Jim MacPhee, chief executive of Kalamazoo County State Bank, in Michigan, says that at a community bank your credit score isn't the only criterion: "We look the customer in the eye. We try to analyze their credit situation so we understand what they can afford."

Some credit unions offer even lower rates on auto loans. Pentagon Federal Credit Union charges 3.99% for loans from 12 to 60 months. Georgia's Own Credit Union offers loans as low as 5.2% for 60 months. It will also lower your rate by 0.5 point if you buy a hybrid car, and promises members $100 if it can't lower their monthly payments when it refinances their car loan. ■

BUSINESS MATH ISSUE

Credit unions are always a better choice for CD's than large banks.

1. List the key points of the article and information to support your position.
2. Write a group defense of your position using math calculations to support your view.

PROJECT A

Go to the Web and find out the latest rates for 6-month, 1-year, and 5-year CDs along with the current rates for markets.

GETTING GOING

If You Don't Know Your Math, You'll End Up Taking a Bath

Maybe we're just lousy at math.

The official savings rate remains stubbornly close to zero, mortgage and consumer debt leapt 7.4% in the 12 months through September, and the Pew Research Center recently reported that half of Americans rate their personal finances as fair or poor.

It's tempting to blame all this on financial recklessness. But consider another culprit: Our feeble math skills.

Here's a look at where we go wrong—and how we can do better.

By Jonathan Clements

■ **Losing interest.** In a recent study, marketing professors Eric Eisenstein and Stephen Hoch found that most folks underestimated how much savings would grow and how much debt would end up costing.

The problem: People think in terms of simple interest, not compound interest. For instance, if our investments clock 8% a year for 10 years, we don't earn 80%, as many people assume. Rather, we would notch a cumulative 116%. Remember, we earn returns not only on our original investment, but also on the investment gains earned in earlier years. Similarly, with credit-card debt, we pay interest both on our original purchases and on any monthly interest charges we didn't pay off in full.

"People use simple interest because they don't know to use anything else," says Prof. Eisenstein, of Cornell University's Johnson Graduate School of Management. "The higher the interest rate and the longer the time horizon, the worse the error." He argues that this basic math mistake helps explain why people delay saving for retirement and why they postpone paying off credit-card debt.

■ **Guessing wrong.** It isn't just credit cards that trip us up. We also don't appreciate how much interest we're paying on loans that promise "low monthly payments," according to new research by Dartmouth College economics professors Victor Stango and Jonathan Zinman.

The two authors analyzed data from the Federal Reserve's 1983 Survey of Consumer Finances. For that survey, consumers were asked how much they would expect to repay in total, assuming 12 monthly payments, if they took out a $1,000 one-year loan to buy furniture.

$$a = P(1+i)^N$$
$$i = 8\%, N = 4$$
$$P = 1500$$
$$1500 \times 1.3604\,9$$
$$\$213$$

In response, folks gave answers such as $1,200, which means the effective interest rate was 35%. Yet, when consumers were asked what interest rate was implied, 98% underestimated the rate.

The fewer the number of monthly payments, the more we're likely to underestimate the interest rate charged. Why? When we do our mental calculation, we overlook the fact that, with each monthly payment, we're reducing the loan balance. With a short-term loan, these principal repayments are a big chunk of each monthly payment.

"We know these are hard problems," says Prof. Stango, of Dartmouth's Tuck School of Business. "It isn't surprising that people get the answers wrong. What's really surprising is that people are almost always wrong in the same direction. They underestimate the interest rate and they underestimate the costs of borrowing."

■ **Getting better.** What can we do to avoid these mistakes? Try three strategies:

■ If you're considering a loan with "low monthly payments," ask the lender what the finance charge is as an annual percentage rate. That will tell you whether the monthly payments are truly low.

"People are scared to ask the tough questions," Prof. Stango says. "They're worried about not getting approved for the loan. They don't want to seem naive."

■ To get a handle on the costs of borrowing and the benefits of saving, try playing around with some online financial calculators. You can find a great collection of calculators at www.dinkytown.com.

■ As you toy with whether to spend or save, keep in mind the rule of 72. If you divide 72 by the rate of return you expect to earn, that will tell you how long it takes to double your money.

Think you can earn 7% a year? Divide that into 72, and you will learn that doubling your money takes 10.2 years. The implication: If you saved $1,000, rather than spending it, you would have roughly $2,000 after 10 years, $4,000 after 20 years—and an impressive $8,000 after 30 years.

WSJ.com

ONLINE TODAY: Jonathan Clements answers a question about investing 100% in stocks, at **WSJ.com/Video**.

PROJECT B

List the key points of this article.
Do you disagree with any of these points?

Internet Projects: See text Web site (www.mhhe.com/slater10e) and The Business Math Internet Resource Guide.

Classroom Notes

Additional Homework by Learning Unit

Name _____ Date _____

Learning Unit 1–1 :   Reading, Writing, and Rounding Whole Numbers

DRILL PROBLEMS

1. Express the following numbers in verbal form:
   a. 6,448 _____
   _____

   b. 160,501 _____
   _____

   c. 2,098,767 _____
   _____

   d. 58,003 _____
   _____

   e. 50,025,212,015 _____
   _____

2. Write in numeric form:
   a. Seventy thousand, two hundred eighty-one _____
   b. Fifty-eight thousand, three _____
   c. Two hundred eighty thousand, five _____
   d. Three million, ten _____
   e. Sixty-seven thousand, seven hundred sixty _____

3. Round the following numbers:
   a. To the nearest ten:
      64 _____   379 _____   855 _____   5,981 _____   206 _____
   b. To the nearest hundred:
      9,664 _____   2,074 _____   888 _____   271 _____   75 _____
   c. To the nearest thousand:
      21,486 _____   621 _____   3,504 _____   9,735 _____

4. Round off each number to the nearest ten, nearest hundred, nearest thousand, and round all the way. (Remember that you are rounding the original number each time.)

		Nearest ten	Nearest hundred	Nearest thousand	Round all the way
a.	4,752	_____	_____	_____	_____
b.	70,351	_____	_____	_____	_____
c.	9,386	_____	_____	_____	_____
d.	4,983	_____	_____	_____	_____
e.	408,119	_____	_____	_____	_____
f.	30,051	_____	_____	_____	_____

5. Name the place position (place value) of the underlined digit.
   a. 8,3<u>4</u>8 _____
   b. <u>9</u>,734 _____
   c. 3<u>4</u>7,107 _____
   d. 7<u>2</u>3 _____

   e. 28,200,000,121 _____

   f. 706,359,005 _____

   g. 27,563,530 _____

WORD PROBLEMS

6. Gim Smith was shopping for an Apple computer. He went to three different Web sites and found the computer he wanted at three different prices. At Web site A the price was $2,018, at Web site B the price was $1,985, and at Web site C the price was $2,030. What is the approximate price Gim will have to pay for the computer? Round to the nearest thousand. (Just one price.)

7. Amy Parker had to write a check at the bookstore when she purchased her books for the new semester. The total cost of the books was $384. How will she write this amount in verbal form on her check?

8. Matt Schaeffer was listening to the news and heard that steel production last week was one million, five hundred eighty-seven thousand tons. Express this amount in numeric form.

9. Jackie Martin is the city clerk and must go to the aldermen's meetings and take notes on what is discussed. At last night's meeting, they were discussing repairs for the public library, which will cost three hundred seventy-five thousand, nine hundred eighty-five dollars. Write this in numeric form as Jackie would.

10. A government survey revealed that 25,963,400 people are employed as office workers. To show the approximate number of office workers, round the number all the way.

11. Bob Donaldson wished to present his top student with a certificate of achievement at the end of the school year in 2004. To make it appear more official, he wanted to write the year in verbal form. How did he write the year?

12. Nancy Morrissey has a problem reading large numbers and determining place value. She asked her brother to name the place value of the 4 in the number 13,542,966. Can you tell Nancy the place value of the 4? What is the place value of the 3?
   The 4 is in the _____ place.
   The 3 is in the _____ place.

Learning Unit 1-2 :   Adding and Subtracting Whole Numbers

DRILL PROBLEMS

1. Add by totaling each separate column:

a.	668	b.	43	c.	493	d.	36	e.	716	f.	535	g.	751	h.	75,730
	338		58		826		76		458		107		378		48,531
			96				43		397		778		135		15,797
							24		139		215		747		
									478		391		368		

2. Estimate by rounding all the way, then add the actual numbers:

a.	580	b.	1,470	c.	475
	971		7,631		837
	548		4,383		213
	430				775
	506				432

Name _____ Date _____

Learning Unit 2–1 : Types of Fractions and Conversion Procedures

DRILL PROBLEMS

1. Identify the type of fraction—proper, improper, or mixed number:

    a. $8\dfrac{1}{8}$ **b.** $\dfrac{31}{29}$ **c.** $\dfrac{29}{27}$

    d. $9\dfrac{3}{11}$ **e.** $\dfrac{18}{5}$ **f.** $\dfrac{30}{37}$

2. Convert to a mixed number:

    a. $\dfrac{29}{4}$ **b.** $\dfrac{137}{8}$ **c.** $\dfrac{27}{5}$

    d. $\dfrac{29}{9}$ **e.** $\dfrac{71}{8}$ **f.** $\dfrac{43}{6}$

3. Convert the mixed number to an improper fraction:

    a. $8\dfrac{1}{5}$ **b.** $12\dfrac{3}{11}$ **c.** $4\dfrac{3}{7}$

    d. $20\dfrac{4}{9}$ **e.** $10\dfrac{11}{12}$ **f.** $17\dfrac{2}{3}$

4. Tell whether the fractions in each pair are equivalent or not:

    a. $\dfrac{3}{4}\quad\dfrac{9}{12}$ _____   **b.** $\dfrac{2}{3}\quad\dfrac{12}{18}$ _____   **c.** $\dfrac{7}{8}\quad\dfrac{15}{16}$ _____

    d. $\dfrac{4}{5}\quad\dfrac{12}{15}$ _____   **e.** $\dfrac{3}{2}\quad\dfrac{9}{4}$ _____   **f.** $\dfrac{5}{8}\quad\dfrac{7}{11}$ _____

    g. $\dfrac{7}{12}\quad\dfrac{7}{24}$ _____   **h.** $\dfrac{5}{4}\quad\dfrac{30}{24}$ _____   **i.** $\dfrac{10}{26}\quad\dfrac{12}{26}$ _____

5. Find the greatest common divisor by the step approach and reduce to lowest terms:

    a. $\dfrac{36}{42}$

    b. $\dfrac{30}{75}$

    c. $\dfrac{74}{148}$

    d. $\dfrac{15}{600}$

    e. $\dfrac{96}{132}$

f. $\dfrac{84}{154}$

6. Convert to higher terms:

   a. $\dfrac{8}{10} = \dfrac{}{70}$

   b. $\dfrac{2}{15} = \dfrac{}{30}$

   c. $\dfrac{6}{11} = \dfrac{}{132}$

   d. $\dfrac{4}{9} = \dfrac{}{36}$

   e. $\dfrac{7}{20} = \dfrac{}{100}$

   f. $\dfrac{7}{8} = \dfrac{}{560}$

WORD PROBLEMS

7. Ken drove to college in $3\frac{1}{4}$ hours. How many quarter-hours is that? Show your answer as an improper fraction.

8. Mary looked in the refrigerator for a dozen eggs. When she found the box, only 5 eggs were left. What fractional part of the box of eggs was left?

9. At a recent meeting of a local Boosters Club, 17 of the 25 members attending were men. What fraction of those in attendance were men?

10. By weight, water is two parts out of three parts of the human body. What fraction of the body is water?

11. Three out of 5 students who begin college will continue until they receive their degree. Show in fractional form how many out of 100 beginning students will graduate.

12. Tina and her friends came in late to a party and found only $\frac{3}{4}$ of a pizza remaining. In order for everyone to get some pizza, she wanted to divide it into smaller pieces. If she divides the pizza into twelfths, how many pieces will she have? Show your answer in fractional form.

13. Sharon and Spunky noted that it took them 35 minutes to do their exercise routine. What fractional part of an hour is that? Show your answer in lowest terms.

14. Norman and his friend ordered several pizzas, which were all cut into eighths. The group ate 43 pieces of pizza. How many pizzas did they eat? Show your answer as a mixed number.

Learning Unit 2–2 : Adding and Subtracting Fractions

DRILL PROBLEMS

1. Find the least common denominator (LCD) for each of the following groups of denominators using the prime numbers:

a. 8, 16, 32   **b.** 9, 15, 20

c. 12, 15, 32   **d.** 7, 9, 14, 28

2. Add and reduce to lowest terms or change to a mixed number if needed:

a. $\dfrac{1}{8} + \dfrac{4}{8}$ **b.** $\dfrac{5}{12} + \dfrac{8}{15}$

c. $\dfrac{7}{8} + \dfrac{5}{12}$ **d.** $7\dfrac{2}{3} + 5\dfrac{1}{4}$

e. $\dfrac{2}{3} + \dfrac{4}{9} + \dfrac{1}{4}$

3. Subtract and reduce to lowest terms:

a. $\dfrac{5}{9} - \dfrac{2}{9}$ **b.** $\dfrac{14}{15} - \dfrac{4}{15}$ **c.** $\dfrac{8}{9} - \dfrac{5}{6}$ **d.** $\dfrac{7}{12} - \dfrac{9}{16}$

e. $33\dfrac{5}{8} - 27\dfrac{1}{2}$ **f.** $9 - 2\dfrac{3}{7}$ **g.** $15\dfrac{1}{3} - 9\dfrac{7}{12}$

h. $92\dfrac{3}{10} - 35\dfrac{7}{15}$ **i.** $93 - 57\dfrac{5}{12}$ **j.** $22\dfrac{5}{8} - 17\dfrac{1}{4}$

WORD PROBLEMS

4. Dan Lund took a cross-country trip. He drove $5\frac{3}{8}$ hours on Monday, $6\frac{1}{2}$ hours on Tuesday, $9\frac{3}{4}$ hours on Wednesday, $6\frac{3}{8}$ hours on Thursday, and $10\frac{1}{4}$ hours on Friday. Find the total number of hours Dan drove in the first 5 days of his trip.

5. Sharon Parker bought 20 yards of material to make curtains. She used $4\frac{1}{2}$ yards for one bedroom window, $8\frac{3}{5}$ yards for another bedroom window, and $3\frac{7}{8}$ yards for a hall window. How much material did she have left?

6. Molly Ring visited a local gym and lost $2\frac{1}{4}$ pounds the first weekend and $6\frac{1}{8}$ pounds in week 2. What is Molly's total weight loss?

7. Bill Williams had to drive $46\frac{1}{4}$ miles to work. After driving $28\frac{5}{6}$ miles he noticed he was low on gas and had to decide whether he should stop to fill the gas tank. How many more miles does Bill have to drive to get to work?

8. Albert's Lumber Yard purchased $52\frac{1}{2}$ cords of lumber on Monday and $48\frac{3}{4}$ cords on Tuesday. It sold $21\frac{3}{8}$ cords on Friday. How many cords of lumber remain at Albert's Lumber Yard?

9. At Arlen Oil Company, where Dave Bursett is the service manager, it took $42\frac{1}{3}$ hours to clean five boilers. After a new cleaning tool was purchased, the time for cleaning five boilers was reduced to $37\frac{4}{9}$ hours. How much time was saved?

Learning Unit 2–3 :   Multiplying and Dividing Fractions

DRILL PROBLEMS

1. Multiply (use cancellation technique):

a. $\dfrac{6}{13} \times \dfrac{26}{12}$

b. $\dfrac{3}{8} \times \dfrac{2}{3}$

c. $\dfrac{5}{7} \times \dfrac{9}{10}$

d. $\dfrac{3}{4} \times \dfrac{9}{13} \times \dfrac{26}{27}$

e. $6\dfrac{2}{5} \times 3\dfrac{1}{8}$

f. $2\dfrac{2}{3} \times 2\dfrac{7}{10}$

g. $45 \times \dfrac{7}{9}$

h. $3\dfrac{1}{9} \times 1\dfrac{2}{7} \times \dfrac{3}{4}$

i. $\dfrac{3}{4} \times \dfrac{7}{9} \times 3\dfrac{1}{3}$

j. $\dfrac{1}{8} \times 6\dfrac{2}{3} \times \dfrac{1}{10}$

2. Multiply (do not use canceling; reduce by finding the greatest common divisor):

a. $\dfrac{3}{4} \times \dfrac{8}{9}$

b. $\dfrac{7}{16} \times \dfrac{8}{13}$

3. Multiply or divide as indicated:

a. $\dfrac{25}{36} \div \dfrac{5}{9}$

b. $\dfrac{18}{8} \div \dfrac{12}{16}$

c. $2\dfrac{6}{7} \div 2\dfrac{2}{5}$

d. $3\dfrac{1}{4} \div 16$

e. $24 \div 1\dfrac{1}{3}$

f. $6 \times \dfrac{3}{2}$

g. $3\frac{1}{5} \times 7\frac{1}{2}$

h. $\frac{3}{8} \div \frac{7}{4}$

i. $9 \div 3\frac{3}{4}$

j. $\frac{11}{24} \times \frac{24}{33}$

k. $\frac{12}{14} \div 27$

l. $\frac{3}{5} \times \frac{2}{7} \div \frac{3}{10}$

WORD PROBLEMS

4. Mary Smith plans to make 12 meatloafs to store in her freezer. Each meatloaf requires $2\frac{1}{4}$ pounds of ground beef. How much ground beef does Mary need?

5. Judy Carter purchased a real estate lot for $24,000. She sold it 2 years later for $1\frac{5}{8}$ times as much as she had paid for it. What was the selling price?

6. Lynn Clarkson saw an ad for a camcorder that cost $980. She knew of a discount store that would sell it to her for a markdown of $\frac{3}{20}$ off the advertised price. How much is the discount she can get?

7. To raise money for their club, the members of the Marketing Club purchased 68 bushels of popcorn to resell. They plan to repackage the popcorn in bags that hold $\frac{2}{21}$ of a bushel each. How many bags of popcorn will they be able to fill?

8. Richard Tracy paid a total of $375 for lumber costing $9\frac{3}{8}$ per foot. How many feet did he purchase?

9. While training for a marathon, Kristin Woods jogged $7\frac{3}{4}$ miles per hour for $2\frac{2}{3}$ hours. How many miles did Kristin jog?

10. On a map, 1 inch represents 240 miles. How many miles are represented by $\frac{3}{8}$ of an inch?

11. In Massachusetts, the governor wants to allot $\frac{1}{6}$ of the total sales tax collections to public education. The total sales tax collected is $2,472,000; how much will go to education?

Name _Sam Corum_   Date _4/17/13_

Learning Unit 3–1 : Rounding Decimals; Fraction and Decimal Conversions

DRILL PROBLEMS

1. Write in decimal:
   a. Forty-one hundredths ___.41___
   b. Six tenths ___.6___
   c. Nine hundred fifty-three thousandths ___.953___
   d. Four hundred one thousandths ___.401___
   e. Six hundredths ___.06___

2. Round each decimal to the place indicated:
   a. .4326 to the nearest thousandth ___.433___
   b. .051 to the nearest tenth ___.1___
   c. 8.207 to the nearest hundredth ___8.21___
   d. 2.094 to the nearest hundredth ___2.09___
   e. .511172 to the nearest ten thousandth ___.5112___

3. Name the place position of the underlined digit:
   a. .8_2_6 ___hundredth___
   b. .91_4_ ___thousandth___
   c. 3._1_169 ___tenths___
   d. 53.17_5_ ___ten thousandths___
   e. 1.017_4_ ___ten thousandths___

4. Convert to fractions (do not reduce):
   a. .83 ___$\frac{83}{100}$___
   b. .426 ___$\frac{426}{1000}$___
   c. 2.516 ___$\frac{2516}{1000}$___
   d. .62$\frac{1}{2}$ ___$\frac{62500}{100000}$___
   e. 13.007 ___$13\frac{7}{1000}$___
   f. 5.03$\frac{1}{4}$ ___$\frac{50325}{10000}$___

5. Convert to fractions and reduce to lowest terms:
   a. .4 ___$\frac{4}{10} = \frac{2}{5}$___
   b. .44 ___$\frac{44}{100} = \frac{22}{50} = \frac{11}{25}$___
   c. .53 ___$\frac{53}{100}$___
   d. .336 ___$\frac{336}{1000}$___
   e. .096 ___$\frac{96}{1000}$___
   f. .125 ___$\frac{125}{1000}$___
   g. .3125 ___$\frac{3125}{10000}$___
   h. .008 ___$\frac{8}{1000}$___
   i. 2.625 ___$2\frac{625}{1000}$___
   j. 5.75
   k. 3.375
   l. 9.04

6. Convert the following fractions to decimals and round your answer to the nearest hundredth:
   a. $\frac{1}{8}$ ___.13___
   b. $\frac{7}{16}$ ___.44___
   c. $\frac{2}{3}$ ___.67___
   d. $\frac{3}{4}$ ___.75___

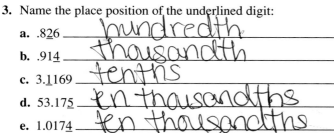

whole number   thousandths
tenths hundreths ten thousand

e. $\dfrac{9}{16}$ *56*

f. $\dfrac{5}{6}$ *.83*

g. $\dfrac{7}{9}$ *.78*

h. $\dfrac{38}{79}$ *.48*

i. $2\dfrac{3}{8}$ *$\dfrac{19}{8}$ 2.38*

j. $9\dfrac{1}{3}$ *$\dfrac{28}{3}$ 9.33*

k. $11\dfrac{19}{50}$ *$\dfrac{569}{50}$ 11.38*

l. $6\dfrac{21}{32}$ *$\dfrac{213}{32}$ 6.66*

m. $4\dfrac{83}{97}$ *$\dfrac{471}{97}$ 4.88*

n. $1\dfrac{2}{5}$ *$\dfrac{7}{5}$ 1.4*

o. $2\dfrac{2}{11}$ *$\dfrac{24}{11} = 2.18$*

p. $13\dfrac{30}{42}$ *$\dfrac{576}{42}$ 13.71*

WORD PROBLEMS

7. Alan Angel got 2 hits in his first 7 times at bat. What is his average to the nearest thousandths place?

   2/7 .286

8. Bill Breen earned $1,555, and his employer calculated that Bill's total FICA deduction should be $118.9575. Round this deduction to the nearest cent. *$118.96*

9. At the local college, .566 of the students are men. Convert to a fraction. Do not reduce.

   $\dfrac{566}{1000}$

10. The average television set is watched 2,400 hours a year. If there are 8,760 hours in a year, what fractional part of the year is spent watching television? Reduce to lowest terms.

    $\dfrac{240}{876}$

11. On Saturday, the employees at the Empire Fish Company work only $\frac{1}{3}$ of a day. How could this be expressed as a decimal to nearest thousandths?

    .333

12. The North Shore Cinema has 610 seats. At a recent film screening there were 55 vacant seats. Show as a fraction the number of filled seats. Reduce as needed.

    $\dfrac{555}{610}$

13. Michael Sullivan was planning his marketing strategy for a new product his company had produced. He was fascinated to discover that Rhode Island, the smallest state in the United States, was only twenty thousand, five hundred seven ten millionths the size of the largest state, Alaska. Write this number in decimal. *.0020507*

14. Bull Moose Company purchased a new manufacturing plant, located on an acre of land, for a total price of $2,250,000. The accountant determined that $\frac{3}{7}$ of the total price should be allocated as the price of the building. What decimal portion is the price of the building? Round to the nearest thousandth.

    967,500 or .43

    .429

3. In reconciling the checking account for Nasser Enterprises, Beth Accomando found that the bank had collected a $3,000 promissory note on the company's behalf and had charged a $15 collection fee. There was also a service charge of $7.25. What amount should be added/subtracted from the checkbook balance to bring it up to date?

   Add: _____   Deduct: _____

4. In reconciling the checking account for Colonial Cleaners, Steve Papa found that a check for $34.50 had been recorded in the check register as $43.50. The bank returned an NSF check in the amount of $62.55. Interest income of $8.25 was earned and a service charge of $10.32 was assessed. What amount should be added/subtracted from the checkbook balance to bring it up to date?

   Add: _____   Deduct: _____

5. Matthew Stokes was completing the bank reconciliation for Parker's Tool and Die Company. The check register balance was $1,503.67. Matthew found that a $76.00 check had been recorded in the check register as $67.00; that a note for $1,500 had been collected by the bank for Parker's and the collection fee was $12.00; that $15.60 interest was earned on the account; and that an $8.35 service charge had been assessed. What should the check register balance be after Matthew updates it with the bank reconciliation information?

6. Consumers, community activists, and politicians are decrying the new line of accounts because several include a $3 service charge for some customers who use bank tellers for transactions that can be done through an automated teller machine. Bill Wade banks at a local bank that charges this fee. He was having difficulty balancing his checkbook because he did not notice this fee on his bank statement. His bank statement showed a balance of $822.18. Bill's checkbook had a balance of $206.48. Check No. 406 for $116.08 and Check No. 407 for $12.50 were outstanding. A $521 deposit was not on the statement. Bill has his payroll check electronically deposited to his checking account—the payroll check was for $1,015.12 (Bill's payroll checks vary each month). There are also a $1 service fee and a teller fee of $6. Complete Bill's bank reconciliation.

7. At First National Bank in San Diego, some customers have to pay $25 each year as an ATM card fee. John Levi banks at First National Bank and just received his bank statement showing a balance of $829.25; his checkbook balance is $467.40. The bank statement shows an ATM card fee of $25.00, teller fee of $9.00, interest of $1.80, and John's $880 IRS refund check, which was processed by the IRS and deposited to his account. John has two checks that have not cleared—No. 112 for $620.10 and No. 113 for $206.05. There is also a deposit in transit for $1,312.10. Prepare John's bank reconciliation.

Classroom Notes

Name _____ Date _____

Learning Unit 5–1 :   Solving Equations for the Unknown

DRILL PROBLEMS

1.   Write equations for the following situations. Use N for the unknown number. Do not solve the equations.
   a. Four times a number is 120.
   b. A number increased by 13 equals 25.
   c. Seven less than a number is 5.
   d. Fifty-seven decreased by 3 times a number is 21.
   e. Fourteen added to one-third of a number is 18.

   f. Twice the sum of a number and 4 is 32.

   g. Three-fourths of a number is 9.

   h. Two times a number plus 3 times the same number plus 8 is 68.

2.   Solve for the unknown number:
   a. $B + 10 = 45$

   b. $29 + M = 44$

   c. $D - 77 = 98$

   d. $7N = 63$

   e. $\dfrac{X}{12} = 11$

   f. $3Q + 4Q + 2Q = 108$

   g. $H + 5H + 3 = 57$

   h. $2(N - 3) = 62$

   i. $\dfrac{3R}{4} = 27$

   j. $E - 32 = 41$

   k. $5(2T - 2) = 120$

   l. $12W - 5W = 98$

   m. $49 - X = 37$

   n. $12(V + 2) = 84$

   o. $7D + 4 = 5D + 14$

   p. $7(T - 2) = 2T - 9$

Learning Unit 5–2 : Solving Word Problems for the Unknown

WORD PROBLEMS

1. A blue denim shirt at the Old Navy was marked down $20. The sale price was $40. What was the original price?

Unknown(s)	Variables(s)	Relationship

2. Goodwin's Corporation found that $\frac{2}{3}$ of its employees were vested in their retirement plan. If 124 employees are vested, what is the total number of employees at Goodwin's?

Unknown(s)	Variables(s)	Relationship

3. Eileen Haskin's utility and telephone bills for the month totaled $180. The utility bill was 3 times as much as the telephone bill. How much was each bill?

Unknown(s)	Variables(s)	Relationship

4. Ryan and his friends went to the golf course to hunt for golf balls. Ryan found 15 more than $\frac{1}{3}$ of the total number of golf balls that were found. How many golf balls were found if Ryan found 75 golf balls?

Unknown(s)	Variables(s)	Relationship

5. Linda Mills and Sherry Somers sold 459 tickets for the Advertising Club's raffle. If Linda sold 8 times as many tickets as Sherry, how many tickets did each one sell?

Unknown(s)	Variables(s)	Relationship

6. Jason Mazzola wanted to buy a suit at Giblee's. Jason did not have enough money with him, so Mr. Giblee told him he would hold the suit if Jason gave him a deposit of $\frac{1}{5}$ of the cost of the suit. Jason agreed and gave Mr. Giblee $79. What was the price of the suit?

Unknown(s)	Variables(s)	Relationship

7. Peter sold watches ($7) and necklaces ($4) at a flea market. Total sales were $300. People bought 3 times as many watches as necklaces. How many of each did Peter sell? What were the total dollar sales of each?

Unknown(s)	Variables(s)	Price	Relationship

8. Peter sold watches ($7) and necklaces ($4) at a flea market. Total sales for 48 watches and necklaces were $300. How many of each did Peter sell? What were the total dollar sales of each?

Unknown(s)	Variables(s)	Price	Relationship

9. A 3,000 piece of direct mailing cost $1,435. Printing cost is $550, about $3\frac{1}{2}$ times the cost of typesetting. How much did the typesetting cost? Round to the nearest cent.

Unknown(s)	Variables(s)	Relationship

10. In 2012, Tony Rigato, owner of MRM, saw an increase in sales to $13.5 million. Rigato states that since 2009, sales have more than tripled. What were his sales in 2009?

Unknown(s)	Variables(s)	Relationship

Classroom Notes

Name _____ Date _____

Learning Unit 6–1 : Conversions

DRILL PROBLEMS

1. Convert the following to percents (round to the nearest tenth of a percent if needed):

   a.   .03 _____ %   b.   .729 _____ %   c.   .009 _____ %

   d.   8.3 _____ %   e.   5.26 _____ %   f.   6 _____ %

   g.   .0105 _____ %   h.   .1180 _____ %   i.   5.0375 _____ %

   j.   .862 _____ %   k.   .2615 _____ %   l.   .8 _____ %

   m.   .025 _____ %   n.   .06 _____ %

2. Convert the following to decimals (do not round):

   a.   33% _____   b.   .09% _____

   c.   4.7% _____   d.   9.67% _____

   e.   .2% _____   f. $\frac{1}{4}$% _____

   g.   .76% _____   h.   110% _____

   i. $12\frac{1}{2}$% _____   j.   5% _____

   k.   .004% _____   l. $7\frac{5}{10}$% _____

   m. $\frac{3}{4}$% _____   n.   1% _____

3. Convert the following to percents (round to the nearest tenth of a percent if needed):

   a. $\frac{4}{10}$ _____ %   b. $\frac{1}{5}$ _____ %

   c. $1\frac{5}{8}$ _____ %   d. $\frac{2}{7}$ _____ %

   e.   2 _____ %   f. $\frac{14}{100}$ _____ %

   g. $\frac{1}{6}$ _____ %   h. $\frac{1}{2}$ _____ %

   i. $\frac{3}{5}$ _____ %   j. $\frac{3}{25}$ _____ %

   k. $\frac{5}{16}$ _____ %   l. $\frac{11}{50}$ _____ %

   m. $4\frac{3}{4}$ _____ %   n. $\frac{3}{200}$ _____ %

4. Convert the following to fractions in simplest form:

   a.   40% _____   b.   15% _____

   c.   50% _____   d.   75% _____

   e.   35% _____   f.   85% _____

   g. $12\frac{1}{2}$% _____   h. $37\frac{1}{2}$% _____

   i. $33\frac{1}{3}$% _____   j.   3% _____

   k.   8.5% _____   l. $5\frac{3}{4}$% _____

   m.   100% _____   n.   10% _____

5. Complete the following table by finding the missing fraction, decimal, or percent equivalent:

	Fraction	Decimal	Percent		Fraction	Decimal	Percent
a.		.25	25%	h.	$\frac{1}{6}$	$.16\overline{6}$	
b.	$\frac{3}{8}$		$37\frac{1}{2}\%$	i.		$.083\overline{3}$	$8\frac{1}{3}\%$
c.	$\frac{1}{2}$	.5		j.	$\frac{1}{9}$		$11\frac{1}{9}\%$
d.	$\frac{2}{3}$		$66\frac{2}{3}\%$	k.		.3125	$31\frac{1}{4}\%$
e.		.4	40%	l.	$\frac{3}{40}$	.075	
f.	$\frac{3}{5}$	.6		m.	$\frac{1}{5}$		20%
g.	$\frac{7}{10}$		70%	n.		1.125	$112\frac{1}{2}\%$

WORD PROBLEMS

6. If in 2011, Mutual of New York reported that 60% of its new sales came from existing clients. What fractional part of its new sales came from existing clients? Reduce to simplest form.

7. Six hundred ninety corporations and design firms competed for the Industrial Design Excellence Award (IDEA). Twenty were selected as the year's best and received gold awards. Show the gold award winners as a fraction; then show what percent of the entrants received gold awards. Round to the nearest tenth of a percent.

8. If in the first half of 2010, stock prices in the Standard & Poor's 500-stock index rose 3.2%. Show the increase as a decimal.

9. In the recent banking crisis, many banks were unable to cover their bad loans. Citicorp, the nation's largest real estate lender, was reported as having only enough reserves to cover 39% of its bad loans. What fractional part of its loan losses was covered?

10. Dave Mattera spent his vacation in Las Vegas. He ordered breakfast in his room, and when he went downstairs to the coffee shop, he discovered that the same breakfast was much less expensive. He had paid 1.884 times as much for the breakfast in his room. What was the percent of increase for the breakfast in his room?

11. Putnam Management Company of Boston recently increased its management fee by .09%. What is the increase as a decimal? What is the same increase as a fraction?

12. Joel Black and Karen Whyte formed a partnership and drew up a partnership agreement, with profits and losses to be divided equally after each partner receives a $7\frac{1}{2}\%$ return on his or her capital contribution. Show their return on investment as a decimal and as a fraction. Reduce.

Learning Unit 6–2 :   Application of Percents—Portion Formula

DRILL PROBLEMS

1. Fill in the amount of the base, rate, and portion in each of the following statements:

  a. The Logans spend $3,000 a month on food, which is 20% of their monthly income of $15,000.

    Base _____ Rate _____ Portion _____

  b. Rocky Norman got a $15 discount when he purchased a new camera. This was 20% off the sticker price of $75.

    Base _____ Rate _____ Portion _____

  c. Mary Burns got a 12% senior citizens discount when she bought a $7.00 movie ticket. She saved $0.84.

    Base _____ Rate _____ Portion _____

  d. Arthur Bogey received a commission of $13,500 when he sold the Brown's house for $225,000. His commission rate is 6%.

    Base _____ Rate _____ Portion _____

  e. Leo Davis deposited $5,000 in a certificate of deposit (CD). A year later he received an interest payment of $450, which was a yield of 9%.

    Base _____ Rate _____ Portion _____

  f. Grace Tremblay is on a diet that allows her to eat 1,600 calories per day. For breakfast she had 600 calories, which is $37\frac{1}{2}$% of her allowance.

    Base _____ Rate _____ Portion _____

2. Find the portion; round to the nearest hundredth if necessary:

  a. 7% of 74 _____   **b.** 12% of 205 _____   **c.** 16% of 630 _____

  d. 7.5% of 920 _____   **e.** 25% of 1,004 _____   **f.** 10% of 79 _____

  g. 103% of 44 _____   **h.** 30% of 78 _____   **i.** .2% of 50 _____

  j. 1% of 5,622 _____   **k.** $6\frac{1}{4}$% of 480 _____   **l.** 150% of 10 _____

  m. 100% of 34 _____   **n.** $\frac{1}{2}$% of 27 _____

3. Find the rate; round to the nearest tenth of a percent as needed:

  a. 30 is what percent of 90? _____   **b.** 6 is what percent of 200? _____

  c. 275 is what percent of 1,000? _____   **d.** .8 is what percent of 44? _____

  e. 67 is what percent of 2,010? _____   **f.** 550 is what percent of 250? _____

  g. 13 is what percent of 650? _____   **h.** $15 is what percent of $455? _____

  i. .05 is what percent of 100? _____   **j.** $6.25 is what percent of $10? _____

4. Find the base; round to the nearest tenth as needed:

  a. 63 is 30% of _____   **b.** 60 is 33% of _____   **c.** 150 is 25% of _____

  d. 47 is 1% of _____   **e.** $21 is 120% of _____   **f.** 2.26 is 40% of _____

  g. 75 is $12\frac{1}{2}$% of _____   **h.** 18 is 22.2% of _____   **i.** $37.50 is 50% of _____

  j. 250 is 100% of _____

5. Find the percent of increase or decrease. Round to nearest tenth percent as needed:

Last year	This year	Amount of change	Percent of change
a. 5,962	4,378	_____	_____
b. $10,995	$12,250	_____	_____
c. 120,000	140,000	_____	_____
d. 120,000	100,000	_____	_____

WORD PROBLEMS

6. A machine that originally cost $5,000 was sold for $500 at the end of 5 years. What percent of the original cost is the selling price?

7. Joanne Byrne invested $75,000 in a candy shop and is making 12% per year on her investment. How much money per year is she making on her investment?

8. There was a fire in Bill Porper's store that caused 2,780 inventory items to be destroyed. Before the fire, 9,565 inventory items were in the store. What percent of inventory was destroyed? Round to nearest tenth percent.

9. Elyse's Dress Shoppe makes 25% of its sales for cash. If the cash receipts on January 21 were $799, what were the total sales for the day?

10. The YMCA is holding a fund-raiser to collect money for a new gym floor. So far it has collected $7,875, which is 63% of the goal. What is the amount of the goal? How much more money must the YMCA collect?

11. Leslie Tracey purchased her home for $51,500. She sold it last year for $221,200. What percent profit did she make on the sale? Round to nearest tenth percent.

12. Maplewood Park Tool & Die had an annual production of 375,165 units this year. This is 140% of the annual production last year. What was last year's annual production?

Name _____   Date _____

Learning Unit 7–1 : Trade Discounts—Single and Chain*

DRILL PROBLEMS

1. Calculate the trade discount amount for each of the following items:

Item	List price	Trade discount	Trade discount amount
a. BlackBerry	$ 250	30%	_____
b. Flat-screen TV	$1,200	30%	_____
c. Suit	$ 500	10%	_____
d. Bicycle	$ 800	$12\frac{1}{2}$	_____
e. David Yurman bracelet	$ 950	40%	_____

2. Calculate the net price for each of the following items:

Item	List price	Trade discount amount	Net price
a. Home Depot table	$600	$250	_____
b. Bookcase	$525	$129	_____
c. Rocking chair	$480	$ 95	_____

3. Fill in the missing amount for each of the following items:

Item	List price	Trade discount amount	Net price
a. Sears electric saw	_____	$19	$56.00
b. Electric drill	$90	_____	$68.50
c. Ladder	$56	$15.25	_____

4. For each of the following, find the percent paid (complement of trade discount) and the net price:

	List price	Trade discount	Percent paid	Net price
a.	$45	15%	_____	_____
b.	$195	12.2%	_____	_____
c.	$325	50%	_____	_____
d.	$120	18%	_____	_____

5. In each of the following examples, find the net price equivalent rate and the single equivalent discount rate:

	Chain discount	Net price equivalent rate	Single equivalent discount rate
a.	25/5	_____	_____
b.	15/15	_____	_____
c.	15/10/5	_____	_____
d.	12/12/6	_____	_____

*Freight problems to be shown in LU 7–2 material.

6. In each of the following examples, find the net price and the trade discount:

List price	Chain discount	Net price	Trade discount
a. $5,000	10/10/5	_____	_____
b. $7,500	9/6/3	_____	_____
c. $898	20/7/2	_____	_____
d. $1,500	25/10	_____	_____

7. The list price of a handheld calculator is $19.50, and the trade discount is 18%. Find the trade discount amount.

8. The list price of a silver picture frame is $29.95, and the trade discount is 15%. Find the trade discount amount and the net price.

9. The net price of a set of pots and pans is $65, and the trade discount is 20%. What is the list price?

10. Jennie's Variety Store has the opportunity to purchase candy from three different wholesalers; each of the wholesalers offers a different chain discount. Company A offers 25/5/5, Company B offers 20/10/5, and Company C offers 15/20. Which company should Jennie deal with? *Hint:* Choose the company with the highest single equivalent discount rate.

11. The list price of a television set is $625. Find the net price after a series discount of 30/20/10.

12. Mandy's Accessories Shop purchased 12 purses with a total list price of $726. What was the net price of each purse if the wholesaler offered a chain discount of 25/20?

13. Kransberg Furniture Store purchased a bedroom set for $1,097.25 from Furniture Wholesalers. The list price of the set was $1,995. What trade discount rate did Kransberg receive?

14. Susan Monk teaches second grade and receives a discount at the local art supply store. Recently she paid $47.25 for art supplies after receiving a chain discount of 30/10. What was the regular price of the art supplies?

Learning Unit 8–2 :   Markups Based on Selling Price (100%)

DRILL PROBLEMS

1. Calculate the markup based on the selling price.

	Selling price	Markup (percent of selling price)	Dollar markup
a.	$18.00	30%	_____
b.	$230.00	25%	_____
c.	$81.00	42.5%	_____
d.	$72.88	$37\frac{1}{2}\%$	_____
e.	$1.98	$7\frac{1}{2}\%$	_____

2. Calculate the dollar markup and the markup as a percent of selling price (to the nearest tenth percent). Verify your answer, which may be slightly off due to rounding.

	Cost	Selling price	Dollar markup	Markup (percent of selling price)	Verify
a.	$2.50	$4.25	_____	_____	_____
b.	$16.00	$24.00	_____	_____	_____
c.	$45.25	$85.00	_____	_____	_____
d.	$0.19	$0.25	_____	_____	_____
e.	$5.50	$8.98	_____	_____	_____

3. Given the *cost* and the markup as a percent of *selling price*, calculate the selling price.

	Cost	Markup (percent of selling price)	Selling price
a.	$5.90	15%	_____
b.	$600	32%	_____
c.	$15	50%	_____
d.	$120	30%	_____
e.	$0.29	20%	_____

4. Given the selling price and the percent markup on selling price, calculate the cost.

	Cost	Markup (percent of selling price)	Selling price
a.	_____	40%	$6.25
b.	_____	20%	$16.25
c.	_____	19%	$63.89
d.	_____	$62\frac{1}{2}\%$	$44.00

5. Calculate the equivalent rate of markup (round to the nearest hundredth percent).

Markup on cost	Markup on selling price		Markup on cost	Markup on selling price
a. 40%	_____		**b.** 50%	_____
c. _____	50%		**d.** _____	35%
e. _____	40%			

WORD PROBLEMS

6. Fisher Equipment is selling a Wet/Dry Shop Vac for $49.97. If Fisher's markup is 40% of the selling price, what is the cost of the Shop Vac?

7. Gove Lumber Company purchased a 10-inch table saw for $225 and will mark up the price 35% on the selling price. What will the selling price be?

8. To realize a sufficient gross margin, City Paint and Supply Company marks up its paint 27% on the selling price. If a gallon of Latex Semi-Gloss Enamel has a markup of $4.02, find **(a)** the selling price and **(b)** the cost.

9. A Magnavox 20-inch color TV cost $180 and sells for $297. What is the markup based on the selling price? Round to the nearest hundredth percent.

10. Bargain Furniture sells a five-piece country maple bedroom set for $1,299. The cost of this set is $700. What are **(a)** the markup on the bedroom set, **(b)** the markup percent on cost, and **(c)** the markup percent on the selling price? Round to the nearest hundredth percent.

11. Robert's Department Store marks up its sundries by 28% on the selling price. If a 6.4-ounce tube of toothpaste costs $1.65, what will the selling price be?

12. To be competitive, Tinker Toys must sell the Nintendo Control Deck for $89.99. To meet expenses and make a sufficient profit, Tinker Toys must add a markup on the selling price of 23%. What is the maximum amount that Tinker Toys can afford to pay a wholesaler for Nintendo?

13. Nicole's Restaurant charges $7.50 for a linguini dinner that costs $2.75 for the ingredients. What rate of markup is earned on the selling price? Round to the nearest hundredth percent.

Learning Unit 8-3 : Markdowns

DRILL PROBLEMS

1. Find the dollar markdown and the sale price.

	Original selling price	Markdown percent	Dollar markdown	Sale price
a.	$100	30%	_____	_____
b.	$2,099.98	25%	_____	_____
c.	$729	30%	_____	_____

2. Find the dollar markdown and the markdown percent on original selling price.

	Original selling price	Sale price	Dollar markdown	Markdown percent
a.	$19.50	$9.75	_____	_____
b.	$250	$175	_____	_____
c.	$39.95	$29.96	_____	_____

3. Find the original selling price.

	Sale price	Markdown percent	Original selling price
a.	$328	20%	_____
b.	$15.85	15%	_____

4. Calculate the final selling price.

	Original selling price	First markdown	Second markdown	Final markup	Final selling price
a.	$4.96	25%	8%	5%	_____
b.	$130	30%	10%	20%	_____

WORD PROBLEMS

5. Speedy King is having a 30%-off sale on their box springs and mattresses. A queen-size, back-supporter mattress is priced at $325. What is the sale price of the mattress?

6. Murray and Sons sell a personal fax machine for $602.27. It is having a sale, and the fax machine is marked down to $499.88. What is the percent of the markdown?

7. Coleman's is having a clearance sale. A lamp with an original selling price of $249 is now selling for $198. Find the percent of the markdown. Round to the nearest hundredth percent.

8. Johnny's Sports Shop has advertised markdowns on certain items of 22%. A soccer ball is marked with a sale price of $16.50. What was the original price of the soccer ball?

9. Sam Grillo sells seasonal furnishings. Near the end of the summer a five-piece patio set that was priced $349.99 had not been sold, so he marked it down by 12%. As Labor Day approached, he still had not sold the patio set, so he marked it down an additional 18%. What was the final selling price of the patio set?

10. Calsey's Department Store sells their down comforters for a regular price of $325. During its white sale the comforters were marked down 22%. Then, at the end of the sale, Calsey's held a special promotion and gave a second markdown of 10%. When the sale was over, the remaining comforters were marked up 20%. What was the final selling price of the remaining comforters?

Classroom Notes

Classroom Notes

Name _____   Date _____

Learning Unit 9–1 :   Calculating Various Types of Employees' Gross Pay

DRILL PROBLEMS

1. Fill in the missing amounts for each of the following employees. Do not round the overtime rate in your calculations and round your final answers to the nearest cent.

Employee	Total hours	Rate per hour	Regular pay	Overtime pay	Gross pay
a. Ed Slope	40	$9.20	_____	_____	_____
b. Casey Guitare	43	$9.00	_____	_____	_____
c. Norma Harris	37	$7.50	_____	_____	_____
d. Ed Jackson	45	$12.25	_____	_____	_____

2. Calculate each employee's gross from the following data. Do not round the overtime rate in your calculation but round your final answers to the nearest cent.

Employee	S	M	Tu	W	Th	F	S	Total hours	Rate per hour	Regular pay	Overtime pay	Gross pay
a. L. Adams	0	8	8	8	8	8	0	_____	$8.10	_____	_____	_____
b. M. Card	0	9	8	9	8	8	4	_____	$11.35	_____	_____	_____
c. P. Kline	2	$7\frac{1}{2}$	$8\frac{1}{4}$	8	$10\frac{3}{4}$	9	2	_____	$10.60	_____	_____	_____
d. J. Mack	0	$9\frac{1}{2}$	$9\frac{3}{4}$	$9\frac{1}{2}$	10	10	4	_____	$9.95	_____	_____	_____

3. Calculate the gross wages of the following production workers.

Employee	Rate per unit	No. of units produced	Gross pay
a. A. Bossie	$0.67	655	_____
b. J. Carson	$0.87\frac{1}{2}$	703	_____

4. Using the given differential scale, calculate the gross wages of the following production workers.

Units produced	Amount per unit
From 1–50	$.55
From 51–100	.65
From 101–200	.72
More than 200	.95

Employee	Units produced	Gross pay
a. F. Burns	190	_____
b. B. English	210	_____
c. E. Jackson	200	_____

5. Calculate the following salespersons' gross wages.
   a. Straight commission:

Employee	Net sales	Commission	Gross pay
M. Salley	$40,000	13%	_____

b. Straight commission with draw:

Employee	Net sales	Commission	Draw	Commission minus draw
G. Gorsbeck	$38,000	12%	$600	_____

c. Variable commission scale:

Up to $25,000	8%
Excess of $25,000 to $40,000	10%
More than $40,000	12%

Employee	Net sales	Gross pay
H. Lloyd	$42,000	_____

d. Salary plus commission:

Employee	Salary	Commission	Quota	Net sales	Gross pay
P. Floyd	$2,500	3%	$400,000	$475,000	_____

WORD PROBLEMS

For all problems with overtime, be sure to round only the final answer.

6. In the first week of December, Dana Robinson worked 52 hours. His regular rate of pay is $11.25 per hour. What was Dana's gross pay for the week?

7. Davis Fisheries pays its workers for each box of fish they pack. Sunny Melanson receives $.30 per box. During the third week of July, Sunny packed 2,410 boxes of fish. What is Sunny's gross pay?

8. Maye George is a real estate broker who receives a straight commission of 6%. What would her commission be for a house that sold for $197,500?

9. Devon Company pays Eileen Haskins a straight commission of $12\frac{1}{2}\%$ on net sales. In January, Devon gave Eileen a draw of $600. She had net sales that month of $35,570. What was Eileen's commission minus draw?

10. Parker and Company pays Selma Stokes on a variable commission scale. In a month when Selma had net sales of $155,000, what was her gross pay based on the following schedule?

Net sales	Commission rate
Up to $40,000	5%
Excess of $40,000 to $75,000	5.5%
Excess of $75,000 to $100,000	6%
More than $100,000	7%

11. Marsh Furniture Company pays Joshua Charles a monthly salary of $1,900 plus a commission of $2\frac{1}{2}\%$ on sales over $12,500. Last month, Joshua had net sales of $17,799. What was Joshua's gross pay for the month?

12. Amy McWha works at Lamplighter Bookstore where she earns $7.75 per hour plus a commission of 2% on her weekly sales in excess of $1,500. Last week, Amy worked 39 hours and had total sales of $2,250. What was Amy's gross pay for the week?

Learning Unit 9-2 : Computing Payroll Deductions for Employees' Pay; Employers' Responsibilities

DRILL PROBLEMS

Use tables in the *Business Math Handbook* (assume FICA rates in text).

Employee	Allowances and marital status	Cumulative earnings	Salary per week	Taxable earnings S.S.	Taxable earnings Medicare
1. Pete Small	M—3	$106,300	$2,300	a. _____	b. _____
2. Alice Hall	M—1	$90,000	$1,100	c. _____	d. _____
3. Jean Rose	M—2	$100,000	$2,000	e. _____	f. _____

4. What is the tax for Social Security and Medicare for Pete in Problem 1?

5. Calculate Pete's FIT by the percentage method.

6. What would employer's contribute for this week's payroll for SUTA and FUTA?

WORD PROBLEMS

7. Cynthia Pratt has earned $105,300 thus far this year. This week she earned $3,500. Find her total FICA tax deduction (Social Security and Medicare).

8. If Cynthia (Problem 7) earns $1,050 the following week, what will be her new total FICA tax deduction?

9. Roger Alley, a service dispatcher, has weekly earnings of $750. He claimed four allowances on his W-4 form and is married. Besides his FIT and FICA deductions, he has deductions of $35.16 for medical insurance and $17.25 for union dues. Calculate his net earnings for the third week in February. Use the percentage method.

10. Nicole Mariotte is unmarried and claimed one withholding allowance on her W-4 form. In the second week of February, she earned $707.35. Deductions from her pay included federal withholding, Social Security, Medicare, health insurance for $47.75, and $30.00 for the company meal plan. What is Nicole's net pay for the week? Use the percentage method.

11. Gerald Knowlton had total gross earnings of $106,500 in the last week of November. His earnings for the first week in December were $804.70. His employer uses the percentage method to calculate federal withholding. If Gerald is married, claims two allowances, and has medical insurance of $52.25 deducted each week from his pay, what is his net pay for the week?

Name _____ Date _____

Learning Unit 10–1 : Calculation of Simple Interest and Maturity Value

DRILL PROBLEMS

1. Find the simple interest for each of the following loans:

Principal	Rate	Time	Interest
a. $9,000	3%	1 year	_____
b. $3,000	12%	3 years	_____
c. $18,000	$8\frac{1}{2}\%$	10 months	_____

2. Find the simple interest for each of the following loans; use the exact interest method. Use the days-in-a-year calendar in the text when needed.

Principal	Rate	Time	Interest
a. $900	4%	30 days	_____
b. $4,290	8%	250 days	_____
c. $1,500	8%	Made March 11 Due July 11	_____

3. Find the simple interest for each of the following loans using the ordinary interest method (Banker's Rule).

Principal	Rate	Time	Interest
a. $5,250	$7\frac{1}{2}\%$	120 days	_____
b. $700	3%	70 days	_____
c. $2,600	11%	Made on June 15 Due October 17	_____

WORD PROBLEMS

4. On October 17, Gill Iowa borrowed $6,000 at a rate of 4%. She promised to repay the loan in 7 months. What are **(a)** the amount of the simple interest and **(b)** the total amount owed upon maturity?

5. Marjorie Folsom borrowed $5,500 to purchase a computer. The loan was for 9 months at an annual interest rate of $12\frac{1}{2}\%$. What are **(a)** the amount of interest Marjorie must pay and **(b)** the maturity value of the loan?

6. Eric has a loan for $1,200 at an ordinary interest rate of 9.5% for 80 days. Julie has a loan for $1,200 at an exact interest rate of 9.5% for 80 days. Calculate **(a)** the total amount due on Eric's loan and **(b)** the total amount due on Julie's loan.

7. Roger Lee borrowed $5,280 at $13\frac{1}{2}$% on May 24 and agreed to repay the loan on August 24. The lender calculates interest using the exact interest method. How much will Roger be required to pay on August 24?

8. On March 8, Jack Faltin borrowed $10,225 at $9\frac{3}{4}$%. He signed a note agreeing to repay the loan and interest on November 8. If the lender calculates interest using the ordinary interest method, what will Jack's repayment be?

9. Dianne Smith's real estate taxes of $641.49 were due on November 1, 2009. Due to financial difficulties, Dianne was unable to pay her tax bill until January 15, 2010. The penalty for late payment is $13\frac{3}{8}$% ordinary interest. What is the penalty Dianne will have to pay, and what is Dianne's total payment on January 15?

10. On August 8, Rex Eason had a credit card balance of $550, but he was unable to pay his bill. The credit card company charges interest of $18\frac{1}{2}$% annually on late payments. What amount will Rex have to pay if he pays his bill 1 month late?

11. An issue of *Your Money* discussed average consumers who carry a balance of $2,000 on one credit card. If the yearly rate of interest is 18%, how much are consumers paying in interest per year?

12. AFBA Industrial Bank of Colorado Springs, Colorado, charges a credit card interest rate of 11% per year. If you had a credit card debt of $1,500, what would your interest amount be after 3 months?

Learning Unit 10–2 :   Finding Unknown in Simple Interest Formula

DRILL PROBLEMS

1. Find the principal in each of the following. Round to the nearest cent. Assume 360 days. *Calculator hint:* Do denominator calculation first, do not round; when answer is displayed, save it in memory by pressing [M+]. Now key in the numerator (interest amount), [÷], [MR], [=] for the answer. Be sure to clear memory after each problem by pressing [MR] again so that the M is no longer in the display.

	Rate	Time	Interest	Principal
a.	8%	70 days	$68	_____
b.	11%	90 days	$125	_____
c.	9%	120 days	$103	_____
d.	$8\frac{1}{2}$%	60 days	$150	_____

Name _____ Date _____

Learning Unit 11–1 : Structure of Promissory Notes; the Simple Discount Note

DRILL PROBLEMS

1. Identify each of the following characteristics of promissory notes with an **I** for simple interest note, a **D** for simple discount note, or a **B** if it is true for both.

   ___ Interest is computed on face value, or what is actually borrowed.

   ___ A promissory note for a loan usually less than 1 year.

   ___ Borrower receives proceeds = Face value − Bank discount.

   ___ Maturity value = Face value + Interest.

   ___ Maturity value = Face value.

   ___ Borrower receives the face value.

   ___ Paid back by one payment at maturity.

   ___ Interest computed on maturity value, or what will be repaid, and not on actual amount borrowed.

2. Find the bank discount and the proceeds for the following (assume 360 days):

	Maturity value	Discount rate	Time (days)	Bank discount	Proceeds
a.	$7,000	2%	90	_____	_____
b.	$4,550	8.1%	110	_____	_____
c.	$19,350	12.7%	55	_____	_____
d.	$63,400	10%	90	_____	_____
e.	$13,490	7.9%	200	_____	_____
f.	$780	$12\frac{1}{2}$%	65	_____	_____

3. Find the effective rate of interest for each of the loans in Problem 2. Use the answers you calculated in Problem 2 to solve these problems (round to the nearest tenth percent).

	Maturity value	Discount rate	Time (days)	Effective rate
a.	$7,000	2%	90	_____
b.	$4,550	8.1%	110	_____
c.	$19,350	12.7%	55	_____
d.	$63,400	10%	90	_____

e. $13,490   7.9%   200   _____

f. $780 $12\frac{1}{2}$%   65   _____

WORD PROBLEMS

Assume 360 days.

4. Mary Smith signed a $9,000 note for 135 days at a discount rate of 4%. Find the discount and the proceeds Mary received.

5. The Salem Cooperative Bank charges an $8\frac{3}{4}$% discount rate. What are the discount and the proceeds for a $16,200 note for 60 days?

6. Bill Jackson is planning to buy a used car. He went to City Credit Union to take out a loan for $6,400 for 300 days. If the credit union charges a discount rate of $11\frac{1}{2}$%, what will the proceeds of this loan be?

7. Mike Drislane goes to the bank and signs a note for $9,700. The bank charges a 15% discount rate. Find the discount and the proceeds if the loan is for 210 days.

8. Flora Foley plans to have a deck built on the back of her house. She decides to take out a loan at the bank for $14,300. She signs a note promising to pay back the loan in 280 days. If the note was discounted at 9.2%, how much money will Flora receive from the bank?

9. At the end of 280 days, Flora (Problem 8) must pay back the loan. What is the maturity value of the loan?

10. Dave Cassidy signed a $7,855 note at a bank that charges a 14.2% discount rate. If the loan is for 190 days, find (a) the proceeds and (b) the effective rate charged by the bank (to the nearest tenth percent).

11. How much money must Dave (Problem 10) pay back to the bank?

Learning Unit 11–2 : Discounting an Interest-Bearing Note before Maturity

DRILL PROBLEMS

1. Calculate the maturity value for each of the following promissory notes (use 360 days):

Date of note	Principal of note	Length of note (days)	Interest rate	Maturity value
a. April 12	$4,000	160	4%	_____
b. August 23	$15,990	85	13%	_____
c. December 10	$985	30	11.5%	_____

2. Find the maturity date and the discount period for the following; assume no leap years. *Hint:* See Exact Days-in-a-Year Calendar, Chapter 7.

Date of note	Length of note (days)	Date of discount	Maturity date	Discount period
a. March 11	200	June 28	_____	_____
b. January 22	60	March 2	_____	_____
c. April 19	85	June 6	_____	_____
d. November 17	120	February 15	_____	_____

3. Find the bank discount for each of the following (use 360 days):

Date of note	Principal of note	Length of note	Interest rate	Bank discount rate	Date of discount	Bank discount
a. October 5	$2,475	88 days	11%	9.5%	December 10	_____
b. June 13	$9,055	112 days	15%	16%	August 11	_____
c. March 20	$1,065	75 days	12%	11.5%	May 24	_____

4. Find the proceeds for each of the discounted notes in Problem 3.

   a. _____

   b. _____

   c. _____

WORD PROBLEMS

5. Connors Company received a $4,000, 90-day, 10% note dated April 6 from one of its customers. Connors Company held the note until May 16, when the company discounted it at a bank at a discount rate of 12%. What were the proceeds that Connors Company received?

6. Souza & Sons accepted a 9%, $22,000, 120-day note from one of its customers on July 22. On October 2, the company discounted the note at Cooperative Bank. The discount rate was 12%. What were (a) the bank discount and (b) the proceeds?

7. The Fargate Store accepted an $8,250, 75-day, 9% note from one of its customers on March 18. Fargate discounted the note at Parkside National Bank at $9\frac{1}{2}\%$ on March 29. What proceeds did Fargate receive?

8. On November 1, Marjorie's Clothing Store accepted a $5,200, $8\frac{1}{2}\%$, 90-day note from Mary Rose in granting her a time extension on her bill. On January 13, Marjorie discounted the note at Seawater Bank, which charged a 10% discount rate. What were the proceeds that Majorie received?

9. On December 3, Duncan's Company accepted a $5,000, 90-day, 12% note from Al Finney in exchange for a $5,000 bill that was past due. On January 29, Duncan discounted the note at The Sidwell Bank at 13.1%. What were the proceeds from the note?

10. On February 26, Sullivan Company accepted a 60-day, 10% note in exchange for a $1,500 past-due bill from Tabot Company. On March 28, Sullivan Company discounted at National Bank the note received from Tabot Company. The bank discount rate was 12%. What are (a) the bank discount and (b) the proceeds?

11. On June 4, Johnson Company received from Marty Russo a 30-day, 11% note for $720 to settle Russo's debt. On June 17, Johnson discounted the note at Eastern Bank whose discount rate was 15%. What proceeds did Johnson receive?

12. On December 15, Lawlers Company went to the bank and discounted a 10%, 90-day, $14,000 note dated October 21. The bank charged a discount rate of 12%. What were the proceeds of the note?

Name _____   Date _____

Learning Unit 12–1 :   Compound Interest (Future Value)—The Big Picture

DRILL PROBLEMS

1. In the following examples, calculate manually the amount at year-end for each of the deposits, assuming that interest is compounded annually. Round to the nearest cent each year.

	Principal	Rate	Number of years	Year 1	Year 2	Year 3	Year 4
a.	$530	4%	2	_____	_____		
b.	$1,980	12%	4	_____	_____	_____	_____

2. In the following examples, calculate the simple interest, the compound interest, and the difference between the two. Round to the nearest cent; do not use tables.

	Principal	Rate	Number of years	Simple interest	Compound interest	Difference
a.	$4,600	10%	2	_____	_____	_____
b.	$18,400	9%	4	_____	_____	_____
c.	$855	$7\frac{1}{5}\%$	3	_____	_____	_____

3. Find the future value and the compound interest using the Future Value of $1 at Compound Interest table or the Compound Daily table. Round to the nearest cent.

	Principal	Investment terms	Future value	Compound interest
a.	$10,000	6 years at 8% compounded annually	_____	_____
b.	$10,000	6 years at 8% compounded quarterly	_____	_____
c.	$8,400	7 years at 12% compounded semiannually	_____	_____
d.	$2,500	15 years at 10% compounded daily	_____	_____
e.	$9,600	5 years at 6% compounded quarterly	_____	_____
f.	$20,000	2 years at 6% compounded monthly	_____	_____

4. Calculate the effective rate (APY) of interest using the Future Value of $1 at Compound Interest table.

Investment terms	Effective rate (annual percentage yield)
a. 12% compounded quarterly	_____
b. 12% compounded semiannually	_____
c. 6% compounded quarterly	_____

WORD PROBLEMS

5. John Mackey deposited $5,000 in his savings account at Salem Savings Bank. If the bank pays 6% interest compounded quarterly, what will be the balance of his account at the end of 3 years?

6. Pine Valley Savings Bank offers a certificate of deposit at 12% interest compounded quarterly. What is the effective rate (APY) of interest?

7. Jack Billings loaned $6,000 to his brother-in-law Dan, who was opening a new business. Dan promised to repay the loan at the end of 5 years, with interest of 8% compounded semiannually. How much will Dan pay Jack at the end of 5 years?

8. Eileen Hogarty deposits $5,630 in City Bank, which pays 12% interest compounded quarterly. How much money will Eileen have in her account at the end of 7 years?

9. If Kevin Bassage deposits $3,500 in Scarsdale Savings Bank, which pays 8% interest compounded quarterly, what will be in his account at the end of 6 years? How much interest will he have earned at that time?

10. Arlington Trust pays 6% compounded semiannually. How much interest would be earned on $7,200 for 1 year?

11. Paladium Savings Bank pays 9% compounded quarterly. Find the amount and the interest on $3,000 after three quarters. Do not use a table.

12. David Siderski bought a $7,500 bank certificate paying 16% compounded semiannually. How much money did he obtain upon cashing in the certificate 3 years later?

13. An issue of *Your Money* showed that the more frequently the bank compounds your money, the better. Just how much better is a function of time. A $10,000 investment for 6% in a 5-year certificate of deposit at three different banks can result in different interest being earned.
   a. Bank A (simple interest, no compounding)
   b. Bank B (quarterly compounding)
   c. Bank C (daily compounding)
   What would be the interest for each bank?

Learning Unit 12–2 :   Present Value—The Big Picture

DRILL PROBLEMS

1. Use the *Business Math Handbook* to find the table factor for each of the following:

Future value	Rate	Number of years	Compounded	Table value
a. $1.00	10%	5	Annually	_____
b. $1.00	12%	8	Semiannually	_____
c. $1.00	6%	10	Quarterly	_____
d. $1.00	12%	2	Monthly	_____
e. $1.00	8%	15	Semiannually	_____

2. Use the *Business Math Handbook* to find the table factor and the present value for each of the following:

Future value	Rate	Number of years	Compounded	Table value	Present value
a. $1,000	14%	6	Semiannually	_____	_____
b. $1,000	16%	7	Quarterly	_____	_____
c. $1,000	8%	7	Quarterly	_____	_____
d. $1,000	8%	7	Semiannually	_____	_____
e. $1,000	8%	7	Annually	_____	_____

3. Find the present value and the interest earned for the following:

Future value	Number of years	Rate	Compounded	Present value	Interest earned
a. $2,500	6	8%	Annually	_____	_____
b. $4,600	10	6%	Semiannually	_____	_____
c. $12,800	8	10%	Semiannually	_____	_____
d. $28,400	7	8%	Quarterly	_____	_____
e. $53,050	1	12%	Monthly	_____	_____

4. Find the missing amount (present value or future value) for each of the following:

Present value	Investment terms	Future value
a. $3,500	5 years at 8% compounded annually	_____
b. _____	6 years at 12% compounded semiannually	$9,000
c. $4,700	9 years at 14% compounded semiannually	_____

WORD PROBLEMS

Solve for future value or present value.

5. Paul Palumbo assumes that he will need to have a new roof put on his house in 4 years. He estimates that the roof will cost him $18,000 at that time. What amount of money should Paul invest today at 8%, compounded semiannually, to be able to pay for the roof?

6. Tilton, a pharmacist, rents his store and has signed a lease that will expire in 3 years. When the lease expires, Tilton wants to buy his own store. He wants to have a down payment of $35,000 at that time. How much money should Tilton invest today at 6%, compounded quarterly, to yield $35,000?

7. Brad Morrissey loans $8,200 to his brother-in-law. He will be repaid at the end of 5 years, with interest at 10% compounded semiannually. Find out how much he will be repaid.

8. The owner of Waverly Sheet Metal Company plans to buy some new machinery in 6 years. He estimates that the machines he wishes to purchase will cost $39,700 at that time. What must he invest today at 8%, compounded semiannually, to have sufficient money to purchase the new machines?

9. Paul Stevens's grandparents want to buy him a car when he graduates from college in 4 years. They feel that they should have $27,000 in the bank at that time. How much should they invest at 12%, compounded quarterly, to reach their goal?

10. Gilda Nardi deposits $5,325 in a bank that pays 12% interest compounded quarterly. Find the amount she will have at the end of 7 years.

11. Mary Wilson wants to buy a new set of golf clubs in 2 years. They will cost $775. How much money should she invest today at 9%, compounded annually, so that she will have enough money to buy the new clubs?

12. Jack Beggs plans to invest $30,000 at 10%, compounded semiannually, for 5 years. What is the future value of the investment?

13. Ron Thrift has a 2000 Honda that he expects will last 3 more years. Ron does not like to finance his purchases. He went to First National Bank to find out how much money he should put in the bank to purchase a $20,300 car in 3 years. The bank's 3-year CD is compounded quarterly with a 4% rate. How much should Ron invest in the CD?

14. The Downers Grove YMCA had a fund-raising campaign to build a swimming pool in 6 years. Members raised $825,000; the pool is estimated to cost $1,230,000. The money will be placed in Downers Grove Bank, which pays daily interest at 6%. Will the YMCA have enough money to pay for the pool in 6 years?

Classroom Notes

Chapter 1

LU 1-1A

1. **a.** Eight thousand, six hundred eighty-two
   b. Fifty-six thousand, two hundred ninety-five
   c. Seven hundred thirty-two billion, three hundred ten million, four hundred forty-four thousand, eight hundred eighty-eight

2. **a.** $43 = 40$ **b.** $654 = 700$ **c.** $7,328 = 7,000$ **d.** $5,980 = 6,000$

3. Kellogg's sales and profit:

The facts	Solving for?	Steps to take	Key points
Sales: Three million, two hundred ninety-one thousand dollars. *Profit:* Four hundred five thousand dollars.	Sales and profit rounded all the way.	Express each verbal form in numeric form. Identify leftmost digit in each number.	Rounding all the way means only the leftmost digit will remain. All other digits become zeros.

Steps to solving problem

1. Convert verbal to numeric.
   Three million, two hundred ninety-one thousand ⟶ $3,291,000
   Four hundred five thousand ⟶ $ 405,000

2. Identify leftmost digit of each number.
   $3,291,000 $405,000
      ↓   ↓
   $3,000,000 $400,000

LU 1-2A

1.
```
   10
   18
   19
   24
26,090
```

2.
Estimate	Actual
3,000	3,482
7,000	6,981
+ 5,000	5,490
15,000	15,953

3.
```
   8 17717
   9,787
 −5,968
   3,819
```
Check
```
   3,819
 + 5,968
   9,787
```

4. Jackson Manufacturing Company over- or underestimated sales:

The facts	Solving for?	Steps to take	Key points
Projected 2011 sales: $878,000 *Major clients:* $492,900 *Other clients:* $342,000	How much were sales over- or underestimated?	Total projected sales − Total actual sales = Over- or underestimated sales.	Projected sales (minuend) − Actual sales (subtrahend) = Difference.

Steps to solving problem

1. Calculate total actual sales.
```
  $492,900
 + 342,000
  $834,900
```

2. Calculate over- or underestimated sales.
```
  $878,000
 − 834,900
  $ 43,100  (overestimated)
```

LU 1-3A

1.
Estimate	Actual	Check

$$\begin{array}{r} 5,000 \\ \times\ 20 \\ \hline 100,000 \end{array}$$

$$\begin{array}{r} 4,938 \\ \times\ 19 \\ \hline 44442 \\ 4938 \\ \hline 93,822 \end{array}$$

$$\begin{array}{r} 9 \times 4,938 =\ \ 44,442 \\ 10 \times 4,938 = +49,380 \\ \hline 93,822 \end{array}$$

2. $86 \times 19 = 1,634 + 5$ zeros $= 163,400,000$

3. $86 + 4$ zeros $= 860,000$

4.
Rounding	Actual	Check

$$\begin{array}{r} 200 \\ 30\overline{)6,000} \\ 6\ 0 \\ \hline \end{array}$$

$$\begin{array}{r} 245 \quad R24 \\ 26\overline{)6,394} \\ 52 \\ \hline 119 \\ 104 \\ \hline 154 \\ 130 \\ \hline 24 \end{array}$$

$$\begin{array}{r} 25 \times 255 = 6,375 \\ + 19 \\ \hline 6,394 \end{array}$$

5.   Drop 3 zeros $= 3\overline{)99}^{\,33}$

6.   General Motors' total cost per year:

The facts	Solving for?	Steps to take	Key points
Cars produced each workday: 850 Workweek: 5 days Cost per car: $7,000	Total cost per year.	Cars produced per week × 52 = Total cars produced per year. Total cars produced per year × Total cost per car = Total cost per year.	Whenever possible, use multiplication and division shortcuts with zeros. Multiplication can be checked by division.

Steps to solving problem

1. Calculate total cars produced per week. $5 \times 850 = 4,250$ cars produced per week

2. Calculate total cars produced per year. $4,250$ cars $\times 52$ weeks $= 221,000$ total cars produced per year

3. Calculate total cost per year. $221,000$ cars $\times \$7,000 = \$1,547,000,000$ (multiply 221×7 and add zeros)

   Check $\$1,547,000,000 \div 221,000 = \$7,000$ (drop 3 zeros before dividing)

Chapter 2

LU 2-1A

1.   a. Proper
     b. Improper
     c. Mixed
     d. Improper

2. $$\begin{array}{r} 22\ 1/7 \\ 7\overline{)155} \\ 14 \\ \hline 15 \\ 14 \\ \hline 1 \end{array}$$

3. $$\frac{(9 \times 8) + 7}{9} = \frac{79}{9}$$

4.   a. $$42\overline{)70}^{\,1} \qquad 28\overline{)42}^{\,1} \qquad 14\overline{)28}^{\,2}$$
$$\phantom{42\overline{)70}}\ \frac{42}{28} \qquad \phantom{28\overline{)42}}\ \frac{28}{14} \qquad \phantom{14\overline{)28}}\ \frac{28}{0}$$

   14 is greatest common divisor

$$\frac{42 \div 14}{70 \div 14} = \frac{3}{5}$$

b. $96\overline{)182}^{\,1}$ $\nearrow86\overline{)96}^{\,1}$ $\nearrow10\overline{)86}^{\,8}$
$\quad\quad\dfrac{96}{86}\quad\quad\quad\dfrac{86}{10}\quad\quad\quad\dfrac{80}{6}$

$\quad\quad 6\overline{)10}^{\,1}\quad\nearrow4\overline{)6}^{\,1}\quad\nearrow2\overline{)4}^{\,2}$
$\quad\quad\dfrac{6}{4}\quad\quad\quad\dfrac{4}{2}\quad\quad\quad\dfrac{4}{0}$

$$\frac{96 \div 2}{182 \div 2} = \frac{48}{91}$$

5. **a.** $\dfrac{300}{30} = 10 \times 16 = 160$ **b.** $\dfrac{60}{20} = 3 \times 9 = 27$

LU 2-2A

1.
2/10	15	9	4
3⧸ 5	15	9	2
5⧸ 5	5	3	2
1	1	3	2

$\text{LCD} = 2 \times 3 \times 5 \times 1 \times 1 \times 3 \times 2 = 180$

2. **a.** $\dfrac{2}{25} + \dfrac{3}{5} = \dfrac{2}{25} + \dfrac{15}{25} = \dfrac{17}{25}$ $\left(\begin{array}{c}\dfrac{3}{5} = \dfrac{?}{25} \\ 25 \div 5 = 5 \times 3 = 15\end{array}\right)$

b. $\begin{array}{r}3\frac{3}{8} \\ +6\frac{1}{32} \\ \hline \end{array}$ $\begin{array}{r}3\frac{12}{32} \\ +6\frac{1}{32} \\ \hline 9\frac{13}{32}\end{array}$ $\dfrac{3}{8} = \dfrac{?}{32}$

$\qquad\qquad\qquad\qquad\qquad\qquad 32 \div 8 = 4 \times 3 = 12$

3. **a.** $\begin{array}{r}\frac{5}{6} = \frac{5}{6} \\ -\frac{1}{3} = \frac{2}{6} \\ \hline \frac{3}{6} = \frac{1}{2}\end{array}$ **b.** $9\frac{1}{8} = \quad 9\frac{4}{32} = \quad 8\frac{36}{32} \leftarrow \left(\dfrac{32}{32} + \dfrac{4}{32}\right)$
$\qquad\qquad\qquad\qquad -3\frac{7}{32} = -3\frac{7}{32} = -3\frac{7}{32}$
$\qquad\qquad\qquad\qquad\qquad\qquad\qquad\qquad 5\frac{29}{32}$

c. Note how we showed the 6 as $5\frac{5}{5}$

$\begin{array}{r}5\frac{5}{5} \\ -1\frac{2}{5} \\ \hline 4\frac{3}{5}\end{array}$

4. $\begin{array}{r}209\frac{1}{8} \\ +382\frac{1}{4} \\ \hline\end{array}\quad\begin{array}{r}209\frac{1}{8} \\ +382\frac{2}{8} \\ \hline 591\frac{3}{8}\text{ sq. feet}\end{array}\quad\begin{array}{r}985\frac{1}{4} \\ 591\frac{3}{8} \\ \end{array}\quad\begin{array}{r}985\frac{2}{8} \\ -591\frac{3}{8} \\ \hline\end{array}\quad\begin{array}{r}984\frac{10}{8} \\ -591\frac{3}{8} \\ \hline 393\frac{7}{8}\text{ sq. feet}\end{array}$

13. $150\% = 150 \times \dfrac{1}{100} = \dfrac{150}{100} = 1\dfrac{50}{100} = 1\dfrac{1}{2}$

14. $\dfrac{1}{4}\% = \dfrac{1}{4} \times \dfrac{1}{100} = \dfrac{1}{400}$

15. $17\dfrac{8}{10}\% = \dfrac{178}{10} \times \dfrac{1}{100} = \dfrac{178}{1,000} = \dfrac{89}{500}$

LU 6-2A

1. $504 = 1,200 \times .42$
$(P) = (B) \times (R)$

2. $\$560 = \$8,000 \times .07$
$(P) = (B) \times (R)$

3. $\dfrac{(P)510}{(B)6,000} = .085 = 8.5\%$

4. $\dfrac{(P)400}{(B)900} = .444 = 44.4\%$

5. $\dfrac{(P)30}{(R).60} = 50(B)$

6. $\dfrac{(P)1,200}{(R).035} = 34,285.7(B)$

7. Percent of Professor Ford's class that did not receive the A grade:

The facts	Solving for?	Steps to take	Key points
10 As. 25 in class.	Percent that did not receive A.	Identify key elements. Base: 25 Rate: ? Portion: 15(25 − 10). Rate $= \dfrac{\text{Portion}}{\text{Base}}$	Portion (15) Base × Rate (25) (?) The whole Portion and rate must relate to same piece of base.

Steps to solving problem

1. Set up the formula. $\text{Rate} = \dfrac{\text{Portion}}{\text{Base}}$

2. Calculate the rate. $R = \dfrac{15}{25}$
$R = 60\%$

8. Abby Biernet's original order:

The facts	Solving for?	Steps to take	Key points
70% of the order not in. 90 lobsters received.	Total order of lobsters.	Identify key elements. Base: ? Rate: 30 (100% − 70%) Portion: 90. Rate $= \dfrac{\text{Portion}}{\text{Rate}}$	Portion (90) Base × Rate (?) (.30) 90 lobsters represent 30% of the order Portion and rate must relate to same piece of base.

Steps to solving problem

1. Set up the formula. $\text{Rate} = \dfrac{\text{Portion}}{\text{Rate}}$

2. Calculate the base. $B = \dfrac{90}{.30}$ ◄——— 90 lobsters are 30% of base
$B = 300$ lobsters

9. Dunkin' Donuts Company sales for 2010:

The facts	Solving for?	Steps to take	Key points
2009: $400,000 sales. *2010:* Sales up 35% from 2009.	Sales for 2010.	Identify key elements. *Base:* $300,000 *Rate:* 1.35. Old year 100% New year + 35 _____ 135% *Portion:* ? Portion = Base × Rate	2010 sales Portion (?) Base × Rate ($400,000) (1.35) 2009 sales When rate is greater than 100%, portion will be larger than base.

Steps to solving problem

1. Set up the formula.   Portion = Base × Rate

2. Calculate the portion. $P = \$400,000 \times 1.35$
                             $P = \$540,000$

10. Percent decrease in Apple Computer price:

The facts	Solving for?	Steps to take	Key points
Apple Computer was $1,800; now $1,000.	Percent decrease in price.	Identify key elements. *Base:* $1,800 *Rate:* ? *Portion:* $800 ($1,800 − $1,000) $Rate = \dfrac{Portion}{Base}$	Difference in price Portion ($800) Base × Rate ($1,800) (?) Original price

Steps to solving problem

1. Set up the formula. $Rate = \dfrac{Portion}{Base}$

2. Calculate the rate. $R = \dfrac{\$800}{\$1,800}$
                            $R = 44.44\%$

11. Percent increase in Boston Celtics ticket:

The facts	Solving for?	Steps to take	Key points
$14 ticket (old). $75 ticket (new).	Percent increase in price.	Identify key elements. *Base:* $14 *Rate:* ? *Portion:* $61 ($75 − $14) $Rate = \dfrac{Portion}{Base}$	Difference in price Portion $61 Base × Rate ($14) (?) Original price When portion is greater than base, rate will be greater than 100%.

Steps to solving problem

1. Set up the formula. $Rate = \dfrac{Portion}{Base}$

2. Calculate the rate.

$R = \dfrac{\$61}{\$14}$

$R = 435,714 = 435.71\%$

Chapter 7

LU 7-1A

1. Dining room set trade discount amount and net price:

The facts	Solving for?	Steps to take	Key points
List price: $16,000. *Trade discount rate*: 30%.	Trade discount amount. Net price.	Trade discount amount = List price × Trade discount rate. Net price = List price × Complement of trade discount rate.	Trade discount amount Portion (?) Base × Rate ($16,000) (.30) List price Trade discount rate

Steps to solving problem

1. Calculate the trade discount. $\$16,000 \times .30 = \$4,800$ Trade discount amount

2. Calculate the net price. $\$16,000 \times .70 = \$11,200$ (100% − 30% = 70%)

2. Video system list price:

The facts	Solving for?	Steps to take	Key points
Net price: $400. *Trade discount rate*: 20%.	List price.	List price = $\dfrac{Net\ price}{Complement\ of\ trade\ discount}$	Net price Portion $400 Base × Rate (?) (.80) List price 100% −20%

Steps to solving problem

1. Calculate the complement of trade discount

$\begin{array}{r} 100\% \\ -\ 20\% \\ \hline 80\% = .80 \end{array}$

2. Calculate the list price. $\dfrac{\$400}{.80} = \$500$

3. Lamps Outlet's net price and trade discount amount:

The facts	Solving for?	Steps to take	Key points
List price: $14,000. *Chain discount*: 4/8/20.	Net price. Trade discount amount.	Net price = List price × Net price equivalent rate. Trade discount amount = List price × Single equivalent discount rate.	Do not round off net price equivalent rate or single equivalent discount rate.

Steps to solving problem

1. Calculate the complement of each chain discount.

100%	100%	100%
− 4	− 8	− 20
96%	92%	80%

2. Calculate the net price equivalent rate.

$$.96 \times .92 \times .80 = .70656$$

3. Calculate the net price.

$$\$14,000 \times .70656 = \$9,891.84$$

4. Calculate the single equivalent discount rate.

```
  1.00000
− .70656
  .29344
```

5. Calculate the trade discount amount.

$$\$14,000 \times .29344 = \$4,108.16$$

LU 7-2A

1. End of discount period: July 8 + 10 days =   July 18
   End of credit period: By Table 7.1, July 8 =

   ```
     189 days
   + 30 days
     219 → search → Aug. 7
   ```

2. End of discount period: June 12 + 10 days = June 22
   End of credit period: By Table 7.1, June 12 =

   ```
     163 days
   + 30 days
     193 → search → July 12
   ```

3. End of discount period: By Table 7.1, May 12 =

   ```
     132 days
   + 30 days
     162 → search → June 11
   ```

   End of credit period: By Table 7.1, May 12 =

   ```
     132 days
   + 60 days
     192 → search → July 11
   ```

4. End of discount period: May 10
   End of credit period: May 10 + 20 = May 30

5. End of discount period: June 10
   End of credit period: June 10 + 20 = June 30

6. Vasko Corporation's cost of equipment:

The facts	Solving for?	Steps to take	Key points
List price: $9,000.	Cost of equipment.	Net price = List price × Complement of trade discount rate.	Trade discounts are deducted before cash discounts are taken.
Trade discount rate: 30%.			
Terms: 2/10 EOM.		EOM before 25th: Discount period is 1st 10 days of month that follows sale.	Cash discounts are not taken on freight or returns.
Invoice date: 6/29			
Date paid: 8/9			

Steps to solving problem

1. Calculate the net price.

   $\$9,000 \times .70 = \$6,300$ 100%
             − 30%

2. Calculate the discount period.

   Until Aug. 10

3. Calculate the cost of office equipment.

   $\$6,300 \times .98 = \$6,174$ 100%
             − 2%

7. $\dfrac{\$600}{.98} = \$612.24$ Credited

   $\$700 − \$612.24 = \$87.76$ Balance outstanding

2. Selling price of doll and dollar markup:

The facts	Solving for?	Steps to take	Key points
Doll cost: $14 each. Markup on selling price: 38%.	% $ C 62% $14.00 + M 38 8.58² = S 100% $ 22.58¹ ¹Selling price. ²Dollar markup.	$S = C + M$ or $S = \dfrac{\text{Cost}}{1 - \begin{array}{l}\text{Percent markup} \\ \text{on selling price}\end{array}}$	Cost Portion $14 Base × Rate (?) (.62) Selling price 100% −38%

Steps to solving problem

1. Calculate the selling price.

$$S = C + M$$
$$S = \$14.00 + .38S$$
$$\underline{-.38S} \qquad\qquad \underline{-.38S}$$
$$\frac{.62S}{.62} = \frac{\$14.00}{.62}$$
$$S = \$22.58$$

2. Calculate the dollar markup.

$$M = S - C$$
$$\$8.58 = \$22.58 - \$14.00$$

Check

$$\text{Selling price } (B) = \frac{\text{Cost } (P)}{1 - \text{Percent markup on selling price } (R)} = \frac{\$14.00}{.62} = \$22.58$$

3. Cost and dollar markup:

The facts	Solving for?	Steps to take	Key points
Selling price: $16. Markup on selling price: 42%.	% $ C 58% $ 9.28¹ + M 42 6.72² = S 100% $16.00 ¹Dollar markup. ²Cost.	$S = C + M$ or $\text{Cost} = \text{Selling price} \times$ $\left(1 - \begin{array}{l}\text{Percent markup} \\ \text{on selling price}\end{array}\right)$	Cost Portion (?) Base × Rate ($16) (.58) Selling price 100% −42%

Steps to solving problem

1. Cost = Selling price × (1 − Percent markup on selling price) = $16.00 × .58 = $9.28
   (P)   (B)   (R)

   (1.00 − .42)

2. Dollar markup = $16.00
   $\underline{\quad\; -9.28}$
   $ 6.72

4. Cost $= \dfrac{\$5}{\$7} = 71.4\%$ $\dfrac{.417}{1 - .417} = \dfrac{.417}{.583} = 71.5\%$

Selling price $= \dfrac{\$5}{\$12} = 41.7\%$ $\dfrac{.714}{1 + .714} = \dfrac{.714}{1.714} = 41.7\%$ (due to rounding)

LU 8-3A

1. $$S = \frac{\text{Cost}}{1 - \text{Percent markup on selling price}}$$

$$S = \frac{\$800}{1 - .30} = \frac{\$800}{.70} = \$1,142.86$$

First markdown: $.90 \times \$1,142.86 = \$1,028.57$ selling price
Second markdown: $.95 \times \$1,028.57 = \$977.14$
Markup: $1.02 \times \$977.14 = \$996.68$ final selling price

$$\$1,142.86 - \$996.68 = \frac{\$146.18}{\$1,142.86} = 12.79\%$$

Chapter 9

LU 9-1A

1. 40 hours $\times$ \$12.00 = \$480.00
    14 hours $\times$ \$18.00 = $\underline{\$252.00}$ (\$12.00 $\times$ 1.5 = \$18.00)
                            \$732.00

2. \$210,000 $\times$ .08 =   \$16,800
                      $\underline{-\ \ 4,000}$
                      \$12,800

3. Gross pay = \$1,200 + (\$3,000 $\times$ .01) + (\$8,000 $\times$ .03) + (\$20,000 $\times$ .05) + (\$20,000 $\times$ .08)
                 = \$1,200 +   \$30   +   \$240   +   \$1,000   +   \$1,600
                 = \$4,070

LU 9-2A

1. **Social Security**

$106,800
− 106,300
$\overline{\quad}$
$\quad\ \ $500 × .062 = $31

Medicare

$10,000 × .0145 = $145.00

FIT

Percentage method: $10,000.00
$304.17 × 1 = \quad − 304.17 (Table 9.1)
$\overline{\quad}$
$ 9,695.83

$7,025 to $14,467 → $1,395.80 plus 28% of excess over $7,025 (Table 9.2)

$9,695.83 \qquad\quad $1,395.80
− 7,025.00 \qquad + \ \ 747.83 ($2,670.83 × .28)
$\overline{\quad}$ \qquad\quad $\overline{\quad}$
$2,670.83 \qquad\quad $2,143.63

2. 13 weeks × $200 = $ 2,600
13 weeks × $800 = \ \ 10,400 ($10,400 − $7,000) → $3,400
13 weeks × $950 = \ \ 12,350 ($12,350 − $7,000) → \ \ 5,350 } Exempt Wages (not taxed
$\overline{\quad}$ \qquad\qquad\qquad\qquad\qquad $\overline{\quad}$ for FUTA or SUTA)
$25,350 \qquad\qquad\qquad\qquad\qquad $8,750

$25,350 − $8,750 = $16,600 taxable wages
SUTA = .051 × $16,600 = $846.60
FUTA = .008 × $16,600 = $132.80

Note: FUTA remains at .008 whether SUTA rate is higher or lower than standard.

Chapter 10

LU 10-1A

1. $16,000 × .03 × $\dfrac{8}{12}$ = $320

2. $15,000 × .06 × 6 = $5,400

3. $50,000 × .07 × $\dfrac{18}{12}$ = $5,250

4. August 14 → \quad 226 \qquad\qquad $20,000 × .07 × $\dfrac{100}{365}$ = $383.56
   May 6 \quad → − 126
   $\overline{\qquad}$
   \qquad\qquad\qquad 100 \qquad\qquad $MV = $20,000 + $383.56 = $20,383.56

5. $20,000 × .07 × $\dfrac{100}{360}$ = $388.89 \qquad $MV = $20,000 + $388.89 = $20,388.89

LU 10-2A

1. $\dfrac{\$9,000}{.04 \times \dfrac{90}{360}} = \dfrac{\$9,000}{.01} = \$900,000 \qquad P = \dfrac{I}{R \times T}$

2. $\dfrac{\$280}{\$6,000 \times \dfrac{180}{360}} = \dfrac{\$280}{\$3,000} = 9.33\% \qquad R = \dfrac{I}{P \times T}$

3. $\dfrac{\$190}{\$900 \times .06} = \dfrac{\$190}{\$54} = 3.52 \times 360 = 1{,}267 \text{ days} \qquad T = \dfrac{I}{P \times R}$

LU 10-3A

$$\$4,000 \times .04 \times \frac{15}{360} = \$6.67$$

$$
\begin{array}{r}
\$2,000.00 \\
-\quad 9.19 \\
\hline
\$1,990.81
\end{array}
\qquad
\begin{array}{r}
\$3,306.67 \\
-1,990.81 \\
\hline
\$1,315.86
\end{array}
$$

$$
\begin{array}{r}
\$\ 700.00 \\
-\quad 6.67 \\
\hline
\$\ 693.33
\end{array}
\qquad
\begin{array}{r}
\$\ 4,000.00 \\
-\quad 693.33 \\
\hline
\$\ 3,306.67
\end{array}
$$

$$\$1,315.86 \times .04 \times \frac{20}{360} = \$2.92$$

$$\$3,306.67 \times .04 \times \frac{25}{360} = \$9.19$$

$$
\begin{array}{r}
\$\quad 2.92 \\
+\ 1,315.86 \\
\hline
\$1,318.78
\end{array}
$$

Chapter 11

LU 11-1A

1. a. Maturity value = Face value = $14,000
    b. Bank discount = $MV \times$ Bank discount rate $\times$ Time

    $$= \$14,000 \times .045 \times \frac{60}{360}$$

    $$= \$105$$

    c. Proceeds = $MV -$ Bank discount

    $$= \$14,000 - \$105$$

    $$= \$13,895$$

    d. Effective rate $= \dfrac{\text{Interest}}{\text{Proceeds} \times \text{Time}}$

    $$= \dfrac{\$105}{\$13,895 \times \dfrac{60}{360}}$$

    $$= 4.53\%$$

2. $\$10,000 \times .04 \times \dfrac{13}{52} = \$100$ interest $\dfrac{\$100}{\$9,900 \times \dfrac{13}{52}} = 4.04\%$

LU 11-2A

1. a. $I = \$40,000 \times .05 \times \dfrac{170}{360} = \$944.44$

    $MV = \$40,000 + \$944.44 = \$40,944.44$

    b. Discount period = $170 - 61 = 109$ days.

April	30	**or by table:**	
	− 10	June 8	161
	20	April 8	− 100
May	+ 31		61
	51		
June	+ 10		
	61		

    c. Bank discount $= \$40,944.44 \times .02 \times \dfrac{109}{360} = \$247.94$

    d. Proceeds $= \$40,944.44 - \$247.94 = \$40,696.50$

Chapter 12

LU 12-1A

1. a. $4(4 \times 1)$ b. $541.21   c. $41.27 ($541.27 − $500)

    $\$500 \times 1.02 = \$510 \times 1.02 = \$520.20 \times 1.02 = \$530.60 \times 1.02 = \$541.21$

2. $\$500 \times 1.0824$ (4 periods at 2%) = $541.20

3. 16 periods, 2%, $7,000 × 1.3728 = $9,609.60

4. 4 periods, $1\frac{1}{2}$%

$8,000 × 1.0614 = $8,491.20 $\dfrac{$491.20}{$8,000}$ = 6.14%
               − 8,000.00
                $ 491.20

5. $1,800 × 1.3498 = $2,429.64

LU 12-2A

1. 14 periods (7 years × 2) $2\frac{1}{2}$% (5% ÷ 2)   .7077 $6,369.30 ($9,000 × .7077)

2. 20 periods (20 years × 1)   4% (4% ÷ 1)   .4564 $9,128 ($20,000 × .4564)

3. 6 years × 4 = 24 periods $\dfrac{8\%}{4}$ = 2%   .6217 × $40,000 = $24,868

4. 4 × 4 years = 16 periods $\dfrac{4\%}{4}$ = 1%   .8528 × $28,000 = $23,878.40

Check Figures

Odd-Numbered Drill and Word Problems for End-of-Chapter Problems.

Challenge Problems.

Summary Practice Tests (all).

Cumulative Reviews (all).

Odd-Numbered Additional Assignments by Learning Unit from Appendix A.

9. $\dfrac{566}{1,000}$

11. .333

13. .0020507

LU 3–2

1. **a.** 31.608 **b.** 5.2281 **d.** 3.7736

3. **a.** .3 **b.** .1 **c.** 1,480.0 **d.** .1

5. **a.** 6,870 **c.** .0272
e. 34,700 **i.** 8,329.8

7. $4.53

9. $111.25

11. 15

LU 4–1

1. **a.** $430.64 **b.** 3 **c.** $867.51

3. **a.** Neuner Realty Co.
b. Kevin Jones
h. $2,756.80

LU 4–2

1. $1,435.42

3. Add $3,000; deduct $22.25

5. $2,989.92

7. $1,315.20

LU 5–1

1. **a.** $4N = 120$ **e.** $14 + \dfrac{N}{3} = 18$
h. $2N + 3N + 8 = 68$

LU 5–2

1. $60

3. $45 telephone; $135 utility

5. 51 tickets—Sherry;
408 tickets—Linda

7. 12 necklaces ($48);
36 watches ($252)

9. $157.14

LU 6–1

1. **a.** 3% **b.** 72.9% **i.** 503.8% **l.** 80%

3. **a.** 40% **c.** 162.5%
h. 50% **n.** 1.5%

5. **a.** $\dfrac{1}{4}$ **b.** .375 **c.** 50%
d. $.66\overline{6}$ **n.** $1\dfrac{1}{8}$

7. 2.9%

9. $\dfrac{39}{100}$

11. $\dfrac{9}{10,000}$

LU 6–2

1. **a.** $15,000; 20%; $3,000
c. $7.00; 12%; $.84

3. **a.** 33.3% **b.** 3% **c.** 27.5%

5. **a.** −1,584; −26.6%
d. −20,000; −16.7%

7. $9,000

9. $3,196

11. 329.5%

LU 7–1

1. **a.** $75 **b.** $360 **c.** $50
d. $100 **e.** $380

3. **a.** $75 **b.** $21.50; $40.75

5. **a.** .7125; .2875 **b.** .7225; .2775

7. $3.51

9. $81.25

11. $315

13. 45%

LU 7–2

1. **a.** February 18; March 10
d. May 20; June 9
e. October 10; October 30

3. **a.** .98; $1,102.50
c. .98; $367.99

5. **a.** $16.79; $835.21

7. $14,504

9. **a.** $439.29 **b.** $491.21

11. $209.45

13. **a.** $765.31 **b.** $386.99

LU 8–1

1. **a.** $15.35 **b.** $2.72
c. $4.35 **d.** $90 **e.** $116.31

3. **a.** $2; 80% **b.** $6.50; 52%
c. $.28; 28.9%

5. **a.** $1.52 **b.** $225
c. $372.92 **d.** $625

7. **a.** $139.65 **b.** $538.65

9. **a.** $258.52 **b.** $90.48

11. **a.** $212.50 **b.** $297.50

13. $8.17

LU 8–2

1. **a.** $5.40 **b.** $57.50
c. $34.43 **d.** $27.33 **e.** $.15

3. **a.** $6.94 **b.** $882.35 **c.** $30
d. $171.43

5. **a.** 28.57% **b.** 33.33% **d.** 53.85%

7. $346.15

9. 39.39%

11. $2.29

13. 63.33%

LU 8–3

1. **a.** $30.00; $70
b. $525; $1,574.98

3. **a.** $410 **b.** $18.65

5. **a.** $216; $324; $5.14
b. $45; $63.90; $1.52

7. 17%

9. $21.15

11. $273.78

13. $.79

LU 8–4

1. **a.** $7.00 **b.** $11.11

3. **a.** 16,667 **b.** 7,500

5. 5,070

7. 22,222

LU 9–1

1. **a.** $368; 0; $368
b. $360; $40.50; $400.50

3. **a.** $438.85 **b.** $615.13

5. **a.** $5,200 **b.** $3,960
c. $3,740 **d.** $4,750

7. $723.00

9. $3,846.25

11. $2,032.48

LU 9–2

1. **a.** $500; $2,300

3. $2,000; $2,000

5. $338.41

7. $143.75

9. $608.27

11. $660.98

LU 10–1

1. **a.** $270 **b.** $1,080 **c.** $1,275

3. **a.** $131.25 **b.** $4.08 **c.** $98.51

5. **a.** $515.63 **b.** $6,015.63

7. **a.** $5,459.66

9. $659.36

11. $360

LU 10–2

1. **a.** $4,371.44 **b.** $4,545.45
c. $3,433.33

3. **a.** 60; .17 **b.** 120; .33
c. 270; .75 **d.** 145; .40

5. 5%

7. $250

9. $3,000

11. 119 days

LU 10–3

1. **a.** $2,568.75; $1,885.47; $920.04

3. $4,267.59

5. $4,715.30; $115.30

LU 11–1

1. I; B; D; I; D; I; B; D

3. **a.** 2%
c. 13%

5. $15,963.75

7. $848.75; $8,851.25

9. $14,300

11. $7,855

LU 11–2

1. **a.** $4,071,11
   b. $16,480.80
   c. $994.44
3. **a.** $14.76
   b. $223.25
   c. $3.49
5. $4,031.67
7. $8,262.74
9. $5,088.16
11. $721.45

LU 12–1

1. **a.** $573.25 year 2
   b. $3,115.57 year 4
3. **a.** $15,869; $5,869
   b. $16,084; $6,084
5. $5,980
7. $8,881.20
9. $2,129.40
11. $3,207.09; $207.09
13. $3,000; $3,469; $3,498

LU 12–2

1. **a.** .6209 **b.** .3936 **c.** .5513
3. **a.** $1,575,50; $924.50
   b. $2,547.02; $2,052.98
5. $13,152.60
7. $13,356.98
9. $16,826.40
11. $652.32
13. $18,014.22